THE BIOGRAPHY OF
LEO TOLSTOY

Tolstoy at the time of his departure for the Caucasus, 1851.

LEO TOLSTOY

HIS LIFE AND WORK

AUTOBIOGRAPHICAL MEMOIRS, LETTERS, AND BIOGRAPHICAL MATERIAL, COMPILED BY PAUL BIRUKOFF, AND REVISED BY LEO TOLSTOY

TRANSLATED FROM THE RUSSIAN

VOLUME I

CHILDHOOD AND EARLY MANHOOD

ILLUSTRATED

NEW YORK
CHARLES SCRIBNER'S SONS
1906

No Rights Reserved

WITH FEELINGS OF SINCERE GRATITUDE
I DEDICATE THIS VOLUME TO

MY WIFE

WHO BY HER SELF-SACRIFICING LABORS
SECURED ME THE NECESSARY LEISURE FOR PREPARING

THIS BOOK

AS WELL AS TO ALL THOSE UNKNOWN WORKERS
WHO WERE ENGAGED IN LABOR OF A HEAVIER NATURE
WHILST I HAD THE PRIVILEGE OF
THIS PLEASANT WORK

PAUL BIRUKOFF

CONTENTS

	PAGE
PREFACE	xi
BIBLIOGRAPHY	xix
INTRODUCTION TO HIS REMINISCENCES, BY LEO TOLSTOY	xxiii

PART I

THE FAMILY ORIGIN OF LEO TOLSTOY

CHAPTER
I. THE ANCESTORS OF LEO TOLSTOY ON HIS FATHER'S SIDE	3
II. THE ANCESTORS OF LEO TOLSTOY ON HIS MOTHER'S SIDE	11
III. TOLSTOY'S PARENTS	18

PART II

CHILDHOOD, BOYHOOD, AND YOUTH (1828–1850)

IV. CHILDHOOD	33
V. BOYHOOD	58
VI. YOUTH	80

CONTENTS

PART III

MILITARY SERVICE (1851–1857)

CHAPTER		PAGE
VII.	THE CAUCASUS	119
VIII.	THE DANUBE AND SEBASTOPOL	166
IX.	ST. PETERSBURG	196
X.	ROMANCE	225

PART IV

TRAVELS, LITERARY AND SOCIAL ACTIVITY

XI.	THE FIRST JOURNEY ABROAD—LIFE IN MOSCOW—BEAR-HUNTING	237
XII.	THE SECOND JOURNEY ABROAD—HIS BROTHER'S DEATH	268
XIII.	TOLSTOY AND TURGENEF—EMANCIPATION OF THE SERFS—MEDIATION	303
XIV.	EDUCATIONAL ACTIVITY OF TOLSTOY—FOUNDATION OF THE SCHOOL—THEORIES	320
XV.	THE WORK OF THE YASNAYA POLYANA SCHOOL	339
XVI.	MARRIAGE—SHORT REVIEW OF TOLSTOY'S WORKS	360
XVII.	CONCLUSION	369

ILLUSTRATIONS

Tolstoy at the time of his departure for the Caucasus, 1851 . . . . *Frontispiece*

FACING PAGE

Count Peter Andreyevich Tolstoy, the first Count Tolstoy . 4

Count Ilya Andreyevich Tolstoy, Leo Tolstoy's paternal grandfather 8

Prince Nicolas Sergeyevich Volkousky, Tolstoy's maternal grandfather 12

Tolstoy's mother and her sister 20

Count Nicolas Ilyich Tolstoy, Tolstoy's father . . . 26

The house in which Tolstoy was born at Yasnaya Polyana, since removed to Dolgoye 34

The old entrance to Yasnaya Polyana Park . . . 36

The present entrance to Yasnaya Polyana Park . . . 38

Avenue of birch trees leading to the house . . . 42

A view in Yasnaya Polyana Park 46

A view in the village of Yasnaya Polyana . . . 50

Leo Tolstoy (in skull cap) and his brother Count Sergius Nicolayevich, shortly before the death of the latter; taken at about the time Leo Tolstoy wrote his reminiscences for this volume 54

V. J. Yushkof, Tolstoy's uncle 66

The Kayan University at the time of Tolstoy's student years 82

Tolstoy at the time of his leaving the University, 1848 . 94

The country house of Tolstoy's aunt, Yushkof . . . 132

ILLUSTRATIONS

                                                                    FACING PAGE

Tolstoy and his brothers before he left to join the Danube Army, 1854	160
Tolstoy, 1854	170
Group of contributors to the "Sovremennik" (The Contemporary Magazine)	198
Another group of contributors to the "Sovremennik"	202
Caricature of the "Inevitable Contributors" of the "Sovremennik"	206
Tolstoy at the time of his retirement from military service, 1856	220
Tolstoy during his second stay abroad, 1860	284
A facsimile of a letter written by Tolstoy in 1860	288
The house at Yasnaya Polyana used by Tolstoy as a school, 1860–62	324
Tolstoy during his educational activity	340
The Countess S. A. Tolstoy in 1860, before her marriage	362

PREFACE

Reasons for writing the biography—Correspondence with Countess S. A. Tolstoy—The definition of biography—Collection of materials—Division of the sources of materials into four parts, according to their importance—Correspondence with Tolstoy—Assistance of V. Tchertkoff—Unfavorable conditions of the work—Letters of Tolstoy concerning his participation in the work—The division of the biography into periods of seven years—Reminiscences of Tolstoy—The division of the whole biography into three volumes—The true significance of Leo Tolstoy—P.S.—The list of materials used in the first three parts in the alphabetic order of the authors' names.

CONSCIOUS of my inability, it is with diffidence and hesitation that I approach this work, sacred in my eyes—the life-story of my teacher, the aged prophet, Leo Tolstoy.

Only a few years ago I was so far from dreaming of this undertaking that, while living much of my time in close proximity to Tolstoy, and often staying in his house for hours or even whole days, it never entered into my mind to make any note or record of what I heard from Tolstoy himself or from those about him. Now, an exile[1] for my religious opinions, living far from my country and far from Tolstoy, I have set myself to accomplish this important task.

I was first encouraged to do it by the French publisher Stock, who, when taking in hand a complete publication of Tolstoy's works in French, asked me if I would revise the Russian texts and write a biography of the author.

I knew very well that it was impossible to write the biography of a man still living without the consent of himself and his family, so, before accepting Stock's offer, I wrote to Countess Tolstoy, asking if she had any objection to my undertaking the biography of her husband. I received from her a kind and encouraging reply, from which I will quote a few lines:

" . . . Of course you ought to write the biography, and

---

[1] See P.S. to this Introduction.

Lyof Nicolayevich could answer many of your questions, only you must not delay. The life so precious to us all was on the point of passing away. But now Lyof Nicolayevich is progressing favorably and is again at work."

This letter bears the date July 19, 1901, and was written directly after Tolstoy's severe illness.

On receipt of this letter I did not trouble Tolstoy himself, being convinced beforehand that he would not stand in my way; I accepted Stock's offer and set to work.

When I began to look into my materials and to consider the nature and the plan of the work I was undertaking, I grew alarmed on the one hand at its magnitude, while on the other I felt more and more fascinated by it, and, carried away as I was with the subject, I became so much engrossed with it that at the present moment I look upon it as my life's work, and heed no considerations which are offered from a publisher's point of view.

Some preliminary labor had to be spent in the collection of materials. These I divide into four categories, according to their importance and value.

In the first category I place Tolstoy's own autobiographical notes, as well as his letters and diaries. Such notes can be turned to much better account in the lifetime of the author, for the reason that any discrepancies between them and information derived from other sources can be explained by the author himself.

In the second category I place reminiscences and notices generally of Tolstoy by those who knew him personally, such as relations, friends, and acquaintances who had immediate intercourse with him. It may also include various kinds of official documents, such as certificates of birth, documents of the educational authorities, official records of State service, copies from judicial and administrative documents, and so on.

The third category includes notices of Tolstoy from outside sources, as well as works of his own in which real facts are intermingled with fiction by the play of the artistic imagination. But these, when looked at from a biographer's point of view, must be treated with great caution.

Lastly, the fourth category consists of sundry short articles, not to speak of whole books, which, though badly or clumsily written, or coming from authors who are not wholly trustworthy, yet have a certain comparative value where there is a gap left by other works. These I do not consider it necessary to enumerate.

Foreign literature gives us very few facts, especially in relation to the first period of Tolstoy's life. For this reason I do not make a separate list of foreign works, but include them in the general catalogue.

At the end of this Introduction is appended a list of all the written materials I have used.

After my first few steps in the examination of the collected materials, I found it necessary to seek personal intercourse with Tolstoy, as he alone could explain a number of obscure points by which I was puzzled. For a long while I hesitated, wondering whether it was right to trouble him, but at last I made up my mind to write to him and say that I had resolved to approach him with a few questions. Being aware that he permitted artists to take his portrait or make busts of him and amateur photographers to take his likeness, though all this gave him no pleasure, I requested him to sit for me too, as I wished to make a picture of him in words. To this he returned his kind consent in the following terms in a letter of December 2, 1901:

" . . . I shall be very glad to give you a sitting and will categorically answer your questions."

My friend V. Tchertkoff rendered me an important service by consenting to lay open for my work his rich archive of Tolstoy's private correspondence and of extracts from his diaries.

One great drawback to my labor was the fact that, through a senseless administrative order,[1] I was exiled from Russia, and have thus been deprived of an opportunity of consulting the man whose life I was writing, as well as prevented from working in Russian public libraries and archives, a circumstance which greatly hindered my work so far as dependent on the use of extracts from old periodicals, although, owing to the kindness of some owners of private Russian libraries and to the literary wealth of the Russian Department of the British Museum, this obstacle has been to some extent overcome. I have done my best in accordance with conscience and reason to meet these difficulties; I even petitioned the Minister of Interior to be

[1] See P.S. to this Introduction.

allowed to visit Russia for two months, but I received a distinct refusal. I therefore cannot look upon my task as complete.

As to the first volume, which I am now publishing, I may state that the readers will find there something perfectly new—I mean Tolstoy's memories of his childhood, and of his relations, as well as a great many of his private letters.

In order to illustrate for the reader the difficulty which Tolstoy had in writing his Reminiscences, as well as the way in which to treat them, I will quote a few extracts from our correspondence upon the subject.

I had written several times to Tolstoy and also to his intimate friends begging the latter to write down anything that, during quiet evening conversations, they might hear from him about his childhood.

At last I received the following communication from Tolstoy:

" . . . At first I thought that I should not be able to help you with my biography, notwithstanding all my desire to do so. I was afraid of the insincerity incidental to every autobiography, but now I seem to have found a form in which I can meet your wish by pointing out the distinguishing features of the consecutive periods of my life, in childhood, youth, and manhood. As soon as I find it possible, I will devote some hours to this work, and will endeavor to carry it out."

In one of his subsequent letters he writes:

" . . . I am afraid that it was in vain I gave you hopes by my promise to write my Reminiscences. I have tried to think about it, and I saw what a dreadful difficulty it is to avoid the Charybdis of self-praise (by keeping silence about all that is bad) and the Scylla of cynical frankness about all the abomination of one's life. Were a man to describe all his odiousness, stupidity, viciousness, vileness— quite truthfully, even more truthfully than Rousseau—it would be a seductive book or article. People would say: 'Here is a man whom many place high, but look what a scoundrel he was; if so, then for us ordinary folk it is all the more admissible.'

" Seriously, when I began to recall vividly to my mind all my life and saw all its stupidity (sheer stupidity) and

PREFACE

abomination, I thought, 'What then are other men if I, praised by many, am such a stupid worm?' And yet this could be explained by the fact that I am more cunning than others. I tell you all this not for the sake of verbal display, but quite sincerely. I have personally experienced it."

Seeing his hesitation and being alive to the great importance of the subject, I still insisted, and I sent him the outlines of the intended biography by way of canvas for him to embroider.

In my scheme I set forth the plan of dividing human life into periods of seven years' duration. I heard once from Tolstoy that he believed that, as physiologists divide human life into periods of seven years, so psychological life has the same periods of growth, and that each period of seven years' duration has its own moral physiognomy.

In arranging thus briefly the facts of Tolstoy's life we arrive at the following scheme:

YEARS.	TOLSTOY'S AGE.	CONTENTS OF THE PERIODS.
(1) 1828–35.	From birth to 7 years.	Childhood.
(2) 1835–42.	" 7 to 14 years.	Boyhood.
(3) 1842–49.	" 14 to 21 "	Youth, studies university, country life, and farming.
(4) 1849–56.	" 21 to 28 "	The beginning of a literary career: the Caucasus, Sebastopol, St. Petersburg.
(5) 1856–63.	" 28 to 35 "	Retirement from service. Travels, death of a brother, educational activity, services as a "Mediator," marriage.
(6) 1863–70.	" 35 to 42 "	Married life. *War and Peace.* Farming.
(7) 1870–77.	" 42 to 49 "	The famine in Samara. *Anna Karenina.* The summit of literary fame, family happiness, and wealth.
(8) 1877–84.	" 49 to 56 "	Crisis. *How I Came to Believe* (My Confession). New Testament. *What I Believe.*
(9) 1884–91.	" 56 to 63 "	Moscow. *What shall we do?* Literature for the people. *Posrednik.* Spread of ideas in the classes and the masses. The Critics.
(10) 1891–98.	" 63 to 70 "	Famine. *The Kingdom of God is Within You.* The Doukhobors. The persecutions of the supporters of these views.
(11) 1898–1905.	" 70 to 77 "	*Resurrection.* Excommunication. The latest period. Appeal to the military, the people, the clergy, and social reformers. The war.

On even a cursory glance at this scheme the reader must notice the spiritual tendency of each period. And this scheme or plan has not remained without results. Before long I received a letter from Tolstoy in which, among other things, he writes:

"... With regard to my biography, I may tell you that I very much desire to help you and to write at least what is most essential. I decided that I might write it, because I can understand that it may be interesting and possibly useful to men were I to show all the abomination of the life I led before my awakening, and—speaking without false modesty—what was good in it (were it only in intentions, which, owing to my weakness, were not being always realized) after the awakening. It is in this spirit that I should like to write it for you. Your programme of seven-year periods is useful to me and does indeed suggest thoughts. I will endeavor to occupy myself with this as soon as I complete the work I am now engaged in."

Finally, in a few more months, I received a rough draft of the first part of his reminiscences written by Tolstoy. I hastened to make use of them, putting his own vivid descriptions in the place of colorless passages of the biography I had begun. At the first opportunity which I had I forwarded to Tolstoy the early chapters of my work, asking him to give his opinion of it. In his answer he says:

"... My general impression is that you make very good use of my notes, but I avoid entering into details, as this might draw me into the work of correcting, which I wish to avoid. So I leave it all to you, merely requesting that in your biography, when citing extracts from my notes, you should add that *they are taken from uncorrected draft notes sent to you and put at your disposal by me.*"

I relate all this here in order to free Tolstoy from all literary responsibility, and, in accordance with his wish, I quote the italicized sentence both in the Introduction and with all the extracts from his notes.

With this encouragement I continued my labors.

The first volume, now published, contains the story of his origin and the earlier periods of his life—childhood, youth, and manhood, and ends with his marriage.

This limit is, I think, very appropriate, the more so as Tolstoy himself looks upon his marriage as the beginning of a new life. It happens also to have one practical convenience—its contents make up an ordinary-sized volume.

In the second volume will be described the period of Tolstoy's greatest literary success, family happiness, and material welfare, followed by an important crisis which led to his birth into a new spiritual life. The period is that of the years 1863-84, corresponding to his age, 35-56.

In the third and last volume will be presented the life which he lives now, and which I hope will continue to our joy for many years.

It is well remarked by one of Tolstoy's biographers that his life may be compared to a pyramid with its top downward and the base upward, growing higher and wider. The biographical material is distributed in a corresponding proportion: there is very little of it during his childhood, but, as we approach the present time, its growth becomes enormous.

Tolstoy's name is so well known that I am relieved of the difficult and responsible task of giving his general characteristics in order to introduce him to the public. It is my sole aim and endeavor to adhere to the simple facts.

October 15, 1905.

ONEX, NEAR GENEVA, VILLA RUSSE,
SWITZERLAND.

P.S.—I had already reached the end of my first volume, when, in consequence of a temporary relaxation of repressive measures in Russia, I received permission to revisit my country. I went to Russia, accordingly, and have there been able adequately to enlarge the biographical material of the first volume, thanks to my personal intercourse with Tolstoy himself, and also by reading his diaries and correspondence, for which privilege I am deeply grateful to Countess S. Tolstoy. She gave me access to the valuable collections of biographical materials collected by her and placed in the Historical Museum of Moscow, in the room called after Tolstoy's name.

Had my work been begun under more favorable circumstances, it would probably appear in a different and less imperfect shape. But it is impossible to go back and begin again from the beginning; I therefore leave it in its

PREFACE

original form, introducing only such changes as are rendered necessary by the additional material newly collected in Russia.

I also leave unchanged the Introduction to the work, as it truly represents the conditions under which I have done it.

Two more words. I hope the reader will understand under what peculiar conditions I had to labor and still am laboring. I am writing the biography not only of a living man, but also of one who leads a strenuous and energetic life, and hence, as a biographer, I am unable to say the last word or give my judgment on the stream of life which is still flowing so forcibly.

I must therefore be content simply to call my work, as I most sincerely do, a Collection of those materials for the Biography of Leo Tolstoy which are accessible to me. I desired not to delay the publication of this volume, which is more or less complete in itself, as I thought that its publication might indicate to every one a centre to which information and reminiscences, as well as any documents concerning Tolstoy, could be forwarded, and for all help and advice I shall be very grateful.

August 23, 1905. P. BIRUKOFF.

BIBLIOGRAPHY

List of materials used for the writing of Volume I.

First Division.

(1) *A Short Biography*, written by Tolstoy at the request of N. Strakhof for the Stassulevich publication, *Russian Library*, Issue IX. Count L. Tolstoy, St. Petersburg, 1879.

(2) *How I Came to Believe*, L. Tolstoy. Complete Edition of Tolstoy's Works, vol. i. Published by The Free Age Press, Christchurch, Hants.

(3) *First Reminiscences.* A Fragment. Complete Edition of Leo Tolstoy's Works, vol. xiii, tenth edition. Moscow, 1897.

(4) A rough draft of uncorrected notes intrusted to me by Tolstoy.

(5) Private letters of Tolstoy to his friends and relations.

(6) *The Diary of Leo Tolstoy.*

(7) *The Memoirs of Countess S. A. Tolstoy.*

(8) *Autobiographical Tales*, printed in vol. iv. Complete Edition of Tolstoy's Works (Articles on Education).

(9) *My Reminiscences*, 1848–1889, by A. Fet. Moscow, 1890. (Many letters by Tolstoy.)

(10) "A Few Words in Connection with the Book, *War and Peace*." An article by Tolstoy. *The Russian Archive*, 1868, vol. iii.

Second Division.

(11) S. A. Bers, *Reminiscences of Count L. N. Tolstoy.* Smolensk, 1894.

(12) Paul Boyer, *Chez Tolstoy: Trois jours à Yasnaya Polyana.* Le Temps, August 27–29, 1901.

(13) A. E. Golovachof-Panayef, *Russian Writers and Artists: Reminiscences,* 1824–1870. St. Petersburg, 1890. Published by Gubinsky.

(14) D. V. Grigorovich, *Literary Reminiscences.* Complete Works, vol. xii, p. 326.

(15) G. P. Danilevsky, *A Journey to Yasnaya Polyana. Historical Messenger,* March, 1886.

(16) From the Papers of A. V. Druzhinin: *Twenty-Five Years.* Magazine published by the Friendly Society of Needy Writers and Scholars. St. Petersburg, 1884.

(17) N. P. Zagoskin, *Count Leo Tolstoy and his Life as a Student. Historical Messenger,* January, 1894.

(18) Zakharyin (Yakunin), Dr., *Countess A. A. Tolstoy: Personal Impressions and Reminiscences. Messenger of Europe,* June, 1904.

(19) R. Loewenfeld, *Count Leo Tolstoy; his Life and Works.* Translated from the German by A. V. Pereligin (with notes by the Countess S. A. Tolstoy). Moscow, 1897.

(20) R. Loewenfeld, *Gespraeche mit und ueber Tolstoy.* Leipzig.

(21) Eugene Markof, *The Living Soul in School. Thoughts and Reminiscences of an old Educationist. Messenger of Europe,* February, 1900.

(22) M. O. Menshikof, *The First Work of Tolstoy.* Booklets of "Nedelya." October, 1892.

(23) N. K. Mikhailovsky, *Literary Reminiscences and the Contemporary Muddle,* vol. i. Published by the *Russian Wealth.* St. Petersburg, 1900.

(24) "Opinion of One Hundred and Five Noblemen of the Tula Province upon the Question of Allotting Land to Peasants." *The Contemporary,* 1858, vol. lxxii.

(25) N. A. Nekrassof, *Four Letters to Count Leo Tolstoy.* "Niva." N. 2, 1898.

(26) L. P. Nikiforof, *Biographical Sketch. The Courier,* September, 1902.

(27) Prince D. D. Obolensky, *Reminiscences and Characteristics. The Russian Archive,* 1894.

(28) J. J. Panayef, *Literary Reminiscences, including Letters.* St. Petersburg, 1888. Published by Martinof.

(29) S. Plaksin, *Count Leo Tolstoy among Children.* Moscow, 1903.

BIBLIOGRAPHY

(30) V. A. Poltoratsky, *Reminiscences. Historical Messenger,* June, 1893.

(31) A. Rumyantsef, *Letter to D. D. Titoff. The Polar Star,* iv. Published by Herzen, London, 1857.

(32) *The Sebastopol Song.* Related by one of the authors of the song. *Russian Olden Times,* February, 1884.

(33) P. A. Sergeyenko, *How Leo Tolstoy Lives and Works.* Moscow, 1898.

(34) Eugene Schuyler, *Reminiscences of Count Leo Tolstoy. Russian Olden Times,* October, 1890. Translated from the English (*Scribner's Magazine,* 1889).

(35) I. S. Turgenef, *First Collection of Letters,* 1840–1883. Published by the Literary Fund, St. Petersburg, 1885.

(36) D. Oospensky, *Archive Materials for Tolstoy's Biography. Russian Thought,* September, 1903.

(37) Private letters of Tolstoy's friends and relations about him.

(38) N. K. Schilder, *Episode of the Battle of Austerlitz. Russian Olden Times,* vol. lxviii, 1890.

Third Division.

(39) Eugene Bogoslavsky, *Turgenef on Lyof Tolstoy, Seventy-five Opinions.* Tiflis, 1894.

(40) Wilh. Bode, *Tolstoy in Weimar. Der Saemann,* Monatschrift, Leipzig, September, 1905.

(41) M. I. Venukof, *Sebastopol Song. Russian Olden Times,* February, 1875.

(42) Princess E. G. Volkonsky, *The Family of the Princes' Volkonsky.* Materials collected and edited by Princess E. G. Volkonsky. St. Petersburg, 1900.

(43) Prince S. G. Volkonsky (decembrist). *Memoirs.* Published by M. S. Volkonsky.

(44) Eugene Garshin, *Reminiscences of I. S. Turgenef. Historical Messenger,* November, 1883.

(45) P. D. Draganof, *Count L. N. Tolstoy;* as a writer of world-wide fame, and the circulation of his works in Russia and abroad.

(46) A. F. Kony, *A Biographical Sketch: "I. F. Gorbunof"* (preface to the edition of his works).

(47) V. N. Lyaskovsky, A. S. Khomiakof, *His Biography and Teaching*. The Russian Archive, No. 11, 1896.
(48) V. N. Nazaryef, *Life and Men of the Past Time*. Historical Messenger, November, 1900.
(49) Eugene Solovyof, *L. N. Tolstoy; his Life and Literary Activity*. Published by Pavlenkof.
(50) M. A. Yanzhul, *To Tolstoy's Biography*. Russian Olden Times, February, 1900.

Books of Reference, Articles in Newspapers, Notes.

(51) *Brockhaus and Effron. Encyclopædic Dictionary.*
(52) Yuri Bitoft. *Count Tolstoy in Literature and Art. Bibliographical Indicator.* Published by Sytin. Moscow, 1903.
(53) *Russian Literature, Eleventh to Nineteenth Century inclusive,* by A. V. Mezyer.
(54) V. Zelinsky, Criticism in *Russian Literature* of Tolstoy's Works. Moscow, 1896.

INTRODUCTION TO HIS REMINISCENCES

By Leo Tolstoy.

Reason for writing the Reminiscences—Pushkin's verses—A quotation from Tolstoy's diary—The general review of his life—Tolstoy's attitude to his novels: *Childhood, Boyhood,* and *Youth.*

MY friend, Paul Birukoff, having undertaken to write my biography (for the complete edition of my works), has asked me to furnish him with some particulars of my life.

I very much wished to fulfil his desire, and in my imagination I began to compose my autobiography. At first, I involuntarily began in the most natural way with only that which was good in my life, merely adding to this good side, like shade on a picture, its dark, repulsive features. But upon examining the events of my life more seriously I saw that such an autobiography, though it might not be a direct lie, would yet be a lie, owing to the biassed exposure and lighting up of the good and the hushing up or smoothing down of the evil. Yet when I thought of writing the whole truth without concealing anything that was bad in my life, I was shocked at the impression which such an autobiography was bound to produce. At that time I fell ill, and during the unavoidable idleness of an invalid, my thoughts kept continually turning to my reminiscences, and dreadful these reminiscences were.

I experienced with the utmost force what Pushkin says in his verses, " Memory ":

> "When, for mankind, the weary day grows still,
> And on the City's silent heart there fall
> The half transparent shadows of the night
> With sleep, the sweet reward of daily work—
> Then is the time when in the hush I wear
> Through dragging hours of heavy watchfulness:

> When, idle in the dark, most keen I feel
> The stinging serpent of my heart's remorse:
> Reflection seethes—and on my o'erwhelmed mind
> Rushes a multitude of woful thoughts,
> While memory, her unending roll unfolds
> In silence, and with sick recoil I read
> The story of my life, and curse myself,
> And bitterly bewail with bitter tears—
> But not one woeful line can I wash out!"

In the last line I would only make this alteration: instead of "woeful line" I would say "shameful line can I wash out."

Under this impression I wrote the following in my diary:

6th January, 1903.—I am now suffering the torments of hell: I am calling to mind all the infamies of my former life—these reminiscences do not pass away and they poison my existence. Generally people regret that the individuality does not retain memory after death. What a happiness that it does not! What an anguish it would be if I remembered in this life all the evil, all that is painful to the conscience, committed by me in a previous life. And, if one remembers the good, one has to remember the evil too. What a happiness that reminiscences disappear with death and that there only remains consciousness, a consciousness which, as it were, represents the general outcome of the good and the evil, like a complex equation reduced to its simplest expression: $x =$ a positive or a negative, a great or a small quantity.

Yes, the extinction of memory is a great happiness; with memory one could not live a joyful life. As it is, with the extinction of memory we enter into life with a clean white page upon which we can write afresh good and evil.

It is true that not all my life was so fearfully bad. That character prevailed only for a period of twenty years. It is also true that even during that period my life was not the uninterrupted evil that it appeared to me during my illness; for even during that period there used to awake in me impulses toward good, although they did not last long and were soon stifled by unrestrained passions.

Still these reflections, especially during my illness, clearly showed me that my autobiography—as autobiographies are generally written—if it passed over in silence all the abomination and criminality of my life, would be a lie, and that, when a man writes his life, he should write the whole and exact truth. Only such an autobiography, however humiliating it may be for me to write it, can have a true and fruitful interest for the readers.

Thus recalling my life to mind, *i. e.*, examining it from the point of view of the good and evil which I had done, I saw that all my long life breaks up into four periods: that splendid—especially in comparison with what comes after—that innocent, joyful, poetic period of childhood up to fourteen; then the second, those dreadful twenty years, the period of coarse dissoluteness, of service of ambition and vanity, and, above all, of sensuousness; then the third period of eighteen years, from my marriage until my spiritual birth, a period which, from the worldly point of view, one might call moral; I mean that during these eighteen years I lived a regular, honest family life, without addicting myself to any vices condemned by public opinion, but a period all the interests of which were limited to egotistical family cares, to concern for the increase of wealth, the attainment of literary success, and the enjoyment of every kind of pleasure; and lastly, there is the fourth period of twenty years in which I am now living and in which I hope to die, and from the standpoint of which I see all the significance of my past life, and which I do not desire to alter in anything except in those habits of evil which were acquired by me in the previous periods.

Such a history of my life during all these four periods, I should like to write quite, quite truthfully, if God will give me the power and the time. I think that such an autobiography, even though very defective, would be more profitable to men than all that artistic prattle with which the twelve volumes of my works are filled, and to which men of our time attribute an undeserved significance.

And I should now like to do this. I will begin by describing the first joyful period of my childhood, which attracts me with special force; then, however ashamed I may be to do so, I will also describe, without hiding anything, those dreadful twenty years of the following period; then the third period, which may be of the least interest of all; and, finally, the last period of my awakening to the

BIOGRAPHY OF LEO TOLSTOY

PART I

THE FAMILY ORIGIN OF LEO TOLSTOY

CHAPTER I

THE ANCESTORS OF LEO TOLSTOY ON HIS FATHER'S SIDE [1]

The Counts Tolstoy-Indris—The first Count P. A. Tolstoy—His rise, service, and fall—Restoration of the title of count to his grandson, Andrey Ivanovich Tolstoy—An episode in the life of A. I. Tolstoy—Tolstoy's recollections of his grandparents—Their characters and mutual relations—Soap-bubbles—Nut-gathering—The narrator of fairy tales, Lyof Stepanovich—Genealogical table—The more eminent representatives of the Tolstoy family—Their family relations to L. Tolstoy.

THE history of the Counts Tolstoy presents a picture of an ancient and noble family descending, according to the accounts of genealogists, from the good and true man Indris, who came from Germany to Tchernigof in 1353 with his two sons and a retinue of 3,000 men; he was baptized and received the name of Leonty; he became the founder of several noble families. His great-grandchild, Andrey Kharitonovich, who moved from Tchernigof to Moscow and received from the Grand Duke Vassili Tyomny the surname of Tolstoy, was the founder of the branch known to us as the Tolstoys (in which branch Count Lyof Tolstoy was born in the twentieth generation from the founder Indris).

One of his descendants, Peter Andreyvich Tolstoy, became a dignitary at the Russian court in 1683, and was

---

[1] Wherever I quote the words of Tolstoy from his Reminiscences, I shall mention it and put them in inverted commas.—*P. B.*

afterward one of the chief actors in the rebellion of the Streltsi. The fall of the Tsarevna Sophia caused this Tolstoy abruptly to change his attitude and pass over to the Tsar Peter; but the latter behaved to him for a long time with coldness, and a considerable period passed before Peter Andreyvich enjoyed the full confidence of the Tsar. It is said that at their merry banquets Tsar Peter delighted to pull the big wig off Peter Tolstoy's head, and tapping him on the bald crown to repeat: "Little head, little head, if you were not so clever, you would have parted from your body long ago."

The Tsar's suspicions were not allayed even by the military achievements of Peter Tolstoy during the second Azof campaign (1696).

In 1697 the Tsar sent "volunteers" to study in foreign countries, and Peter Tolstoy, already a middle-aged man, offered himself to go abroad to study naval matters. Two years which he spent in Italy gave him an opportunity of seeing something of the culture of Western Europe. At the end of 1701 Peter Tolstoy was appointed ambassador in Constantinople, an important but very difficult post. During the complications of 1710–1713 Peter Tolstoy was twice confined in the Castle of the Seven Towers, a fact which accounts for this castle being represented in the Tolstoy coat-of-arms.

In 1717 Tolstoy rendered an important service to the Tsar, and so strengthened his position for all subsequent time. Having been sent to Naples, where the Tsarevitch Alexis was hiding with his mistress Euphrosyne in the Castle of St. Elmo, Peter Tolstoy, with the help of the lady, adroitly outwitted the Tsarevitch, and by means of threats and false promises induced him to return to Russia. For his active participation in the subsequent trial and secret execution of the Tsarevitch carried out by Peter Tolstoy, with the aid of Rumyantsef,[1] Oshakof, and Buturlin, his accomplices, at the direction of Peter I Peter Tolstoy received a present of land, and was appointed Chief of the Secret Chamber, where there was soon a great deal to be done in consequence of the rumors and agitations provoked among the people by the fate of Alexis. From that time Peter

[1] Rumyantsef. Letter to D. T. Titof. *The Polar Star*, IV. Herzen's publication, London, 1857.

Count Peter Andreyevich Tolstoy, the first Count Tolstoy.

Tolstoy is conspicuous as one of the most intimate and trusted persons about the Emperor. The affair of the Tsarevitch brought Peter into favor with the Empress Catherine, and on the day of her coronation, May 7, 1724, he was made a Count. After the death of Peter I Tolstoy, together with Menshikof, greatly aided Catherine's accession to the throne, and consequently enjoyed much favor during her reign. But on Peter II's accession his fall ensued. In spite of his advanced age—he was eighty-two years old—he was exiled to the Solovetsky Convent, where, however, he did not live long. He died in 1729.

We still possess the diary of Peter Tolstoy's journey abroad in 1697-1699, a characteristic exhibition of the impression made on men of his period by their acquaintance with Western Europe. Besides this, in 1706 Peter Tolstoy wrote a detailed description of the Black Sea. There also exist two translations he made: *Ovid's Metamorphoses,* and *Administration of the Turkish Empire.*

Peter Tolstoy had a son, Ivan Petrovich, who was himself deprived of his office, that of President of the Court, at the same time as his father, and was exiled to the same convent, where he died soon after him.

It was not till May 26, 1760, when the Empress Elisabeth Petrovna was already on the throne, that the descendants of Peter Andreyevich were restored to the rank of counts in the person of Peter's grandson, Andrey Ivanovich, the grandfather of Lyof Tolstoy.

"I heard from my aunt the following story about Andrey Ivanovich, who whilst very young married the Princess Schetinin. For some reason or other his wife had to go to a ball without her husband. Having started on her way, probably in a covered sledge, from which the seat had been removed in order that her high headgear should not be injured, the young countess, perhaps seventeen years old, remembered that she had not said good-by to her husband, and returned home.

"When she arrived, she found him in tears; he was so much distressed at his wife's leaving the house without bidding him good-by."[1]

In his Reminiscences Tolstoy speaks of his grandfather and grandmother on his father's side as follows:

[1] Note added by Tolstoy when revising the MS. of this work.

"My grandmother, Pelageya Nicolayevna, was the daughter of the blind Prince Nicolay Ivanovich Gorchakof, who had amassed a large fortune. As far as I can form an idea of her character, she was not very intelligent, poorly educated—like all at that time, she knew French better than Russian (and to this her education was limited) —and exceedingly spoilt, first by her father, then by her husband, and lastly, in my time, by her son. Besides this, as a daughter of the elder branch, she enjoyed great regard from all the Gorchakofs: from the former Minister of War, Nicolay Ivanovich, from Andrey Ivanovich and the sons of Dmitri Petrovich, the freethinker, Peter, Sergey, and Michael of Sebastopol.

"My grandfather, Ilya Andreyevich, her husband, was, according to my view of him, a man of limited intelligence, gentle in manner, merry, and not only generous, but carelessly extravagant, and above all, trustful. In his estate, Polyani, in the Belyefski district—not Yasnaya Polyana, but Polyani—incessant fêtes, theatrical performances, balls, banquets, and excursions were kept up, which, largely owing to my grandfather's tendency to play for high stakes at lomber and whist without knowing the game, and his readiness either to give or lend to any one who asked, both in loan and donation, and above all with the speculations and monopolies he used to start, resulted in his wife's large estate being so involved in debts, that at last there was no means of livelihood, and my grandfather had to procure the post of governor in Kazan, which he did easily owing to his connections.

"My grandfather, as I have been told, would not accept bribes, except from wine merchants, though it was then a universal custom, and he was angry when any were offered to him. But my grandmother, as I am informed, accepted presents unknown to her husband.

"In Kazan, my grandmother gave her youngest daughter Pelageya in marriage to Yushkof; the eldest, Alexandra, while yet in St. Petersburg, had married Count Osten-Saken.

"After the death of her husband in Kazan, and the marriage of my father, my grandmother settled down with my father in Yasnaya Polyana, and here I knew her as an old woman, and well remember her.

"My grandmother passionately loved my father and us, her grandchildren, and amused herself with us. She was fond of my aunts, but I think she did not quite love my mother; she considered her unworthy of my father, and was jealous of her in regard to him. With the servants she could not be exacting, because all knew she was the first person in the house, and tried to please her, but with her maid, Gasha, she gave herself up to her caprices and tormented her, calling her 'You, my dear,' and demanding of her what she had not asked for, and in every way worrying her. Strange to say, Gasha or Agafia Michaelovna,[1] whom I knew well, became infected with my grandmother's capricious ways, and with her little daughter, with her cat, and in general with all those beings with whom she could be exacting, was as capricious as my grandmother was with herself.

"My earliest reminiscences of my grandmother, before our removal to Moscow and our life there, amount to three strong impressions concerning her. One was how my grandmother washed, and with some kind of special soap produced on her hands wonderful bubbles, which, so it seemed to me, she alone could produce. We used to be purposely brought to her—probably our delight and wonder at her soap-bubbles amused her—in order to see how she washed. I remember the white jacket, petticoat, white aged hands, and the enormous bubbles rising on them, and her satisfied, smiling, white face.

"The second recollection is how she was drawn out, my father's valets acting as horses, in the yellow cabriolet on springs—in which we used to go for drives with our tutor, Feodor Ivanovich—into the small coppice for gathering nuts, of which there was a specially great quantity that year. I remember the dense thicket of hazel trees into which, thrusting aside and breaking the branches, Petrusha and Matyusha, the house valets, dragged the cabriolet with my grandmother, how they pulled down to her branches with clusters of ripe nuts, sometimes dropping off, how my grandmother herself gathered them into a bag, and how we either ourselves bent down branches, or else were astonished by the strength of Feodor Ivanovich, who bent down thick

---

[1] Agafia Michaelovna died an old woman a few years ago in Yasnaya Polyana, where she had been living in retirement for many years.

stems, while we gathered nuts on all sides, and always noticed that there yet remained nuts ungathered by us when Feodor Ivanovitch let go the stems, and the bushes slowly catching in one another straightened up again. I remember how hot it was in the open spaces, how pleasantly fresh in the shade, how one breathed the sharp odor of the hazel-tree foliage, how the nuts cracked on all sides under the teeth of the girls who were with us, and how we, without ceasing, chewed the fresh, full, white kernels.

"We gathered the nuts into our pockets, into the skirts of our jackets, into the cabriolet, and our grandmother took them from us and praised us. How we came home, and what happened after, I do not remember. I remember only that grandmother and the hazel trees, the peculiar odor of the foliage of the hazel bushes, the valets, the yellow cabriolet, and the sun were blended into one joyful impression. It seemed to me that, as the soap-bubbles could be produced only by my grandmother, so also the wood, the nuts, the sun, could only be in connection with my grandmother in her yellow cabriolet drawn by Petrusha and Matyusha.

"But the strongest impression connected with my grandmother was a night passed in her bedroom with Lyof Stepanovich. Lyof Stepanovich was a blind story-teller (he was already an old man when I came to know him)—the survival of ancient luxury, the luxury of my grandfather. He was bought merely for the purpose of narrating stories, which, owing to the extraordinary memory peculiar to blind people, he could retell word for word after they had been twice read to him.

"He lived somewhere in the house, and during the whole day he was not seen. But in the evenings he came up into my grandmother's bedroom (this bedroom was a low little room into which one had to enter up two steps), and he seated himself on a low window ledge, where they used to bring him supper from the master's table. Here he waited for my grandmother, who might with impunity perform her night toilet in the presence of a blind man. On the day when it was my turn to sleep in my grandmother's bedroom, Lyof Stepanovich, with his white eyes, clad in a long blue coat with puffs on the shoulders, was already sitting on the window ledge having his supper. I don't remember where my grandmother undressed, whether in this room or another,

Count Ilya Andreyevich Tolstoy, Leo Tolstoy's paternal grandfather.

or how I was put to bed, I remember only the moment when the candle was put out and there remained only a little light in front of the gilded icons, and my grandmother, that same wonderful grandmother who produced the extraordinary soap-bubbles, all white, clothed in white, lying on white, and covered with white, in her white nightcap, lay high on the cushions, and from the window was heard the even quiet voice of Lyof Stepanovich. 'Will it please you for me to continue?' 'Yes, continue.' '"Dearest sister," she said,' recommenced Lyof Stepanovich, with his quiet, even, aged voice, '"tell us one of those most interesting stories which you know so well how to narrate." "Willingly," answered Shaheresada, "would I relate the remarkable history of Prince Kamaralzaman, if our lord will express his consent." Having received the consent of the Sultan, Shaheresada began thus: A certain powerful king had an only son"'... and, evidently word for word, according to the book, Lyof Stepanovich began the history of Kamaralzaman. I did not listen, I did not understand what he said, so absorbed was I by the mysterious appearance of the white grandmother, by her swaying shadow on the wall, and the appearance of the old man with white eyes whom I could not now see, but whom I realized as sitting immovably on the window ledge, and who was saying with a slow voice some strange words, which seemed to me very solemn as they alone resounded through the darkness of the little room lighted by the trembling of the image-lamp. I probably immediately fell asleep, for I remember nothing further, and in the morning I was again astonished and enraptured by the soap-bubbles which my grandmother when washing produced on her hands.

"According to Marie's recollections, the blind Lyof Stepanovich's sense of hearing was so perfect that he could distinctly hear mice running about and could tell in which direction they were going. In grandmother's room one of the special attractions for the mice was the oil used for the image-lamp, which they drank up. At night while telling stories he would say, without changing his tone of voice: 'There, your excellency, a little mouse has just run to the image-lamp to get at the oil.' After that he would go on again with his story-telling in the same monotone."

The following genealogical table gives the reader a view of the nearest ancestors and relations of Lyof Nicolayevich Tolstoy:

The Counts Tolstoy

Number of Generations from "Indris."	
15	Peter Andreyevich Tolstoy, the first Count (died **1729**).
16	Ivan Petrovich (died 1728).
17	Andrey Ivanovich (died 1803).
18	Ilya Andreyevich, Governor of Kazan (died 1820).
19	Alexandra, married to Count Osten-Saken. Nicolay (died 1837).
19	Pelageya, married V. P. Yushkof. Ilya (died childless).
20	Nicolay (born 1823). Sergey (born 1826). Dmitri (born 1827). Lyof (born 1828). Marie (born 1830).[1]

The Counts Tolstoy are known in many branches of social activity. It would probably interest the reader to know the degree of relationship which some of these bear to Tolstoy. For example, let us take Feodor Petrovitch Tolstoy, the well-known artist, medallist, and vice-president of the Imperial Academy of Arts, his nephew the poet, Alexey Konstantinovich Tolstoy, and the ex-minister Dmitri Andreyevich Tolstoy, well known for his reactionary measures. These three members of the Tolstoy family were distantly related to our Tolstoy, their common ancestor being Ivan Petrovitch Tolstoy, son of the first Count Tolstoy, Peter Andreyevich, who died with his father in exile at the Solovetsky Convent.[2]

I ought here to mention Theodore Tolstoy, an original man, called the American. He was known for his very unusual adventures, and the following words in Griboyedof's comedy, called "Come to Grief through being too Clever," refer to him: "Exiled to Kamchatka, he returned an Aleoute." Tolstoy speaks of him in his reminiscences of his childhood, and it was his individuality which partly suggested the character of Dolokhof in *War and Peace*. He was Tolstoy's first cousin once removed.

---

[1] "Count L. N. Tolstoy and his University Life." N. P. Zagoskin *Istoricheski Vestnik*. Jan., 1894, p. 81.

[2] Information given by Lyof Tolstoy. See also Brockhaus and Effron's Encyclopædia, vol. xxxiii, p. 462.

CHAPTER II

THE ANCESTORS OF LEO TOLSTOY ON HIS MOTHER'S SIDE

The Princes Volkonsky—The origin of the family—Its more important representatives—Prince Sergey Feodorovich Volkonsky—Legend about the icon—Prince N. S. Volkonsky—The Bleak Hills—Tolstoy's recollections of his grandfather Volkonsky—The offer of Potemkin—The governorship in Archangel—Nicolay Sergeyevich as landowner and as man—Princess V. A. Volkonsky—Tolstoy's reminiscences of her—Prince Sergey Grigoryevich Volkonsky, the Decembrist—Prince Nicolay Grigoryevich Volkonsky-Repnin—The battle of Austerlitz.

THE Princes Volkonsky trace their descent from Rurik. Since the days of Prince Volkonsky (Tolstoy's grandfather) the genealogical tree of the Princes Volkonsky, painted in oil colors, has been preserved[1] at Yasnaya Polyana. In this the founder of the line, St. Michael, Prince of Tchernigov, is represented as holding in his hand a tree whose branches exhibit an enumeration of his descendants.

At the beginning of the fourteenth century Prince Ivan Turyevich, in the thirteenth generation from Rurik, had received the Volkonsky property, situated on the Volkona; this river flows through the present province of Kaluga and to some extent through Tula. Hence the family was known as that of the Princes Volkonsky.[2]

His son, Feodor Ivanovich, was killed in the battle of Mamai in 1380.

Among other ancestors of Tolstoy we may mention his great-grandfather, Prince Sergey Feodorovich Volkonsky, who is the hero of the following legend:

" The prince took part in the Seven Years' War as Major-General. During the campaign his wife dreamed that a voice commanded her to have a small icon painted, showing on one side the source of life and on the other Nicolay the Thaumaturgist, and to send it to her husband. She

---
[1] This picture has been destroyed, according to latest information
[2] *The Family of the Princes Volkonsky*, p. 7.

selected a wooden plate, on which she ordered that the icon should be painted, and this she sent to Prince Sergey by the hands of Field-Marshal Apraxin. The same day Sergey received by the courier an order to go out in search of the enemy; and having appealed for God's help, he put on the sacred image. In a cavalry attack a bullet struck him on the breast, but it knocked against the icon and did not hurt him, and in this way the icon saved his life. It was treasured in later years by his younger son, Nicolay Sergeyevich. Prince Sergey Feodorovich died March 10, 1784." [1]

Tolstoy was no doubt acquainted with this legend, and made use of it in *War and Peace* to illustrate the character of the devout princess Marie Volkonsky, as it is made to appear in an incident represented as occurring before Prince Andrey's departure for the war. The reader will remember that the princess persuaded her brother to wear the image, handing it to Prince Andrey with the words: "You may think what you like, but do this for my sake. Please do it! The father of my father, our grandfather, wore it during all his wars...." [2]

We see here artistic truth interwoven with historical, and if the latter gives the former an air of truthfulness, so it receives from it in return that touch of human nature which makes all the characters of *War and Peace* so lifelike and so irresistibly soul-stirring.

The younger son of Sergey Feodorovich, Nicolay Sergeyevich, was Tolstoy's grandfather on his mother's side. What we learn about him from the genealogy is as follows:

"Nicolay Sergeyevich, an infantry general, youngest son of Sergey Feodorovich and Princess Marie Dmitryevna, *née* Chaadaef, was born March 30, 1753. In 1780 he was in the suite of the Empress Catharine II when she was in Mogilef, and was present at her first interview with the Emperor Joseph II. In 1786 he accompanied the Empress to Taurida. On the occasion of the wedding of the hereditary prince, afterward King Frederick William III, he was appointed special envoy to Berlin. He died on February 3, 1821, on his estate, where he lived throughout those last years of his life which have been immortalized

---

[1] *The Family of the Princes Volkonsky*, p. 697.
[2] *War and Peace*, vol. i., p. 167, tenth edition.

Prince Nicolas Sergeyevich Volkousky, Tolstoy's maternal grandfather.

by his grandson in his novel *War and Peace*. His remains rest in the Troitsko-Sergey monastery."[1]

In his Reminiscences Tolstoy speaks of his maternal grandfather as follows:

"As for my grandfather, I know that having attained the high position of Commander-in-chief during the reign of Catherine, he suddenly lost it by refusing to marry Potemkin's niece and mistress, Varenka Engelhardt. To Potemkin's suggestion he answered: 'What makes him think that I'll marry his strumpet?'

"In consequence of this exclamation, not only was his career checked, but he was nominated Governor of Archangel, where he remained, I believe, until Paul's accession, when he retired; and having after that married Princess Catherine Trubetskoy, he settled down in his estate, Yasnaya Polyana, which he had inherited from his father, Sergey Feodorovich.

"The Princess Catherine died early, leaving my grandfather an only daughter, and with this dearly beloved child and her friend, a Frenchwoman, he lived until his death about 1821. He was regarded as a very exacting master, but I never heard instances of his cruelty or of his inflicting the severe punishments which were usual at that time. I believe that such cases did occur on his estate, but that the enthusiastic respect for his character and intelligence was so great among the servants and the peasants of his time, whom I have often questioned about him, that although I have heard condemnation of my father, I heard only praises of my grandfather's intelligence, business capacities, and interest in the welfare of the peasants and of his enormous household. He erected splendid accommodation for his servants, and took care that they should always be not only well fed, but also well dressed and happy. On fête days he arranged recreations for them, swings, dancing, etc.

"Like every intelligent landowner of that time, he was concerned with the welfare of the peasants, and they prospered, the more so that my grandfather's high position, inspiring respect as it did in the police and local authorities, exempted them from oppression from this quarter.

"He probably possessed refined æsthetic feeling. All

[1] *The Family of the Princes Volkonsky*, p. 707.

his buildings were not only durable and commodious, but also of considerable beauty; and these last words would apply also to the park which he laid out in front of the house. He probably was very fond of music, for he kept a small but excellent orchestra, merely for himself and my mother. I still remember an enormous elm tree which grew near the avenue of limes and was surrounded by benches with stands for the musicians. In the mornings he used to walk in the avenue and listen to the music. He could not bear sport, and he loved flowers and hot-house plants.

"A strange fate brought him into contact with that same Varenka Engelhardt whom he had refused to marry, for which refusal he had suffered during his service. Varenka married Prince Sergey Golitsin, who consequently received various promotions, decorations, and rewards. With this Sergey Golitsin and his family, consequently also with Varvara Vassilyevna (Varenka), my grandfather entered into so close a friendship that my mother was betrothed in her childhood to one of Golitsin's ten sons, and the two old princes exchanged portrait galleries (that is, of course, copies made by serf artists). These Golitsin portraits are all still in our house, among them Prince Sergey Golitsin wearing the ribbon of St. Andrew, and the red-haired, fat Varvara Vassilyevna dressed as a high lady of the Court. The alliance, however, was not destined to be concluded: 'My mother's betrothed, Lyof Golitsin,[1] died from fever before the marriage.'"[2]

In going through the genealogy of the Princes Volkonsky one comes across another interesting personage, a cousin of Tolstoy's mother, the Princess Varvara Alexandrovna Volkonsky, a woman who saw much that went on in the house of Tolstoy's grandfather. We find the following said about her:

"The Princess Varvara Alexandrovna Volkonsky, daughter of Prince Alexander Sergeyevich, after her mother's death frequently made long visits with her father to the house of his brother Nicolay Sergeyevich. Here

---

[1] An aunt of mine told me that this Golitsin's surname was Leo, but this is evidently a mistake, as Sergey Golitsin had no son Leo. I therefore think that the story about my mother being betrothed to one of the Golitsins is correct, as well as that he died; but that the name of Leo is not correct. (Note by Leo Tolstoy.)

[2] From Tolstoy's uncorrected draught Reminiscences sent to me and put at my disposal by himself.

she met the persons described by Count Leo Tolstoy in his novel *War and Peace,* and many details relating to them and to the events of their time remained fresh in her memory in her old age. Toward the close of her life she moved into a neighboring village, Sogalevo, which also belonged to her parents. Here she had a house built for herself close to the church, and in the society of a few old women house servants, who did not care to part from her, she passed her life there, full of memories of the past, reading and rereading *War and Peace.* Long forgotten by others, the aged princess remained an object of respect and devotion to the local peasants. To one casual visitor, who called on her in 1876, she related with delight how peasants of villages long before sold and handed over to strangers, had nevertheless on her ninetieth birthday presented her with a sack of flour and a silver rouble, while the women brought her a rouble, fowls, and some linen. She told this not only with a feeling of gratitude, but also with pride, since it was a proof that a kindly recollection of her parents was still cherished among the peasants.[1]

"I knew the dear old lady, my mother's cousin. I made her acquaintance when living in Moscow in the fifties. Tired of the dissipated worldly life I was then leading in Moscow, I went to stay with her on her little estate in the district of Klin, and passed a few weeks there. She embroidered, managed her household work in her little farm, treated me to sour cabbage, cream cheese, and fruit marmalades, such as are only made by housewives on such small estates; and she told me about old times, about my mother, my grandfather, and the four coronations at which she had been present. During my stay with her I wrote the *Three Deaths.*

"And this visit has remained one of the pure, bright reminiscences of my life."

Let us finally mention one more personality of the Volkonsky family, who, though not an ancestor of Tolstoy's in the direct line, is yet one of his kinsmen, Prince Sergey Grigoryevich Volkonsky, the Decembrist. He is a second cousin of Tolstoy's mother and a grandson of Simon Feodorovich Volkonsky, brother of Prince Sergey Feodorovich, mentioned above.

The Family of the Princes Volkonsky, p. 720

The prince was born in 1788, took part in the campaign of 1812, and afterward joined the southern secret society; and for participation in the conspiracy of the Decembrists he was exiled to Eastern Siberia, where he remained for thirty years; the earlier years he spent doing hard labor in irons, but afterward he lived there in Siberia as a settler.[1] The journey and arrival of his wife, Princess Marie Nicolayevna, are described in the well-known poem of Nekrassof.

In 1801 his brother Prince Nicolay Grigoryevich Volkonsky took, by order of the Emperor Alexander I, the surname of Repnin, that of his grandfather on his mother's side, whose family in the direct line had died out. "Let not the family of the princes Repnin," said the ukase, "which so gloriously served its country, become extinct with the death of the last of them, but let it be renewed, and remain with its name and example never to be obliterated in the remembrance of the Russian nobility."

Prince Nicolay Grigoryevich took part in all the campaigns against Napoleon and in the national war. For his share in the battle of Austerlitz he was rewarded by St. George's Order of the fourth class. In the battle he commanded a squadron and took part in the well-known attack of the cavalry guards described in *War and Peace*, in which he was wounded in the head and otherwise severely hurt. The French bore him from the battlefield and carried him to the hospital tent. On hearing of this, Napoleon ordered that he should be brought on the following day to his quarters, and out of respect for his valor he offered to set him free with all the officers under his command, on the sole condition that they should not take part in the war for two years. Nicolay Grigoryevich thanked Napoleon for the offer, but said that "he had given his oath to serve his emperor to the last drop of his blood, and therefore could not accept the proposal."

Shortly afterward, on his return from captivity, he was given leave of absence out of consideration for his wounds.[2]

In the Russian periodical entitled *Olden Times* of 1890, p. 209, appears a letter from Prince Repnin to Michail-

The Memoirs of S. G. Volkonsky (the Decembrist)
[2] *The Family of the Princes Volkonsky*, pp. 704, 714, 715.

ovsky-Danilevsky, a veteran of the national war. In this letter Prince Repnin relates in detail the episode described in *War and Peace,* and quotes the actual words of his conversation with Napoleon. The first part of this conversation is exactly reproduced in the novel *War and Peace.*

CHAPTER III

TOLSTOY'S PARENTS

Information about his mother in Tolstoy's Reminiscences—Her moral personality—Her gentleness and toleration—Her attitude to his father—Mlle. Enissienne—Her girl friends—Her love for the elder son and for Leo—The general character of the family during the mother's lifetime—Reminiscences of the father—Military service—Captivity—Civil service—Marriage—Management of the estate—General character and appearance of his father—Family life—List of services—An episode in his father's life—Autobiographical importance of *Childhood, Boyhood, Youth,* and *War and Peace.*

IN speaking of his parents, Tolstoy's Reminiscences follow a certain chronological order. First he tells us of the faintly seen features of his mother, supplementing his description by accounts furnished by surviving members of her family; after this he gives his fresher and more exact recollections of his father and of his aunts. We propose to follow his example, endeavoring to change as little as possible the order of his narrative. In giving his account of his father and mother we have omitted only what he says of his grandfather Volkonsky, which we have already quoted in the chapter dealing with the ancestors.

" My mother I do not at all remember. I was a year and a half old when she died. Owing to some strange chance no portrait whatever of her has been preserved, so that, as a real physical being, I cannot represent her to myself. I am in a sense glad of this, for in my conception of her there is only her spiritual figure, and all that I know about her is beautiful, and I think this is so, not only because all who spoke to me of my mother tried to say only what was good, but because there was actually very much of this good in her.

" However, not only my mother, but also all those who surrounded my infancy, from my father to the coachman, appear to me as exceptionally good people. Probably my pure loving feeling, like a bright ray, disclosed to me in people their best qualities (such always exist); when all these people seemed to me exceptionally good, I was much nearer truth than when I saw only their defects.

"My mother was not handsome. She was very well educated for her time. Besides Russian, which, contrary to the national illiterateness then current, she wrote correctly, she knew four other languages, French, German, English, and Italian, and was probably sensitive to art. She played well on the piano, and her friends have told me that she was a great hand at narrating most attractive tales invented at the moment. But the most valuable quality in her was that she was, according to the words of the servants, although hot-tempered, yet self-restrained. 'She would get quite red in the face, even cry,' her maid told me, 'but would never say a rude word.' Indeed she did not know such words.

"I have preserved several of her letters to my father and aunts, and her diary concerning the conduct of Nikolenka (my eldest brother), who was six years old when she died, and I think resembled her more than the rest of us. They both possessed a feature very dear to me, which I infer from my mother's letters, but personally witnessed in my brother: their indifference to the opinion of others, and their modesty in their endeavors to conceal those mental, educational, and moral advantages which they had in comparison with others. They were, as it were, ashamed of these advantages.

"I well knew these qualities in my brother, about whom Turgenef very correctly remarked that he did not possess those faults which are necessary in order to become a great writer.

"I remember once how a very silly and bad man, an adjutant of the governor, when out shooting with him, ridiculed him in my presence, and how my brother smiled good-humoredly, evidently greatly relishing the position.

"I remark the same feature in my mother's letters. She evidently stood on a higher spiritual level than my father and his family, with the exception, perhaps, of Tatiana Yergolsky, with whom I passed half my life, and who was a woman remarkable for her moral qualities.

"Besides this, they both had yet another feature which I believe contributed to their indifference to the judgment of men—it was that they never condemned any one. This I know most certainly about my brother, with whom I lived half my life. The utmost extreme expression of his negative relation to a man consisted with my brother in good-natured humor and a similar smile. I observe the same in my mother's letters, and have heard of it from those who knew her.

"In the *Lives of the Saints*, by Dmitri Rostovsky, there is a short narrative which has always exceedingly touched me, of the life of a certain monk who had, to the knowledge of all his brethren, many faults, and, notwithstanding this, appeared to an old monk in a dream among the saints in a place of honor. The astonished old man asked: 'How could this monk, so unrestrained in many respects, deserve such a reward?' The answer was: 'He never condemned any one.'

"If such rewards did exist, I think that my brother and my mother would have received them.

"A third feature which distinguishes my mother among her circle was her truthfulness and the simple tone of her letters. At that time the expression of exaggerated feelings was especially cultivated in letters: 'Incomparable, divine, the joy of my life, unutterably precious,' etc., were the most usual epithets between friends, and the more inflated the less sincere.

"This feature, although not in a strong degree, is noticeable in my father's letters. He writes: '*Ma bien douce amie, je ne pense qu'au bonheur d'être auprès de toi.*' This could hardly be quite sincere. Whereas she addresses her letters invariably in the same way, '*Mon bon ami,*' and in one of her letters she frankly says: '*Le temps me paraît long sans toi, quoiqu'à dire vrai, nous ne jouissons pas beaucoup de ta société quand tu es ici,*' and she always subscribes herself in the same way: '*Ta devouée Marie.*'

"My mother passed her childhood partly in Moscow, partly in the country with a clever and talented, though proud man, my grandfather Volkonsky. I have been told that my mother loved me very much, and called me '*Mon petit Benjamin.*'

"I think that her love for her deceased betrothed, precisely because it was terminated by death, was that poetic love which girls feel only once. Her marriage with my father was arranged by her relatives and my father's. She was a rich orphan, no longer young, whereas my father was a merry, brilliant young man with name and connections, but

Tolstoy's mother and her sister.

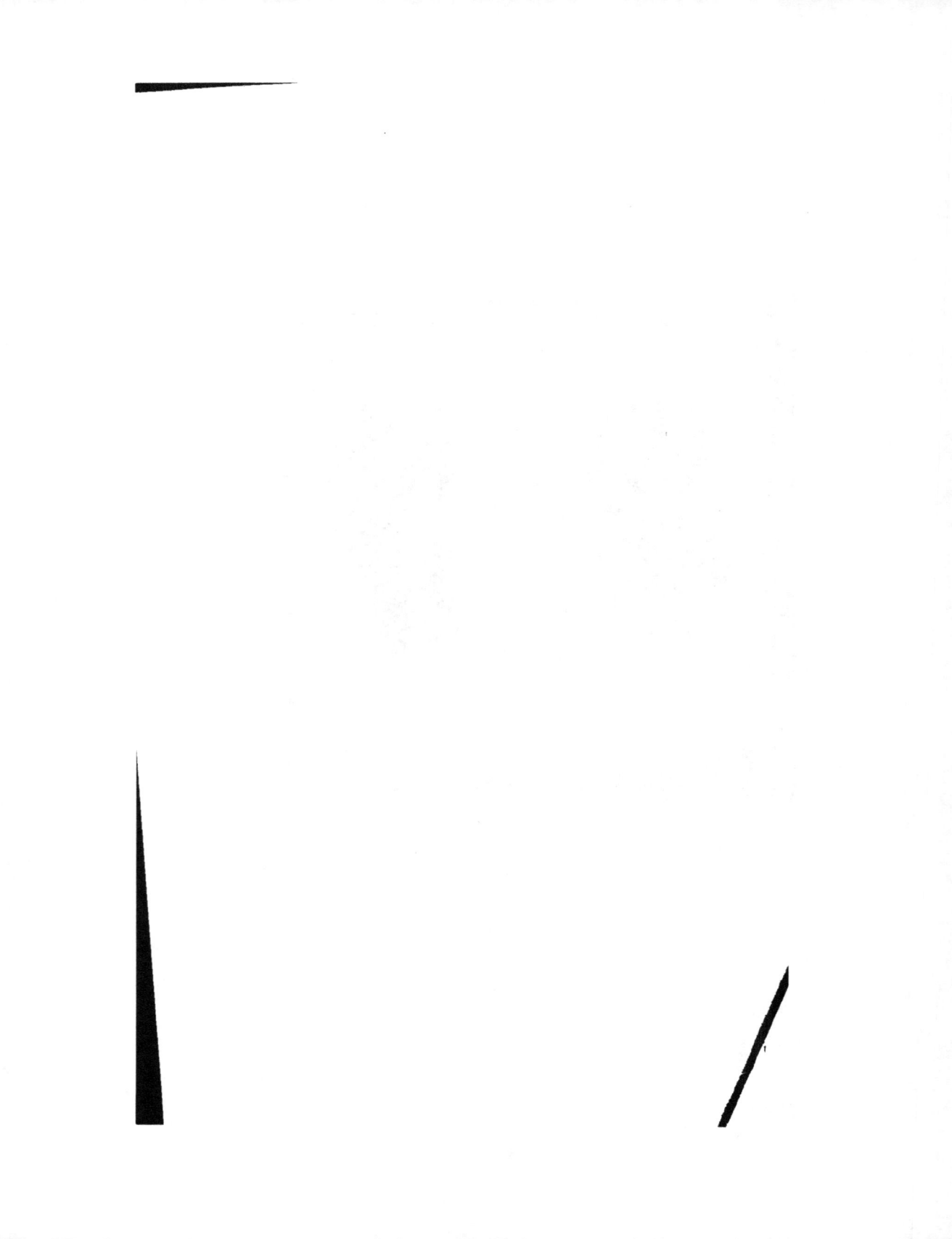

the family fortune was much impaired by my grandfather Tolstoy—indeed my father even refused to accept the heritage. I think that my mother loved my father, but more because he was her husband and especially as he was the father of her children; she was never in love with him. Of real loves she had, as I understand, experienced three or four: there was her love to her deceased betrothed; then a passionate friendship for a Frenchwoman, Mlle. Enissienne, about which I heard from my aunts and which I believe was terminated by a disillusionment. Mlle. Enissienne married a cousin of my mother's, Prince Michael Volkonsky, the grandfather of the present-day writer of that name.

"This is what my mother writes about her friendship with this lady. She is referring to two girls who were living in her house:

"'I get on very well with both of them. I do some music, I laugh and joke with the one, and I talk sentiment and condemn the frivolous world with the other. I am passionately loved by both and am the confidante of each; I reconcile them when they have quarrelled, for there never was friendship more quarrelsome and funny to witness than theirs; it is a series of sulks, tears, reconciliations, and reproaches, and then of transports of affection; in a word, I see as in a mirror the exalted and romantic friendship which had animated and troubled my life during several years. I contemplate them with an indefinable feeling; sometimes I envy them their illusion which I no longer possess, but of which I know the sweetness. Let us ask frankly whether the solid and real happiness of ripe years is worth the charming illusions of youth, when everything is embellished by the all-powerful imagination. And sometimes I smile at their childishness.'

"Her third strong feeling, perhaps the most passionate, was her love for my eldest brother Koko, the diary of whose conduct she kept in Russian—putting down in it his bad conduct—and then read to him. From this diary one can see that while she had a passionate desire to do all that was possible toward giving Koko the best education, she had a very indefinite idea as to what was necessary for this purpose. Thus, for instance, she rebukes him for being too sensitive and being moved to tears at the sight of animals suffering. A man, according to her ideas, should be firm.

Another fault which she endavors to correct in him is that he is absorbed in his thoughts, and instead of '*Bon soir,*' or '*Bon jour,*' says to his grandmother, '*Je vous remercie.*'

"The fourth strong feeling which did perhaps exist, as my aunts told me—I earnestly hope that it did exist—was her love for me, which took the place of her love for Koko, who at the time of my birth had already detached himself from his mother and been transferred into male hands. It was a necessity for her to love what was not herself, and one love took the place of another.

"Such was the figure of my mother in my imagination. She appeared to me a creature so elevated, pure, and spiritual that often in the middle period of my life, during my struggle with overwhelming temptations, I prayed to her soul, begging her to aid me, and this prayer always helped me much.

"My mother's life in her father's family was a very good and happy one, as I may conclude from letters and stories.

"My father's household consisted of his mother, an old lady; of her daughter, my aunt Countess Alexandra Osten-Saken, and her ward Pashenka; of another aunt, as we used to call her, although she was a very distant relative, Tatiana Yergolsky, who had been educated in my grandfather's house and had passed all her later life in my father's; and the tutor, Feodor Ivanovich Resselier, fairly correctly described by me in *Childhood*. We were five children—Nicolay, Sergey, Dmitri, myself, the youngest boy, and our younger sister Mashenka, at whose birth my mother died. My mother's very short married life—I think it lasted not more than nine years—was very full, and adorned by every one's love to her and hers to every one who lived with her. Judging by the letters, I see that she lived at that time in great solitude. Scarcely any one visited Yasnaya Polyana except our intimate friends the Ogarefs and some relatives who, if casually travelling along the high-road, might look in upon them.

"My mother's life was passed in occupations with the children, in reading novels aloud of an evening to my grandmother, and in serious readings, such as *Emile*, by Rousseau, and discussions about what had been read; in playing the piano, teaching Italian to one of her aunts, walks, and household work. In all families there are periods when illness and death are yet unknown, and the members live peacefully. Such a period, it seems to me, my mother was living through in her husband's family until her death. No one died, no one was seriously ill, my father's disordered affairs were improving. All were healthy, happy, and friendly. My father amused every one with his stories and jokes. I did not witness that time. At the time with which my remembrances begin, my mother's death had already laid its seal upon the life of our family.

"All this I have described from what I have heard and from letters. Now I shall begin about what I have myself experienced and remember. I shall not speak about the vague, indistinct recollections of infancy, in which one cannot yet distinguish reality from dream-land. I will commence with what I clearly remember, with the circumstances and the persons that surrounded me from my first years. The first place among them is occupied, of course, by my father, if not owing to his influence upon me, yet from my feeling toward him.

"My father from his early years had remained his parents' only son. His younger brother, Ilenka, was injured, became a cripple, and died in childhood. In the year 1812, my father was seventeen years old, and, notwithstanding the horror and fear and pleading of his parents, he entered the military service. At that time Prince Nicolay Gorchakof, a near relative of my grandmother, Princess Gorchakof, was Minister of War, his brother Andrew was a general in command of troops in the field, and my father was attached to him as adjutant. He went through the campaigns of the years '13 and '14, and in '14, having somewhere in Germany been despatched as a courier, he was taken prisoner by the French, and was liberated only in the year '15, when our troops entered Paris. Even at the age of twenty my father was not a chaste youth, but before he entered the military service, consequently when he was sixteen years old, a connection had been arranged by his parents between him and a servant-girl, as such a union was at that time deemed necessary for health. A son was born, Mishenka, who was made a postilion, and who, during my father's life, lived well, but afterward went wrong and often applied for help to us, his half-brothers. I remember my strange feeling of consternation when this brother of mine, fallen into destitution, bearing a greater resemblance to our father than any of us, begged help of us and was thankful for ten or fifteen roubles which were given him.

"After the campaign, my father, disillusioned as to military service, as is evident from his letters, resigned and came to Kazan, where my grandfather, already completely ruined, was governor, and where also resided my father's sister, who was married to Yushkof. My grandfather soon died in Kazan, and my father remained with an inheritance which was not equal to all the debts, and with an old mother accustomed to luxury, as well as a sister and a cousin, on his hands. At this time his marriage with my mother was arranged for him, and he removed to Yasnaya Polyana, where, after living nine years with my mother, he became a widower, and within my memory lived with us.

"My father was a lively man of sanguine temperament; he was of medium height, well built, with a pleasant face, and eyes of a constantly serious expression. His life was passed in attending to the estate, a business in which he, as it seems, was not very expert, but in which he exercised a virtue great for that time: he not only was not cruel, but was, perhaps, even weak. So that during his time, too, I never heard of corporal punishment. Probably it was administered, for it is difficult to imagine at that time the management of an estate without the use of such punishments, but the cases were probably so rare, and my father took so little part in them, that we children never came to hear of them. It was only after my father's death that I learned for the first time that such punishments took place at home.

"We children with our tutor were returning home from a walk, when by the barn we met the fat steward, Andrey Flyin, followed by the coachman's assistant—'Squinting Koozma,' as he was called—with a sad face. He was a married man, no longer young. One of us asked Andrey Flyin where he was going, and he quietly answered that he was going to the barn, where Koozma had to be punished. I cannot describe the dreadful feeling which these words and the sight of the good-natured, crestfallen Koozma produced on me. In the evening I related this to my aunt, Tatiana Alexandrovna, who had educated us and hated corporal punishment, never having allowed it for us any more than for the serfs, wherever she had influence. She was greatly revolted at what I told her, and rebuking me said: 'And why did you not stop him?' Her words grieved me still more . . . I never thought that we could interfere in such things, and yet it appeared that we could. But it was too late, and the dreadful deed had been committed.

"I return to what I knew about my father, and how I represent to myself his life. His occupation consisted in managing the estate, and above all in litigation, which was very frequent at that time, and I think particularly so with my father, who had to disentangle my grandfather's affairs. These lawsuits often compelled my father to leave home, besides which he used often to go out shooting and hunting. His chief sporting companions were his old friend, a wealthy bachelor, Kireyevsky, Yazikof, Glebof, and Islenyef. My father, in common with other landowners of that time, had special favorites among the house serfs. Of these there were two brothers, Petrusha and Matyusha, both handsome, smart fellows, who helped in the sport. At home my father, besides his occupations with his business and with us children, was greatly given to reading. He collected a library consisting, in accordance with the taste of the time, of French classics, historical works, and books on natural history by Buffon, Cuvier, etc. My aunt told me that my father had made a rule not to buy new books until he had read those previously purchased. But although he read much, it is difficult to believe that he mastered all these *Histoires des Croisades* and *des Papes* which he purchased for his library. As far as I can judge, he had no leanings toward science, but was on a level with the educated people of his time. Like most men of the first period of Alexander's reign, who served in the campaigns of the years '13, '14, and '15, he was not what is now called a Liberal, but, merely as a matter of self-respect, he regarded it as impossible to serve either during the latter part of Alexander's reign or during the reign of Nicholas. Not only did he never serve himself, but even all his friends were similarly people of independent character, who did not serve, and who were in some opposition to the government of Nicholas I. During all my childhood and even youth, our family had no intimate relations with any government official. Naturally I understood nothing about this in childhood, but I did understand that my father never humbled himself before any one, nor altered his brisk, merry, and often chaffing tone. And this feeling of self-respect which I witnessed in him increased my love, my admiration for him. I remember him in his study, where we used to come to say good-night to him and sometimes merely to play, where he with a pipe in his mouth used to sit on a leather couch and caress us, and sometimes, to our immense delight, used to allow us to mount the couch behind his back, while he would continue reading, or talking to the steward standing by the door, or to S. I. Yazikof, my godfather, who often stayed with us. I remember how he used to come downstairs to us and draw pictures which appeared to us the height of perfection, as well as how he once made me declaim to him some verses of Pushkin, which had taken my fancy, and which I had learned by heart: ' To the Sea,' ' Fare thee well, free element,' and to Napoleon, ' The wonderful fate is accomplished, the great man is extinguished,' and so on. He was evidently impressed by the pathos with which I recited these verses, and, having listened to the end, he in a significant way exchanged glances with Yazikof, who was there. I understood that he saw something good in this recitation of mine, and at this I was very happy. I remember his merry jokes and stories at dinner and supper, and how my grandmother and aunt and we children laughed listening to him. I remember also his journeys to town, and the wonderfully fine appearance he had when he put on his frock-coat and tight-fitting trousers. But I principally remember him in connection with hunting. I remember his departures from the house for the hunt. It afterward always seemed to me that Pushkin took his description of the departure for the hunt in *Count Nulin* from my father. I remember how we used to go for walks with him, how the young greyhounds who had followed him gambolled on the unmown fields in which the high grass flicked them and tickled their bellies, how they flew round with their tails on one side, and how he admired them. I remember how, on the day of the hunting festival of the 1st September, we all drove out in a lineyka[1] to the cover, where a fox had been let loose, and how the foxhounds pursued him, and, somewhere out of our sight, the greyhounds

---

[1] A Russian country vehicle, somewhat resembling a low, four-wheeled jaunting-car.—*Trans.*

Count Nicolas Ilyich Tolstoy, Tolstoy's father.

caught him.[1] I particularly well remember the baiting of a wolf. It was quite near the house. We all came out to look. A big gray wolf, muzzled, and with his legs tied, was brought out in a cart. He lay quietly, only looking through the corners of his eyes at those who approached him. At a place behind the garden the wolf was taken out, held to the ground with pitchforks, and his legs untied. He began to struggle and jerk about, fiercely biting the bit of wood tied into his mouth. At last this was untied at the back of his neck, and some one called out, 'Off!' The forks were lifted, the wolf got up and stood still for about ten seconds, but there was a shout raised, and the dogs were let loose. The wolf, the dogs, and the horsemen all flew down the field; and the wolf escaped. I remember how my father, scolding and angrily gesticulating, returned home.

"But the pleasantest recollections of him were those of his sitting with grandmother on the sofa and helping her to play Patience. My father was polite and tender with every one, but to grandmother he was always particularly tenderly subservient. They used to sit, grandmother, with her long chin, in a cap with ruche and a bow, on the sofa, playing Patience, and from time to time taking pinches from a gold snuffbox. Close to the sofa, in an arm-chair, sat Petrovna, a Tula tradeswoman who dealt in fire-arms, dressed in her military jacket, and spinning thread, and at intervals tapping her reel against the wall, in which she had already knocked a hole. My aunts are sitting in arm-chairs, and one of them is reading out loud. In one of the arm-chairs, having arranged a comfortable depression in it, lies black-and-tan Milka, my father's favorite fast greyhound, with beautiful black eyes. We come to say good-night, and sometimes sit here. We always take leave of grandmother and our aunts by kissing their hands. I remember once, in the middle of the game of Patience and of the reading, my father interrupts my aunt, points to the looking-glass, and whispers something. We all look in the same direction. It was the footman Tikhon, who, knowing that my father was in the drawing-room, was going into his study to take some tobacco from a big, leather, folding tobacco-pouch. My father

[1] In Russia, owing to local conditions, the methods of sport are necessarily different from those in England. Thus foxes, abounding in great numbers, are hunted out of the woods by foxhounds, and then sometimes caught by greyhounds in the surrounding fields.

sees him in the looking-glass, and examines his figure, carefully stepping on tiptoe. My aunts are laughing. Grandmother for a long time does not understand, and when she does she cheerfully smiles. I am enchanted by my father's kindness, and taking leave of him with special tenderness, kiss his white muscular hand. I loved my father very much, but did not know how strong this love of mine for him was until he died." [1]

To the above valuable information about his parents, given by Tolstoy himself, we need add only a few facts taken from historical documents.

Count Nicolay Ilyich Tolstoy, the father of Lyof Tolstoy, was born in 1797. In the documents of the Kazan University, among the papers connected with Tolstoy's admission as a student, one of some interest is the certificate of the military service of his father, Nicolay Ilyich

We give the material part of the text of this document, dated January 29, 1825.[2]

"The bearer of this, Lieutenant-Colonel Count Nicolay Ilyich, the son of Tolstoy, as appears by the official documents, is twenty-eight years old, has the order of St. Vladimir of the fourth class, belongs to the nobility, owns no serfs. Being a government secretary, he entered his Majesty's service as a cornet in 1812, June 11, in the Irkutsk regular regiment of Cossacks, whence he was transferred to the Irkutsk regiment of hussars in 1812, August 18; he distinguished himself and was promoted lieutenant in 1813, April 27; and in the same year was promoted second cavalry captain. He further distinguished himself, and was transferred in the same rank to the regiment of horse-guards in 1814, August 8. From this he was transferred to the regiment of the Prince of Orange with the rank of major in 1817, December 11. Having resigned, owing to illness, he was rewarded with the rank of lieutenant-colonel in 1819, March 14. He received an appointment in the Military Orphanage as assistant to the superintendent in 1821, December 15. During his service he took part in various campaigns. In 1813 he was often in action; on April 2 he was taken prisoner by the enemy before the fall of Paris, and, for his distinguished conduct in battle, was rewarded as

[1] From a draught of uncorrected memoirs by L. Tolstoy in my possession.—*P. B.*
[2] "Count L. N. Tolstoy and his University Life." N. P. Zagoskin *Istoricheski Vestnik*, January, 1894.

above described with the ranks of lieutenant and captain of cavalry, and the order of St. Vladimir of the fourth class, with ribbon."

From the same document we learn that Count N. I. Tolstoy resigned his post in the Military Orphanage and definitely retired from service, " for family reasons," January 8, 1824.

After his resignation Count Nicolay Ilyich Tolstoy settled in Yasnaya Polyana. At that time he and his wife had only one child, their son Nicolay, one year old, born in 1823, In the country the family quickly increased. On February 17, 1826, a son, Sergey, was born; on April 23, 1827, Dmitri; on August 28, 1828, a third son, Lyof.

The peaceful and calm country life of the family did not last long. In 1830, having brought into the world a daughter, Marie (born March 7), the Countess Tolstoy died, leaving her husband with five children.

After the death of their mother the children were left under the care of a distant relation, the above-mentioned Miss Tatiana Alexandrovna Yergolsky, who had been practically brought up in the house of Count Ilyia Andreyvich, the grandfather of our Count Tolstoy.

An interesting episode in the life of the father of Tolstoy is remembered in the family.

In 1813, after the blockade of Erfurt, he was sent to St. Petersburg with despatches, and on his way back, near the village of St. Obie, he was taken prisoner together with his orderly, but the latter managed to hide in his boot all his master's gold coins. For several months, while they were kept prisoners, he never took off his boots, for fear he should reveal his secret. He had to bear extreme discomfort; he had, for instance, a bad sore on his foot, still he showed no sign of pain. When Nicolay Ilyich arrived in Paris he could, thanks to his orderly, live in luxury. He long retained a grateful recollection of his devoted servant.[1]

Any one who has read Tolstoy's personal reminiscences will readily agree that the parents whom he describes in the novel *Childhood* are not his own. In fact, so far as we know, in the father was represented A. M. Islenef, a neighboring landowner and a friend of Tolstoy's father. The mother is an imaginary character. But in *War and Peace* it

---

[1] Sergeyenko, *How L. N. Tolstoy Lives and Works*, p. 40. Moscow, 1898.

is not difficult to find an artistic description of his parents in the persons of Count Nicolay Ilyich Rostof and Princess Marya Volkonsky.

Almost every member of the Rostof family, from Count Ilya Andreych to Sonya the adopted, corresponds to some personage in the Tolstoy family; and the inhabitants of the *Bleak Hills* can be similarly brought into comparison. The reading of this novel therefore may add much to our knowledge of the manners and characters of the ancestors and parents of Tolstoy.

PART II

CHILDHOOD, BOYHOOD, AND YOUTH
(1828–1850)

PART II

CHILDHOOD, BOYHOOD, AND YOUTH (1828–1850)

CHAPTER IV

CHILDHOOD

Yasnaya Polyana—The house where Tolstoy was born—The church register—First recollections of Tolstoy: the swaddling, the trough—The unconsciousness of early childhood—Periods of the infinite—Nature and child at one—Yeremeyevna—Feodor Ivanovich and the laundress—The game of " Milashki "—Passing from the women's quarters to Feodor Ivanovich, downstairs—Tatiana Alexandrovna Yergolsky—Tolstoy's recollections of her—Mucius Scaevola—A note of Tatiana found by Tolstoy in her portfolio—Tolstoy's attitude to Tatiana—The atmosphere of love surrounding Tatiana—Her room—Her influence on Tolstoy—Other persons who surrounded Tolstoy in his childhood—F. I. Mauer—The imbeciles—Dunechka-Temeshof, her history, the inheritance—Reminiscences of the servants: Praskovya Issayevna—Anna Ivanovna—Tatiana Philipovna—Nicolay Philipovich, the coachman—Vassili Trubetskoy—Brother Nicolenka—Fanfaronof Hill, the " Ant Brothers," the Green Wand—A few more childish reminiscences—Conclusion (from the novel *Childhood*).

"I WAS born and I spent my earliest childhood in the village Yasnaya Polyana."
With these words Tolstoy opens his Reminiscences, and before we begin the description of his childhood we think it well to say a few words about this little corner of the earth, destined to become of world-wide interest. What a variety of visitors have called at Yasnaya Polyana! Natives of the Malay Archipelago, Australians, Japanese and Americans, Siberian runaways, and representatives of all the European nations, have visited this village and spread abroad a description of it, as well as the words and thoughts of the aged prophet, its inhabitant.

Yasnaya Polyana, the family estate of the Princes Volkonsky, is situated in the Krapivensk district of the province of Tula, almost on the border line of the district of Tula, fifteen versts to the south of the town of the same name. Three high-roads of three different periods cross one another in its neighborhood; the old Kief road, overgrown with grass, the new Kief macadamized road, and the Moscow-Kursk Railway line, the nearest station of which, Kozlovka-Zasseka, is at three and a half versts distance from Tolstoy's home.

The beautiful hilly neighborhood surrounding Yasnaya Polyana is divided from east to west by a long belt of Crown forest, called the Abattis. This name points back to ancient times, when in that place the Slavs had to repel the attacks of the Crimean Tartars and other Mongolian tribes, and were obliged to cut trees and make barriers which formed a natural and impenetrable defence against the enemies' hordes.

The house in which Tolstoy was born no longer stands in Yasnaya Polyana. The work of building it was started by his grandfather, Prince Volkonsky, and finished by his father; after which the house was sold to a neighboring landowner, Gorokhof, and was removed to the village Dolgoye, where it now stands. It was in the early fifties, when Tolstoy was in great need of money, that he requested one of his relatives to sell this house. The large-sized residence with columns and balconies was sold for the comparatively insignificant price of about five thousand roubles in paper money. From Tolstoy's letters to his brother it is evident that he was very sorry to part with it, and only dire necessity induced him to do so. At present nobody lives in it. It stands neglected, with its window-shutters nailed up. The present two houses of Yasnaya Polyana consist of the two wings, formerly standing at the sides of the main body of the old house which was sold. The place occupied by the old house is partly planted with trees, partly cleared and turned into a croquet ground and a small square which is used as a dining-place when weather permits.

In front of the house there is at present a flower-bed, and beyond that spreads an old garden with ponds and aged lime-tree avenues. The garden is surrounded by a ditch and a rampart. At the entrance of this garden stand two brick towers, painted white. Old people say that in

The house in which Tolstoy was born at Yasnaya Polyana, since removed to Dolgoye.

the time of the grandfather, Prince Volkonsky, sentries used to stand there. A birch avenue, the so-called "Prospect," begins at the towers and leads up to the house.

To the old garden are added new fruit gardens planted under Tolstoy's own supervision. The whole residence is situated on rising ground and surrounded by a luxurious growth of shrubs.

It is unfortunate that there exist no details of interest relating to Tolstoy's birth besides the following extract from the church register, quoted by Zagoskin in his reminiscences:

"In the year 1828, on August 28, in the village of Yasnaya Polyana, a son, Lyof, was born to Count Nicolay Ilyich Tolstoy and baptized on the 29th of August by the priest Vassili Mozhaisky, deacon Arkhip Ivanof, chanter Alexander Feodorof, and sexton Feodor Grigoryef. The sponsors at the baptism were the landowner of the Belevsky district, Simon Ivanovich Yazikof, and Countess Pelageya Tolstova."[1]

The countess Pelageya Tolstova was in fact the grandmother of Lyof Tolstoy on his father's side, Pelageya Nicolayevna Tolstoy.

It is seldom that a biographer has the good fortune to learn facts of such an early age. In his *First Memories,* Tolstoy relates his vague sensations on being swathed, sensations, that is, felt during the first year of his life.

We quote these reminiscences as they stand:

"Here are my first reminiscences, which I am unable to arrange in order, not knowing what came before and what after; of some of them I do not even know whether they happened in reality or in a dream. Here they are: I am bound; I wish to free my arms and I cannot do it and I scream and cry, and my cries are unpleasant to myself, but I cannot cease. Somebody bends down over me, I do not remember who. All is in a half light. But I remember that there are two people. My cries affect them; they are disturbed by my cries, but do not unbind me as I desire, and I cry yet louder. They think that this is necessary (*i. e.* that I should be bound), whereas I know it is not necessary and I wish to prove it to them, and am con-

---

[1] N. P. Zagoskin, "Count L. N. Tolstoy and his Student Years." *Historic Review,* Jan. 1894, p. 87.

vulsed with cries, distasteful to myself but unrestrainable. I feel the injustice and cruelty, not of human beings, for they pity me, but of fate, and I feel pity for myself. I do not and never shall know what it was, whether I was swathed when a babe at the breast and tried to get my arm free, or whether I was swathed when more than a year old, in order that I should not scratch myself; or whether, as it happens in dreams, I have collected into this one reminiscence many impressions; but certain it is that this was my first and most powerful impression in life. Nor is it my cries that are impressed upon my mind, nor my sufferings, but the complexity and contrast of the impression. I desire freedom, it interferes with no one else, and I, who require strength, am weak, whilst they are strong.

"Another impression is a joyful one. I am sitting in a wooden trough, and am enveloped by the new and not unpleasant smell of some kind of stuff with which my little body is being rubbed. It was probably bran, and most likely I was having a bath, but the novelty of the impression from the bran aroused me, and for the first time I remarked and liked my little body with the ribs showing on the breast, and the smooth, dark-colored trough, my nurse's rolled-up sleeves, and the warm steaming bran-water, and its sound, and especially the feeling of the smoothness of the trough's edges when I passed my little hands along them.

"It is strange and dreadful to think that from my birth until the age of three years, during the time when I was fed from the breast, when I was weaned, when I began to crawl, to walk, to speak, however much I may seek them in my memory, I can find no other impressions save these two: When did I originate? When did I begin to live? And why is it joyous to me to imagine myself as at that time, and yet has been dreadful to me, as it is still dreadful to many, to imagine myself again entering that state of death of which there will be no recollections that can be expressed in words? Was I not alive when I learned to look, to listen, to understand, and to speak, when I slept, took the breast, kissed it, and laughed and gladdened my mother? I lived, and lived blissfully! Did I not then acquire all that by which I now live, and acquire it to such an extent and so quickly, that in all the rest of my life

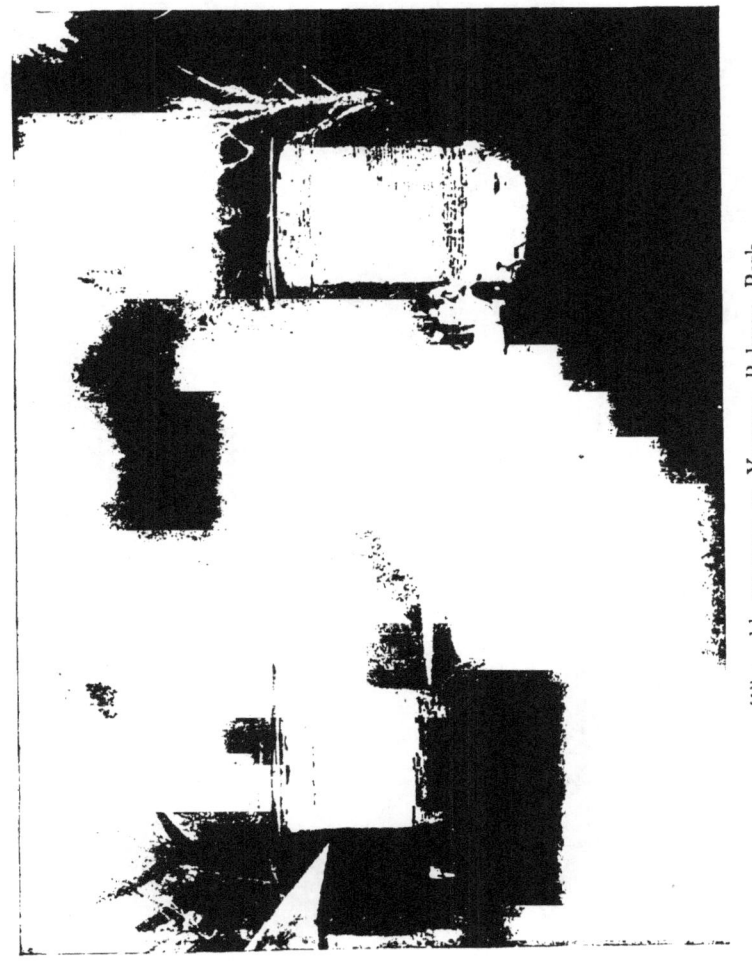

The old entrance to Yasnaya Polyana Park.

I have not acquired a hundredth part of the amount? From a five-year-old child to my present self there is only one step. From a new-born infant to a five-year-old child there is an awesome distance. From the germ to the infant an unfathomable distance. But from non-existence to the germ the distance is not only unfathomable, but inconceivable. Not only are space and time and causation forms of thought, and not only is the essence of life outside these forms, but all our life is a greater and greater subjection of oneself to these forms, and then again liberation from them.

" The next reminiscences refer to the time when I was already four or five years old, but of these I have very few, and not one of them concerns life outside the walls of the house. Nature, up to five years old, did not exist for me. All that I remember takes place in my little bed in a room. Neither grass nor leaves nor sky nor sun exists for me. It cannot be that I was not given flowers or leaves to play with, that I did not see the grass, was not shaded from the sun; still, up to five or six years, I have no recollection of what we call nature. Probably one has to leave it in order to see it, and I was nature itself.

" After that of the trough, the next reminiscence is one about 'Yeremeyevna.' 'Yeremeyevna' was a word with which we children were threatened, but my recollection of it is this: I am in my little bed, happy and content as always, and I should not remember this were it not that my nurse, or some person who formed part of my childish world, says something in a voice new to me, and goes away, and, besides being merry, I become afraid. And I call to mind that I am not alone, but with some one else who is like myself; this probably was my sister Mashenka, a year younger than myself, whose bed stood in the same room as mine. I recall that my bed has a curtain, and my sister and I are happy, and afraid of something extraordinary which has happened among us, and I hide under my pillow, both hide and watch the door, from which I expect something new and amusing, and we laugh and hide and wait. And lo! there appears some one in a dress and cap quite unlike anything I have ever seen, but I recognize that it is the same person who is always with me (whether my nurse or my aunt I do not know), and in a gruff voice which I recognize, this some one says something dreadful about naughty children and "Yeremeyevna." I shriek with fear and joy, and am indeed horrified and yet delighted to be horrified, and I wish the one who is frightening me not to know I have recognized her. We quiet down, but then purposely begin whispering to each other to recall 'Yeremeyevna.'

"I have another recollection of 'Yeremeyevna,' probably of a later period, for it is more distinct, although it has forever remained incomprehensible to me. In this reminiscence the chief part is played by the German, Feodor Ivanovich, our tutor; but I know for certain that I am not yet under his supervision; therefore that this takes place before I am five. And this is my first impression of Feodor Ivanovich, and it happened so early that I do not as yet remember any one, neither my brothers nor my father. If I have an idea of any separate person, it is only my sister, and that simply because she is, like me, afraid of 'Yeremeyevna.' With this reminiscence is connected my first recognition that our house has a second story. How I got up there, whether I mounted alone or was carried up, I don't at all remember, but I remember that there were many of us, and that we were all moving in a circle, holding each other's hands. Among us there were women, strangers to us (I somehow remember that they were washerwomen), and we all begin to circle round and jump, and Feodor Ivanovich jumps, lifting his legs too high, flinging about and making a great noise, and I feel at one and the same moment that this is not right, and that it is wicked, and I rebuke him, and I think I begin to cry, and everything ceases."

The account given by Marie, Tolstoy's sister, of their childish games belongs to this period.

"Three of us slept in the same room—I, Lyovochka, and Dunechka [1]—and we often played with one another, making a children's party apart from our elder brothers, who lived with the tutor downstairs.

"'Milashki' was one of our favorite games. One of us would pretend to be the 'milashki,' *i. e.*, a child who was specially petted by others, put to bed, fed, given medical treatment, and generally made much fuss about. This 'milashki' (favorite), according to the rules of the game,

[1] The governess; see concerning her further on in the following chapter.

The present entrance to Yasnaya Polyana Park.

had to submit without complaining to all the tricks that were played with him, and to act his part submissively.

"I remember how grieved and vexed we were during the game when our 'milashki' (generally Lyof Nicolayevich) really fell asleep after having been put to bed. According to the rules of the game, he had to cry, then to be doctored, given medicine, rubbed, etc. And thus his sleep put an end to our play, and called us back from illusions to reality.

"This is all I remember till I was five years old," continues Tolstoy. "As for my nurses, my aunts, brothers, sisters, father, the rooms, and the playthings—of all these I remember nothing. My definite reminiscences commence from the time when I was transferred downstairs to Feodor Ivanovich and my elder brothers.

"With Feodor Ivanovich and the boys I experienced for the first time, and therefore more powerfully than ever after, that feeling which is called the feeling of duty—the feeling of the Cross, which every man is called to bear. I was sorry to abandon what I was used to (used to from eternity), I was sorry, poetically sorry, to separate not so much from persons, from my sister, my nurse, and my aunt, as from my little bed, with its curtain and the pillow, and I was afraid of the new life into which I entered. I tried to find what was joyful in the new life which confronted me; I tried to believe the caressing words with which Feodor Ivanovich sought to attract me; I tried not to see the contempt with which the boys received me, the younger one; I tried to think that it was shameful for a big boy to live with girls, and that there was nothing good in the upstairs life with the nurse. But inwardly I felt dreadfully sad, I knew that I was irretrievably losing innocence and happiness, and only the feeling of self-respect, the consciousness that I was fulfilling my duty, supported me. Many times later on I had to live through such moments at the parting of the ways in life, when I entered on a new road. I experienced a quiet grief at the irretrievableness of what was being lost, I kept disbelieving that it was really happening. Although I had been told that I was to be transferred to the boys, yet I remember that the dressing-gown, with belt sewn to the back, which was put on me, cut me off as it were forever from upstairs, and then for the first time I was impressed, not by all those with whom I had lived upstairs, but by the principal person with whom I lived and whom I did not previously understand. This was my aunt, Tatiana Alexandrovna. I remember a short, stout, black-haired, kind, affectionate, solicitous woman. She put the dressing-gown on to me, and tightened the belt while embracing and kissing me, and I saw that she felt as I did; that it was sad—dreadfully sad—but necessary. For the first time I felt that life was not a plaything, but a difficult task. Shall I not feel the same when I am dying? I shall understand that death or future life is not a plaything, but a difficult task."[1]

Of this aunt, Tatiana Alexandrovna, Tolstoy gives the following interesting information in his Memoirs:

"The third person, after my father and mother, as regards influence upon my life, was my 'Aunty,' as we called her, Tatiana Alexandrovna Yergolsky. She was a very distant relation of my grandmother through the Gorchakofs. She and her sister Lisa, who afterward married Count Peter Ivanovich Tolstoy, remained poor little orphan girls after the death of their parents. There were also several brothers whom my parents managed to get adopted. But it was decided that one of the girls should be taken to be educated by Tatiana Semyonovna Skuratof, powerful, important, famous in her time and circle of the Chern district, and the other by my grandmother. Scraps of paper were folded and put under the icons, and after prayer they were chosen, when Lizenka fell to the lot of Tatiana Semyonovna, and the little dark one (Tanichka) to my grandmother. Tanichka, as we called her, was of the same age as my father. She was born in 1795, was brought up exactly on equal lines with my aunts, and was tenderly loved by all; and indeed it was impossible not to love her for her firm, resolute, energetic, and at the same time self-sacrificing character, a character very well displayed in an incident with a ruler, about which she used to tell us, showing the scar of a burn on her arm, almost as big as the palm of the hand, between the elbow and the wrist. The children had been reading the story of Mucius Scaevola, and they disputed as to whether any of them could make up his mind

---

[1] *First Reminiscences* (from unpublished autobiographical sketches). Tolstoy's Complete Works, tenth Russian edition. vol. xiii, p. 515.

to do the same. 'I will do it,' she said. 'You will not,' said Yazikof, my godfather, and also characteristically to himself he burned a ruler on the candle, so that it became charred and smoked all over. 'There, place this on your arm,' he said. She stretched out her white arm (at that time girls were always dressed *décolleté*) and Yazikof applied the charred ruler. She frowned, but did not withdraw her arm; she groaned only when the ruler with the skin was torn away. When the older people saw her wound and asked how it was caused, she said she had done it herself, wishing to experience what Mucius Scaevola had done.

"So resolute and self-sacrificing was she in everything.

"She must have been very attractive, with her crisp, black, curling hair in its enormous plait, her jet black eyes, and vivacious, energetic expression. V. Yushkof, the husband of my Aunt Pelageya Ilyinishna, a great flirt, even when an old man, used often, when recalling her, to say with the feeling with which those who have been in love speak about the object of their previous affections: '*Toinette, oh! elle était charmante!*'[1]

"When I remember her she was more than forty, and I never thought about her being pretty or not pretty. I simply loved her—loved her eyes, her smile, and her dusky, broad little hand with its energetic little cross vein.

"She probably loved my father and my father loved her, but she did not marry him in youth, in order that he might marry my rich mother, and later she did not marry him because she did not wish to spoil her pure poetic relations with him and us. In her papers, in a little beaded portfolio, there lies the following note, written in 1836, six years after my mother's death:

"'16th August, 1836.—*Nicolas m'a fait aujourd'hui une étrange proposition—celle de l'épouser, de servir de mère à ses enfants et de ne jamais les quitter. J'ai refusé la première proposition, j'ai promis de remplir l'autre tant que je vivrai.*'[2]

"Thus she recorded it, but she never spoke of this either to us or to any one. After my father's death she

---

[1] "Toinette, oh! she was charming!"
[2] "16th August 1836.—Nicolas has to-day made me a strange proposal—that I should marry him, be a mother to his children, and never desert them. I refused the first proposal, I have promised to fulfil the other as long as I live."

fulfilled his second desire. We had two aunts and a grandmother; they all had more right to us than Tatiana Alexandrovna—whom we called aunt only by habit, for our kinship was so distant that I could never remember it—but she, by right of love to us, like Buddha with the wounded swan, took the first place in our bringing up. And this we felt.

"I had fits of passionately tender love for her.

"I remember how once on the sofa in the drawing-room, when I was about five, I squeezed in behind her, and she caressingly touched me with her hand. I caught this hand and began to kiss it and to cry from tender love toward her.

"She had been educated like a young lady of a rich house; she spoke and wrote French better than Russian, and played the piano admirably, but for thirty years she did not touch it. She resumed playing only when I had grown up and learned to play, and sometimes in playing duets she astonished me by the correctness and refinement of her performance. Toward the servants she was kind; she never spoke to them angrily and could not bear the idea of blows or flogging, yet she regarded serfs as serfs and treated them as their superior. Notwithstanding this, all the servants distinguished her from others and loved her. When she died and was being borne through the village, peasants came out from all the houses and paid for *Te Deums.* Her principal characteristic was love, but how I could wish that this had not been all for one person—for my father. Still, starting from this centre her love spread on all around. We felt that she loved us for his sake, that through him she loved every one, because all her life was love.

"She, owing to her love for us, had the greatest right to us, but our aunts, especially Pelageya Ilyinishna, when the latter took us away to Kazan, had the external rights, and 'Auntie' submitted to them, but her love did not thereby diminish. She lived with her sister, the Countess L. A. Tolstoy, but in her soul she lived with us, and, whenever possible, she would return to us. The fact that the last years of her life, about twenty years, were passed with me at Yasnaya Polyana was a great joy to me. But how incapable we were of appreciating our happiness, the more

Avenue of birch trees leading to the house.

so that true happiness is never loud nor manifest! I appreciated it, but far from sufficiently. 'Auntie' liked to keep sweets in her room in various little dishes—dried figs, gingerbread, dates; she liked to buy them and to treat me first to them. I cannot forget, and cannot call to mind without a cruel twinge of conscience, how several times I refused her money for the sweets, and how she, sadly sighing, desisted. It is true I was then in straitened circumstances, but now I cannot recall without remorse how I refused her!

"When I was already married and she had begun to fail, she once, having waited for the opportunity when I was in her room, turning her face away, said to me (I saw she was ready to shed tears): 'Look here, *mes chers amis*, my room is a very good one and you will require it. But if I die in it,' she went on with a trembling voice, 'the memory of that will be unpleasant, so move me to another that I may not die here.' Such she was from the earliest time of my childhood, when as yet I could not understand. . . .

"Her room was thus. In the left corner stood a worktable with innumerable little articles valuable only to her, in the right corner a glass cupboard with icons and one big one—that of the Saviour—in a silver setting; in the middle the couch on which she slept, in front of it a table. To the right a door for her maid.

"I have said that Aunty Tatiana Alexandrovna had the greatest influence on my life. This influence consisted first, in that ever since childhood she taught me the spiritual delight of love. She taught me this, but not in words: by her whole being she filled me with love. I saw, I felt, how she enjoyed loving, and I understood the joy of love. This was the first thing.

"Secondly, she taught me the delights of an unhurried, lonely life.

"But about this we will speak later.

"Although this reminiscence is not of childhood but of adult life, I cannot refrain from recalling my bachelor life with her at Yasnaya Polyana."[1]

In the chapter dealing with Tolstoy's parents we have already mentioned that his novels, *Childhood*, *Boyhood*, and

---

[1] From Tolstoy's rough Memories and uncorrected notes intrusted to me.

Youth, are not to be considered autobiographical; but this remark only applies to their external facts and scenery, created by the author to give greater completeness to his picture.

As to the description of the inner life of the child-hero, we can say with confidence that, in one way or another, the author lived through all the experiences of his hero, and therefore we consider that we have a right to use them as furnishing hints for our biography.

Further, we know that certain of the characters which we meet with in this work are copies from life. We will mention them here as they will throw some further light on the group of persons among whom Tolstoy's childhood was spent.

Thus, the German, Carl Ivanovitch Mauer, is certainly Feodor Ivanovitch Kessel, the German tutor, who really lived in Tolstoy's home, and whom we have mentioned before. Tolstoy speaks of him in his *Earliest Memories*. He must undoubtedly have influenced the spiritual life of the child, and we may presume that the influence had been for good, since the author of *Childhood* speaks with great love of him, where he sketches his " honest, straightforward, and loving nature."

It is not without reason that Tolstoy begins the story of his childhood with a description of this character. Feodor Ivanovitch died in Yasnaya Polyana, and was buried in the parish church-yard.

Another real character in *Childhood* is the half-crazy Grisha. Though he is not a real person, many traits of his character are true to life; he had evidently left a deep trace in the child's soul. To him Tolstoy dedicates the following pathetic words describing the evening prayer of the pilgrim, which he overheard:

" His words were incorrect, but touching. He prayed for all his benefactors (thus he called all who received him), among them for my mother, and for us; he prayed for himself and asked the Lord to forgive him his heavy sins, and repeated, ' O Lord, forgive mine enemies!' He arose with groans, still repeating the same words, prostrated himself upon the ground, and again arose, in spite of the weight of the chains that emitted a grating, penetrating sound as they struck the ground. . . .

"Grisha was for a long time in this attitude of religious ecstasy, and he improvised prayers. Now he repeated several times in succession, 'The Lord have mercy upon me,' but every time with new strength and expression; now, again, he said, 'Forgive me, O Lord, instruct me what to do, instruct me what to do, O Lord!' with an expression as if he expected an immediate answer to his prayer; now, again, were heard only pitiful sobs. He rose on his knees, crossed his arms on his breast, and grew silent.

"'Thy will be done!' he suddenly exclaimed with an inimitable expression, knocked his brow against the floor, and began to sob like an infant.

"Much water has flowed since then, many memories of the past have lost all meaning for me and have become dim recollections, and pilgrim Grisha has long ago ended his last pilgrimage; but the impression which he produced on me, and the feeling which he evoked, will never die in my memory.

"O great Christian Grisha! Your faith was so strong that you felt the nearness of God; your love was so great that words flowed of their own will from your lips, and you did not verify them by reason. And what high praise you gave to the majesty of God, when, not finding any words, you prostrated yourself on the ground."

Are we not entitled to regard this man as the first who taught Tolstoy that faith of the people, which, after his fruitless wanderings through the labyrinths of theology, philosophy, and positive science, satisfied his soul. A faith which he in his turn has lighted with his own light of reason, purified and intensified in the struggle and sufferings which unavoidably accompany the search for truth. He gives a few indications of this in his Reminiscences.

Of other secondary characters in the novel we will mention Mimi and her daughter Katenka, "something like the first love." Under the name Mimi is presented the governess of a neighboring house, and Katenka is Dunechka Temeshof, an adopted member of the Tolstoy family. Tolstoy, in his Reminiscences, speaks of her thus:

"Besides my brothers and my sister, a girl of my age, Dunechka Temeshof, grew up with us, and I must tell who she was and how she came to be in our house. The visitors whom I remember in childhood were my aunt's husband

Yushkof, of an appearance strange to children, with black mustaches and whiskers and wearing spectacles (I shall yet have much to say about him); and my godfather, S. Yazikof, a remarkably ugly man, saturated with the smell of tobacco, his big face possessing a superfluity of skin which he kept twisting incessantly into the strangest grimaces, and our neighbors Ogaref and Islenef. Besides these we were also visited by a distant relative through the Gorchakofs, a wealthy bachelor Temeshof, who addressed my father as brother, and had a peculiarly enthusiastic love for him. He lived forty versts from Yasnaya Polyana, in the village Pirogovo, and once brought with him from there some sucking pigs, with tails twisted into rings, which were placed on a tray on the table in the servants' hall. Temeshof, Pirogovo, and sucking pigs are blended into one in my imagination.

"Besides this, Temeshof retained a place in the memory of us children by his playing on the piano in the hall some dancing tune—it was all he could play—and making us dance to this music, and when we used to ask him what dance we were to dance, he would say that all dances could be danced to that music. And we liked to take advantage of this.

"It was a winter evening. Tea was over, we were soon going to be taken to bed, and my eyes were already blinking, when from the servants' hall into the drawing-room, where we were all sitting, and where only two candles were burning, and it was half dark, there came suddenly and quickly through the big open door a man in soft boots who, having reached the middle of the room, fell down on his knees. The lighted pipe with its long stem, which he held in his hand, struck against the floor, and the sparks flew out lighting the face of the kneeling man—it was Temeshof. What Temeshof told my father, while kneeling before him, I do not remember nor indeed did I hear, but only afterward I learned that he had fallen on his knees before my father because he had brought with him his illegitimate daughter, Dunechka, concerning whom he had previously spoken, and arranged that my father should accept her and bring her up with his own children. Thenceforth a broadfaced girl appeared among us, of the same age as myself, Dunechka, with her nurse Eupraxia, a tall, wrinkled old

A view in Yasnaya Polyana Park.

CHILDHOOD

woman with a hanging chin, like a turkey, in which there was a ball which she used to let us feel.

"The introduction of Dunechka into our house was connected with a complicated business agreement between my father and Temeshof. The agreement was of this sort:

"Temeshof was very wealthy. He had no legitimate children; he only had two little girls, Dunechka and Verochka, the latter a little hunchback, born of a former serf girl, Marfusha, who was subsequently set free. The heirs of Temeshof were his sisters. He made over to them all his estates except Pirogovo, in which he lived, and this he desired to transfer to my father, on the understanding that my father should remit to the two girls its value, £30,000. It was always said of Pirogovo that it was as good as a gold mine, and was worth much more than that sum. In order to arrange this matter the following method was devised: Temeshof drew up a conveyance according to which he sold Pirogovo to my father for £30,000, while my father gave promissory notes to three unconcerned persons—Islenef, Yazikof, and Glebof—to the amount of £10,000 each. On Temeshof's death my father was to take possession of the estate, and having previously explained to Glebof, Islenef, and Yazikof for what purpose the notes were given them, he was to pay them the £30,000 which were to go to the two girls.

"Perhaps I may be mistaken in the description of the whole plan, but I positively know that the estate of Pirogovo passed over to us after my father's death, and that there were three promissory notes payable to Islenef, Glebof, and Yazikof, that our guardians redeemed these notes, and that the amount of the first two was paid to the girls, £10,000 to each; whereas Yazikof misappropriated the other £10,000; but about this later.

"Dunechka lived with us, and was a nice, simple, quiet, but not clever girl, and much disposed to weep. I remember how, when I had already learned French, I was made to teach her the alphabet. At first it went well (we were each five years old), but later she probably became tired, and ceased to name correctly the letter I pointed out. I insisted. She began to cry. I also. And when the elders came we could not pronounce anything owing to our hopeless tears. I remember another incident about her. When a plum was found to be missing from a plate and the culprit could not be discovered, Feodor Ivanovich, with a serious face and not looking at us, said that its being eaten did not much matter, but that any one who swallowed the stone might die. Dunechka could not restrain her terror, and said that she had spat out the stone. I further remember her tears of despair when she and my brother Mitenka got up a game which consisted in spitting into each other's mouth a little copper chain, and she spat so strongly, while Mitenka opened his mouth wide, that he swallowed the chain. She cried inconsolably until the doctor arrived and reassured every one. . . ."

This brief but valuable information Tolstoy gives concerning the servants who surrounded him during his childhood. The information forms a supplement to what is described in his published story *Childhood*. We borrow this description also from his Reminiscences:

"I have described Praskovya Issayevna fairly correctly in *Childhood*. All I there wrote about her was actual truth. She was the housekeeper, a venerable personage. I remember one of the pleasantest impressions was that of sitting in her room after or during a lesson and talking with and listening to her. She probably liked to see us at these moments of specially happy and touching expansiveness: 'Praskovya Issayevna, how did grandfather fight? On horseback?' one would ask her.

"'He fought in various ways, on horseback and on foot, and in consequence he was General-in-Chief,' she would answer, opening a cupboard and getting out a burning tablet which she called the 'Ochakovsky smoke.' According to her words, it appeared that this tablet grandfather brought from Ochakof. She would ignite a taper at the little lamp in front of the icons, and with it would light the tablet, which smouldered with a pleasant scent.

"Besides her devotion and honesty, I especially loved her because, with Anna Ivanovna, she was connected in my eyes with that mysterious side of my grandfather's life —with the 'Ochakovsky smoke.'

"Anna Ivanovna lived in retirement, but once or twice she visited the house, and I saw her. It was said that she was a hundred years old, and that she remembered Pougacheff.[1] She had very black eyes and one tooth. She was in that stage of old age which inspires children with fear.

"Nurse Tatiana Philipovna, small, dusky, and with plump little hands, was the young assistant of our old nurse Annushka, whom I scarcely recall precisely, because at the time I was with Annushka I was conscious of myself only. And as I did not observe myself nor understand myself as I then was, so also I do not remember Annushka.

"And as I did not look at myself, and don't remember how I looked, so I cannot recall to mind Annushka, but Dunechka's nurse, Eupraxia, with a little ball on her neck, is well preserved in my memory.

"Nurse Tatiana Philipovna I remember because she was afterward the nurse of my nieces and of my eldest son. She was one of those pathetic beings from among the people who so identify themselves with the families of their nurslings that they transfer all their interests to those families, and so that their own relatives see in them only an opportunity for extortion or await the inheritance of the money they earned. Such have always spendthrift brothers, husbands, or sons. Such were, so far as I can remember, Tatiana Philipovna's husband and son. I remember how he painfully, quietly, and meekly died in the very place where I am now sitting writing these Reminiscences. Her brother, Nicolay Philipovich, was a coachman, whom we not only loved, but for whom, as gentlemen's children generally do, we felt a great reverence. He had peculiar thick boots; he always carried with him the pleasant smell of the stables, and his voice was tender and musical.[2]

"The butler, Vassili Trubetskoy, should be mentioned. He was a pleasant, kindly man, who evidently loved children, and therefore loved us, especially Seryozha, at whose house he afterward served, and where he died. I remember the kind, one-sided smile of his beaming face with its wrinkles, and his neck, which we saw close, and his peculiar smell when he took us in his arms and seated us on the tray (it was one of our great pleasures; 'And me, now me!') and carried us about the pantry—a place mysterious in our eyes

---

[1] The leader of a widespread and bloody rebellion in the reign of Catherine II.—*Trans.*

[2] From Tolstoy's draught Reminiscences.

with its strange underground passage. One poignant reminiscence connected with him was his departure to Sherbachovka, an estate in the government of Kursk, inherited by my father from a relative. This (Vassili's departure) happened during Yule-tide, at the time when all the children and some of the household servants were playing at 'Rublik' in the hall. I must say a word about those Yule-tide amusements. They took place thus: all the household servants—and there were many of them, about thirty—used to dress up, come into the house, play various games, and dance to the accompaniment of the fiddle of old Gregory, who only appeared in the house on these occasions. It was very amusing. Those masquerading usually represented a bear with its leader, a goat, Turks and Turkish women, Tyrolese, brigands, peasant men and women. I remember how beautiful some of the characters appeared to me, and especially so Masha, the Turkish woman. Sometimes Auntie dressed us up also. Especially desirable to us was a belt with stones and a muslin towel, embroidered with silver and gold; and I thought myself very grand with mustaches painted with burnt cork. I remember that looking in the mirror at my face, with black mustaches and eyebrows, I could not refrain from a smile of delight, though I had to assume the fierce expression of a Turk. All these characters walked about the rooms and were treated to various refreshments. During one of the Yule-tides of my earlier childhood all the Islenefs came to us dressed up: the father, who was my wife's grandfather, with his three sons and three daughters. They all had on costumes which appeared most extraordinary to us; there was a toilet, there was a boot, there was a cardboard belt, and something else besides. The Islenefs, having driven thirty miles, changed dress in the village, and on entering our hall Islenef sat down to the piano and sang some verses he had invented, to a tune which I can still remember. The verses were: 'We have come here to congratulate you on the New Year; should we succeed in amusing you we shall be happy!' This was all very extraordinary, and probably entertaining to the elders, but for us children the most amusing were the household servants. Such entertainments took place during Christmas and at New Year, sometimes even later, up to the day of Baptism;[1]

---

[1] Sixth of January.—*Trans.*

A view in the village of Yasnaya Polyana.

but after New Year few people came and the amusements slackened. So it was on the day when Vassili was leaving for Scherbachovka. I remember we were sitting in a circle in the corner of the dimly lighted hall on home-made chairs of imitation mahogany with leather cushions and playing at 'Rublik.' One of us was walking about searching for the rouble, while we, passing it on from hand to hand, were singing, ' Pass on Rublik, pass on Rublik.' I remember one of the servant-girls kept singing these words with an especially pleasant and true voice. Suddenly the door of the pantry opened, and Vassili, buttoned up in an unusual way, without his tray and china, passed along the end of the hall into the study. Then only did I learn that Vassili was going as overseer to Scherbachovka. I understood it was a promotion, and was glad for Vassili, and at the same time I was not only sorry to part from him, to know that he would no longer be in the pantry and would no longer carry us on his tray, but I did not even understand, did not believe, that such an alteration could take place. I became dreadfully and mysteriously sad, and the chant of ' Pass on Rublik ' grew pathetically touching. And when Vassili left my aunt, and with his dear one-sided smile approached us, and kissed us on the shoulder, I experienced for the first time horror and fear in the presence of the inconstancy of life, and pity and love toward dear Vassili. When I afterward used to meet Vassili I saw in him merely a good or a bad overseer of my brother's, a man whom I respected, but there was no longer any trace of the former sacred, brotherly, human feeling.

"In a mysterious way, incomprehensible to the human mind, the impressions of early childhood are preserved in one's memory, and not only are they preserved, but they grow in some unfathomed depth of the soul, like seed thrown on good ground, and after many years all of a sudden thrust their vernal shoots into God's world."

Such a seed-time in Tolstoy's early childhood were the days of his eldest brother Nicolenka's games with the younger brothers. His great influence on Tolstoy's life is referred to in his Reminiscences more than once, for example, in the stories about the Fanfaronof Hill, Ant Brothers, and the Green Wand.

"Yes, the Fanfaronof Hill is one of the earliest, pleasantest, and most important memories. My eldest brother, Nicolenka, was six years older than I. He was consequently ten or eleven when I was four or five, namely, at the time when he *led* us on to the Fanfaronof Hill. In our earlier youth we used to address him (I don't know how it happened) as ' you.' [1] He was a wonderful boy, and later a wonderful man. Turgenef used very truly to say about him that but for the lack of certain faults he would have been a great writer. For instance he was deficient in vanity; he was not in the least interested in what people thought of him. Whereas the qualities of a writer which he did possess were, first of all, a fine artistic sense, an extremely developed sense of proportion, a good-natured, gay human, an extraordinary, inexhaustible imagination, and a truthful and highly moral view of life—and all this without the slightest conceit. His imagination was such that he could during whole hours narrate ghost stories or humorous tales in the spirit of Mrs. Radcliffe without pause or hesitation, and with such vivid realization of what he was narrating that one forgot it was all invention. When he was not narrating or reading (he read a great deal) he used to draw. He almost invariably drew devils with horns and pointed mustaches, intertwined in the most varied attitudes and occupied in the most various ways. These drawings were also full of imagination and humor.

"Well, it was he who, when I and my brothers were, myself five years old, Mitenka six, Seryozha seven, announced to us that he possessed a secret by means of which, when it should be disclosed, all men would become happy: there would be no diseases, no troubles, no one would be angry with any one, all would love each other, all would become 'Ant brothers.' He probably meant 'Moravian brothers,' about whom he had heard and had been reading, but in our language they were 'Ant brothers.' [2] And I remember that the word Ant especially pleased us, as reminding us of ants in an ant-hill. We even organized a game of ant brothers, which consisted in our sitting down under chairs, sheltering ourselves with boxes, screening ourselves with handkerchiefs, and, thus crouching in the dark, pressing ourselves against each other. I remember experiencing

---

[1] Instead of in the singular, "thou," as is usual in Russian between near relatives or friends.—*Trans.*
[2] The word for Ant in Russian is "Mouravey," whence the similarity.—*Trans.*

a special feeling of love and pathos and liking this game very much. The ant brotherhood was revealed to us, but the chief secret as to the way for all men to cease suffering any misfortune, to leave off quarrelling and being angry, and to become continuously happy, this secret, as he told us, was written by him on a green stick, which stick he had buried by the road on the edge of a certain ravine, at which spot, since my corpse must be buried somewhere, I have asked to be buried in memory of Nicolenka. Besides this little stick, there was also a certain Fanfaronof Hill up which he said he could lead us, if only we would fulfil all the appointed conditions. These conditions were: first, to stand in a corner and not think of the white bear. I remember how I used to get into a corner and endeavor, but could not possibly manage, not to think of the white bear. The second condition was to walk without wavering along a crack between the boards of the floor; and the third, for a whole year not to see a hare either alive or dead or cooked; and it was necessary to swear not to reveal these secrets to any one. He who should fulfil these conditions and others more difficult which Nicolenka was going to communicate later, would have his desire fulfilled, whatever it might be. We had to express our desires. Seryozha desired to be able to model horses and hens out of wax. Mitenka desired to be able to draw all kinds of things like an artist on a large scale. I could not devise anything but to be able to draw small pictures. All this, as it happens with children, was very soon forgotten and no one ascended the Fanfaronof Hill, but I remember the profound importance with which Nicolenka initiated us into these mysteries, and our respect and awe in regard to the wonderful things which were revealed. But I have especially kept a strong impression of the 'Ant Brotherhood' and the mysterious green stick connected with it destined to make all men happy.

"As I now conjecture, Nicolenka had probably read or heard of the Freemasons—about their aspiration toward the happiness of mankind, and about the mysterious initiatory rites on entering their order; he had probably also heard about the Moravian brothers, and linking all into one by his active imagination, his love to men, and his aptness to kindness, he invented all these tales, enjoyed them himself, and mystified us with them.

"The ideals of ant brothers lovingly cleaving to each other, though not beneath two arm-chairs curtained with handkerchiefs, but of all mankind under the wide dome of the sky, has remained the same for me. As then I believed that there existed a little green stick whereon was written that which could destroy all the evil in men and give them great welfare, so do I now also believe that such truth exists, and that it will be revealed to men and will give them all that it promises." [1]

Later on we shall refer to Tolstoy's memories of his brother Dmitri. Here we will quote another extract from his Reminiscences concerning his brother Sergius, also relating to his early childhood: "Mitenka was for me a companion, Nicolenka I respected, but Seryozha I enthusiastically admired and imitated. I loved him and wished to be like him; I admired his handsome appearance, his singing—he was always singing—his drawing, his cheerful mirth, and especially, however strange it may be to say so, the spontaneity of his egotism. I always realized myself, was always conscious of myself; I always felt whether others' thoughts and feelings about me were just or not, and this spoiled my joy of life. This probably is why I especially liked in others the opposite feature, spontaneity of egotism. And for this I especially loved Seryozha. The word *loved* is not correct. I loved Nicolenka, but for Seryozha I was filled with admiration as for something quite apart and incomprehensible to me. It was a human life, a very fine one, but completely incomprehensible to me, mysterious, and therefore specially attractive.

"A few days ago he died, and in his last illness and his death he was to me as unfathomable and as dear as in our bygone days of childhood. In more advanced age, his latter days, he loved me more, valued my attachment, was proud of me, wished to agree with me, but could not, and remained the same as he had been, entirely original, altogether himself, handsome, high-spirited, proud, and above all and to such an extent a truthful and sincere man that I have never seen his like. He was what he was; he concealed nothing, and did not desire to appear anything.

"With Nicolenka I wished to associate, to talk, to think; Seryozha I only wished to imitate. This imitation began in

[1] From Tolstoy's personal reminiscences.

Leo Tolstoy (in skull cap) and his brother Count Sergius Nicolayevich, shortly before the death of the latter, taken at about the time Leo Tolstoy wrote his reminiscences for this volume.

our first childhood. He took to keeping his own hens and chickens, and I did the same. This was perhaps my first insight into animal life. I remember chickens of various breeds—gray, spotted, or tufted, how they used to run to us at our call, how we fed them and hated the big Dutch cock which maltreated them. Seryozha had begged these chickens for himself; I did the same in imitation of him. Seryozha used to draw and paint on long strips of paper (and as it appeared to me wonderfully well) rows of hens and cocks of various colors, and I did the same but not so well. (In this I hoped to perfect myself by the means of the Fanfaronof Hill.) Seryozha, when the double doors were removed in spring, had the idea of feeding the hens through the keyhole in the door by means of long thin sausages of black and white bread, and I did the same."[1]

Let us add here a few more fragmentary reminiscences related by Tolstoy himself, which, like most of the stories of his early childhood, it is impossible to arrange in a chronological order, though it would be a pity to omit them, as they give some interesting traits descriptive of his childhood.

"One childish memory of an insignificant event left a strong impression on me," said Tolstoy. "It was, I see it now, in our nursery rooms upstairs. Temeshof was sitting talking to Feodor Ivanovich. I do not remember why the conversation turned upon keeping the fasts, and Temeshof, the good-natured Temeshof, very quietly said: 'My cook (or servant, I do not remember which) took it into his head to eat meat during fast time. I sent him to be a soldier.'[2] The reason why I now remember this is, that at the time it seemed to me something strange and incomprehensible.

"Another event was the Perof inheritance. I remember a caravan, with horses and carts loaded high, which arrived from Nerucha,[3] when the lawsuit concerning this estate had been won, thanks to Glya Mitrovich.

"He was a tall old man with long hair, addicted to fits of drinking, a former serf of the owner, and a great specialist, such as there used to be in olden times, in dealing with various cases that might lead to litigation. He directed the

---

[1] From Tolstoy's draught Reminiscences.
[2] In Russia, in the days of serfdom, the enlisting of a serf into the ranks for the fifteen years was regarded as the severest punishment short of flogging him to death.—*Trans.*
[3] This estate of 900 acres which we received by inheritance was sold for the purpose of feeding the starving during the great famine of 1840.

case, and in return he was kept until his death in Yasnaya Polyana.

"Other memorable impressions are: the arrival of Peter Tolstoy, the father of my sister's husband, Valerian; he used to come into the drawing-room in his dressing-gown; we did not understand why, but later we learned that it was because he was in the last stage of consumption. Another impression: the arrival of his brother, the famous traveller in America, Feodor Tolstoy. I remember how he drove up in a post-chaise, entered my father's study, and ordered his special dry French bread to be brought. He did not eat any other. At this time my brother Sergey was suffering from a very bad toothache. He asked what was the matter, and, having ascertained, said that he could cure the pain by magnetism. He entered the study and locked the door after him. In a few minutes he came out with two cambric pocket handkerchiefs—I remember they had a fancy violet edge—and he gave the handkerchiefs, saying: 'When he puts on this one the pain will cease, and this one is for him to sleep with.' The handkerchiefs were taken, put on Seryozha, and we carried away and kept the impression that everything took place as he had said.

"I remember his fine, bronzed face, shaven, save for thick white whiskers down to the corners of the mouth and similarly white curly hair. I should like to relate much about this extraordinary, guilty, and attractive man!"

Here, unfortunately, these reminiscences stop short.

Let us conclude this chapter on the childhood of Tolstoy with the poetic memory in his published story.

"Happy, happy, irrevocable period of childhood! How can one help loving and cherishing its memories? These memories refresh and elevate my soul and serve me as a source of my best enjoyments. . . .

"After the prayer I rolled myself into my coverlet, and my heart felt light and cheerful. One dream chased another, but what were they about? They were intangible, but filled with pure love and hope for bright happiness. I thought of Karl Ivanovich and his bitter fate, of the only man whom I knew to be unhappy, and I felt so sorry for him, and so loved him, that the tears gushed from my eyes, and I thought: God grant him happiness, and me an opportunity of helping him, and alleviating his sorrow; I was ready to sacrifice everything for him. Then I stuck my favorite china toy—a hare or a dog—into the corner of the down pillow, and I was happy seeing how comfortable and snug the toy was there. I also prayed the Lord that He would give happiness to everybody, and that all should be satisfied, and that to-morrow should be good weather for the outing, and then I turned on my other side, my thoughts and dreams became mixed and disturbed, and I fell softly, quietly asleep, my face wet with tears.

"Will that freshness, carelessness, need of love, and strength of faith, which one possesses in childhood, ever return? What time can be better than that when all the best virtues—innocent merriment and limitless need of love—are the only incitements in life?

"Where are all those ardent prayers, where is the best gift—those tears of contrition? The consoling angel came on his pinions, with a smile wiped off those tears, and fanned sweet dreams to the uncorrupted imagination of the child.

"Is it possible life has left such heavy traces in my heart that these tears and that ecstasy have forever gone from me? Is it possible, nothing but memories are left?"

CHAPTER V

BOYHOOD

Removal to Moscow—Father's death—Its influence on Tolstoy—Grandmother's death—Prosper St. Thomas—His influence—St. Thomas' opinion of Tolstoy's gifts—Division of the family—Countess A. T. Osten-Saken as guardian—Tolstoy's recollections of her—Unhappy marriage—Madness of her husband—The adopted daughter Pashenka—The moral physiognomy of the Countess—The housemaid Gasha—Father's jokes—The death of the Countess in the Optin Convent—The second guardian—Natalya Ilynishna Yushkof—Removal of Kazan—Boats, horse carts—Serfs—Life during the journey—The husband of Pelageya Ilyinishna, Vladimir Ivanovich Yushkof—Pelageya Ilyinishna's death—Inner development of Tolstoy during his boyhood—His self-consciousness and shyness—His opinion on his own appearance—Love for his brothers—Seryozha Ivin or the Count Alexander Pushkin—The change in his views on men—The beginning of philosophic reasoning—The ascetic experiment—The epicurean period—The reasoning on symmetry and eternity—Scepticism, non-existence—Friendship with Nekhludof-Dyakof—The adoration of virtue—Religious education—The destruction of outward religious ideas—Recollection of it in the *Confession*—The list of literary works which influenced Tolstoy. *Several episodes of his boyhood narrated by Tolstoy and his relatives:* Mitka Kopilof—Christmas-tree at Shipofs'—Astashof's garden—Fall from the window—Cutting of the eyebrows—Race with a troika—Peculiarities—Poor learning—Jealousy—The flying experiment. *Episodes as related in the books for reading:* The old horse—A lesson in riding.

WITH the beginning of Tolstoy's boyhood came the time for the more serious education of his elder brothers, Nicolay and Sergey. For this purpose, in autumn of 1836, the Tolstoy family moved to Moscow, and settled down at Pluschikha, in a house belonging to one Scherbachof. This house is still in use, and stands back opposite St. Mary the Virgin's Church, Smolensky, its façade forming an acute angle with the direction of the street.

In this house they lived during the winter of 1836-7, and after their father's death they remained there for the summer.

Once in the summer of 1837 Tolstoy's father went to Tula on business, and in the street on his way to the house of one

Temeshof, a friend, all at once he staggered, fell on the ground, and died of apoplexy. Some people said he was poisoned by his man-servant, because, though his money disappeared, yet some unnegotiable bonds he had on him were brought to the Tolstoys in Moscow by an unknown beggar.

His body was taken by his sister Alexandra and his eldest son Nicolay to Yasnaya Polyana, in Tula, where he was buried.

His father's death was the event which left the deepest impression on Tolstoy in his childhood. He used to say that this death called forth in him a feeling of religious awe, bringing the question of life and death vividly before him for the first time. As he was not present when his father died, he would not believe for a long time that he was no longer alive. For a long time afterward, if he looked at the faces of strangers in the streets of Moscow, he not only fancied, but was almost certain, that he might, at any moment, come upon his father alive. And this mixed attitude of hope and unbelief called forth in him a special feeling of tenderness. After their father's death the Tolstoys remained for the summer in Moscow, and this was the first and last time that Tolstoy spent a summer in town.

They sometimes made excursions to places near the city in a carriage drawn by four bay horses driven abreast, according to custom. These occasions, on which they were unattended by a post-boy, made a strong impression on him —attributable, it may be, not only to the beauty of Kuntsef-Neskuchny, but in some measure to escape from the unpleasant smells emitted by the factories which even then were disfiguring the suburbs of Moscow.

"The death of her son quite killed my grandmother, Pelageya Nicolayevna; she wept perpetually, and every evening ordered the door into the next room to be opened, and said that she saw her son there and talked with him. Sometimes she asked with horror of her daughters: 'Is it really, really true that he is no longer?' She died at the end of nine months from a broken heart and grief."

His grandmother's death reminded Tolstoy anew of the religious import of life and death—it may be without his being fully conscious of it, but the impression was there, and that a strong one. His grandmother suffered for a long time, till at last she was seized with dropsy, and Tolstoy remembers the horror he felt when he was admitted to take leave of her, and how she, lying in her lofty white bed, all in white, looked round with difficulty on her grandchildren, and without making a motion let them kiss her white hand which had swollen up like a pillow. But, as is usual with children, the sense of fear and pity in the presence of death was soon succeeded by playfulness, thoughtlessness, and love of mischief. On one holiday, little Vladimir Milutin, a friend of Tolstoy's of the same age, came to stay in the house; it was he who made to the Tolstoys while they were still in the gymnasium the remarkable statement—though the information did not make a strong impression—that there was no God.

Just before dinner the wildest and strangest merrymaking was going on in the children's room, in which Sergey, Dmitri, and Lyof were taking part, though Milutin and Nicolay had more sense than the rest and kept aloof. The fun consisted in burning paper in pots behind a partition where the *commode* stood. It is difficult to imagine where all the amusement was, but no doubt the sport was greatly enjoyed. All of a sudden in the midst of the merrymaking, the light-haired, wiry, and energetic little tutor, St. Thomas, described in *Boyhood* as St. Jerome, came in with a quick step, and, without paying any attention to their doings, and without scolding them, said to them, with the lower jaw of his white face trembling: "*Votre grand'mère est morte!*"

"I remember," related Tolstoy, "how at that time new jackets of black material, bound with white braid, were made for all of us. It was dreadful to see the undertaker's workmen hurrying about the house, and then the coffin brought with a lid covered with glazed brocade, and my grandmother's severe face with its crooked nose, in a white cap, with a white kerchief on her neck, lying high in the coffin on the table, and it was piteous to see the tears of our aunts and of Pashenka, but at the same time the new braided jackets and the soothing attitude taken toward us by those around gratified us. I do not remember why we were removed to the aisle during the funeral, and I remember how pleasant it was to me to overhear a conversation of some gossiping female guests near us, who said: 'Completely orphans, the father has only just died, and now the grandmother is gone too.'"

BOYHOOD

Tolstoy has mixed recollections of good and evil about Prosper St. Thomas, the French tutor.

"I do not now remember for what," says Tolstoy in his Reminiscences, "but it was for something utterly undeserving of punishment that St. Thomas first locked me up in a room and secondly threatened to flog me. Hereupon I had a dreadful feeling of anger, indignation, and disgust, not only toward St. Thomas himself, but toward the violence which it was intended to inflict upon me. Very likely this incident was the cause of the dreadful horror and repulsion toward every kind of violence which I have experienced all my life."[1]

However, the tutor, St. Thomas, watched attentively the manifestation of gifts in his little pupil. He probably had noticed something extraordinary in the boy, for he used to say about him: "*Ce petit a une tête, c'est un petit Molière.*"[2]

After the death of Tolstoy's grandmother, complicated transactions in connection with the Court of Wards making it imperative that expenses should be cut down, part of the family returned to the estates, namely, Dmitri, Lyof, and Marie, with their aunt, Tatiana Alexandrovna Yergolsky. Here the children's tutors were replaced by new German teachers and Russian students from theological seminaries. Their guardian was the Countess Alexandra Ilyinishna Osten-Saken.

Of this remarkable woman Tolstoy thus writes in his memoirs:

"My aunt Alexandra Ilyinishna was very early given in marriage in St. Petersburg to a wealthy Count Osten-Saken of the Baltic Provinces. The match appeared very brilliant, but from the conjugal point of view it terminated very sadly for my aunt, although perhaps the consequences of this marriage were beneficial to her soul. Aunt Aline, as we called her in the family, was probably very attractive, with her large blue eyes and the meek expression of her pale face, as she is depicted in a very good portrait taken when she was a girl of sixteen. Soon after the marriage, Osten-Saken went with his young wife to his great estate in the Baltic Provinces, and there he increasingly manifested his diseased mental condition, which at first showed itself only in a very

[1] An interpolation by Tolstoy when looking through the MS.
[2] From Countess S. A. Tolstoy's Reminiscences.

marked and causeless jealousy. During the very first year of the marriage, when my aunt was already nearing childbirth, the husband's malady increased to such an extent that spells of complete aberration used to take possession of him, during which he thought that his foes, desirous of carrying away his wife, were surrounding him, and that his only way of escape was in flight. This was in summer. Having got up early in the morning, he announced to his wife that the only means of safety was to flee, that he had ordered the calesh, that they were to start immediately, and that she must get ready. And indeed the calesh drove up, he placed my aunt inside, and ordered the coachman to drive as quickly as possible. On the way he got two pistols out of a box, cocked the trigger, and having given one to my aunt, told her that if his foes found out about his flight they would catch him up, and then they were lost, and the only thing which would then remain for them to do would be to kill each other. My frightened and bewildered aunt took the pistol and tried to dissuade her husband, but he did not listen to her, and only kept turning round, anticipating pursuit, and urging the coachman to speed. Unfortunately, out of a lane converging upon the high-road there appeared a carriage. He called out that all was lost, and ordered my aunt to shoot herself, and himself shot point-blank into my aunt's breast. Startled by what he had done, and seeing that the carriage which had frightened him had turned in another direction, he stopped, lifted my wounded and bleeding aunt from the carriage, put her down on the road, and galloped away. Fortunately for my aunt, some peasants soon came across her, raised her, and drove her to the pastor, who bound up her wounds as well as he could, and sent for the doctor. The wound was in the right side of the chest, passing completely through the body (my aunt showed me the scar remaining), but was not serious. When she was recovering, and still lying enceinte at the pastor's house, her husband, having come to himself, hurried to her, and after explaining to the doctor how she was unfortunately wounded, he sought an interview with her. This interview was dreadful. He, cunning as are all the mentally diseased, pretended repentance for his act, and concern only about her health. Having remained with her some time talking quite rationally about everything, he profited by a moment when they were left alone together to attempt to fulfil his intention. As if concerned with her health, he asked her to show him her tongue, and when she put it out, he caught hold of it with one hand, and with the other brought out a razor he had in readiness, with the intention of cutting the tongue off. A struggle ensued—she tore herself away from him, screamed; people rushed in, seized him, and led him away.

"Thenceforth his insanity took a thoroughly definite form, and he lived for a long time in some institution for lunatics, having no communication with my aunt. Soon after this, my aunt was removed to her parents' house in St. Petersburg, and there she gave birth to a dead child. For fear of the consequences of grief at her child's death, she was told that it was alive, and a girl who was at the same time born of a servant known to the family, the wife of a court cook, was brought to her. This girl, Pashenka, who lived with us, was already grown up when I begin myself to remember. I do not know when the history of her birth was disclosed to Pashenka, but when I knew her she was already aware she was not my aunt's daughter. Aunt Alexandra Ilyinishna, after what had happened to her, lived first with her parents, and then at my father's. After his death she was our guardian, but when I was twelve she died in the convent of Optin Pustin.

"My aunt was a truly religious woman. Her favorite occupation was reading the lives of the saints, conversing with pilgrims, crazy devotees, monks, and nuns, of whom some always lived in our house, while others only visited my aunt. Among the constant residents was the nun Marya Gerassimovna, my sister's godmother, who had in her youth undertaken pilgrimages in the character of 'crazy Ivanushka.' She was my sister's godmother, because my mother had promised this to her, should she by prayer obtain from God for my mother a daughter, a boon which my mother greatly desired after bearing four sons. A daughter was born, and Marya Gerassimovna became her godmother, living partly in the Tula convent and partly at our house.

"Aunt Alexandra Ilyinishna was not only outwardly religious, keeping the fasts, praying much, and associating with people of saintly life, such as was in her time the hermit Leonid in the Optin Pustin, but she herself lived a truly Christian life, endeavoring not only to avoid all luxury and acceptance of service, but also, as much as possible, to serve others. She never had any money, because she gave away all she had to those who asked.

"The maid Gasha, who after my grandmother's death passed over to my aunt, has related to me how during their Moscow life my aunt, in going to Matins, used carefully to pass on tiptoe by her sleeping maid, and herself discharged all the functions which according to the then received custom should have been done by the maid. In food and dress she was as simple and unexacting as it is possible to imagine. However unpleasant it is to me to say so, I remember from childhood the specific acrid smell connected with my aunt, probably due to negligence in her toilet, and this was that graceful, poetic Aline with beautiful blue eyes who used to like to read and copy French verses, who played on the harp, and always had great success at the biggest balls! I remember how she was always as affectionate and kind to all the most important men and women as to nuns and pilgrims. I remember how her brother-in-law, Yushkof, liked to make fun of her, and how he once sent from Kazan a big box directed to her. In the box another box was found, in that one a third, and so on until there appeared quite a tiny one, in which, wrapped in cotton-wool, lay a china monk. I remember how my father laughed good-naturedly, showing this parcel to my aunt. I also remember my father relating at table how she, according to his assertion, with her cousin Molchanova, ran after a priest whom they reverenced that they might get his benediction. My father described this, comparing it to coursing, saying that Molchanova cut the priest off from the gates before the altar; he then threw himself toward the north gates, she in pursuit made a miss, and here it was that Aline caught him. I remember her dear, good-natured laugh and face shining with pleasure. The religious feeling which filled her soul was evidently so important to her, so much higher than all the rest, that she could not be angry or annoyed by anything, she could not attribute to worldly matters the importance which is generally given to them. She took care of us when she was our guardian, but all she did did not absorb her soul, all was subdued to the service of God as she understood that service."[1]

[1] From Tolstoy's draught Reminiscences.

BOYHOOD

As has been stated before, the younger children, *i. e.*, Dmitri, Marie, and Leo, lived with Aunt Tatiana in the country after their grandmother's death, and the elder, Nicolay and Sergey, remained with their guardian, Alexandra Ilyinishna, in Moscow. In the summer the whole family met at Yasnaya Polyana. Thus passed the years 1838–9, and the year 1840 began a year of famine; the crops were so poor that the Tolstoys had to buy corn to feed their serfs, and the means for this purpose were obtained from the sale of the Neruch estate which they had inherited.

The food for the horses was cut short and the free supply of oats was stopped. Tolstoy recollects how sorry the children were for their favorite horses, and how they secretly ran to the peasants' field of oats and, without being aware of the crime they were committing, plucked the oat stems, gathered the grain in their skirts, and treated their horses to it.

In the autumn of 1840 the whole family moved to Moscow where they spent the winter of 1840–41; for the summer they returned to Yasnaya again. In the autumn of 1841 their guardian, the Countess A. T. Osten-Saken, died.

She died in the convent Optina Pustin. During her stay there the children remained in Yasnaya Polyana with their Aunt Tatiana. But when the news reached her that Alexandra Ilyinishna was on her death-bed, Tatiana went to the convent.

After her death her sister, Pelageya Ilyinishna, who was then the wife of V. T. Yushkof, a Kazan landowner, arrived at Moscow from Kazan. Aunt Tatiana and all the children came there in the autumn. The elder brother of Tolstoy, who at that time was already a student of the first year in the university, greeted his aunt with the words: "*Ne nous abandonnez pas, chère tante, il ne nous reste que vous au monde.*" Her eyes filled with tears and she made up her mind "*se sacrifier.*" What she meant by this no one knew; the result was that she at once began preparations for a journey to Kazan. For this purpose she ordered some boats which she loaded with everything she could carry away from Yasnaya Polyana. All the servants had to follow—carpenters, tailors, locksmiths, chefs, upholsterers, etc. Moreover, to each of the four brothers Tolstoy was attached a serf of about the same age, as man-servant. One of these was Vanyusha, who afterward accompanied Tolstoy to the Caucasus and who now spends his old age at his daughter's house in Tula.

At this time Tolstoy was twelve years old. Masters and servants started for the journey in autumn, and in numerous carriages and other vehicles crept slowly from Tula to Kazan. During the journey something like regular habits were maintained. Sometimes they stopped in the fields, sometimes in the woods, bathed, walked about and gathered mushrooms. The parting with Aunt Tatiana Alexandrovna was distressing, but she had never been on friendly terms with Aunt Pelageya Ilyinishna, and, after the death of Alexandra Ilyinishna, she settled with her sister, Helena Alexandrovna Tolstoy, in the village of Pokrovskoye. The want of a good understanding between Tatiana Alexandrovna and Pelageya Ilyinishna arose from the fact that the husband of the latter had been in love with Tatiana in his youth and made her an offer of marriage, which she rejected. Pelageya Ilyinishna could never forgive her husband's love for the other and hated her for it, though in public they appeared to be on thoroughly friendly terms.

Pelageya's husband, V. J. Yushkof, a retired colonel of hussars, has left behind him in Kazan the memory of an educated, witty, and kind-hearted man, who loved jokes and lively conversation, and such he remained until his death.

Pelageya herself was remembered in Kazan as a very kind, but not particularly clever woman. She was very pious, and after the death of her husband in 1869 she retired to the convent Optin Pustin. Later on she lived in a convent in Tula and finally moved to Yasnaya Polyana, where she fell ill and died.

All through her long life she strictly observed all the rites of the orthodox church; but in her eightieth year, before her death, which she greatly feared, she declined to take the communion and grew angry with other people on account of the misery which she suffered herself in the presentiment of her end.

Let us now point out certain stages in the moral development of children which we find in such of Tolstoy's

V. J. Yushkof, Tolstoy's uncle.

novels as are descriptive of that period of life, and which carry, in our opinion, a real autobiographical character.

One trait often observable in children, and which perhaps existed in Tolstoy himself in a high degree, is extreme shyness—the outcome of self-consciousness.

People very often make a distinction between these two characteristics—self-consciousness and shyness. They find fault with the one and encourage the other, or *vice versa*, but these traits are merely the reverse sides of the same medal, and are related to one another as cause and effect. A man is often shy because he is self-conscious, and as the shyness increases it intensifies his self-consciousness. The former manifests itself on any trifling ground, for instance in consequence of misgivings as to one's appearance. This is how Tolstoy speaks of it in himself under the character of Nicolenka:

"I had the oddest conceptions of beauty—I even regarded Carl Ivanovich as the first beau in the world; but I knew full well that I was not good-looking, and in this opinion was not mistaken. Therefore, every reference to my looks was offensive to me. . . .

"Moments of despair frequently came over me. I imagined that there was no happiness in the world for a man with such a broad nose, fat lips, and small gray eyes, as mine were. I asked God to do a miracle, and to change me into a handsome boy, and everything I then had, and everything I should ever have in the future, I would gladly have given for a pretty face." [1]

As soon as man turns his glance upon himself, a conflict of most varied feelings rises in him. If he is a man of intelligence and morality, he is bound to feel dissatisfaction, and the feeling must call forth a longing for improvement in things external, as well as in his own heart. As he has no power to improve the former, *e. g.,* to make his nose more shapely, therefore it is perhaps painful to think about the matter. But, if the mind be strong, it will lead one to the path of inward self-perfecting, and thereby open the way of endless progress.

This is exactly the conflict of feeling and thought which we can follow in the child, boy, and youth presented to us by Tolstoy in Nicolenka Irtenef. In describing his develop-

[1] In *Childhood*.

ment the author endows him with his own deep, rich inner world.

In a conversation with one of his friends, Tolstoy said that his early youth was spent under the influence of his brother Seryozha, and in attempts to imitate him. This brother he specially loved and admired. In somewhat riper years he was chiefly influenced by his brother Nicolay, whom he loved, not indeed so passionately as he did Seryozha, but still very dearly, and whom he respected more.[1]

Glancing through the novel *Childhood,* we find the account of a similar feeling in the description of the love of Nicolenka Irtenef for Seryozha Ivin.

These are the glowing words in which he depicts this affection:

"I felt unconquerably attracted by him. It was enough for my happiness to see him, and all the powers of my soul were concentrated upon this desire. When I passed three or four days without seeing him, I grew lonely, and felt sad enough to weep. All my dreams, waking and sleeping, were of him. When I lay down to sleep, I wished that I might dream of him; when I closed my eyes, I saw him before me, and I treasured this vision as my greatest pleasure. I did not dare intrust this feeling to any one in the world, I valued it so.

"Perhaps he was tired of feeling my restless eyes continually directed toward him, or he did not feel any sympathy for me, but he visibly preferred to play and to talk with Volódya, rather than with me. I was, nevertheless, satisfied, wished for nothing, demanded nothing, and was ready to sacrifice everything for him.

"Under the name of the Ivins, I have described the Count's Pushkin boys, one of whom, Alexander, has just died—the one whom I liked so much in childhood. Our favorite game was playing at soldiers."[2]

Tolstoy thus depicts the turning-point in his development, the transition from childhood to boyhood:

"My reader, have you ever happened to notice at a certain stage of your life how your view of things completely changed, as though all the things which you used

[1] From a private letter.
[2] Interpolation by Tolstoy in the MS. of this work.

to know, heretofore, suddenly turned a different, unfamiliar side to you? Some such moral transformation took place in me for the first time, during our journey, and from this I count the beginning of my boyhood.

"I obtained for the first time a clear idea of the fact that we, that is, our family, were not alone in the world, that not all interests centred about us, and there was another life for people who had nothing in common with us, who did not care for us, and who even did not have any idea of our existence. To be sure, I knew it before; but I did not know it in the same manner as now—I was not conscious of it, did not feel it."[1]

At an early age the child had taken up philosophic argument, and even in his boyhood the path is foreshadowed by which his powerful mind was to be developed and to influence so many others.

"People will hardly believe what the favorite and most constant subjects of my thoughts were during the period of my boyhood—for they were inconsistent with my age and station. But, according to my opinion, the inconsistency between a man's position and his moral activity is the surest token of truth. . . .

"At one time it occurred to me that happiness did not depend on external causes, but on our relation to them; that a man who is accustomed to bear suffering could not be unhappy. To accustom myself to endurance, I would hold for five minutes at a time the dictionaries of Tatishchev in my outstretched hands, though it caused me unspeakable pain, or I would go into the lumber room and strike my bare back so painfully with a rope that the tears would involuntarily appear in my eyes.

"At another time, I happened to think that death awaited me at any hour and at any minute, and wondering how it was people had not seen this before me, I decided that man cannot be happy otherwise than by enjoying the present and not caring for the future. Under the influence of this thought, I abandoned my lessons for two or three days, and did nothing but lie on my bed and enjoy myself reading some novel and eating honey cakes which I bought with my last money.

"At another time, as I was standing at the blackboard

[1] *Boyhood.*

and drawing various figures upon it with a piece of chalk, I was suddenly struck by the idea, Why is symmetry pleasant to the eye? What is symmetry? It is an implanted feeling, I answered myself. What is it based upon? Is symmetry to be found in everything in life? Not at all. Here is life—and I drew an oval figure on the board. After life the soul passes into eternity. Here is eternity—and I drew, on one side of the figure, a line to the very edge of the board. Why is there no such line on the other side of the figure? Really, what kind of eternity is that which is only on one side? We have no doubt existed before this life, although we have lost the recollection of it. . . .

"By none of these philosophic considerations was I so carried away as by scepticism, which at one time led me to a condition bordering on insanity. I imagined that nothing existed in the whole world outside of me, that objects were no objects, but only images which appeared whenever I turned my attention to them, and that these images would immediately disappear when I no longer thought of them. In short, I held the conviction with Schelling that objects do not exist, but only my relation to them. There were moments when, under the influence of this fixed idea, I reached such a degree of absurdity that I sometimes turned in the opposite direction, hoping to take nothingness by surprise, where I was not."[1]

Boyhood ends by a description of Nicolenka Irtenef's friendship with Nekhludof.[2]

The conclusion of this novel expresses in a few words that ideal of man which Tolstoy has sought and followed all his life, and which he still seeks in the sunset of his days.

"Of course, under the influence of Nekhludof I involuntarily appropriated his point of view, the essence of which was an ecstatic worship of the ideal of virtue, and the conviction that a man's destiny is continually to perfect himself. At that time it seemed a practicable affair to correct humanity at large, to destroy all human vices and misfortunes—and therefore it looked easy and simple to correct oneself, to appropriate to oneself all virtues and be happy."[1]

[1] *Boyhood.*
[2] The material for the description of this friendship I owe to my later friendship with Dyakof, during the last year of my university life at Kazan.

It is evident that this tendency toward abstract thought, this timidity and shyness, this striving after an ideal—that all these qualities manifested in the child were the primitive elements which gradually formed the harmonious soul of the artist-thinker. We now see the full bloom of these spiritual germs which were planted in Tolstoy's boyhood.

Brought up in a patriarchally aristocratic and, in its way, religious atmosphere, Tolstoy, in his childhood, with his responsive soul, absorbed all he could and was sincerely religious. Hints of this we see in *Childhood*. But this "habitual" religiousness fell away at the first breeze of rationalism.

He speaks thus in his *Confession* about his religious education, given as it was in accordance with the views of those days:

"I was christened and educated in the faith of the Orthodox Greek Church; I was taught it in my childhood, and I learned it in my youth. Nevertheless, at eighteen years of age, when I quitted the university, I had discarded all belief in everything that I had been taught. To judge by what I can now remember, I could never have had a very serious belief; it must have been a kind of trust in this teaching, based on a trust in my teachers and elders, and a trust, moreover, not very firmly grounded.

"I remember once, in my eleventh year, a boy, now long since dead, Vladimir M——, a pupil in a gymnasium, spent a Sunday with us, and brought us the news of the last discovery in the gymnasium, namely, that there was no God, and that all we were taught on the subject was a mere invention. This was in 1838. I remember well how interested my elder brothers were in this news. I was admitted to their deliberations, and we all eagerly accepted the theory as something particularly attractive and possibly quite true."

But of course this rationalism could not shake the foundations of his soul. These foundations withstood terrible life-storms and brought him to the path of truth.

Tolstoy gives interesting information concerning those literary works which, as far as he remembers, had great influence on his moral development during his childhood and boyhood, *i. e.*, up to about fourteen years of age. Here is the list of the works:

The Titles.	The Degree of Influence.
The Story of Joseph, from the Bible	Powerful.
Thousand and One Night Tales: The Forty Thieves, Prince Kamaralzaman	Great.
The Black Fowl, by Pogorelsky	Very great.
Russian Legends: Dobrinya Nikitich, Ilya Muromets, Alyosha Popovich	Powerful.
Popular Tales, Pushkin's Verses: Napoleon.	Great.

We shall now give a few episodes from Tolstoy's boyhood, partly written down from his own words, partly gathered from his relatives, but also borrowed from other sources which have already appeared in print, and which we have ourselves edited. In doing as above mentioned, we shall make a selection, being guided therein by authentic information which is in our possession. It is impossible to arrange the stories in a chronological order.

"It was quite at the beginning of our Moscow life, during my father's lifetime," Tolstoy once observed in describing his reminiscences, "that we had a pair of very spirited horses of our own breeding. My father's coachman was Mitka Kopilof. He was also my father's groom, a good horseman, sportsman, and excellent coachman, and, above all, an invaluable postilion. He was invaluable in this respect that a boy cannot manage spirited horses and an elderly man is too heavy and not suitable for a postilion, so that Mitka combined the rare qualities necessary for the purpose, which were: small stature, lightness, strength, and agility. I remember once the phaeton was brought to the door for my father, and the horses bolted out of the yard gate. Some one shouted, 'The Count's horses have run away!' Pashenka was overcome. My aunts rushed to my grandmother to reassure her, but it turned out that my father had not yet entered the carriage, and Mitka cleverly arrested the horses and returned into the yard.

"Well, it was this same Mitka who, after the reduction of our expenses, was given freedom on ransom. Rich merchants competed in endeavoring to engage his services, and would have given him a big salary, as he already flaunted silk shirts and velvet jackets. It so happened that the turn came for his brother to be enlisted as a soldier, and his father, already aged, summoned Mitka home to do laborer's work for the master. And this small-sized, elegant Dmitri in a month's time became transformed into a modest peasant, in bast shoes, working for the landlord, and cultivating his own two allotments, mowing, ploughing, and, in general, doing all the heavy peasant's task of that time. And all this was done without the slightest murmur, with the consciousness that this should be so, and could not be otherwise."

This was one of the events that fostered that love and respect for the people which Tolstoy used to feel even in childhood.

Here are two episodes which Tolstoy related to me, and which, according to his words, planted in his youthful mind germs of doubt and dissatisfaction—with the injustice and cruelty of those very people whom he still regarded as his "elders," and who always appeared to him as invested with a certain kind of authority. The authority of these people was being undermined even then.

While still a child, he was shown the unfairness, the worship of appearances, and the fashionable contempt for everything that is modest, the exhibition of which is so painful to childhood and directs the little ones especially to serious thoughts and promotes the development of their spiritual perception.

One illustration of the above was furnished by an incident connected with the Christmas-tree at Shipof's to which the Tolstoy children were invited, as they were related to the family. They had just lost their father and their grandmother and were orphans, cared for by an aunt who was in rather poor circumstances, and hence they did not possess much attraction or importance in fashionable society.

To the same Christmas-tree were invited the princes Gorchakof, nephews of the then Minister of War, and the Tolstoys observed with annoyance the difference which was made in the choice of presents for them and for the other more honored guests; the Tolstoys received presents of cheap wooden things, while the others had magnificent and expensive toys.

Another case took place in Moscow.

Once they went for a walk with their German tutor.

Tolstoy, who was then nine or ten years old, his brothers, and a girl named Yuzenka, a daughter of the French governess, who lived with their neighbors, the Islenefs, were among the children. Yuzenka was a very good-looking and attractive girl. While walking along Bolshaya Bronnaya Street, they found themselves near a garden gate leading to Polyakof's house. The gate was not shut and they entered with some hesitation, not knowing what would happen; the garden seemed to them of an unusual beauty. There were a pond with boats, flags, and flowers, small bridges, paths, bowers, etc.; they walked round the garden as if it was enchanted, till they were met by a gentleman who appeared to be Astashof, the owner of the place. He greeted them affably and invited them to look round, gave them a row in a boat, and was so amiable that they thought their presence actually gave pleasure to the owner of the garden. Encouraged by their good fortune, they decided to visit this garden again in a few days. When they entered the gate they were stopped by an old man who asked whom they wanted to see. They gave their surname and begged to be announced to the master. Yuzenka was not with them. The old man returned with the answer that the garden belonged to a private individual and the public was forbidden to enter. They went away disappointed, and were unable to understand why their friend's pretty face should have made so great a difference in the attitude of strangers toward them.

Here are a few stories which indicate the originality, not to say eccentricity, of his boyish character.

"We were once assembled at dinner," said Marie (Tolstoy's sister) to me; "it was in Moscow, during their grandmother's illness, when etiquette was adhered to and everybody had to appear in good time before grandmother came, and wait for her, so that all were surprised to see that Lyovochka was not there. When all were seated at the table, the grandmother, who had noticed his absence, asked St. Thomas, the tutor, what was the reason of it, and whether Leo had been punished. The tutor declared with some confusion that he did not know, but that he was certain that Leo would appear in a minute, that he was probably detained in his room getting ready for dinner. The grandmother was put at her ease, but, before long, the assistant tutor entered and whispered something to St. Thomas, who immediately jumped up and hurriedly left the room. This was so unusual, considering the strict etiquette observed at dinner, that everybody concluded that some great misfortune had taken place; as Lyovochka was absent, every one was sure that he was the person who had met with a misfortune, and all anxiously awaited the return of St. Thomas.

"Soon the matter was cleared up and we learned what had happened.

"For some unknown reason, Lyovochka (as he now tells us himself, simply to do something extraordinary and surprise the others) had conceived the idea of jumping from a second-story window, a height of several yards. And in order not to have this achievement hindered, he remained in the room alone when everybody else went to dinner. He climbed up to the open window in the attic and jumped into the yard. In the basement was the kitchen, and the cook was standing by the window, when, before she realized what was happening, Lyovochka struck the ground with a thud. She then informed the steward, and, stepping outside, they found Lyovochka lying in the yard in a state of unconsciousness. Luckily no bones were broken, and the injury was limited to a slight concussion of the brain; unconsciousness changed into sleep; he slept eighteen hours at a stretch and woke up quite sound. You may imagine what fear and anxiety were caused by the queer little fellow's unpremeditated act.

"Once the idea struck him that he would clip his eyebrows; and he carried it out, thus disfiguring a face which was never strikingly beautiful and causing himself a great deal of grief.

"'Another time,' related Marie, 'we were driving in a troika from Pirogovo to Yasnaya. During a pause in our journey, Lyovochka ·got down and walked on on foot. When the carriage was ready to set off again, he could not be found. Soon, however, the coachman beheld from his seat his disappearing figure on the road ahead of him, so the party started, believing he had gone on only with the intention of resuming his seat as soon as the troika caught him up; but this was a mistake. As the carriage approached, he quickened his pace, and when the horse was made to trot he began to run, apparently not desiring to take his seat. The troika advanced at a rapid pace and he also ran as hard as he could, and kept on running for about three versts, till at last he was tired out and gave it up. They got him to take his seat; but he was gasping for breath, perspiring, and broken down with fatigue.'"

Sofya Andreyevna, Tolstoy's wife, has many a time busied herself with putting down particulars of his life, asking him questions about his childhood, and listening to stories told by his relations. Unfortunately these notes are incomplete, but nevertheless they are very valuable. We quote a few extracts from them, availing ourselves of the kind permission of their writer.

"Judging by tales of old aunts who have told me a few things about my husband's childhood, and also by what my grandfather Islenef has said (he was very friendly with Nicolay Ilyich, Tolstoy's father), little Lyovochka was a peculiar child, in fact quite an odd little fellow. For instance, he once entered the saloon and made a bow to everybody backward, bending his head and courtesying.

"When I asked Tolstoy himself and also others if he studied well, I was answered that he 'did not.'"

S. A. Bers, Tolstoy's brother-in-law, relates the following in his reminiscences:

"P. I. Yushkof, Tolstoy's late aunt, declared that in his boyhood he was very frolicsome, and as a boy he was marked for his oddity, sometimes also for his impulsive acts, as well as for a noble heart.

"My mother related to me that in describing his first love in his work *Childhood* he omitted to say that, being jealous, he pushed the object of his love off the balcony. This was my mother, nine years old, who had to limp for a long time afterward. He did this because she was not talking to him but to somebody else. Later on, she used to laugh and say to him: 'Evidently you pushed me off the terrace in my childhood that you might marry my daughter afterward.'"[1]

Tolstoy himself used to relate in the family circle, in my presence, that when he was a child of seven or eight years, he had an ardent desire to fly. He imagined that it

[1] S. A. Bers *Reminiscences of Count L. N. Tolstoy*

was quite possible if you sat down on your heels and hugged your knees, and that the harder the knees were clasped the higher you could fly.

Several stories by Tolstoy, published in his *Books for Reading,* are autobiographical. We reproduce some characteristic passages from them.

In the tale, *The Old Horse,* Tolstoy relates how he and his three brothers got permission to have a ride. They were only allowed to ride on a quiet old horse called Voronok. The three elder brothers, after riding to their hearts' content and exhausting the horse, handed it over to him.

" When my turn came, I wanted to surprise my brothers and to show them how well I could ride, so I began to drive Raven with all my might, but he did not want to get away from the stable. And no matter how much I beat him, he would not run, but only shied and turned back. I grew angry at the horse, and struck him as hard as I could with my feet and with the whip. I tried to strike him in places where it would hurt most; I broke the whip, and began to strike his head with what was left of the whip. But Raven would not run. Then I turned back, rode up to the valet, and asked him for a stout switch. But the valet said to me:

" ' Don't ride any more, sir! Get down! What use is there in torturing the horse?'

" I felt offended, and said:

" ' But I have not had a ride yet. Just watch me gallop! Please, give me a good-sized switch! I will heat him up.'

" Then the valet shook his head and said:

" ' Oh, sir, you have no pity; why should you heat him up? He is twenty years old. The horse is worn out; he can barely breathe, and is old. He is so very old! Just like Pimen Timofeyich.[1] You might just as well sit down on Timofeyich's back and urge him on with a switch. Now, would you not pity him?'

" I thought of Pimen, and listened to the valet's words. I climbed down from the horse and, when I saw how his sweaty sides hung down, how he breathed heavily through his nostrils, and how he switched his bald tail, I understood that it was hard for the horse. I felt so sorry for Raven

[1] A man ninety years old.

that I began to kiss his sweaty neck and to beg his forgiveness for having beaten him."

In the tale, *How I Was Taught to Ride Horseback,* Tolstoy recalls how together with his brothers he went to a riding-school.

"Then they brought a pony. It was a red horse, and his tail was cut off. He was called Ruddy. The master laughed and said to me:

"'Well, young gentleman, get on your horse!'

"I was both happy and afraid, and tried to act in such a manner as not to be noticed by anybody. For a long time I tried to get my foot into the stirrup, but could not do it because I was too small. Then the master raised me up in his hands and put me on the saddle. He said:

"'The young master is not heavy; about two pounds in weight, that is all.'

"At first he held me by my hand, but I saw that my brothers were not held, and so I begged him to let go of me. He said:

"'Are you not afraid?'

"I was very much afraid, but I said that I was not. I was so much afraid because Ruddy kept dropping his ears. I thought he was angry with me. The master said:

"'Look out, don't fall down!' and let go of me. At first Ruddy went at a slow pace, and I sat up straight. But the saddle was smooth, and I was afraid I should slip off. The master asked me:

"'Well, are you fast in the saddle?'

"I said:

"'Yes, I am.'

"'If so, go at a slow trot!' and the master clicked his tongue.

"Ruddy started at a slow trot, and began to jog me. But I kept silent, and tried not to slip to one side. The master praised me:

"'Oh, a fine young gentleman, indeed!'

"I was very glad to hear it.

"Just then the master's friend went up to him and began to talk with him, and the master stopped looking at me.

"Suddenly I felt that I had slipped a little to one side on my saddle. I wanted to straighten myself up, but was unable to do so. I wanted to call out to the master to stop the horse, but I thought it would be a disgrace if I did it, and so kept silence. The master was not looking at me, and Ruddy ran at a trot, and I slipped still more to one side. I looked at the master and thought that he would help me, but he was still talking with his friend, and, without looking at me, kept repeating:

"'Well done, young gentleman!'

"I was now altogether on one side, and was very much frightened. I thought I was lost, but I felt ashamed to cry. Ruddy shook me up once more, and I slipped off entirely and fell to the ground. Then Ruddy stopped, and the master looked at the horse and saw that I was not on him. He said:

"'I declare, my young gentleman has dropped off!' and walked over to me.

"When I told him that I was not hurt, he laughed and said:

"'A child's body is soft.'

"I felt like crying. I asked him to put me again on the horse, and I was lifted on. After that I did not fall down any more."

Thus developed this remarkable child, thoughtful, impressionable, shy, affectionate, very lonely owing to the immense power of inner life in him which found no response in his surroundings.

CHAPTER VI

YOUTH

Kazan University: The Tolstoy brothers taking a course—Tolstoy's entrance at the university—Failure in his first examination—A fresh examination—Kazan society according to Zagoskin and Tolstoy—The half-yearly examination during his first year of study—His failure in examinations at the end of the year—His change to the faculty of law—Interest taken in the discourses of Vogel and the lectures of Meyer—Entrance upon the second year of his studies in law—His punishment and discussion with Nazaryef—Removal to new lodgings—The petition for leave to quit the university—Testimonial given by the university—Departure from Kazan—Causes of leaving the university. *Reminiscences about his brother Dmitri:* His appearance—His peculiarities—How he differed from his brothers—Irritability—His contempt for public opinion.—His piety—The prison priest—His friend Poluboyarinof—Impulsiveness—Lubov Sergeyevna—Mitenka's immortality—Sketch of inner development of Tolstoy during this period—Critical age—Indications of inner life and ideal aspirations in the tale *Youth*—"She"—"The love of love"—The hope of conceited happiness—Repentance—The guiding voice—The poetical contemplation of nature—Influence of literature—Influence of environment—University work—The beginning of the diary—Rules—Visions of country life—His attitude to women—First philosophic experiments. *Religious state of his soul:* Falling away from faith—The part of religion in the life of a society man—Repentance. *Beginning of the management of his country estate:* A letter to his aunt—Failure. *Departure to St. Petersburg:* A letter to his brother concerning his plans—His loss at play, debts—Letter to his brother—His final examination—Return to Yasnaya Polyana—Period of carousals with intervals of asceticism—Entries in his diary, rules—His attitude to gambling. *Life in Moscow:* Letters to Tatiana—Literary experiments.

TOLSTOY and his brothers had spent five years at Kazan. In the summer the whole family, accompanied by Pelageya Ilyinishna, used to move to Yasnaya Polyana, and every autumn they returned to Kazan.

Tolstoy spent the greater part of his youth in Yushkof's home.

The brothers Tolstoy moved there in 1841. The elder brother, Nicolay, who left the Moscow University for that of Kazan, had in 1841-42 been already for the second year in the second division of the same faculty of philosophy in which he graduated in 1844. The two next brothers, Sergey and Dmitri, had chosen the same division of the faculty of philosophy which now is the same thing as the faculty of mathematics.

Both matriculated in 1843, and graduated in the spring of 1847.

Tolstoy had chosen the faculty of Oriental languages, probably having the diplomatic service in view. To enter this faculty he worked very hard during the years 1842-44, for the entrance examinations were not easy, as one had to know the Arabic and Turco-Tartarian languages, which at that time were taught in the Kazan gymnasium. The difficulties were successfully overcome by Tolstoy.

In the archives of the Kazan University are kept all the documents relating to Tolstoy's entrance and stay in that university as well as his departure from it.

All these papers are carefully collected and printed in the Reminiscences of Zagoskin.[1] We will present here only the more interesting.

The petition of Tolstoy at entering the university.

"A Petition.

"*To His Excellency the Rector of the Imperial Kazan University, the Councillor of State, and Cavalier Nicolay Ivanovitch Lobachevsky.*

"Desiring to enter as a student of the Oriental Section (Turco-Arab category) of the Kazan University, I beg your Excellency to allow me to appear before the Board of Examination. My papers: the certificate of birth from the Tula Theological Consistory under N 252, and the certificate of my noble origin from the Tula noblemen's Board of Deputies under N 267, I have the honor to present herewith.— Count Lyof Tolstoy."

[1] N. P. Zagoskin. "Count L. N. Tolstoy and his University Life." *Historical Review*, January, 1894.

In reply to this petition he was allowed to come up for the examinations, which, however, did not come off quite satisfactorily, as appears from the following statement of his marks.

Here are the marks [1] received by Tolstoy at his preliminary examinations for the university.

Religion	4
History, general and Russian	1 — "I knew nothing."—*Remark by Tolstoy.*
Statistics and geography	1 — "Still less."—*Remark by Tolstoy.*
Mathematics	4
Russian literature	4
Logic	4
Latin	2
French	5
German	5
Arabic	5
Turco-Tartar	5
English	4

"I remember I was questioned concerning France, Pushkin, the curator, who was present, examining me. He was a caller at our house, and evidently wanted to assist me. '*Please name the seaports in France.*' 'I could not name a single one.'"—*Tolstoy's note.*

In the minutes of the Board of Examination relating to Tolstoy's entrance at the university it is stated that Count Tolstoy "has been examined upon the section of Oriental literature, but was not admitted into the university." It was added: "His papers to be returned."

This happened in the spring of 1844. Tolstoy resolved to appeal for another examination to take place in the autumn in those subjects for which he had received unsatisfactory marks.

Accordingly, in the beginning of August, in the same year, 1844, another petition reached the Rector of the university, written in Tolstoy's own hand.

"Petition.

"*To His Excellency the Rector of the Imperial University of Kazan, Professor N. J. Lobachevsky, from Count L. N. Tolstoy.*

"In the month of May of the present year, together with the pupils of the first and second Kazan gymnasiums, I un-

---

[1] In Russia 5 represents highest marks.

The Kazan University at the time of Tolstoy's student years.

derwent an examination for the purpose of becoming a student of the Kazan University in the department of Arabo-Turkish languages. But at this examination I failed to show sufficient knowledge in history and statistics. I humbly beg your Excellency to allow me to be now re-examined in these subjects. Herewith I have the honor to present the following documents: (1) My birth certificate from the Consistory of Tula; (2) A copy of the resolution of the Tula Board of Deputy Noblemen, Aug. 3rd, 1844. To this petition the above-named petitioner, L. N. Tolstoy, has put his hand."

On this petition the following remark was made:

"Presented Aug. 4, 1844. To be allowed to come to the supplementary examinations. Aug. 4, 1844.

"Rector LOBACHEVSKY."

Precisely when or how Tolstoy passed these additional examinations no one knows. But this time all ended well, for at the bottom of his petition was written the following memorandum:

"Tolstoy to be admitted to the university as an extern student in the section of Turco-Arabic literature."

Thus Tolstoy entered the university. But he spent there only the hours taken up with lectures. For the rest of his time he moved in the social circle of his aunt, Mme. Yushkof, in whose house he lived. What were these surroundings, and how were they likely to influence a youth?

In Zagoskin's reminiscences of Tolstoy's life as a student it is stated that the surroundings in which he moved in the Kazan society were demoralizing, and that Tolstoy must have instinctively felt repelled, but he, having seen the manuscript, remarked that this was not the case.

"I did not feel any repulsion," he says, "but very much liked to enjoy myself in the Kazan society, at that time very good."[1]

Enumerating further on in his article the different unfavorable circumstances in Tolstoy's life, Zagoskin is amazed at the moral power shown by him in overcoming all these

[1] Notes made by Tolstoy when reading the MS.

temptations. On this Tolstoy himself made the following remark:

"On the contrary, I am very thankful to fate for having passed my first youth in an environment wherein a young man could be young without touching upon problems beyond his grasp, and for living, although an idle and luxurious life, yet not an evil one."[1]

The winter season of 1844-45, when Tolstoy began as a "young man" to appear in society, was still more gay than previous seasons. Balls, now at the house of the governor of the province, now given by the chief of the nobility, now at the Rodinovsky Institute for the young ladies of nobility (balls which were particularly favored by the matron of the Institution, Mme. E. D. Zagoskin), private dancing soirees, masquerades in the Hall of the Nobles, private theatricals, tableaux-vivants, concerts—all these followed one another in an endless chain. As a titled young man of good birth, with good local connections, the grandson of the ex-governor of Kazan, and an eligible match, Tolstoy was welcome everywhere. The old inhabitants of Kazan remember him as being present at all the balls, soirees, and aristocratic parties, a welcome guest everywhere, and always dancing, but, unlike his high-born fellow-students, far from being a ladies' man. He was always distinguished by a strange awkwardness and shyness; he evidently was ill at ease in the part which he had to play and to which he was involuntarily bound by the detestable surroundings of his life in Kazan. All this was sure to do harm to his studies, and the first half-yearly examination gave rather a poor result, as is seen by the examination sheet of the archive of the Kazan University, produced by Zagoskin:

TOLSTOY, LYOF

	Progress.	Application.
The Church bibl. history	3	2
The history of general literature	(did not appear)	
Arabic language	2	2
French language	5	3

This failure did not change his habits. He continued his gay worldly life, and at Shrovetide, together with his

[1] Notes made by Tolstoy when reading the MS.

brother Sergey, took part in two private theatrical performances with a charitable aim.

The end of all was that Tolstoy did not pass his examinations, and regularly this would have obliged him to follow the same course of study for another year. This is his own account of this unfortunate examination:

"The first year Ivanof, Professor of Russian History, prevented me from being passed to the second course, notwithstanding the fact that I had not missed a single lecture and knew Russian history quite well, because he had a quarrel with my family. Besides, the same professor gave me the lowest mark—1—for German, though I knew the language incomparably better than any student in our division."

But Tolstoy did not care to stay another year, and presented a petition for leave to take another faculty, that of Jurisprudence, which was given him.

After having entered the faculty of law, Tolstoy gave up studying altogether, and plunged with greater zest into the gayeties and distractions of fashionable Kazan society, which were at this time in full swing. The winter season of 1845–46 opened with a fête on the occasion of a two days' visit of Duke Maximilian of Leichtenberg, and an enthusiastic reception was given in his honor.

"Notwithstanding this," Tolstoy remarks, "at the end of this year I began for the first time to study seriously, and even found a certain pleasure in so doing. Among the university subjects the Encyclopædia of Law and Criminal Law were of interest to me; moreover, the German Professor Vogel arranged discussions at the lectures, and I remember that I was interested by one on capital punishment; but besides the university or faculty subjects, Meyer, Professor of Civil Law, set me a task, viz., a comparison between Montesquieu's *Esprit des Lois* and Catherine's *Code*, and this work greatly absorbed me."

The May examinations of 1846 went off well for Tolstoy. His marks were as follows: Logic and psychology, five each; encyclopædia of law, history of Roman law, and Latin, four each; universal and Russian history, theory of rhetoric and German, three each; deportment in each of the three terms, five each. The average mark received was three, and thus Tolstoy passed on to his second year's course.

The same year he was punished by the university authorities. He was put under lock and key. This episode has been described by a student, a fellow-sufferer with Tolstoy, Nazaryef, in his reminiscences. His version is far from true, though what he gives as their conversation corresponded to what really happened. With the help of Tolstoy's remarks we hope to reproduce the incident as it occurred.

Tolstoy was locked up, not in a lecture hall, according to Nazaryef, but in a punishment cell (prison room), with its arches and iron gates; he and his comrade were both there. Tolstoy carried with him a candle and candlestick secreted in his boot, and they spent a day or two very pleasantly.

The coachman, trotter, man-servant, and so on existed in Nazaryef's imagination only. But their conversation as reproduced by him is plausible, and we therefore take it from Nazaryef's article as follows:

"I remember," says Nazaryef, "noticing *Lermontof's Demon.* Tolstoy made an ironical remark about verses in general, and then turning to the *History of Karamzin* lying at my side, he attacked history as the dullest subject and an almost useless one.

"'History,' he declared curtly, 'is nothing but a collection of fables and useless details, sprinkled with a quantity of unnecessary dates and proper names. The death of Igor, the snake that stung Oleg, what are these but fairy tales? And who wants to know that the second marriage of John with the daughter of Temryuk took place on August 21, 1562, and the fourth with Anna Alexeyevna Koltorsky, in 1572? Yet they expect me to learn all this, and, if I don't know it, I get mark one! And how is history written? All is fitted in according to a certain plan invented by the historian. Ivan the Terrible (about whom Professor Ivanhof is at present lecturing), in 1560, from a virtuous and wise man, suddenly changes into a stupid, cruel tyrant. How and why, you need not ask. . . .' This was my companion's strain more or less throughout. I was greatly puzzled by such sharp criticism, the more so as history was my favorite subject.

"This time the (to me) irresistible force of Tolstoy's doubts fell upon the university and the teaching of universities generally. 'The temple of science was continually on his lips. While himself remaining quite serious, he made such caricatures of our professors, that in spite of my endeavor to appear uninterested I simply roared with laughter."

"'Yet,' concluded Tolstoy, 'we both have a right to expect that we shall leave this temple useful men, equipped with knowledge. But what shall we carry from the university? Think a little and answer your conscience. What shall we take from this temple when we return home to the country, what shall we know how to do, to whom shall we be necessary?' So he proceeded, addressing the question to me.

"In conversation of this kind we spent the whole night. Morning had hardly dawned when the door opened, and the sergeant entered. He saluted us and explained that we were free and could retire to our respective homes.

"Tolstoy pulled his cap over his eyes, wrapped himself in his cloak with beaver collar, slightly nodded to me, once more abused 'the temple,' and then disappeared accompanied by his servant and the sergeant. I, too, was in a hurry to be gone. After leaving my companion, I gave a sigh of relief to be in the open frosty air in the midst of the silent street, just beginning to stir.

"My head was heavy and full of doubts and questions brought before me for the first time in my life by this strange and utterly incomprehensible companion in my captivity." [1]

The beginning of the academic year 1846–47 brought certain changes in the life of the brothers Sergey, Dmitri, and Lyof Tolstoy. They left the house of their aunt, Pelageya Ilyinishna Yushkof, and settled in private rooms in the house belonging then to Petondi, and now occupied by Lozhkin's Public Charitable Home. There they had five rooms on the upper floor of the brick lodge, which still remains in the court-yard of this house and is used as one of the wards of the home.

In January, 1847, Tolstoy once more appeared on the day of the half-yearly examinations, but did not enter for all of them, and he evidently treated the whole affair as a hollow formality. Probably the plan of leaving the university was already forming in his mind. Indeed, soon after

[1] V. N. Nazaryef, "Life and Men of the Past." *Historic Review*, November, 1890.

the Easter holidays, he presented a petition to be allowed to leave the university. It was as follows:

" PETITION.

"*To His Excellency the Rector of the Imperial Kazan University, the State Councillor, and Cavalier Ivan Mihailovitch Simonof, from an extern undergraduate in the second year of the faculty of law, Count Lyof Nicolayevich Tolstoy.*

"Prevented from continuing my studies in the university on account of ill-health and family affairs, I humbly beg your Excellency to issue on order authorizing the omission of my name from the roll of university students and the return of all my documents."

To this petition is added in his own handwriting the signature of the student Count Lyof Tolstoy, April 12, 1847.

After this comes the resolution of the administration of the university authorizing "Tolstoy's name to be struck off the roll of students, and a memorandum to be made of the time for which he remained in the university."

In the archives of the university there still exists the duplicate of the testimonial given to Count L. N. Tolstoy. This testimonial is very curious in its way, for it has been so edited as to smooth down Tolstoy's university failures, and to say nothing of the causes which hindered his moving up into his second year's course while he was a student in the division of Oriental languages. It runs as follows:

"The bearer of this, Count Lyof, the son of Nicolay Tolstoy, having received a private education and passed an examination in all the subjects contained in the gymnasium curriculum, was admitted as a student at the Kazan University in the Division of Turco-Arab literature for the first year, but what progress he made during this year is not known, as he did not present himself for the examinations at the end of the year, and had therefore to remain in the same class. By the permission of the Director of the Educational Department of Kazan, dated September 13, 1845, he was transferred under N 3919 from the Division of Turco-Arab literature to the faculty of Law, where he made progress which, in logic and psychology, was excellent; in comparative jurisprudence, history of Roman law, and Latin —good; in universal and Russian history, theory of rhetoric and German—tolerably good; he was then moved to the second year's course, but what progress he made while there is not known, as the yearly examinations have not yet taken place. Tolstoy's conduct while at the university was excellent. Now in compliance with his petition, presented on the 12th instant of April, he is on the ground of ill-health and family affairs discharged from the university. Not having taken a degree, he cannot enjoy the privileges reserved to graduates, but in virtue of paragraph 590, Volume III of the Civil Code (edition 1842), on entering civil service, he will be entitled to the same privileges as to promotion as those who have passed through the gymnasium course of instruction, and will have the same rank as the civil service officials of the second class. In witness hereof this testimonial is given to Count Lyof Tolstoy by the administration of the University of Kazan, duly signed and sealed with the official seal, in accordance with the Imperial Charter granted to Kazan University, on ordinary paper."

"Tolstoy," writes Zagoskin in his reminiscences, " was in a great hurry to leave Kazan, and did not even wait for the final university examinations which his brothers had to pass. The day came when he was to set out for Moscow, which lay on his way to Yasnaya Polyana. In the rooms of the Counts Tolstoy in the wing of Petondi's house, a small party of students gathered to celebrate his departure on a journey which was not free from difficulty in those days of imperfect communications over great distances. One of those present who related to me the incident is still living in Kazan. In accordance with the custom, all drank the traveller's health, and wished him every good fortune. They accompanied him to the ferry across the river Kazanka, which had then overflowed its banks, and for the last time the friends exchanged the farewell kisses."

Few traces are now left of Tolstoy's stay at Kazan.

Prince D. D. Obolensky, who recently paid a visit to the university, told me that in the lecture hall he saw the signature " Count L. N. Tolstoy," undoubtedly cut by himself on the iron bar of his seat during his attendance at the lectures. This, it seems, is the only record of Tolstoy's presence in the Kazan University.

Tolstoy's German biographer, Loewenfeld, while at Yasnaya Polyana, asked him why, considering his inherent thirst for knowledge, he left the university prematurely.

The Count's answer was: "This was perhaps the chief reason why I left it. I was little interested in what our Professors read at Kazan. I first worked a year at Oriental languages, but with little success, though I threw myself enthusiastically into what I did. I read innumerable books, but all in one and the same direction. When any subject interested me, I did not deviate from it either to the right or the left, and I endeavored to become acquainted with everything which might throw a light on this particular subject. So it was with me at Kazan."[1]

"There were two reasons for my leaving the university," says Tolstoy; "first that my brother had finished his course and was leaving; and secondly, however strange it may be to say so, that the work on the *Nakaz* and the *Esprit des Lois* (I have still got it) opened out to me a new sphere of independent mental work, whereas the university with its demands far from aiding such work, only hindered it."[2]

Calling to mind his brother Dmitri, Tolstoy gives interesting details of student life in Kazan, so we insert these reminiscences here.

"Mitenka was a year older than I. Big, black, grave eyes. I hardly remember him as a boy. I only know by hearsay that as a child he was very capricious; it was said that such moods used to seize him that he was angry and cried at his nurse's not looking at him, and next got into a rage and screamed because she was looking at him. I know by what I have been told that my mother had much trouble with him. He was nearest to me by age, and I played with him oftenest, but I did not love him as much as I loved Seryozha, nor as I loved and respected Nicolenka. He and I lived together amicably. I do not recollect that we quarrelled. Probably we did, and may even have fought; but, as it happens with children, these fights did not leave the slightest trace, and I loved him with a simple instinctive love, and therefore did not remark it and do not remember it. I think, nay, I actually know, that according to my experi-

---

[1] R. Loewenfeld, *Gespraeche mit und ueber Tolstoy*. Leipzig.
[2] Interpolation by Tolstoy upon reading the MS.

ence, especially in childhood, love for human beings is a natural state of the soul, or rather a natural attitude toward all men, and, as it is such, one does not remark it. This changes only when one dislikes, when one does not love but is afraid of something, as I was afraid of beggars, and was afraid of one of the Volkonskys who used to pinch me, and, I think, of no one else—and when one loves some one exceptionally, as I loved my aunt Tatiana, my brother Seryozha, Nicolenka, Vassili, my nurse, Issayevna, and Pashenka. As a child I remember nothing special about Mitenka, except his childish merriment. His peculiarities became manifest, and are memorable to me from the time of our life at Kazan, whither we removed in the year '40 when he was thirteen. Till then, in Moscow, I remember that he did not fall in love as did Seryozha and I, did not particularly like dancing, nor military pageants, about which I will speak later, but studied well and strenuously. I remember that a student teacher named Poplonsky, who used to give us lessons, defined the attitude of us three brothers to our studies thus: Sergey both wishes and can, Dmitri wishes but cannot (this was not true), and Lyof neither wishes nor can. I think this was perfectly true.

" So that my real memories concerning Mitenka begin with Kazan. At Kazan I, who had always imitated Seryozha, began to grow depraved (I will relate this later). Not only at Kazan, but even earlier, I used to take pains about my appearance. I tried to be elegant, *comme il faut*. There was no trace of anything of the kind in Mitenka. I think he never suffered from the usual vices of youth; he was always serious, thoughtful, pure, resolute, though hot-tempered, and whatever he did he did to the best of his ability. It happened once that he swallowed a bit of chain; but, as far as I can remember, he was not particularly troubled about the consequences. But as for myself, I remember what terrors I underwent when I swallowed the stone of a French plum which my aunt had given me, and how solemnly, as if in the face of death, I announced the mishap to her. I also remember how, as children, we used to toboggan down a steep hill by the farm-yard, and how some traveller, in order to drive his troika [1] along the road, drove it up this hill. I think Seryozha, with a village boy, had

[1] The Russian three-horse conveyance.—*Trans.*

launched down the hill, and, being unable to stop his sleigh, got under the horses. The boy climbed out without injury. The troika ascended the hill. We were all absorbed in the event, thinking how they got out from under the horses, how the centre horse got frightened, etc., whereas Mitenka (a boy of nine) went up to the traveller and began to upbraid him. I remember how it astonished and displeased me when he said that, in order to keep people from driving where there was no road, it would be necessary to send them to the stables, which, in the language of the time, implied a flogging.

"At Kazan his peculiarities began; he studied well and regularly, and wrote verses with great facility. I remember how admirably he translated Schiller's *Der Jüngling aus Lorche,* but he did not devote himself to this occupation. I remember that once he merrily romped, and how the girls were delighted with it, and how I was envious, and reflected that this was because he was always so serious. And I desired to imitate him in this. Our aunt and godmother had the silly idea of making each of us the gift of a boy, who was eventually to become our devoted servant. To Mitenka was given Vanyusha (he is still living). Mitenka often treated him badly, and I think even beat him. I say I think, because I do not remember it, but only remember his repentance for something done to Vanyusha, and his humble prayers for forgiveness.

"Thus he grew up, associating little with others, always, except in moments of anger, quiet and serious, with thoughtful, grave, large hazel eyes. He was tall, rather thin, and not very strong, with long big hands and round shoulders. His peculiarities began at the time of entering the university. He was a year younger than Sergey, but they entered the university together, in the mathematical faculty, solely because the elder brother was a mathematician. I do not know how or by what he was so early attracted toward a religious life, but it began with the very first year of his university life. His religious aspirations naturally directed him to Church life, and he devoted himself to it as thoroughly as he did to everything. He began to fast, he attended all the Church services, and became especially strict in his conduct.

"In Mitenka there must have existed that valuable characteristic which I believe my mother to have had, and which I knew in Nicolenka, and of which I was altogether devoid —the characteristic of complete indifference to other people's opinion about oneself. Until quite lately I have always been unable to divest myself of concern about people's opinion, but Mitenka was quite free from this. I never remember on his face that restrained smile which involuntarily appears when one is praised. I always remember his serious, quiet, sad, sometimes severe, large, almond-shaped hazel eyes. Only from the Kazan days did we begin to pay particular attention to him, and that merely because, while Seryozha and I attached great importance to what was *comme il faut* —to the external—he was careless and untidy, and for this we condemned him. He did not dance, and did not wish to learn dancing. As a student he did not go into society; he wore a student's suit with a tight tie, and from his very youth he had the habit of jerking his head as if freeing himself from this tie. His peculiarity first revealed itself in our first preparation for communion. He made his devotions, not in the fashionable university church, but in the church of the prison. We lived in a house belonging to a Mr. Gortalof opposite the jail. The prison chaplain of that time was a specially pious and devout man, who, contrary to the ordinary usage of priests, went through the whole of the appointed readings in the Gospels for Passion Week, as was officially required, which made the services last a very long time. Mitenka used to stand them out, and made the priest's acquaintance. The jail church was so arranged that the public was separated from the place where the convicts stood only by a glass partition with a door. Once one of the convicts wished to pass something to one of the vergers —either a candle, or money to buy one; no one in the church cared to undertake the commission, but Mitenka, with a serious expression on his face, immediately took it and passed it on. It turned out that it was forbidden, and he was reprimanded, but, as he thought it was right, he did it again.

" We others, especially Seryozha, kept up acquaintance with our aristocratic comrades and other young men. Mitenka, on the contrary, out of all our comrades, selected a piteous-looking, poor, shabbily dressed student, Poluboyarinof (whom a humorous comrade of ours used to call

Polubezobedof,[1] and we contemptible lads thought this amusing, and laughed at Mitenka). He consorted only with Poluboyarinof, and with him prepared for his examinations.

"We were living in the upper floor, which was divided in two by an inner balcony over the ball-room. In the nearest half on this side of the balcony lived Mitenka, in the room on the other Seryozha and myself. We two were fond of small knick-knacks, we decorated our rooms as grown-up people do, and trifling articles used to be given us for this purpose. Mitenka kept no ornaments at all. The only thing he had taken from our father's things was a collection of minerals: he classified them, ticketed them, and placed them in a case under glass. As we brothers, and even aunt, looked down upon Mitenka with a certain contempt for his low tastes and associations, the same attitude was assumed by our light-minded comrades. One of the latter, a very unintelligent man, an engineer, one E., a friend of ours—not so much by our choice as because he stuck to us—once, on passing through Mitenka's room, took notice of these minerals, and questioned Mitenka about them. E. was not sympathetic, not natural, and Mitenka answered unwillingly. E. moved the box and jerked the minerals. Mitenka said, 'Leave them alone.' E. paid no attention, but made some joke and called him Noah. Mitenka flew in a rage, and with his big hands hit E. in the face. E. ran away and Mitenka after him. As they rushed into our quarters we locked the doors, but Mitenka declared that he would thrash him when he went back. Seryozha and, I think, Schuvalof went to persuade Mitenka to let E. pass, but he took a broom and declared that he would certainly beat him. I don't know what might have happened had E. passed through his room, but E. himself requested us to get him out some other way, and we led him out, almost crawling, by some way through the dusty garret.

"Such was Mitenka in his moments of anger. But this is what he was when nothing put him out. To our family had attached herself (she was taken in from pity) a most strange and piteous being, Lyubof Sergeyevna, a girl; I don't know what surname was given her. She was the fruit of an incestuous connection. How she came into our house

---

[1] An untranslatable play of words, the first name literally meaning "half a noble," and the second "half hungry."—*Trans.*

Tolstoy at the time of his leaving the University, 1848.

I do not know. I have been told that she was pitied and caressed, and that they wished to find her a situation, or even to have her married to Feodor Ivanovich, but nothing of this succeeded. Then she was taken by my aunt to Kazan, and lived with her, so that I came to know her at Kazan. She was a pitiful, meek, oppressed being. She had a little room of her own, and a girl attended her. When I made her acquaintance she was not only pitiful but repulsive to look at. I don't know what her disease was, but her face was all swollen, as faces are when they have been stung by bees. Her eyes appeared in two narrow slits, between swollen shining cushions without brows; similarly swollen and gleaming were her cheeks, nose, lips, and mouth, and she spoke with difficulty, probably having the same swelling within her mouth. In summer flies settled on her face without her feeling it, and it was especially unpleasant to see this. Her hair was still black but scanty, barely concealing the scalp. Vassili Yushkof, my aunt's husband, a sarcastic man, did not conceal his repugnance for her. She always had a bad smell about her, and in her room, where neither window nor ventilator was ever open, the atmosphere was oppressive. Well, it was this Lyubof Sergeyevna who became Mitenka's friend. He used to go to her room, listen to her, talk to her, read to her. And strange to say, we were morally so dense that we only laughed at this, whereas Mitenka was morally so high, so independent of concern about people's opinion, that he never either by word or by hint showed that he regarded what he was doing as something good. He simply did it.

"This was not a passing impulse, but continued the whole time we lived at Kazan.

"How clear it is to me that Mitenka's death did not destroy him, that he existed before I came to know him, before he was born, and that, having died, he still is!"

Let us take a glance at Tolstoy's inner life at this period, so far as we have the materials.

The critical age of man—youth—leads him into the abyss of passion. To an ordinary man it is a period in life when he is carried away by various sensations and passions, when he searches for an ideal; a period of dreams, expectations, and, generally, of unfulfilled hopes. One can imagine the mental excitement through which such a many-sided and powerful nature had to pass, as Tolstoy's was and remains. His soul was tossed to and fro on divers blasts. The wings of vision lifted him to unattainable heights, from which he plunged downward, carried away by the lower impulses of a powerful animal nature.

References are to be found to the tumultuous inner life of this youthful period in two works of Tolstoy's—*Youth* and *My Confession*. In the first we meet with autobiographical traits in Nicolenka Irtenef's reflections. The thoughts taken from *Youth* are chiefly of an ideal character, and expressed in a beautiful poetic form. Here we bring forward only the more important of them.

"I have said that my friendship with Dmitri had opened up to me a new view of life, its aims and relations. The essence of this view consisted in the conviction that it was man's destiny to strive after moral perfection, and that this perfection was easy, possible, and eternal. . . .

"But a time came when these ideas burst upon my reason with such a fresh power of moral discovery that I became frightened at the thought of how much time I had spent in vain, and I wished immediately, that very second, to apply all those ideas to life, with the firm intention of never being false to them.

"This time I regard as the beginning of my youth.

"I was then finishing my sixteenth year. Teachers still came to the house, St. Jérôme looked after my studies, and I was preparing myself with an effort, and against my will, for the university.

. . . . .

"At that date, which I regard as the extreme limit of boyhood and beginning of youth, the basis of my dreams consisted of four sentiments. The first was the love for *her*, an imaginary woman, of whom I dreamed ever in the same way, and whom I expected to meet somewhere at any minute. . . . my second sentiment was the love of love. I wanted everybody to know and love me. I wanted to tell my name, and have every one struck by the information, and surround me and thank me for something. The third sentiment was a hope for some unusual vain happiness— such a strong and firm hope that it passed into insanity. . . . My fourth and chief sentiment was my self-disgust and repentance, but a repentance which was so closely welded with the hope of happiness, that there was nothing sad in it. . . . I even found pleasure in my disgust with the past, and tried to see it blacker than it was. The blacker the circle of my memories of the past, the brighter and clearer stood out from it the bright and clear point of the present, and streamed the rainbow colors of the future. This voice of repentance and passionate desire for perfection was the main new sensation of my soul at that epoch of my development, and it was this which laid a new foundation for my views of myself, of people, and of the whole world.

"Beneficent, consoling voice, which since then has so often been heard suddenly and boldly against all lies, in those sad moments when the soul in silence submitted to the power of deceit and debauchery in life, which has angrily accused the past, has indicated the bright point of the present, causing one to love it, and has promised happiness and well-being in the future—beneficent, consoling voice! will you ever cease to be heard?"

Fortunately for Tolstoy himself and for all of us, we know that that voice was never for a moment silent, and that this beneficent voice still calls to him and to us, guiding us toward a bright and infinite ideal.

Sometimes these dreams vividly expressed the principles of that idealistic naturalism which became the base of the greater part of Tolstoy's works.

"And the moon rose higher and higher, and stood brighter and brighter in the heavens, the rich sheen of the pond, evenly growing, like sound, became more and more distinct, the shadows became blacker and blacker, and the light ever more transparent; and as I looked at it all and listened, something told me that *she*, with her bared arms and passionate embraces, was very far from bearing all the happiness in the world, that the love for her was very far from being all its bliss; and the more I looked at the full moon up on high, the higher did true beauty and goodness appear to me, and the purer and nearer to Him, the source of all that is beautiful and good, and tears of an unsatisfied but stirring joy stood in my eyes.

"And I was all alone, and it seemed to me that mysterious, majestic Nature, the attractive bright disc of the moon, which had for some reason stopped in one high undefined spot in the pale blue sky, and yet stood everywhere and, as it were, filled all the immeasurable space—and myself, insignificant worm, defiled already by all petty, wretched human passions, but with all the immeasurable mighty power of love—it seemed to me in those minutes that Nature and the moon and I were one and the same."[1]

It is interesting to note the literary works which influenced Tolstoy and helped the development of his views during his youth, that is to say, from about fourteen to twenty-one years.

Titles of the Books.	The Degree of their Influence.
The New Testament (Gospel of St. Matthew); The Sermon on the Mount	Powerful.
Sterne's *Sentimental Journey*	Very great.
Rousseau, *Confession*	Powerful.
" *Émile*	Powerful.
" *Nouvelle Héloïse*	Very great.
Pushkin, *Eugene Onegin*	Very great.
Schiller, *Die Räuber*	Very great.
Gogol, *The Overcoat; Iv. Iv. and Iv. Nik; Nevsky Prospect; Vy; Dead Souls*	Great.
Turgenef, *The Memoirs of a Sportsman*	Very great.
Druzhinin, *Polinka Sax*	Very great.
Grigorovitch, *Anton Goremika*	Very great.
Dickens, *David Copperfield*	Powerful.
Lermontof, *The Hero of our Times; Taman*	Very great.
Prescott, *The Conquest of Mexico*	Great.

At the same time Tolstoy had to put up with the worry of the conventionalities to which his life, as one of the gentry, was subjected; to one of which, the so-called *comme il faut*, he dedicates a whole chapter in *Youth*. We will quote from it only the more essential passages.

"I feel myself constrained to devote a whole chapter to a conception that was one of the most disastrous and false ideas with which I was inoculated by education and society.

"My chief and favorite classification at the time of which I am writing was into people *comme il faut* and *comme il ne faut pas*. The second division was subdivided into people more particularly not *comme il faut,* and into the common people. I respected people *comme il faut,* and considered them worthy of being on an equality with me;

[1] *Youth.*

I pretended a contempt for the second, but in reality hated them, cherishing against them a feeling of being personally offended; the third for me did not exist—I disregarded them entirely. My *comme il faut* consisted, first and foremost, in the use of excellent French, more especially in pronunciation. A man who pronounced French badly immediately provoked a feeling of hatred in me. 'Why do you attempt to speak as we do, if you do not know how?' I asked him mentally, with a venomous smile. The second condition for *comme il faut* consisted in long, manicured, and clean nails. The third was the ability to courtesy, dance, and converse. The fourth—and this was very important—was an indifference to everything, and a constant expression of a certain elegant, supercilious ennui. . . .

"It is terrible to think how much invaluable time of my seventeenth year I wasted on the acquisition of this temper of mind. . . .

"But it was not the loss of the golden time, which was employed on the assiduous task of preserving all the difficult conditions of the *comme il faut*, to the exclusion of every serious application, nor the hatred and contempt for nine-tenths of the human race, nor the absence of any interest in all the beauty that existed outside that circle of *comme il faut*, that was the greatest evil which this conception caused me. The greatest evil consisted in the conviction that *comme il faut* was an independent position in society, that a man need not have to try to be an official, or a carriage-maker, or a soldier, or a learned man, if he was *comme il faut*; that, having reached that position, he had already fulfilled his purpose, and even stood higher than most people.

"At a certain period of his youth, every man, after many blunders and transports, generally faces the necessity of taking an active part in social life, chooses some department of labor, and devotes himself to it; but this seldom happens with the man who is *comme il faut*. I know many, very many, old, proud, self-confident people, sharp in their judgments, who to the question which may be asked them in the next world, 'Who are you? And what have you been doing there?' would not be able to answer otherwise than '*Je fus un homme très comme il faut.*'

"This fate awaited me."

As we know from the conversation of Tolstoy with his German biographer, Loewenfeld, along with his university studies (on the whole uninteresting to him) he showed capacity for independent intellectual research. This was called forth by the university inviting an essay comparing the *Esprit des Lois* of Montesquieu and the *Instruction* of the Empress Catherine II.

The diaries of Tolstoy relating to this period are full of thoughts, notes, and commentaries concerning this essay. A swarm of ideas crowded his brain, as if the hitherto sleeping intellect suddenly awoke and began to work actively in all directions.

In March, 1847, Tolstoy was laid up in the Kazan hospital. During his illness, being alone in the hospital, he found time to think of the significance of Reason. Society is but part of the world. Reason must be in harmony with the world, with the whole, so by studying its laws one may become independent of the past, of the world. We see from this remark that this youth of eighteen years had already in him the germ of the future idea of anarchy.

Having observed in himself signs of a passion for knowledge, Tolstoy checks himself at once, and fearing to go too far in theory, he tries to solve the questions of science applied to practice, but chiefly those of the moral ideal and moral conduct.

Among others, he made the following entry in his diary (March, 1847):

"I have greatly changed, but still have not attained that degree of perfection (in my occupations) which I would like to attain. I do not fulfil that which I set myself to do, and what I do fulfil I do not fulfil well, I do not exercise my memory. For this purpose I here put down some rules, which, as it seems to me, would greatly help if I followed them.

"(1) To fulfil despite everything that which I set myself.

"(2) To fulfil well what I do fulfil.

"(3) Never to refer to a book for what I have forgotten, but to endeavor to recall it to mind myself.

"(4) Continually to compel my mind to work with the utmost power it is capable of.

"(5) To read and think always aloud.

"(6) Not to be ashamed of telling those who interrupt me that they hinder me; at first let them only feel it, hit if they do not understand (that they are hindering me), then apologize and tell them so."

His university essay leads him to the conclusion that there are two principles in Catherine's *Instruction*: that of the revolutionary ideas of modern Europe and that of Catherine's despotism and vanity, the latter principle being predominant. The republican ideas are borrowed by her from Montesquieu. In the end Tolstoy comes to the conclusion that the *Instruction* brought with it more glory to Catherine than advantage to Russia.

Having resolved to leave the university and settle in the country, Tolstoy determined that he would study Latin, the English language, and Roman law, the subjects which, in his own opinion, he knew least about.

But as the time of departure drew nearer, the plans and dreams of his new life widened, and finally he wrote this in his diary of April 17, 1847:

"A change must take place in my way of life, but it is necessary that this change should be the result of the soul, and not of external circumstances."

Further:

"The object of life is the conscious aspiration toward the many-sided development of all that exists.

"The object of life in the country during two years:

"(1) To study the whole course of law necessary for the final university examination. (2) To study practical medicine and a part of the theory. (3) To study these languages: French, Russian, German, English, Italian, and Latin. (4) To study agriculture, both theoretically and practically. (5) To study history, geography, and statistics. (6) To study mathematics, gymnasium course. (7) To write my university essay. (8) To attain the highest possible perfection in music and painting. (9) To write down the rules of conduct. (10) To acquire some knowledge of the natural sciences. And (11) to compose essays on all the subjects I shall study."

All the subsequent life of Tolstoy in the country is full of such dreams, good beginnings, and serious and sincere struggles with himself after perfection.

With incomparable sincerity he notes down any digression, every lapse from the rule he intended to follow, and again gathers strength for a new battle.

His relation with women began to disturb him even then, and this is the interesting advice he gave himself:

"Look upon the society of women as upon a necessary unpleasantness of social life, and as much as possible keep away from them.

"Indeed, from whom do we get sensuality, effeminacy, frivolity in everything, and many other vices, if not from women? Who is to blame that we lose out innate qualities of boldness, resolution, reasonableness, justice, and others, if not women? Women are more receptive than men, therefore in virtuous ages women were better than we, but in the present depraved and vicious age they are worse than we."

In all this we already see hints of his later views of life.

His first philosophical essays also belong to this period, and it was at this time, while reading Rousseau, that he wrote commentaries to his *Discourses*. We also meet his original philosophic article, written in 1846–47, when he was eighteen years old. The title of the article is, "On the Aim of Philosophy." Philosophy is thus defined:

"Man aspires—*i. e.*, man is active. To what is his activity directed, how is his activity to be set free? In this consists philosophy in its true sense. In other words, *philosophy is the science of life*."

Besides these, he wrote essays on various subjects, such as: "On Reasoning Concerning Future Life," "Definition of Time, Space, and Number," "Methods," "Division of Philosophy," etc.

The following incident, noted down by the Countess Tolstoy, occurred about this time:

"During his student days Tolstoy was struck by the idea of symmetry, and wrote a philosophical article on the subject in an argumentative form. The article was lying on the table in his room when Shuvalof, a friend of the brothers Tolstoy, came in with bottles in all his pockets, and was going to drink, when he caught sight of the article and read it. He was interested in it, and asked Tolstoy what he had copied it from. Tolstoy replied, with some hesitation, that he had written it himself. Shuvalof laughed, and said that was not true, it could not be, the article was too deep and clever for such a youth. Nothing would convince him of it, and he went away with his conviction unchanged."[1]

This little incident shows how much Tolstoy's intellectual standard already differed from that of those about him, and how superior to them he was.

His *Confession* reveals to us his inner world of that period from another point of view—the religious one.

"I remember, also, that when my elder brother, Dmitri, then at the university, gave himself up to a passionate faith, with the impulsiveness natural to his character, began to attend the Church services regularly, to fast, and to lead a pure and moral life, we all of us, as well as some older than ourselves, never ceased to hold him up to ridicule, and for some incomprehensible reason gave him the nickname of Noah. I remember that Mussin-Pushkin, then curator of the University of Kazan, having invited us to a ball, tried to persuade my brother, who had refused the invitation, by the jeering argument that even David danced before the ark.

"I sympathized then with these jokes of my elders, and drew from them this conclusion—that I was bound to learn my catechism, and go to church, but that it was not necessary to think of my religious duties more seriously. I also remember that I read Voltaire when I was very young, and that his tone of mockery amused without disgusting me. The gradual estrangement from all belief went on in me, as it does, and always has done, in those of the same social position and culture as myself. This falling off, as it seems to me, for the most part takes place as follows: People live as others do, and their lives are guided, not by the principles of the faith which is taught them, but by their very opposite; belief has no influence on life, nor on the relations between men—it is relegated to some other sphere, where life is not; if the two ever come into contact at all, belief is only one of the outward phenomena, and not one of the constituent parts of life.

"By a man's life, by his acts, it was then, as it is now, impossible to know whether he was a believer or not. If there be a difference between one who openly professes the doctrines of the Orthodox Church and one who denies

[1] *The Memoirs of Countess S. A. Tolstoy.*

them, the difference is not to the advantage of the former. An open profession of the orthodox doctrines is mostly found among persons of dull intellects, of stern character, who are much impressed with their own importance. Intelligence, honesty, frankness, a good heart, and moral conduct are oftener met with among those who are disbelievers. A schoolboy of the people is taught his catechism and sent to church; from the grown man is required a certificate of his having taken the Holy Communion. But a man belonging to our class neither goes to school nor is bound by the regulations affecting those in the public service, and may now live through long years—still more was this the case formerly—without being once reminded of the fact that he lives among Christians, and calls himself a member of the Orthodox Church.

"Thus it happens that now, as formerly, the influence of early religious teaching, accepted merely on trust and upheld by authority, gradually fades away under the knowledge and practical experience of later life, which is opposed to all its principles, and a man often believes for years that his early faith is still intact, while all the time not a particle of it remains in him.

"The belief instilled in childhood gradually disappeared in me, as in so many others, but with this difference, that I was conscious of my own disbelief. At fifteen years of age I had begun to read philosophical works. From the age of sixteen I ceased to pray, and ceased also to attend the services of the Church with conviction, or to fast. I no longer accepted the faith of my childhood, but I had a vague belief in *something,* though I did not think I could exactly explain what. I believed in a God, or rather I did not deny the existence of God, but anything relating to the nature of the Deity I could not have described; I denied neither Christ nor His teaching, but wherein that teaching consisted I could not have said.

"Now, when I think over that time, I see clearly that all the faith I had, the only belief which, apart from mere animal instinct, swayed my life, was a belief in a possibility of perfection, though what it was in itself, or what would be its results, I was unable to say. I endeavored to reach perfection in intellectual attainments; my studies were extended in every direction of which my life afforded me a chance; I strove to strengthen my will, forming for myself rules which I forced myself to follow; I did my best to develop my physical powers by every exercise calculated to give strength and agility, and, by way of accustoming myself to patient endurance, subjected myself to many voluntary hardships and trials of privations. All this I looked upon as necessary to obtain the perfection at which I aimed. At first, of course, moral perfection seemed to me the main end, but I soon found myself contemplating instead of it an ideal of conventional perfectibility; in other words, I wished to be better, not in my own eyes, nor in those of God, but in the sight of other men. This feeling again soon led to another—the desire to have more power than others, to secure for myself a greater share of fame, of social distinction, and of wealth."

Further on begins the terrible confession by which Tolstoy, in denouncing his own sins, denounces ours also at the same time, for most of us have been through the same depths of vice, though we may not have plunged into so gigantic an abyss, or the consciousness of our evil lives may not have been so real.

"At some future time I may relate the story of my life, and dwell in detail on the pathetic and instructive incidents of my youth. Many others must have passed through the same experiences. I honestly desired to make myself a good and virtuous man; but I was young, I had passions, and I stood alone, altogether alone, in my search after virtue. Every time I tried to express the longings of my heart for a truly virtuous life, I was met with contempt and derisive laughter; but directly I gave way to the lowest of my passions, I was praised and encouraged. I found ambition, love of power, love of gain, lechery, pride, anger, vengeance, held in high esteem. I gave way to these passions, and becoming like my elders, felt that the place which I filled in the world satisfied those around me. My kind-hearted aunt, a really good woman, used to say to me, that there was one thing above all others which she wished for me—an intrigue with a married woman: '*Rien ne forme un jeune homme, comme une liaison avec une femme comme il faut.*' Another of her wishes for my happiness was, that I should become an adjutant, and, if possible, to the Emperor. The greatest happiness of all for me she thought would be that I should find a wealthy bride who would bring me as her dowry an enormous number of serfs.

"I cannot now recall those years without a painful feeling of horror and loathing.

"I put men to death in war, I fought duels to slay others. I lost at cards, wasted the substance wrung from the sweat of peasants, punished the latter cruelly, rioted with loose women, and deceived men. Lying, robbery, adultery of all kinds, drunkenness, violence, and murder, all were committed by me, not one crime omitted, and yet I was none the less considered by my equals to be a comparatively moral man. Such was my life for ten years.

"During that time I began to write, out of vanity, love of gain, and pride. I followed as a writer the same path which I had chosen as a man. In order to obtain the fame and the money for which I wrote, I was obliged to hide what was good and bow down before what was evil. How often while writing have I cudgelled my brains to conceal under the mask of indifference or pleasantry those yearnings for something better which formed the real problem of my life! I succeeded in my object, and was praised. At twenty-six years of age, on the close of the war, I came to St. Petersburg and made the acquaintance of the authors of the day.

"I met with a hearty reception and much flattery."

This tumultuous period of ten years' duration began in the country.

To this time belong more or less Tolstoy's attempts to arrange the affairs of his estates on new principles, and especially his endeavors to establish reasonable and friendly relations with the peasants. These attempts fell flat, and their failure is vividly pictured in his tale, *A Russian Proprietor*. This tale gives us so much autobiographical material, in the psychological sense, that we consider it as a chapter of his biography, though the incidents related do not agree with the facts of his life.

From it we quote the letter of "Prince Nekhludof" to his aunt:

"DEAR AUNTY: I have made a resolution on which the fate of my whole life must depend. I will leave the university in order to devote myself to country life, because I feel that I was born for it. For God's sake, dear aunty, do not laugh at me! You will say that I am young; and, indeed, I may still be a child, but this does not prevent me from feeling what my calling is, and from wishing to do good, and loving it.

"As I have written you before, I found affairs in indescribable disorder. In trying to straighten them out, and to understand them, I discovered that the main evil lay in the truly pitiable, poverty-stricken condition of the peasants, and that the evil was such that it could be mended by labor and patience alone. If you could only see two of my peasants, Davýd and Iván, and the lives which they lead with their families, I am sure that the mere sight of these unfortunates would convince you more than all I might say to explain my intention to you.

"Is it not my sacred and direct duty to care for the welfare of these seven hundred men, for whom I shall be held responsible before God? Is it not a sin to abandon them to the caprice of rude elders and managers for their plans of enjoyment and ambition? And why should I look in another sphere for opportunities of being useful and doing good when such a noble, brilliant, and immediate duty is open to me?

"I feel myself capable of being a good landed proprietor; and in order to be one, as I understand this word, one needs neither a university diploma nor rank, which you are so anxious I should obtain. Dear aunty, make no ambitious plans for me! Accustom yourself to the thought that I have chosen an entirely different path, which is nevertheless good, and which, I feel, will bring me happiness. I have thought much, very much, about my future duty, have written out rules for my actions, and, if God will grant me life and strength, shall succeed in my undertaking."

If Tolstoy did not really write this letter in his own person, such thoughts and desires agitated his young soul, and gave direction to his life.

Tolstoy's attempts—as we know them from the tale—ended in failure. It could not be otherwise. Tolstoy's sincerity of character could not bear a position in which he posed as benefactor to his serfs, *i. e.*, to men wounded in the most precious thing they possessed—their moral dignity.

Tolstoy revolted against this contradiction: to become a "cool and stern man," as his aunt advised him in her answer to his letter, he could not, and at the first possible opportunity he changed his way of life.

In the autumn of the year 1847, after having spent the summer in Yasnaya Polyana, Tolstoy removed to St. Petersburg, and at the beginning of 1848 he entered upon his examinations for a university degree.

"In 1848 I went to pass my examination as a candidate at the St. Petersburg University, knowing literally nothing, and having prepared myself for one week only. I did not sleep for nights, and received candidates' marks in civil and criminal law."

To Loewenfeld, Tolstoy thus speaks about this time:

"It was very pleasant to live in the country with my aunt Yergolsky, but a vain thirst for knowledge again called me away. It was in 1848, and still I did not know what to undertake. In St. Petersburg two roads were open to me. I might enter the army, and take part in the Hungarian campaign, or I might finish my university studies in order afterward to get a post as a Government official. But my thirst for knowledge conquered my ambition, and I again resumed my studies. I even passed two successful examinations in criminal law, but after that all my good intentions fell to the ground. Spring came on, and the delights of country life again attracted me to the estate."[1]

This period of his Petersburg life we can follow through his letters to his brother Sergey. From these we quote one passage bearing a general interest. On February 13, 1848, he wrote to his brother:

"I am writing you this letter from St. Petersburg, where I intend remaining *forever*. All are urging me to remain and serve, except Ferzen and Lyof. So I have decided to remain here for my examination and then serve; and if I do not pass (everything may happen), then I shall begin to serve, were it even in the fourteenth rank. I know many Government officials of this second category who serve no worse than we of the first. In a word, I will tell you that Petersburg life has a great and good influence

[1] R. Loewenfeld, *Gespraeche mit und ueber Tolstoy*, s. 87.

on me; it accustoms me to activity, and involuntarily takes the place of a curriculum. Somehow one cannot be idle; all are occupied, all are busy; indeed, one cannot find a man with whom one could lead a disorderly life, and one can't do it by oneself.

"I know that you will not believe that I have altered; that you will say: 'This is already the twentieth time, and still no good comes of you; you are the most frivolous fellow—' No, I have altered in quite a different way from what I did. Then I used to say to myself, 'Well, now, I shall change.' But now I see that I have changed, and I say, 'I have changed.'

"Above all, I am now fully convinced that one cannot live by abstract speculation and philosophy, but that it is necessary to live positively, *i. e.*, to be a practical man. This is a great step forward and a great change. This has never once happened with me before. And if one wishes to live and is young, then in Russia there is no other place but St. Petersburg. Whatever tendency any one may have, there all may be satisfied, and all may be developed, and that without any trouble. As to the means of life—for a bachelor life here, it is not at all expensive, and, on the contrary, it is cheaper and better than at Moscow, excepting lodging.

"Tell all our folk that *I love and greet all,* and that in summer I shall perhaps be in the country, but perhaps not. In summer I want to take leave of absence, and visit the neighborhood of St. Petersburg; also I want to go to Helsingfors and Revel. For God's sake, write to me for once in your life. I should like to know how you and all ours will receive this news. As for me, I am afraid of writing to them; I have been so long without writing that they are probably angry, and especially am I ashamed before Tatiana Alexandrovna; ask her to forgive me."

Alas, these good intentions were not to be realized all at once. Strange as it may seem now, yet at that time Tolstoy's brother had a certain right to call him a "frivolous fellow," as Tolstoy himself confessed to him.

Thus in his letter of May 1, 1848, he wrote:

"Seryozha! I think you are already saying I am a most frivolous fellow. And saying the truth. God knows what I have been up to! I went to St. Petersburg without any reason; there I have done nothing necessary, only spent a heap of money and run up debts. Stupid! Insufferably stupid! You can't believe how it torments me. Above all, the *debts,* which I *must* pay and as *quickly as possible,* because if I do not soon pay them, I shall, besides the money, lose my reputation too. Before I get my next year's income I absolutely require 3,500 roubles: 1,200 for the Guardians' Council, 1,600 to pay my debts, 700 for my current expenses. I know you will exclaim—but what is to be done? Such stupidity is accomplished once in a lifetime. I had to do penance for my freedom (there was no one to thrash me, and this was my chief misfortune) and for philosophy, and so I have paid premium. Be so kind as to arrange to get me out of the false and odious position in which I now am, without a penny at my disposal and in debt all round.

"You probably know that our troops are all starting for the campaign, and that a part of the Second Corps have crossed the frontier and, so they say, are already in Vienna.

"I had begun to attend my examinations as 'candidate' for my degree, and have, in fact, successfully passed two, but I have now altered my mind and want to enter the Horse Guards as a volunteer. I am ashamed of writing this to you because I know you love me, and will be grieved over all my silly actions and reckless behavior. Even while writing this letter I have several times got up and blushed, as you also will do on reading it—but what is to be done? The past cannot be altered, and the future is in my hands.

"Please God I will also some day amend myself and become a respectable man; more than all I rely upon the service as volunteer, it will teach me practical life, and—*nolens volens*—I shall have to serve up to an officer's rank. With luck, *i. e.,* if the Guards should be in action, I may be promoted even before the end of the two years' term. The Guards start for the campaign at the end of May. Now I can do nothing, first, because I have no money—I do not need much (again in my own opinion)—and, secondly, my two certificates of birth are at Yasnaya; get them sent as soon as possible. Please do not be angry with me—as it is I feel my nothingness too much—but quickly do what I ask. Good-by. Do not show this letter to Aunty, I do not wish to give her pain."

Soon after, these plans too were dismissed. In one of his subsequent letters to his brother, Tolstoy says:

"In my last letter I wrote you a lot of nonsense, of which the chief was that I intended to enter the Horse Guards; I shall stick to this plan only if I do not succeed in passing the examinations and the war should be a serious one."

He probably did not consider the war sufficiently "serious," for he did not enter military service.

In the spring he came back to Yasnaya Polyana accompanied by a clever German musician, who was, however, fond of drink. He met him first at the house of his friends, the Perfiliefs, and since then had given himself up to music. The German's name was Rudolph.

Up to the time of his departure to the Caucasus in 1851, Tolstoy lived partly in Moscow, and partly in Yasnaya Polyana. During this time he developed a phase of asceticism, but varied with outbreaks of feasting, sports, card-playing, visiting gipsies, etc.

During these three years of his life Tolstoy tasted of everything which a passionate and energetic young man could seize.

At the same time he neglected his diary, for want of time. Only in the middle of 1850 did he recover himself and begin his diary, with confession and self-accusation and expressions of a desire to write down frankly his reminiscences of these "disgracefully spent three years of his life."

In his wish to begin a regular life he made out a programme of each day from morning to night: estate affairs, bathing, diary, music, meals, rest, reading.

But of course the programme and the rules were not adhered to, and in the diary there was again an entry recording how little he was pleased with himself.

This period of struggle would last for whole months, then suddenly a wave of unrestrained passion would break out and bear down all external restraints.

Like a drowning man who clings to a straw, he would, when carried away by his passion, catch at various feelings which might keep him from ruin. One of these was self-respect.

"Men whom I consider morally beneath me can do

wicked things better than I do," he wrote in his diary, whereupon the wicked things would then become odious to him and he would give them up.

Quiet life in the country often helped him to subdue his passions.

It is remarkable that in such everyday occupations as card-playing, his noble and generous nature would assert itself. It was probably one of his most powerful passions, but still he kept himself within limits by making it a rule of honor to play only with the rich, his object being that such gain as he made should not cause material loss, or humiliate and ruin his partner.

Often, not being able to control himself, he would have a fit of despair, and then again would recover himself and write in his diary:

"I am living a completely brutish life, although not an utterly disorderly one. I have abandoned almost all my occupations and have greatly fallen in spirit."

Being at one time in straitened circumstances, he actually intended to start a business of some kind, thinking he would run the mail post in Tula. It was at the end of 1850. Fortunately this enterprise was not carried out, and he thus avoided many disappointments which would have ensued from such uncongenial occupations. Thinking of his failures he once made the following note in his diary:

"These are the causes of my failures:

"(1) Irresolution, *i. e.*, want of energy. (2) Self-deception. (3) Haste. (4) *Fausse-honte*.[1] (5) A bad frame of mind. (6) Instability. (7) The habit of imitation. (8) Fickleness. (9) Thoughtlessness."

The greater part of the winter of 1850–51 he passed in Moscow, from which city he often wrote to his aunt in Yasnaya, and told her various details of his life. In one of the letters he thus describes his lodging and environment:

"It consists of four rooms—a dining-room, where I already have a piano which I have hired; a drawing-room furnished with arm-chairs and tables in walnut, and covered with red cloth and decorated with three large mirrors; a study where I have my writing-table, desk, and arm-chair

---

[1] False shame, *i. e.*, French expression for being ashamed of that which is not shameful.

—which always reminds me of our disputes about this last piece of furniture; and a room big enough to be both bedroom and dressing-room, and besides all this a small anteroom.

"I dine at home on *schi* and *kasha,* with which I am quite content. I am only waiting for the confections and home-made wines in order to have everything in accordance with my country habits.

"For forty roubles I have bought a sleigh of a style which is now very fashionable—Sergey must know the kind. I have bought all that is necessary for the harness, which at the present moment is very elegant."

Evidently his aunt felt great fears about his behavior in Moscow; in fact she gave him advice and warned him against bad acquaintances, for in the next letter he writes to her:

"Why are you so set against Islenief? If it is in order to warn me against him, that is unnecessary, as he is not at Moscow. All you say on the subject of the evil of gambling is very true, and I often recall it, and consequently I think that I will play cards no more. 'I think,' but I soon hope to tell you for certain.

"All you say about society is true, as is everything you say, especially in your letters, first because you write Madame de Sévigné, and secondly because I cannot dispute it in my usual way. You also say much that is kind about myself. I am convinced that praises do as much good as evil. They do good because they maintain one in the good qualities which are praised, and they do evil because they increase vanity. I am sure that yours can only do me good, being dictated by sincere friendship. It goes without saying that this is so, so far as I deserve them.

"I think I have deserved them during all the time of my sojourn at Moscow—I am satisfied with myself."

He also called at Yasnaya, from which place he again went to Moscow in March, 1851; after his return from this trip, he wrote in his diary that, in coming to Moscow, he had three ends in view—card-playing, marriage, and securing an official situation. However, he did not obtain even one of these objects. He conceived a dislike for gambling because he had become conscious of the vileness of this passion; he put off marrying because the three things which he recognized as conducing to marriage—love, reason, and destiny—were not present. He could not secure an appointment, as he had not at hand certain papers which were necessary for this purpose.

During the above-mentioned sojourn in Moscow he wrote to his aunt Tatiana, March 8th:

"Lately, in a book I was reading, the author said that the first symptoms of spring generally act upon men's morals. 'With the new birth of nature one would like to feel oneself also being born again, one regrets the past, the time badly employed, one repents of one's weakness, and the future appears as a bright spot before one; one becomes better—morally better.' This, as far as I am concerned, is perfectly true. Since I have begun to live independently spring has always put me in a good disposition, in which I have persevered for a period more or less extended, but it is always the winter that is a stumbling-block for me—I always then go wrong.

"However, in comparison with past winters, the last is without doubt the pleasantest and most rational I have passed. I have amused myself, have gone out into society, have laid up pleasant impressions, and, at the same time, have not deranged my finances, though, it is true, neither have I arranged them."

The following letter was written by him after his brother Nicholas returned from the Caucasus; he writes:

"The arrival of Nicolay has been an agreeable surprise for me, as I had almost lost all hope of his coming here. I have been so glad to see him that I have even somewhat neglected my duties, or rather my habits.

"I am now once more alone and literally alone—I go nowhere and receive no one. I am making plans for spring and summer—do you approve of them? Toward the end of May I shall come to Yasnaya; I will pass a month or two there, and will endeavor to keep Nicolay there as long as possible, and then I will go with him for a tour in the Caucasus."

In the midst of these disturbing scenes of worldly pleasure, card-playing, sensual indulgence, carousals with gypsies and sport, there would come periods of remorse and humiliation. Thus he would write a sermon while preparing for sacrament, but his sermon remained unread.

At the same time began attempts at serious artistic writing.

Up to 1850 he intended to write a novel of gypsy life. Another plan of the same time was worked out on the lines of the *Sentimental Journey* of Sterne.

" He once sat at the window reflecting and observing all that took place in the street.

"There goes a constable. Who is he and what is his life? And that carriage that went by, who is in it?—and where is he going and what is he thinking about? And who live in this house? What is their inner life? . . . How interesting it would be to describe all this! What an interesting book could be written upon it."

This changeable and dangerous period of life was cut short by his sudden departure for the Caucasus.

PART III

MILITARY SERVICE
(1851–1857)

PART III

MILITARY SERVICE (1851–1857)

CHAPTER VII

THE CAUCASUS

Departure from Yasnaya Polyana—The cause—Letters to Tatiana from Moscow—Tolstoy's reminiscences of his passing through Kazan—Journey on horses—In boats on the river Volga—His letter to Tatiana from Astrakhan—Historical information about the Caucasus—From Astrakhan to Starogladovsky—First impressions of Caucasian nature—The mountains. *The post Starogladovsk—The village Stari Yurt:* The night prayer—The mountains—Dissatisfaction with life—Wherein lies happiness?—The reasoning of Olenin. *His love for the Cossack girl:* The letter of Olenin to his Moscow friends—Letter to Tatiana on novel writing—The meeting of Ilya Tolstoy and Prince Baryatinsky—Petition to enter the military service. *Tiflis:* A letter to his brother Sergey describing the life in Tiflis and in Starogladovsk—A letter to Tatiana concerning his affection for her and the story of a prayer and his loss at play—Friendship with Sado. *The return to Starogladovsk:* A letter to his aunt about his visions of life at Yasnaya—The three passions: card-playing, sensuality, and vanity—The first hint of his vocation. *Pyatigorsk:* A letter to Tatiana—A letter to his brother Sergey describing the life at Pyatigorsk—Thoughts of serving oneself, men, and God—Justice and striving after perfection—Completion of *Childhood* and its despatch to *The Contemporary*—Meeting with his sister and her husband—His passion for spiritualism. *Return to Starogladovsky.* Meditations, during his journey, concerning life in the present—Striving after simplicity. *Letters of Nekrassof:* A letter to Tatiana—Impression made upon his family by *Childhood*—Impression made on the circle of authors by the novel—Silence of the critics—The article of 1854—Dostoyevsky's interest aroused—Maintenance of the "writing name"—Plan of *A Novel of a Russian Landowner. Delay in his promotion:* The campaign—The danger of February 18, 1853—The attitude of the censor to Tolstoy's early works. *An adventure.—The danger of being captured on June* 13, 1853: Reminiscences of Poltoratsky—Reminiscences of Bers—Rules of life—Letters to his brother Sergey complaining of the tiresome waiting for promotion—The writing of *Boyhood*—Completion of the tale, *The Recollections of a Billiard Marker*—The Lord's Prayer—St. George's

Cross—Two failures to get it—Recollections of Yanzhul—Characteristics of Alexeyef—Passing of an officer's examination—Departure to Russia—Tolstoy's attitude to Caucasian life.

THE unsuccessful attempt to keep house, the impossibility of establishing good relations with the peasants, and the passionate, perilous life, full of all kinds of excesses, which was mentioned in the previous chapter, induced Tolstoy to search for a means of changing his mode of life.

According to his own testimony, his life was so insipid and dissipated that he was ready for any change in it. For instance, his brother-in-law, Valerian Petrovich Tolstoy, being engaged, was going back to Siberia to arrange some business matters there before his marriage, and, as he was leaving the house, Tolstoy jumped into his tarantas,[1] without a hat, and in his blouse only; and it seems as if the only reason why he did not join in the journey to Siberia was simply that he found there was no hat on his head.

At last a serious incident took place that induced a change of life. In April, 1851, Nicolas, Tolstoy's eldest brother, arrived from the Caucasus; he was an officer in the Caucasian army and on leave of absence, and had shortly to return. Tolstoy seized this opportunity, and in spring, 1851, started with him for the Caucasus.

They left Yasnaya Polyana on April 20, and spent two weeks in Moscow, and from there he wrote to his aunt Tatiana at Yasnaya:

"I have been to the promenade at Sokolniki during detestable weather, and therefore have not met any of the society ladies I wish to see. As you assert that I am a man of resources, I went among the plebeians in the gypsy tents. You can easily imagine the inner struggle which there took place for and against. However, I came out victorious, *i. e.*, having given nothing but my blessing to the merry descendants of the illustrious Pharaohs. Nicolas has made the discovery that I should be a very agreeable travelling companion, were it not for my cleanliness. He gets irritated over my changing my underclothing, as he says, a dozen times a day. For my part I find him a very pleasant companion, were it not for his uncleanliness. I don't know which of us is right."

[1] Russian travelling-cart.—*Trans.*

THE CAUCASUS

From Moscow they passed through Kazan, where they visited V. T. Yushkof, their guardian-aunt's husband, with whom they had lived in Kazan, and also saw Madame Zagoskin, a friend of this aunt's, the directress of the Kazan Institute, an eccentric and clever woman.

In Zagoskin's house Tolstoy met Z. M., an ex-pupil of the Institute, and conceived for her a sentimental kind of love, which, as usual, owing to his bashfulness, he could not make up his mind to express, and which he took away with him to the Caucasus.

In Madame Zagoskin's house, as that lady always secured the young men who were the most *comme il faut*, he met and almost made friends with a young lawyer, the procurator Ogolin, and took a journey with the latter into the country to pay a visit to V. J. Yushkof. Ogolin was a new type of the official of that period.

Tolstoy used to relate how struck Yushkof was—being accustomed to see a procurator as a grave, respectable, and hoary personage in a uniform, with a cross on his breast and a star—when he beheld Ogolin, and got acquainted with him, under circumstances of ease and freedom.

"When Ogolin and I had arrived and approached the house, opposite which was a group of young birch trees, I suggested to Ogolin that, while the servant was announcing our arrival, we should compete as to which of us would climb these birches best and highest. When Yushkof came out and saw the procurator climbing up a tree, he could not recover himself for a long time."

Tolstoy, as he told me himself, was in his most stupid and worldly mood during this trip. He related to me how his brother made him feel his stupidity in Kazan. They were walking about the town when a gentleman drove past them in a dolgousha,[1] leaning with ungloved hands on a stick resting on the step of the carriage.

"How evident it is that this man is some sort of 'scallywag,'" said Lyof Tolstoy, addressing his brother.

"Why?" asked Nicolas.

"Why, because he has got no gloves."

"Why should he be good-for-nothing because he has no gloves?" asked Nicolay, with his hardly noticeable, kind, clever, and mocking smile.

[1] A kind of jaunting-car on four wheels.

Nicolay always thought and did everything, not because others thought and did so, but because he himself believed it to be right, and he always thought and did what he believed to be right. Thus he planned to go to the Caucasus not *via* Voronzeh and through the territory of the Don Cossacks, as was the rule, but on horseback to Saratof, from Saratof in a boat down the Volga to Astrakhan, and from Astrakhan in a post-chaise to the Stanitsa, and this plan he put in execution.

They hired a fishing-boat, placed the tarantas in it, and being assisted by a pilot and two oarsmen, sailed here and there, sometimes rowing, sometimes carried by the current. The trip lasted about three weeks, when they reached Astrakhan. From thence Lyof wrote to his aunt:

"We are at Astrakhan, and on the point of leaving it, thus having still a journey of 400 versts to do. I have passed a most agreeable week at Kazan. My journey to Saratof was disagreeable, but, as compensation, the passage from there to Astrakhan in a little boat was very poetical and full of charm, owing to the novelty of the locality, and for me even from the very method of travelling. Yesterday I wrote a long letter to Marie, in which I tell her about my sojourn at Kazan. I do not tell you anything about it, for fear of repeating myself, although I am sure you will not confuse the two letters. So far as it has gone, I am exceedingly satisfied with my journey. There are many things which make me think, and then the very change of locality is pleasant. In passing through Moscow, I subscribed to a lending-library, so that I have plenty of reading, which I do even in the tarantas, and, besides, as you can well imagine, Nicolas' society greatly contributes to my enjoyment. I do not cease to think of you and of all ours; sometimes I even reproach myself for having abandoned the life which your affection rendered so sweet; but it is merely a postponement, and I shall have only the more pleasure in seeing you again. Were I not pressed, I would write to Serge; but I put this off until I shall be quietly settled down. Embrace him on my behalf, and tell him that I greatly repent of the coldness which there was between us before my departure, and for which I blame myself alone."

A few words must be said as to what the Caucasus is, to make the reader understand the facts of Tolstoy's Caucasian life, as well as his Caucasian tales.

When the kingdom of Moscow became so strong as to be able to make head against the Tartar tribes, it gradually pushed them to the southeast, and, having conquered the kingdoms of Kazan and Astrakhan, it came into conflict with wild tribes of mountaineers, who inhabited the northern slopes of the Caucasian mountains. To keep them in check, the Russian Government had, about the beginning of the nineteenth century, erected a whole line of Cossack outposts on the left bank of the Terek and the right bank of the Kuban.

On the other hand, the Georgian kingdom, which lies on the southern slope of the Caucasian mountains, and which was up to that time independent, had, with its King Heraclius II, become subject to Russia in the beginning of the nineteenth century. The subjugation of the mountain tribes between Georgia and Russia became indispensable on political grounds, and the struggle went on for over fifty years.

From the Cossack posts along the banks of the Terek and the Kuban, the Russians gradually pushed on farther to the very edge of the mountains. But they confined themselves chiefly to making raids: a military detachment attacked the villages in the mountains, destroyed pastures, drove off cattle, captured as many inhabitants as possible, and with such booty returned to their posts. The mountaineers in their turn made reprisals: they pursued the detachments on their way back, and with their well-aimed carbine shots inflicted on them great losses; they would hide behind the ramparts in the woods and narrow ravines, and sometimes even appear suddenly at the very posts, where they massacred many, and carried off men and women to the mountains. From time to time the struggle abated, but became fiercer when, taking advantage of our ill fortune, there arose leaders who managed to unite under their command the more powerful and warlike tribes. The fanaticism of the latter was then kindled by the preaching of a holy war against the infidels. The Russians had to encounter great difficulties, and suffered heavy losses from the most warlike of the Caucasian tribes, the Tchetchenians, who live on the forest-clad plains of the right bank of the Terek, near its tributaries Sunja, Arguny, and others, and higher up in the mountain gorges of Itchkeria. Our spirit of enterprise grew stronger or slackened, according to the talent and energy of the commander who happened to be directing the military operations.

With the appointment in 1856 of Prince Baryatinsky as governor of the Caucasus, events took a decisive turn. Profiting by his personal influence over the Emperor Alexander II, he summoned an army of 200,000 men, a greater one than was ever before seen in the Caucasus. A considerable part of this army he directed against Tchetchnya, Itchkeria, and Daghestan, then under the leadership of the well-known Shamyl.

The talent and energy of this leader, and the fanaticism of the mountaineers, who recognized him as their Imaum, were all crushed under the weight of this powerful army led by Yevdokimof, whom nothing could stop. In 1857 Shamyl's residence, the village Vedeno in the centre of Itchkeria, capitulated, and in 1859 Shamyl himself surrendered to Prince Baryatinsky in his new Daghestan stronghold—Gooniba.

At the beginning of the fifties, before his appointment as governor of the Caucasus, Prince Baryatinsky appeared in the Northern Caucasus as commander of the left wing of the Russian army.

Just about this time Tolstoy arrived in the Caucasus, and the events described in his Caucasian tales, *The Invaders, The Cossacks, A Wood-Cutting Expedition,* and *An Old Acquaintance,* took place about this time and in this locality.

From Astrakhan both brothers travelled in a post-chaise through Lizliar to the village of Starogladovsky, where the eldest brother was stationed. Tolstoy came to the Caucasus in a private capacity and settled down with his brother.

The first impression which the Caucasus made on him was not a profound one. Shortly after he reached the country he thus describes it in a letter to his aunt:

"I have arrived well and whole, but am now, toward the end of May, at the Starogladovsky. I am feeling rather sad. I have here seen at close quarters the kind of life Nicolas is leading, and I have made the acquaintance of the officers who form the local society. The kind of life led here is not very attractive as it has at first presented itself to me, for the country, which I had expected to find very fine, is not at all so. As the village is situated on low land there is no outlook, and besides the lodgings are bad, as well as everything that constitutes the comfort of life. As to the officers, they are, as you can imagine, people without education, but at the same time very good fellows, and, above all, they are very much attached to Nicolas.

Alexeyef, the commander, is a little chap, with light hair approaching red, with mustaches and whiskers, and a piercing voice, but an excellent Christian, somewhat reminding one of Volkof, but not canting like him. Then B——, a young officer, childish and good-natured, reminding one of Petrusha. Then an old captain, Bilkovsky of the Ural Cossacks, an old soldier, simple but noble, brave and good. I will confess to you that at first many things in this society shocked me, but I have become accustomed to it, without, however, becoming intimate with the gentlemen. I have found a happy medium in which there is neither pride nor familiarity. In this, however, I had merely to follow Nicolay's example.

However, he did not stay very long in Starogladovsky.

He and his brother moved to Stari Yurt, a fortified camp, to shelter the sick in Goryachevodsk, where, shortly before, hot springs possessing strong healing virtues had been discovered. Again we quote the description of this place from Tolstoy's letter to his aunt, written on his arrival there in July, 1851.

"Nicolay left a week after his arrival, and I followed him, so that we have been here for almost three weeks, and we live in a tent, but, as the weather is fine and I am somewhat adapting myself to this kind of life, I am feeling very well. Here there are beautiful views. To begin with the place where the springs are. It is an enormous mountain of rocks lying one upon the other, some of which have become detached, forming a sort of grotto, others remain suspended at a great height. They are all intersected by torrents of warm water, which in some places fall with much noise, and, especially in the morning, cover all the elevated part of the mountain with a white vapor which is continually rising from this boiling water. The water is so hot they can boil eggs hard in it in three minutes. In the middle of the valley, on the chief torrent, there are three watermills, one above the other, constructed in a peculiar and very picturesque way. All day the Tartar women keep coming to wash their clothes above and beneath these mills. I should mention that they wash them with their feet. It's like an ant heap in continual motion. The women are for the most part handsome and well built. The costume of Oriental women is graceful, notwithstanding their poverty; the picturesque groups formed by the women, together with the savage beauty of the place, make a truly beautiful sight. I sometimes remain for hours admiring the landscape. Then the view from the top of the mountain is still finer and of quite another kind, but I am afraid of boring you with my descriptions.

"I am very glad to be at the waters, as I benefit by them. I take mineral baths, and I no longer feel pain in my feet. I always have rheumatism, but during my journey on the water I think I took cold. I have seldom felt so well as now, and notwithstanding the great heat I take much exercise.

"Here the type of officers is the same as that of which I have already spoken to you. There are many of these, I know them all, and my relations with them are the same."

According to Tolstoy, Yurt was a large village with a population of 1,500, and remarkable for its beautiful mountain situation. In the mountains above the village rose a hot sulphur spring. Its temperature was so high that, according to Tolstoy, his brother's dog after falling into the spring scalded himself so much that he died from the effects. The spring divides itself into many small brooklets which run down the mountain-side. These brooklets were so small that it was easy to bank them up. The inhabitants of the village used them for working watermills. The properties of the spring are superior to those of Pyatigorsk.

From this village Tolstoy joined in a raid as a volunteer. Here he had glorious moments of youthful poetical enthusiasm.

Especially memorable to him was one night, which he has described in his diary in terms of unique spiritual beauty.

"STARI YURT, 11*th June*, 1851.

"Yesterday I hardly slept all night. Having written in my diary, I began to pray to God. It is impossible to convey the sweetness of the feeling which I experienced during prayer. I repeated the prayers I generally say: Our Father, to the Virgin, to the Trinity, 'the gates of mercy,' the appeal to the guardian angel, and then I still remained at prayer. If one were to define prayer as petition or thanksgiving, then I did not pray. I longed for something sublime and good, but what, I cannot convey, although I was clearly conscious that I desired it. I wished to blend into unity with the all-enfolding Being. I asked Him to pardon my crimes; yet no, I did not ask this, for I felt that He had given me this blissful moment, He had pardoned me. I asked and at the same time felt that I had nothing to ask, that I could not and did not know how to ask. I thanked Him, but not in words, not in thoughts. I combined all in one feeling, both petition and thanksgiving. The feeling of fear completely vanished. None of the feelings—Faith, Hope, and Love—could I have disengaged from the general feeling. No, here it is, the feeling which I experienced yesterday—it was love to God, an elevated love combining in itself all that is good, and repudiating all that is evil. How dreadful it was for me to look at all the trivial and vicious side of my life. I could not comprehend how it was this had attracted me. How I prayed God from a pure heart to accept me into His bosom. I did not feel the flesh, I was . . . but no, the carnal, trivial side again asserted itself, and an hour had not passed before I almost consciously heard the voice of vice, of vanity, and of the empty side of life. I knew whence this voice came, I knew it had ruined my bliss; I struggled, yet yielded to it. I fell asleep in dreams of fame and of women. But it was not my fault, I could not help it. Eternal bliss *here* is impossible. Sufferings are necessary. Why? I do not know? But how dare I say, I do not know? How dared I think it was possible to know the ways of Fate? It is the source of reason, and reason wishes to fathom it! . . .

"The mind is lost in these depths of wisdom and emotion, and is afraid of insulting Him. I thank Him for the moment of bliss which showed me both my insignificance and my greatness. I wish to pray, but I do not know how. I wish to attain comprehension, but dare not—I surrender myself to Thy will.

"Why have I written all this? How flabbily, how lifelessly, even how senselessly have my feelings found expression; and yet they were so elevated."

These outbursts of religious emotion were often succeeded by periods of depression and apathy. Thus on the 2d of July, while yet living in the Stari Yurt, he put down the following thoughts:

"I am just now meditating, recalling all the unpleasant moments of my life, which in times of depression alone creep into one's mind. . . . No, there is too little delight—man is too capable of imagining happiness and too often in one way or another Fate strikes him, painfully, very painfully catching his tender chord—for us to love life, and, besides, there is something specially sweet and great in indifference to life, and I delight in this feeling. In face of everything, how strong I appear to myself in this firm conviction that there is nothing to expect here except death. . . . Yet at this very moment I am thinking with delight about a saddle I have ordered in which I will ride in Circassian attire, and about how I will flirt with Cossack girls, and feel despair that my left mustache is higher than the right one, and I shall spend two hours arranging it."

Thus Tolstoy often had to change his abode. The headquarters and the staff-battery, where his brother served, were at Starogladovsky, but he was often sent to the outposts, to which Tolstoy accompanied him.

These wild Cossack and Caucasian villages were destined to become historic. Here the artistic forms of Tolstoy's works were conceived, and the first fruit of his creative power came forth. The wonderful scenery of the Northern Caucasus, its mountains, the river Térek, and the Cossack bravery, the almost primitive simplicity of life—all this in one harmonious whole served to cradle these early creations, and to point out the work of the world-wide genius, who was to struggle for an ideal, to search for truth and the meaning of human life.

Here we give a description of Tolstoy's arrival at Stari Yurt, taken from his novel *The Cossacks,* in which he so very vividly depicts the impression made on him by the majesty of the Caucasian Mountains.

"It was a very clear morning. Suddenly he saw, some twenty steps from him, as he thought at first, pure white masses, with their delicate contours, and the fantastic and sharply defined outline of their summits, against the distant sky. And when he became aware of the great distance between him and the mountains and the sky, and of the immensity of the mountains, and felt the immeasurableness of that beauty, he was frightened, thinking that it was a vision, a dream. He shook himself, in order to be rid of his sleep. The mountains remained the same.

"'What is this? What is it?' he asked the driver.

"'The mountains,' the Nogáy answered, with indifference.

"'I have been looking at them myself for a long time,' said Vanyúsha. 'It is beautiful! They will not believe it at home!'

"In the rapid motion of the vehicle over the even road, the mountains seemed to be running along the horizon, gleaming in the rising sun with their rosy summits. At first they only surprised Olenín, but later they gave him pleasure. And later, as he gazed longer at this chain of snow-capped peaks, which were not connected with other black ones, but rose directly from the steppe, he began by degrees to understand their full beauty, and to 'feel' them.

"From that moment everything he saw, everything he thought, everything he felt, assumed for him a new, severely majestic character, that of the mountains. All the Moscow reminiscences, his shame and remorse, all the trite dreams of the Caucasus, everything disappeared, and never returned again. 'Now it has begun,' a solemn voice said to him. And the road, and the distant line of the Térek, and the villages, and the people, all that appeared to him no longer so many trifles.

"He looked at the sky, and he thought of the mountains. He looked at himself, and at Vanyúsha—and again at the mountains. There, two Cossacks rode by, and their muskets in cases evenly vibrated on their backs, and their horses intermingled their chestnut and gray legs—and the mountains. Beyond the Térek was seen the smoke in a native village—and the mountains.

"The sun rose and glistened on the Térek beyond the reeds—and the mountains. From the Cossack village came a native cart, and women, beautiful young women, walking —and the mountains. 'Abréks [1] race through the steppes, and I am travelling, and fear them not: I have a gun, and strength, and youth'—and the mountains."

[1] Mountaineer braves.

In August he is again at Starogladovsky.

From the story *The Cossacks*, which bears an autobiographical character, we can form an approximate idea of how he passed his time in the Cossack village. His attempt to come more in touch with the people—Cossacks, sport, the contemplation of the beauties of nature, and the incessant inner strife which never abandoned this man, and is vividly expressed in his works, such was Tolstoy's life of that period.

"Why am I happy, and why have I lived before?" he thought. "How exacting I used to be! How I concocted and caused nothing but shame and woe for myself!" And suddenly it seemed that a new world was open to him. "Happiness is this," he said to himself: "happiness consists in living for others. This is clear. The desire for happiness is inborn in man; consequently it is legitimate. In attempting to satisfy it in an egotistical manner, that is, by seeking wealth, glory, comforts of life, and love, the circumstances may so arrange themselves that it is impossible to satisfy these desires. Consequently these desires are illegitimate, but the need of happiness is not illegitimate. Now, what desires are these that can always be satisfied, in spite of external conditions? What desires? Love, self-sacrifice!"

He was so rejoiced and excited when he discovered this truth, which seemed to be new, that he leaped up and impatiently began to look around for some one to sacrifice himself for, to do good to, and to love. "I do not need anything for myself," he proceeded in his thought; "then why should I not live for others?"

Already then the voice of love touched a powerful chord in the soul of the young man, who had hardly entered the life of social activity.

But outward events were still running their course, carrying the strong animal nature of man along its customary path.

The life of the passionate young man in the Cossack village was not devoid of romance. The story of his love is described in the tale *The Cossacks*.

All the stages of this unreturned affection are vividly pictured in that story, and even still better presented in a letter to his Moscow friends. That letter shows the author's love of wild nature, his passionate desire to live in perfect harmony with her, and his sufferings from inability to do so. He knew his life in civilized surroundings had torn him away from nature and created between them an abyss impossible to overcome. Here is the most striking and essential part of this letter:

"How contemptible and pitiable you all appear to me! You do not know what happiness nor what life is! You have first to taste life in all its artless beauty; you must see and understand what I see before me each day: the eternal, inaccessible snows of the mountains, and majestic woman in her pristine beauty, as the first woman must have issued from the hands of her Creator—and then it will be clear who it is that is being ruined, and who lives according to the truth, you or I.

"If you only knew how detestable and pitiable you are to me in your delusions! The moment there rise before me, instead of my cabin, my forest, and my love, those drawing-rooms, those women with pomaded hair, through which the false locks appear, those unnaturally lisping lips, those concealed and distorted limbs, and that prattle of the drawing-rooms, which pretends to be conversation, but has no right to be called so—an insufferable feeling of disgust comes over me. I see before me those dull faces, those rich, marriageable girls, with an expression on the face which says, 'That's all right, you may—. Just come up to me, even though I am a rich, marriageable girl'; that sitting down and changing of places; that impudent pairing of people, and that never-ending gossip and hypocrisy; those rules —to this one your hand, to that one a nod, and with that one a chat; and finally, that eternal *ennui* in the blood, which passes from generation to generation (and consciously even then, with the conviction of its necessity). You must understand, or believe it. You must see and grasp what truth and beauty are, and everything which you say and think, all your wishes for your own happiness and for mine, will be dispersed to the winds. Happiness consists in being with Nature, in seeing it, and holding converse with it. 'The Lord preserve him, but he will, no doubt, marry a Cossack woman, and will be entirely lost to society,' I imagine them saying about me, with genuine compassion, whereas it is precisely this that I wish: to be entirely lost, in your sense of the word, and to marry a simple Cossack woman; I dare not do it, because that would be the acme of happiness, of which I am unworthy.

"Three months have passed since I for the first time saw the Cossack maiden, Maryanka. The conceptions and prejudices of the society from which I had issued were still fresh in me. I did not believe then that I could fall in love with this woman. I admired her, as I admired the beauty of the mountains and of the sky, nor could I help admiring her, for she is as beautiful as they. Then I felt that the contemplation of this beauty had become a necessity of my life, and I began to ask myself whether I did not love her; but I did not find in myself anything resembling the feeling such as I had imagined it to be. This sentiment resembled neither the longing for solitude nor the desire for matrimony, nor platonic love, still less carnal love, which I had experienced. I had to see and hear her, to know that she was near, and I was not exactly happy, but calm. After an evening party which I had attended with her, and at which I had touched her, I felt that between this woman and myself existed an indissoluble, though unacknowledged bond, against which it would be vain to struggle. But I did struggle. I said to myself: 'Is it possible for me to love a woman who will never comprehend the spiritual interests of my life? Can I love a woman for her mere beauty, can I love a statue of a woman?' I asked myself, and I was loving her all the time, though I did not trust my own sentiment.

"After the party, when I had spoken to her for the first time, our relations were changed. Before that time she was to me a foreign, but majestic, object of external Nature; after the party she became a human being for me. I have met her and spoken with her; and I have been with her father at work, and have passed whole evenings in their company. And in these close relations she has remained, to my thinking, just as pure, inaccessible, and majestic. To all questions she has answered in the same calm, proud, and gayly indifferent manner. At times she has been gracious, but for the most part every glance, every word, every motion of hers, has expressed the same, not contemptuous, but repressing and enticing indifference.

"Each day I tried, with a feigning smile on my lips, to

The country house of Tolstoy's aunt, Yushkof, where he visited during his student days.

dissemble, and, with the torment of passion and of desires in my heart, I spoke jestingly to her. But she saw that I was dissembling, and yet looked gayly and simply at me. This situation grew intolerable to me. I did not wish to tell lies before her, and wanted to let her know everything I thought and everything I felt. I was very much excited; that was in the vineyard. I began to tell her of my love in words that I am ashamed to recall. I am ashamed to think of them, because I ought never to have dared to tell her that, and because she stood immeasurably above the words and above the feeling which I intended to express to her. I held my tongue, and since that day my situation has been insufferable. I did not wish to lower myself by persisting in the former jocular relations, and I was conscious that I was not yet ripe for straightforward, simple relations with her. I asked myself in despair, 'What shall I do?'

"In my preposterous dreams I imagined her now as my mistress and now as my wife, and I repelled both thoughts in disgust. It would be terrible to make a mistress of her. It would be murder. And it would be still worse to make a lady of her, the wife of Dmítri Andréyevich Olénin, as one of our officers has made a lady of a Cossack girl of this place, whom he has married. If I could turn Cossack, become a Lukashka, steal herds of horses, fill myself with red wine, troll songs, kill people, and, when drunk, climb through the window to pass the night with her, without asking myself who I am and why I am—it would be a different matter; then we could understand each other, and I might be happy."

But he could not become another Lukashka, and could not therefore find happiness in that direction.

In September he writes a letter to his aunt, through which the future writer can already be clearly seen. It is his serious attitude in the expression of thought that particularly strikes one; probably by that time numberless thoughts and images were overcrowding in his mind, and he chose only those which he could set forth on paper. He thus expresses this sensation:

"You have told me several times that you are not in the habit of writing drafts of your letters; I follow your example, but I don't manage it as well as you do, for it very often happens that I tear up my letters after rereading them. I do not do so from vanity—a mistake in spelling, a blot, a sentence badly turned do not trouble me, but it is that I cannot manage to learn to direct my pen and my ideas. I have just torn up a letter to you which I had finished, because I had said in it many things I did not wish to say to you, and nothing of what I did wish to say. Perhaps you will think that this is dissimulation, and you may say that it is wrong to dissimulate with those one loves and by whom one knows one is loved. I agree, but you will also agree that one says everything to a person toward whom one is indifferent, but that the more a person is dear to one, the more things there are one would like to conceal from him."

Feeling an access of youthful energy, and having no outlet for it, Tolstoy often risked his life in taking part in dangerous excursions.

Thus, in company of his friend, the cossack Epishka (described in *The Cossacks* as Yeroshka), he once went to the village Hossaf-Yurt, in the mountains. The journey was a dangerous one, for the mountaineers sometimes attacked travellers.

On his safe return from the excursion Tolstoy met the commander-in-chief of the left wing, Prince Baryatinsky, accompanied by his own relation, Ilya Tolstoy. The latter invited Tolstoy to join their company, and this gave him a chance of getting well acquainted with the commander-in-chief. He expressed on one occasion his satisfaction and praise at Tolstoy's cheerful and brave appearance, which he noticed on seeing him once after a raid. Then and there he advised him to enter military service at once, as Tolstoy still remained a civilian, but took part in all the expeditions as a volunteer. The flattering opinion of the commander-in-chief and the advice of his relations induced Tolstoy at last to hasten his decision and send in his petition to join the army.

He remained at Starogladovsk during August and September. In September he went with his brother Nicolay to Tiflis. His brother soon returned, but Tolstoy stayed on in Tiflis to pass his examinations and enter the service.

"We did indeed leave on the 25th, and after a seven days' journey, very dull owing to the want of horses at almost every posting-house, and very agreeable owing to the beauty of the country through which we passed, we arrived on the first of the present month.

"Tiflis is a very civilized town, which to a great extent apes St. Petersburg, and greatly succeeds in the imitation. The society is choice and rather numerous; there is a Russian theatre and an Italian Opera, of which I avail myself as much as my restricted means allow. I am living in the German colony. It is a suburb, but has for me two great advantages, one of being a very pretty place surrounded by gardens and vineyards, so that one feels more in the country than in town. It is still very warm and very fine, and up to the present there is neither snow nor frost. The second advantage is that for two tolerably clean rooms I pay five roubles a month, whereas in town one could not have similar apartments for less than forty roubles a month. Into the bargain I get practice in the German language for nothing, have books, occupations, and leisure, since no one comes to disturb me, so that on the whole I am not dull.

"Do you remember, good Aunt, some advice you gave me in bygone days—that I should write novels? Well, I am following your advice, and the occupations I am speaking of consist in literary work. I do not know whether what I write will ever see the light, but it is work which amuses me, and in which I have persevered too long to abandon it."

This letter is interesting, because it shows us with what modesty this great talent was developing its unsuspected excellence. He was ailing and doctoring himself for two months, and wrote his first story, availing himself of occasional leisure and solitude. Besides, part of his time was occupied with attempts to get an official appointment, which was a difficult matter owing to the want of the necessary papers.

December 23, 1851, he writes the following letter to his brother Sergius, giving characteristic details concerning life in Tiflis and the village:

"In a few days the long-desired announcement is to be gazetted of my nomination as volunteer private in the 4th Battery, and I shall have the pleasure of saluting and following with my eyes passing officers and generals. Even here, when walking about the streets in my fashionable overcoat and opera hat, which I bought here for ten roubles, despite all my splendor in this attire, I have become so accustomed to the idea of putting on a gray soldier's coat that my hand involuntarily wishes to seize my hat by the springs and flatten it down. However, if my nomination takes place, on that very day I will leave Stargladovskaya and proceed thence immediately for the front, where I will walk or ride in a soldier's cloak or a Sackashan coat and will, according to my powers, contribute, by the aid of the cannon, to the slaughter of the *wild, rebellious Asiatics.*

"*Seryozha.*—You see by my letter that I am at Tiflis, where I arrived as long ago as the 9th of November, so that I have had time to hunt a little with the dogs I bought there (at Stargladovskaya), but the dogs that have been sent here I have not yet seen. Sport here (*i. e.*, in Sackashan village) is splendid: open fields, marshy ground, full of hares, and clusters, not of trees, but of rushes, in which foxes find cover. I have been out hunting nine times in all, about ten or fifteen versts from the village, with two dogs, of which one is excellent and the other a good-for-nothing. I caught two foxes and upward of sixty hares. In course of time I shall attempt to hunt deer. I have more than once been present in shooting expeditions for wild boar and stags, but have killed nothing myself. This sport is also very pleasant, but, after becoming accustomed to hunt with greyhounds, one cannot care for it. Even as he who has become accustomed to smoke Turkish tobacco cannot care for the common zhukof, although one may argue that the latter is the best.

"I know your weakness. You will probably wish to know who have been and are my acquaintances here and in what relations I stand toward them. I must tell you here that this point does not in the least interest me, but I will hasten to satisfy you. In battery here there are not many officers; I am therefore acquainted with all of them, but very superficially, although I enjoy their general cordiality, as Nicolenka and myself always have brandy, wine, and refreshments for visitors. On these same principles my acquaintance has been made and maintained with officers of other regiments with whom I had occasion to become acquainted at Stari Yurt, a watering-place where I lived in summer, and during the expedition in which I took part.

There are among them some more or less decent fellows, yet, as I always have more interesting occupations than talking to officers, I remain with all of them in good relations. Lieutenant-Colonel Alexeyef, commander of the battery I enter, is a very kind and very vain man. By this latter weakness of his I have, I confess, profited and thrown some dust unintentionally in his eyes—I need him. But this also I do involuntarily and repent of it. With vain people one becomes vain oneself.

"Here at Tiflis I have three acquaintances. I did not make more, first, because I did not wish, and secondly because I had not the opportunity—I have been ill almost all the time and it is only since last week that I have been out. My first acquaintance is Bagracion of St. Petersburg (Ferzen's comrade). The second, Prince Baryatinsky. I made his acquaintance during the expedition I took part in under his command and, later, spent a day with him in a fort with Ilia Tolstoy whom I met here. This acquaintance naturally does not afford me much recreation, for you understand on what footing a volunteer private may be acquainted with a general. My third acquaintance is an *apothecary's assistant*, a Pole reduced to the ranks—a most amusing creature. I am sure Prince Baryatinsky never imagined that he could in any kind of list whatever stand by the side of an apothecary's assistant, but so it has happened. Nicolenka is on a very good footing here; the commanders and fellow-officers love and respect him. He enjoys, moreover, the reputation of a brave officer. I love him more than ever, and when I am with him I am completely happy, and without him I feel dull.

"If you want to boast of news from the Caucasus you may announce that the second personage after Shamil, a certain Hadji-Murat, gave himself up the other day to the Russian Government. He was the first horseman and hero in all Tchetchnya, but committed a base act. You may further relate with grief that the other day the well-known brave and clever general, Sleptsoff, was killed. If you wish to know whether *it hurt him*—I cannot tell you."

January 6, 1852, Tolstoy writes a remarkable letter from Tiflis to his aunt, which is full of tenderness and love for his guardian.

"I have just received your letter of the 24th November,

and I am answering you immediately, as is now my custom. Lately, I wrote you that your letter made me shed tears, and I attributed this weakness to my illness. I was wrong. For some time back all your letters have produced the same effect on me. I have always been a cry-baby. Formerly I was ashamed of this weakness, but the tears I shed in thinking of you and your love for us are so sweet that I let them flow without any scruples or false shame. Your letter is too full of sadness for it not to produce the same effect upon me. It is you who have always given me advice, and although, unfortunately, I have not always followed it, I would wish to act all my life only according to your views. For the present allow me to tell you what effect your letter had on me, and the thoughts that came to me upon reading it. If I speak too frankly, I know you will pardon it in view of the love I have for you. In saying that it is your turn to leave us, in order to join those who are no more, and whom you have so loved; in saying that you pray God to put a limit to your existence, which seems to you so insupportable and isolated, pardon me, dear Aunt, but it seems to me, in saying this, you offend God and me and all of us who so love you. You ask God for death, *i. e.*, the greatest misfortune which could happen to me. (This is not a phrase; God is witness that the two greatest misfortunes which could happen to me would be your death or that of Nicolay—the two persons I love more than myself.) What would remain for me were God to fulfil your prayer? To give pleasure to whom would I desire to become better, to be virtuous, to have a good reputation in the world? When I make plans of happiness for myself, the idea that you will share and enjoy my happiness is always present. When I do anything good, I am satisfied with myself, because I know that you will be satisfied with me. When I act badly, what I most fear is to pain you. Your love is everything for me, and you ask God to separate us! I cannot tell you the feeling I have toward you, speech does not suffice to express it, and I am afraid you will think I am exaggerating, and yet I am weeping with burning tears in writing to you. It is to this painful separation I am indebted for knowing what a friend I have in you and how much I love you. But am I the only one who has this feeling for you? and you ask of God to die!

You say you are isolated. Although I am separated from you, yet, if you believe in my love, this idea might counterbalance your pain. As for myself, wherever I am, I shall not feel isolated, as long as I know I am loved by you as I am.

"However, I know that is a bad feeling that dictates these words to me; I am jealous of your grief."

Further on, in the same letter, he relates an incident as interesting for its practical as for its psychological bearing:

"To-day one of those things happened to me which would have made me believe in God, did I not already, for some time past, firmly believe in Him.

"I was at Stari-Yurt. All the officers who were there did nothing but play and at rather high stakes. As it is impossible for us when living in camp not to see each other often, I have very often taken part in card-playing, and, notwithstanding the importunity I was subject to, I had stood firm for a month, but one day for fun I placed a small stake: I lost. I began again: I again lost. I was in bad luck; the passion for play had awakened, and in two days I had lost all the money I had and that which Nicolay had given me (about 250 roubles), and into the bargain 500 roubles for which I gave a promissory note payable in January, '52. I must tell you that near the camp there is a native village inhabited by the Tchetchenians. A young lad from there, Sado, used to come to the camp and play, but, as he could not count or write, there were rascals who cheated him. For this reason I have never wished to play against Sado, and I have even told him that he should not play because he was being cheated, and I have myself offered to play for him. He was very grateful to me for this and made me a present of a purse, it being the custom of these people to give each other mutual presents. I gave him a worthless gun I had bought for eight roubles. I must tell you that, in order to become 'Kunak,' which means *friend,* it is customary to make each other presents and then to have a meal in the house of the 'Kunak.' After this, according to the ancient custom of this people (which now exists almost only by tradition), you become friends for life and for death, *i. e.,* if I demand of him his money or his wife or his arms, or all that is most precious to him, he must give it to me, and I also must refuse him nothing. Sado had engaged me to come to him and become his 'Kunak.' I went, and, after having regaled me in the native manner, he offered to let me choose anything in his house I wished—his arms, his horse, all. . . . I wished to choose what was of the least value there, and I took a horse bridle mounted in silver, but he told me that I offended him and compelled me to take a sword which cost at least a hundred roubles. His father is rather a rich man, but one who keeps his money buried and does not give a penny to his son. The son, in order to have money, goes and steals horses and cows from the enemy; sometimes he has risked his life twenty times over in order to steal something not worth ten roubles, but it is not through greed he does it, but by fashion. The greatest thief is highly esteemed and called 'Dzhighit,' 'plucky fellow.' At one moment Sado has a thousand roubles, at another not a penny. After a visit to him I made him a present of Nicolay's silver watch, and we became the best of friends in the world. Several times he has proved his devotion to me in exposing himself to dangers for me; but this for him is nothing—it has become a habit and a pleasure.

"When I left Stari-Yurt and Nicolay remained there, Sado used to go to him every day saying he did not know what to do without me and that he felt terribly dull. By letter I communicated to Nicolay that, my horse being ill, I begged him to find one at Stari-Yurt. Sado, having learned this, made haste to come to me and to give me his horse, notwithstanding all I did to decline it.

"After my silly action of playing cards at Stari-Yurt I had not touched cards, and I was continually moralizing to Sado, who had a passion for gambling, and although he does not know the game has wonderfully good luck. Yesterday evening I occupied myself in considering my financial affairs and my debts. I was thinking what I could do to pay them. Having thought over these things, I saw that, if I do not spend too much, all my debts would not embarrass me and might be covered little by little in the course of two or three years; but the 500 roubles I had to pay this month threw me into despair. It was impossible for me to pay them, and at that moment they embarrassed me much more than did previously the 4,000 of Ogoref. The stupidity, after having contracted those debts in Russia, of coming here and making new ones cast me into despair. That evening, during my prayers, I begged God to extricate me from this disagreeable position, and prayed with much fervor. 'But how can I get out of this business?' thought I, on going to bed. 'Nothing can happen which can give me any chance of meeting this debt.' I already represented to myself all the unpleasantness I should have to go through in consequence—how my creditor would present the note for payment, how the military authorities would demand an explanation why I do not pay, etc. 'God help me,' I said, and fell asleep.

"The next day I received a letter from Nicolay, together with yours and several others. He wrote:

"'The other day Sado came to see me, he won your notes from Knoring and brought them to me. He was so glad of this prize, so happy, and kept asking so repeatedly, "What do you think? Your brother will be glad I have done this," that I was inspired with a great affection for him. This man is indeed attached to you.'

"Is it not astonishing to see one's desire fulfilled the very next day, *i. e.*, is there anything so astonishing as the divine goodness for a being who deserves it so little as I? And is not this feature of attachment in Sado admirable? He knows I have a brother, Serge, who loves horses, and as I have promised to take him to Russia when I return, he told me that, were it to cost him his life a hundred times over, he would steal the best horse to be found in the mountains and would bring it to him.

"Please get a six-chambered revolver purchased at Tula and send it to me, also a little musical-box, if this does not cost too much; they are things which will give him much pleasure."

This story is especially interesting because it shows what ground Tolstoy has travelled over in his spiritual development. It reaches from his naïve mystical belief in God's interference with his gambling and monetary affairs, to the perfect religious freedom confessed by him now.

Finally, a few days after this letter was written and his official matters arranged, Tolstoy returned to Starogladovskaya. On his journey from Mozdok station, probably while waiting for horses, he wrote a long letter to his aunt, full of the most profound religious thoughts and, as usual, overflowing with tenderness to this beloved relative, and with visions and plans concerning a future of simple family happiness.

"Here are the thoughts which occurred to me. I will try to express them to you, as I was thinking of you. I find myself greatly changed morally, and this has been the case so very often. However I believe such is every one's fate. The longer one lives the more one changes: you who have got experience tell me, is not this true? I think that the defects and the good qualities—the background of one's character—will always remain the same, but the way of regarding life and happiness must change with age. A year ago I thought I should find happiness in pleasure, in movement; now, on the contrary, rest, both physical and moral, is the state I desire. But I imagine that the state of rest without worry, and with the quiet enjoyments of love and friendship, is the acme of happiness for me! But one feels the charm of rest only after fatigue, and of the enjoyment of love only after being without it. Here I am deprived for some time both of the one and of the other; this is why I long for them so keenly. I *must* be deprived of them yet longer—for how long, God knows. I cannot say why, but I feel that I *must*. Religion and the experience I have of life, however small this be, have taught me that life is a trial. In my case it is more than a trial, it is also the expiation of my mistakes.

"I have an inkling that the seemingly frivolous idea I had of going for a journey to the Caucasus was an idea inspired in me from above. It was the hand of God which guided me—I do not cease to be thankful for it. I feel I have become better here (though that is not saying much, since I had been very bad), and I am firmly persuaded that all that can happen to me here will only be for my good, since it is God Himself who has willed thus. Perhaps the idea is too presumptuous. Nevertheless I have this conviction. For this reason I bear the fatigues and the privations of which I speak (they are not physical privations—such do not exist for a young man of twenty-three who is in good health) without suffering from them, even with a kind of pleasure in thinking of the happiness awaiting me.

"This is how I represent it to myself:

"After an indefinite number of years, neither young nor old, I am at Yasnaya, my affairs are in order, I have no anxieties, no worries. You are also living at Yasnaya. You have become a little older, but are still fresh and in good health. We lead the life we have led; I work in the morning, but we see each other almost all the day. We dine. In the evening I read to you something which does not weary you, then we talk—I relate to you my life in the Caucasus, you relate your memories of my father and my mother, you tell those 'dreadful' stories which we used to listen to with frightened eyes and open mouth. We remind each other of those who have been dear to us and are with us no longer; you weep, I shall do the same, but these tears shall be sweet; we will talk about my brothers, who will come to see us from time to time; of dear Marie, who will also pass some months of the year with her children at Yasnaya, which she so likes. We shall have no acquaintances—no one will come to bore us and to gossip. It is a fine dream, but it is not yet all I allow myself to dream of. I am married. My wife is a sweet, good, loving person; she has the same affection for you as I have; we have children who call you Grandmamma; you live in the big house upstairs in the same room which Grandmother occupied in past times. All the house is arranged in the same way as it was in Papa's time, and we recommence the same life, only changing our parts. You take the character of Grandmamma, but you are yet better; I take the character of Papa, but I despair of ever deserving it; my wife the place of Mamma, the children ours; Marie the rôle of the Aunts, their misfortunes excepted; even Gasha takes the rôle of Praskovya Ilyinishna. But some one will be wanted to take the part which you have played in our family—never will there be found a soul so beautiful, so loving as yours. You have no successor. There will be three new personages who will appear from time to time on the scene, the brothers, especially the one who will often be with you; Nicolas, an old bachelor, bald, retired from service, always as good as he is noble.

"I can imagine how he will, as in the old days, tell the children stories of his own invention, how the children will kiss his greasy hands (but which are worthy of it), how he will play with them, how my wife will take pains to prepare his dish for him, how he and I will talk over common memories of days long past, how you will sit in your customary place and listen to us with pleasure; how you will call us old men, but, as of yore, Lyovochka and Nicolenka, and will scold me for eating with my fingers and him for his hands not being clean.

"Were I to be made Emperor of Russia, or were some one to give me Peru—in a word, were a fairy with a wand to come and ask me what I would like to have, with my hand on my heart I should answer, I only desire that this dream might become a reality. I know you do not like to forecast, but what harm is there in it? And it gives so much pleasure. I am afraid I have been egotistical and have made your portion of happiness too small. I am afraid that misfortunes which have passed, but have left too tender chords in your heart, will hinder you from enjoying this future which would have made my happiness. Dear Aunt, tell me, would you be happy? All I have said may happen, and hope is such a delicious thing.

"I am weeping again. Why do I weep when I think of you? They are tears of happiness; I am happy to know I love you. Were all calamities to afflict me, I should never call myself quite unhappy as long as you existed. Do you remember our parting in the chapel of Uverskaya when we left for Kazan? Then, as if by inspiration, at the moment of leaving you, I understood all you were to me, and although yet a child, I was able to make you understand what I felt by my tears and a few incoherent words. I have never ceased to love you, but the feeling I experienced in that chapel and the one I now have for you are quite different; this one is much stronger, more elevated, than I have had at any other time. I must confess to you something which makes me feel ashamed, but which I must tell you in order to free my conscience. Formerly, on reading your letters, in which you spoke to me of the feelings you had for us, I thought I saw some exaggeration, but only now, on reading them, do I understand you—your unlimited love for us and your elevated soul. I am sure that any one else but you on reading this letter and the last one would have cast the same reproach on me; but I am not afraid of your doing this, you know me too well, and you know that perhaps sensibility is my only virtue. It is to this quality that I owe the happiest moments of my life. At all events this is the last letter in which I shall allow myself to express such high-flown sentiments, high-flown in the eyes of the indifferent, but you will be able to appreciate them."

In January, 1852, Tolstoy returned to Starogladovsk already a non-commissioned officer, and in the following February he took part as a gunner in a campaign.

In March he was again in Starogladovsk. It is interesting to note the few thoughts written down by him in his diary of that time.

He realized that three passions were hindering him on his way toward the moral idea which he placed before himself. These passions were card-playing, sensuality or lust, and vanity. He thus defined and characterized these respective passions:

"(1) Passion for gambling is a greedy passion which gradually develops a craving for strong excitement. But it is possible to resist it.

"(2) The indulgence of sensual passion is a physical need, a need of the body excited by the imagination; abstinence increases the desire and makes it very difficult to contend with. The best method is labor and occupation.

"(3) Vanity: this passion is the one by which we do least injury to others and the most to ourselves."

Further on are the following reflections:

"For some time back I have been greatly tormented by regrets at the loss of the best years of my life. It may be interesting to describe the progress of my moral development ever since I have begun to feel that I could have done something good; but I will use no more words, even thought itself is insufficient.

"There are no limits for a great thought, but writers have long ago reached the absolute limits of its expression. . . . There is something in me which compels me to believe that I am not born to be like every one."

These last words represent his first vague consciousness of his vocation. It should be observed that they were written before he had finished *Childhood,* and therefore before he had been praised and congratulated on a successful literary performance. It was rather an internal independent consciousness of that mysterious power he had which has since placed him so high as one of the best representatives of the moral consciousness of humanity.

In the month of May he got leave of absence and went to Piatigorsk, to drink the waters and to be treated for rheumatism.

From there he writes a letter to his aunt which gives a picture of his spiritual growth, and points to the incessant activity of his inner life.

"Since my journey and stay at Tiflis my way of life has not changed; I endeavor to make as few acquaintances as possible, and to avoid intimacy with those whose acquaintance I have made. People have become accustomed to my manner, they no longer importune me, and I am sure they say he is a 'strange' or a 'proud' man.

"It is not from pride that I behave thus, but it has come of itself. There is too great a difference between the education, the sentiments, and the point of view of those whom I meet here and my own for me to find any pleasure in their society. It is Nicolas who has the talent, notwithstanding the enormous difference there is between him and all these gentlemen, to amuse himself with them and be liked by all. I envy him this talent, but feel I cannot do the same. It is true that this kind of life is not adapted for one's amusement, and for a very long time I have not thought about pleasures. I think about being quiet and contented. Some time ago I began to appreciate historical reading (it was a point of contention between us, but I am at present quite of your opinion); my literary occupations also advance in their little way although I do not yet contemplate publishing anything. I have written three times over a work I had begun a very long time ago, and I intend rewriting it once more in order to be satisfied with it. Perhaps the task will be like that of Penelope, but that does not deter me, I do not write from ambition, but because I enjoy it; I find pleasure and profit in working, and I work. Although I am far from amusing myself, as I have told you, I am also very far from being dull, as I have got something to do; besides this, I enjoy a pleasure sweeter and more elevated than any that society could have given me—that of feeling at rest in my conscience; of knowing myself, of understanding myself better than I did formerly, and of feeling good and generous sentiments stirring within me.

"There was a time when I was vain of my intelligence, of my position in this world, and of my name, but now I know and feel that if there is anything good in me, and if I have to thank Providence for it, it is a kind heart, sensitive and capable of love, that it has pleased God to give me and to keep for me.

"It is to this alone that I owe the brightest moments I have, and the fact that, notwithstanding the absence of pleasures and society, I am not only at my ease but often happy."

In a letter of June 24, 1852, to his brother Sergey, he gives characteristic details of his life in Piatigorsk:

"What shall I tell you about my life? I have written three letters, and in each have described the same thing. I should like to tell to you the *spirit* of Piatigorsk, but it is as difficult as it is to tell to a stranger in what *Tula* consists, which we unfortunately understand very well. Piatigorsk is also something of a Tula, but of a special kind—the Caucasian; for instance, here the chief feature is *family houses and public promenades.* Society consists of landowners (this is the technical term for all visitors to the place), who look down upon the local civilization, and of officers, who look upon the local pleasures as the height of bliss. Along with me there arrived from headquarters an officer of our battery. You should have seen his delight and excitement when we entered the town! He had already told me a great deal about the distractions of watering-places, how every one walks up and down the boulevards to the sound of music, and then, as he declared, all go to the pastry cook's, and there make acquaintance even with family houses. There is the theatre, there are the clubs, every year marriages take place, duels, etc. . . . —*in one word, it is quite a Parisian life.* The moment we got out of our travelling cart, my officer put on blue trousers with fearfully tight riding-straps, boots with enormous spurs, epaulettes, and so got himself up and went for a walk along the boulevard to the sound of music, then to the pastry cook's, the theatre, and the club, but, so far as I know, instead of an acquaintance with family houses, and a bride who owned 1,000 serfs, he—in the course of a whole month—only made acquaintance with three shabby officers who emptied his pockets to the last penny at cards, and with one family house, in which, however, two families live in one room, and tea is served with little scraps of sugar to put in one's mouth. This officer, moreover, spent in one month about 20 roubles on porter and sweets, and purchased a bronze mirror for the adornment of his toilet table. Now he is walking in an old jacket without epaulettes, is drinking brimstone water as hard as he can, and appears to be taking a serious cure; but he is astonished that, although he walked every day on the boulevard, frequented the pastry cook's and did not spare money on the theatre, as well as on cabs and gloves, he could not get acquainted with the aristocracy (here in every little fort there is an aristocracy), while the aristocracy, as if to spite him, arranges rides and picnics, and he is not admitted anywhere. Almost all the officers who come here suffer a like fate, but they pretend they came only for 'treatment,' so they limp on crutches, wear slings and bandages, get drunk, and tell strange stories about the Cherkessi. Yet at headquarters they will again tell people how they were acquainted with family houses, and amused themselves tremendously; and every season they go to the watering-places in crowds to amuse themselves."

As is evident from his letter to his aunt in Piatigorsk, Tolstoy continued writing *Childhood*. At the same time his self-scrutiny never stopped. On June 29th he wrote in his diary a thought which might well serve as a short expression of his present view of life:

" Conscience is our best and surest guide, but where are the marks distinguishing this voice from other voices? . . . The voice of vanity speaks no less powerfully. For instance —an unrevenged offence.

" The man whose object is his own happiness is bad; he whose aim is to get the good opinion of others is bad too, he is weak; one whose object is the happiness of others is virtuous; he whose object is God is great."

This again is a thought which we find further developed in his later works:

" Justice is the least measure of virtue to which every one is bound. Anything higher than justice shows an aspiration to perfection, anything lower is (no better than) vice."

July 2d Tolstoy finished *Childhood*, and in a few days sent the manuscript to the editor of *The Contemporary* in St. Petersburg.

The original title of his first literary work was *The Story of My Childhood*. It was signed with the three letters L. N. T., and the editor for a considerable time did not know the name of the author.

In Piatigorsk Tolstoy saw his sister and her husband. Marie was undergoing treatment for rheumatism at the watering-place. According to her account, Tolstoy was then carried away by spiritualistic experiments such as the turning of the tables; he even carried this on in the boulevard, taking chairs for it from the café.

On August 5th Tolstoy left Piatigorsk and returned to his outpost.

On his journey he wrote down the following interesting thought, which is one of the leading principles of his present view of life:

"The future occupies us more than the present. This is a good thing if we think of a future in another world. To live in the present, *i. e.*, to act in the best way in the present —that is wisdom."

On August 7th he arrived in Starogladovsk, and on returning to his beloved and familiar patriarchal surroundings of Cossack life, he wrote in his diary:

"Simplicity—that is the virtue I desire above all others to acquire."

On August 28th he at last received the long-expected letter from the editor of *The Contemporary*. "It made me silly with joy," he noted in his diary.

Here is the celebrated letter of Nekrassof, who was the sponsor of the newly born talent:

"Sir—I have read your manuscript (*Childhood*). It is so far interesting, and I will print it. It seems to me, though I cannot say positively, not having seen the continuation, that the author is a man of talent. At any rate, the author's tendencies, the simplicity and lifelike character of the story are incontestable merits. If the following parts contain (as one may expect they will) more vivacity and movement, it will turn out a very good novel. Please forward the continuation. Your novel and your talent interest me. I would advise you not to conceal your identity under initials, but to appear with your full name at once, if only you are not a casual visitor in the domain of literature. I hope to hear from you. Accept my best respects,

"N. Nekrassof."[1]

After this, in a month's time, followed a second letter.

"St. Petersburg, *September* 5, 1852.

"Sir—I wrote to you about your novel, and now I consider it my duty to add a few more words. I sent it to be printed in the ninth number of *The Contemporary*, and, after reading it carefully, this time not in manuscript but in proof form, I came to the conclusion that the novel is much better than it appeared to me at first. I can positively say that the author is a man of talent. It is most important for you yourself to be convinced of this now, when you are a beginner. The number of *The Contemporary* with your contribution in it will appear to-morrow in St. Petersburg, but you will only get it in three weeks' time, not before. I will send it on to your address. I have omitted some parts of your novel, but very little; however. . . . I have not added anything. I will write again before long in detail, but I am busy just now. I expect your answer, and beg you to forward me the continuation, if ready for the press.

"N. Nekrassof.

"*P. S.*—Though I believe I have guessed the name of the author, still I beg you to inform me of it. In fact I must know it, because of the rules of our censorship."

Of this letter Tolstoy wrote in his diary, "September 30, Received a letter from Nekrassof, but no money."

He was in need of money at that time, and expected his honorarium for his first literary work. He probably wrote about it to Nekrassof, for he received a third letter from him, of which the contents were as follows:

"St. Petersburg, *October* 30, 1852.

"Dear Sir—I beg to be excused for my delay in answering your last letter—I was very busy. As to the money

[1] Literary supplement to the magazine *Niva*, February, 1898, p. 337.

matter, I said nothing about it in my previous letters for the following reason; our best periodicals have long made it a custom not to pay anything for the first novel to a commencing author, who is first introduced to the public by the periodical itself. All who began their literary career in *The Contemporary*, such as Gentcharof, Drujinin, Ardeyef, and others, had to submit to this custom. When it came out, my own first work, as well as one of Panayef's, had to submit to the same custom. I propose to you to do the same thing, and you can make it a condition that for your subsequent works I will pay you the best honorarium, which is given only to our best-known (very few) novel writers, that is to say, fifty roubles for sixteen pages of printed matter. I should add that I put off writing to you, because I could not make you such an offer before verifying my impression by the judgment of the reading public. This judgment turned out very favorable to you, and I am very glad to make no mistake in my estimate of your first work, so I offer you now with pleasure the above-mentioned conditions of payment.

"Please let me know what you think about it. In any case I can guarantee that we will come to an agreement on this point. As your novel has had so much success, we should be very glad soon to get your second work. Please send what you have now ready for print.

"I wanted to send you the ninth number of *The Contemporary*, but unfortunately I forgot to order extra copies to be printed, and the whole of this year's issues are sold out. However, if you like, I can send you one or two reprints of your novel—this can be done by making use of the defective copies.

"Once more allow me to ask you to send us a novel, or a tale of some kind. I remain, in expectation of your answer, yours truly, N. NEKRASSOF.

"*P. S.*—We are bound to know the names of all the authors whose works we publish, so please give me exact information concerning this point. If you wish it, no one but the publishers shall know it."

Thus, judging by Nekrassof's letter, on the 6th of September, 1852, an event of great significance occurred in the history of Russian literature: Tolstoy's first work appeared in print that day.

Tolstoy mentions this episode, with his usual modesty, in a letter to his aunt Tatiana, dated October 28, 1852.

"On my return from the baths I passed a month rather disagreeably owing to the review which the general was going to hold. Marching and discharging different kinds of guns are not very pleasant, especially as the exercise interferes with any settled habits of my life. Fortunately it did not last long, and I have again resumed my way of life, consisting in sport, writing, reading, and conversations with Nicolas. I have taken to shooting, and as I have turned out to be a tolerably good shot, this occupation takes up two or three hours a day. In Russia they have no idea how much and what excellent game is to be found here. A hundred yards from where I live I find pheasants, and in half an hour I bag two, three, or four. Besides the pleasure, the exercise is good for my health, which, in spite of the waters, is not in first-rate condition. I am not ill, but I very often suffer from colds, at one time from a bad throat, at another from toothache, which I have still got; at times from rheumatism, so that at least for two days a week I keep my room. Do not think I am concealing anything from you: I am, as I have always been, of a strong constitution, but of weak health. I intend passing next summer again at the waters. If I am not cured by them, I am sure they have done me good—'there is no evil without good.' When I am indisposed, I can work, with less fear of being distracted, at another novel which I have begun. The one I sent to St. Petersburg is published in the September number of the *Sovremennik* for 1852 under the title of *Childhood*. I have signed it L. N. T., and no one except Nicolas knows who is the author. I should not like it to be known."

Marie, Tolstoy's sister, told me about the impression which this thing produced in the family circle. They lived on their estate, not far from that of Turgenef-Spasskoye, who used to visit them. On one occasion Turgenef arrived at their place with the latest number of *The Contemporary*, and read out a novel by an unknown author which he praised highly. Marie heard with surprise the story of events of her own family, wondering who could be aware of the intimate details of their life. How little idea they had that their own Lyovochka might be the author of this novel was shown by the fact of Nicolay Nikolayevich being suspected to have written it; the fact was he had manifested literary inclinations from his childhood, and was a splendid story-teller. Evidently his devoted aunt Tatiana knew how to keep the secret intrusted to her, and it probably leaked out only on Tolstoy's arrival from the Caucasus.

In her reminiscences Mme. Golovachof-Panayef gives an interesting description of the impression made by the first novel of Tolstoy on both readers and authors.

"On all sides praises were showered upon the new author by the reading public, and everybody wanted to know his name. As to the men of letters, they treated the newly born talent more or less indifferently, with the exception of Panayef, who was so delighted with *The History of My Childhood* that he read it aloud every evening to some of his friends. Turgenef laughed at Panayef to his face, and said that his friends, when meeting him at the Nevsky Prospect, hid themselves for fear lest he should start reading passages from the new novel, which he had already managed to learn by heart.

"The literary critics were slow to notice Tolstoy. At least in Zelinsky's volume of literary criticisms upon Tolstoy—a carefully written book—the first critical review is mentioned as having appeared in 1854. It was printed in the monthly serial, *Memoirs of the Fatherland*, in November of that year, that is to say more than two years after *Childhood* appeared in print. The article was written *à propos* of the publication of *Boyhood*, and both novels were reviewed in it.

We quote here the short but striking critique of Tolstoy's first work:

"*Childhood*—an immense chain of various poetical and unconscious conceptions of the surroundings, enabled the author to view country life in the same poetical light. He selected from this life all that strikes the mind and imagination of the child, and with the author's powerful talent this life is presented just as the child sees it. Of the environment he introduces into his story as much as strikes the imagination of the child; that is why all the chapters of the novel, though apparently disconnected, have a perfect unity: they show the child's standpoint of the world. But the great talent of the author is further seen in what follows. It might be thought that in depicting the world from the impressions of a child one could hardly present life and mankind from other than a childish point of view. We are the more surprised to find after reading these tales, that they leave in the imagination the lifelike portraiture of father, mother, nurse, and tutor, in short the whole family, and all represented in the most poetical colors." [1]

In proportion to the growing circulation of *The Contemporary* grew the interest of the reading public in the newly rising talent.

When the copies of *The Contemporary* containing the stories *Childhood* and *Boyhood* reached Dostoyevsky in Siberia they deeply impressed him. In a letter to one of his friends in Semipalatinsk he insisted on being told who this mysterious L. N. T. was.

But the mysterious L. N. T., as if of set purpose, declined to reveal his identity, and only watched from the outside the sensation he had made.

In October, while living in the village Starogladovsk, he sketched the plan for a work, *The Novel of a Russian Landlord,* of which the fundamental idea was as follows:

"The hero seeks for the realization of his ideal of happiness and justice in the conditions of country life. Not finding it, he is disillusioned and searches for it in family life. His friend suggests to him the idea that happiness does not consist in any ideal, but in one's continual work with the happiness of others for its object."

Unfortunately the plan was not realized, but the same ideas are developed in many of his following works.

In spite of his prominent position, a military career proved not to his taste. It was evidently a burden to him, and he only waited to get his commission in order to be allowed to leave.

But this promotion was slow in coming, and it looked as if the delay was intentional. When he entered the service he expected to be promoted in about eighteen months, but after nearly a year's service he received at the end of October, a notice informing him that he must first serve three more years.

[1] *Memoirs of the Fatherland*, 1854, No. 11 (Journalism).

The reason for the delay turned out to be his negligence in sending in his papers.

In the Memoirs of Countess S. A. Tolstoy we read the following:

"The promotion of Tolstoy as well as his service had been full of great difficulties and failures. Before his departure for the Caucasus he lived in Yasnaya Polyana with his aunt Tatiana. He often met his brother Sergey, who at that time was very much interested in gypsies and their singing. The gypsies used to come to Yasnaya Polyana, and would sing, and turn the heads of the two brothers. When Tolstoy realized that this might lead to some foolish action, he suddenly, without warning to any one, left for the Caucasus and took no papers with him."

This carelessness, or rather hatred of all kinds of business documents, more than once caused a great deal of embarrassment to Tolstoy.

In his impatience he sent a complaint to his aunt P. Yushkof, who wrote to certain high officials, and so managed to hasten his promotion to the rank of officer.

On December 24th of the same year he finished his tale *The Invaders*, and two days later sent it to the editor of *The Contemporary*.

In January, 1853, Tolstoy's battery had to march against Shamyl.

In the history of the 20th Artillery Brigade, in the description of this campaign, we find the following passage:

"At one of the guns of the chief detachment at No. 4 Battery there acted as gunner Count L. Tolstoy, afterward author of the immortal works *A Wood-Cutting Expedition, The Cossacks, War and Peace,* etc."

The detachment was settled in the fortress Groznaya where, according to Tolstoy, card-playing and carousals constantly went on.

"January 18, as stated in the history of the brigade, the detachment returned from Kurinskoye. During the last three days the seven guns of the column discharged about 800 volleys, and of these about 600 were discharged by five guns of the Battery No. 4 of the Brigade No. 20, which were under the command of Lieutenant Makalinsky and Sub-Lieutenants Sulimovsky and Ladizhensky, under whose authority Count L. Tolstoy served as gunner of the 4th

Division. On January 19 he was despatched with a howitzer to the fort and village of Gerzel."[1]

Tolstoy also took part in the engagement of February 18th, when he was exposed to great danger, being only a hair's-breadth from death. As he was sighting a gun, the enemy's shell broke the gun-carriage and burst at his feet. Fortunately, it did him no harm.

On April 1st he returned with his detachment to Starogladovsk.

From the first steps of his literary activity Tolstoy had to come into contact with the senseless cruelty of that irresponsible power, which has now for more than a century been obstructing without intermission the free development of Russian thought. I mean what is called the censorship.

In a letter to his brother Sergey of May, 1853, Tolstoy writes:

"I am writing in a hurry, so please excuse this letter being short and disorderly. *Childhood* has been spoiled by the censorship, and *The Expedition* has quite perished under it. All that was good in them is deleted or mutilated. I have handed in my resignation, and one of these days, *i.e.*, in about six weeks, I hope to go as a free man to Pyatigorsk and so on to Russia."

But getting leave of absence was no such easy matter, and in the summer of 1853 Tolstoy was again in a dangerous position, and with great difficulty was saved from being taken prisoner.

We take the description of this incident from the Memoirs of Poltoratsky:

"On June 13, 1853, I joined the 5th and 6th squads of Kurinsky and a company of the battalion of the line with two guns, and we set out on an expedition for which we were drafted off[2] to the fortress of Groznaya. After a halt at Yermolof's Knoll, the column started in marching order. When I came up to the middle of the column, which stretched out along the road, I suddenly noticed, not far from the advanced guard, to the left of the upper plain between Khan Kale and the Tower of Groznaya, a party of

---

[1] Yanzhul, *The History of the Artillery Brigade*, No. 20.
[2] During the war with the mountaineers, military expeditions were very dangerous. Such operations usually took place under the protection of a strong convoy of soldiers. Naturally, all kinds of errands for those in service were combined with these movements, which for that reason were called "occasions."

from twenty to twenty-five Tchetchenzi horsemen heedlessly galloping down the incline and across the line of our column.

"I rushed onward to the advanced guard and soon heard a volley of gun-shots, but before I had time to reach the 5th Company I saw at a distance of about forty yards the gun unlimbered and the linstock over it. 'Put it back, put it back, our men are there!' I shouted at the top of my voice, and fortunately succeeded in stopping the discharge, which was aimed at the group of horsemen huddled together, among whom were evidently some of our men. Upon my order the 3d platoon rushed forward, but they hardly made a few steps when the Tchetchenians turned to flight down the plain to Argun, and then two shells were discharged in their pursuit. At the same time, from the spot where the conflict took place, Baron Rosen, deadly pale and very shaky, rode up to the column. He was almost immediately followed by a horse without a saddle, which was recognized as belonging to a platoon officer. At that moment, from behind the short bushes growing on the road, there appeared the artillery ensign Scherbachof. This young, ruddy-complexioned man of nineteen summers, who only a few months before had left the artillery school and struck everybody by his appearance of good health and his extraordinary frame and strength, at this moment shocked us all.

"He came up with deliberate but firm steps, without limping or groaning, and only when he calmly came quite near did we see how badly he had been hurt by the Tchetchenians. Blood was spouting like a fountain from bullet wounds in his chest and both his legs, from a grape-shot wound in the abdomen, and a slash on the neck from a sabre. With the column there was no doctor and no medical assistant, so the barbers of the company had to do what they could, and one of them skilfully and quickly dressed the wounds. Meanwhile, Rosen, who had recovered a little from his fright, explained that five of them rode on in advance of the column and, at the moment of the attack by the mountaineers, Count Lyof Tolstoy, Pavel Poltoratsky, and the Tartar Sado probably escaped to Groznaya, while he and Scherbachof turned their horses back to the column which was moving up behind them. 'Your honor,' interrupted an artillery soldier lying on a high pile of hay, 'there is another man lying on the road, and I believe he is moving.' I shouted to the third platoon, 'Forward, double quick!' and rushed down the road. At a distance of about one hundred yards from the guns of the advanced guard lay a dead raven-hued horse well known to us, and almost buried beneath him was the maimed body of Pavel.[1] He moaned aloud, and in a heartrending voice begged to be set free from the unbearable weight of the dead horse. I sprang from my horse and, throwing the bridle to a Cossack, with one haul, which cost me an extraordinary effort, I turned over the carcass of the horse and freed the sufferer, who was bleeding to death. He had been wounded by sidearms, having received three blows on the head and four on the shoulder. The latter were so deep that they literally divided the shoulder in two, exposing a wide extent of flesh. I sent by a Cossack an order for the whole column to move on to where we were, and here the dressing of the wounds was begun, and the stretchers were made ready.

"All this happened in a few minutes, during which we managed, however, to render first help to the wounded, while the cavalry of the Groznaya fortress was induced to rush out. The commander of the garrison, seeing from the heights our column in perfect order and the Tchetchenians disappearing in the horizon, concluded that it was useless to pursue them, and ordered the soldiers to return to the fortress. But a few horsemen, having separated from the rest, galloped onward to reach our column, which was at a distance of about four versts from Groznaya. These were Pistolkorse and several of his Circassian friends, from the friendly Tchetchenians inhabiting the villages about Groznaya. By common efforts we constructed a kind of stretcher out of the soldiers' overcoats, placed both the wounded thereon, and started on our journey. Pistolkorse informed us that Count Lyof Tolstoy and the Tartar Sado were hotly pursued by seven of the Tchetchenians, but, thanks to the speed of their horses, they reached the gates of the fortress unhurt, leaving the enemies a trophy in the shape of a saddle cushion.

"Tolstoy and his friend Sado and three companions were impatient to arrive before the rest at Groznaya, and detached themselves from the column at Yermolof's Knoll.

[1] Pavel Poltoratsky, the nephew of the writer.

THE CAUCASUS

This manœuvre is unfortunately only known too well in the Caucasus! Who of us, if mounted on a spirited horse, but obliged to move on step by step in the occasion with the infantry, would not gallop away in advance? This is a temptation to which old and young often yielded, contrary to the strict prohibitions and discipline of the authorities. And our five brave fellows did the same. Leaving the column thirty yards behind them, they agreed that two of them, for the purpose of reconnoitring, should ride along the upper recess and the remaining three by the lower road. No sooner did Tolstoy and Sado mount the ridge than they descried a crowd of Tchetchenian riders, who from the Khan-Kalsky forest were flying straight upon them. Not having time to descend without great risk, Tolstoy shouted from above informing his comrades of the enemy's appearance, and himself with Sado galloped away at full speed along the ridge of the recess to the fortress. Those below did not at first believe the news, and not being able to see the mountaineers had lost a few minutes; when the Tchetchenians (seven of them started pursuing Tolstoy and Sado) appeared on the recess and rushed downward, Baron Rosen turned his horse and galloped back to the column and reached it safely. Scherbachof followed him, but his horse, given by the Government, galloped badly, and the Tchetchenians overtook him, wounded him, and threw him off the saddle, after which he managed to reach the column on foot. Pavel's turned out the worse case. Having caught sight of the Tchetchenians he instinctively rushed forward in the direction of Groznaya, but at once realized that his young, wellfed and petted horse could not in hot weather gallop the five versts dividing him from the fortress, so he abruptly turned backward at the very moment when the enemy had already come down the recess on the road, and, with his sabre unsheathed, as a last resource he intended to force his way back to the column. But one of the mountaineers aimed his carbine well, and, waiting for Pavel's approach, lodged a bullet in the forehead of his raven horse; it fell down dead, burying its rider underneath. One Tchetchenian bent from his horse toward Pavel, and, snatching out of his hands the silver-mounted sabre, he pulled off the sheath, but seeing the third platoon, which was hurrying to Pavel's assistance, he slashed him with his sabre on the head and ran away. His example was followed by the remaining six mountaineers one after another, who, riding by in full speed, each dealt heavy blows on the head and shoulders of Pavel, who lay motionless under the weight of his dead horse and bleeding to death, up to the very moment of our arrival." [1]

In the reminiscences of Bers we learn one more detail of this affair characterizing Tolstoy:

"The peaceful Tchetchenian Sado, with whom Tolstoy rode out that day, was his great friend. They had only recently exchanged horses. Sado had bought a young horse, and after having given it a trial, gave it to his friend Tolstoy, and himself mounted the latter's ambler, which, as it is well known, cannot gallop. When they were overtaken by the Tchetchenians, Tolstoy could have galloped away on the spirited horse of his friend, but he did not leave him. Sado, like all mountaineers, never parted from his gun, but unfortunately this time it was not loaded. Still he aimed it at the pursuers, and shouted threateningly at them. Judging by the actions of the pursuers, they intended to take both as prisoners, especially Sado, out of revenge; for that reason they did not shoot. This saved them. They managed to approach Groznaya, where a vigilant sentinel noticed the pursuit afar and sounded the alarm. The appearance of the Cossacks on the road induced the Tchetchenians to stop the pursuit."

This incident served Tolstoy as a basis for his story, *A Prisoner in the Caucasus*.

But neither the dangers of the military career, nor the fits of vice and gambling which burst like hurricanes into his peaceful life, arrested the general development of Tolstoy's character, and soon after the incident just described he writes down the following thoughts or maxims:

"Be straightforward, and, even if brusque, be frank with all, but not childishly frank without due occasion.

"Refrain from wine and women.

"Delight is rare and imperfect, but repentance is complete.

"Give thyself up completely to every work thou doest. Under a strong feeling pause always before action, but having once made thy mind up, even wrongly, act with resolution."

---

[1] "Reminiscences of V. A. Poltoratsky." *Historical Review*, June, 1893, p. 672.

SERGEY   DIMITRY

NICOLAY   LEO

Tolstoy and his brothers before he left to join the
Danube Army, 1854.

In the middle of July, 1853, Tolstoy went to Pyatigorsk, and remained there till October, returning afterward to Starogladovsk. Evidently the monotonous service began to be very wearisome, and he was looking forward to a change in his life.

Meantime he wrote from Pyatigorsk to his brother as follows:

"I think I have already written to you about my having handed in my resignation. God knows, however, whether it will be accepted, and when, in view of the war with Turkey. This disturbs me very much, as I have now become so accustomed to the happy thought of soon settling down in the country, that to return again to Staroglavosk and wait till eternity, as I do for everything connected with my service, is very unpleasant."

The same frame of mind is perceptible in a letter from Staroglavosk, written in December, 1853.

"Please write to me quickly about my papers. This is necessary. *When shall I arrive?* God only knows, for it will soon be a year since I have considered how I can re-sheath my sword, and still I cannot do it. However, as I must fight somewhere, I find it pleasanter to fight in Turkey than here, and have accordingly applied to Prince Sergey Dmitriyevich, who wrote me that he had already written to his brother, but did not know what the result might be.

"At all events, before the New Year I expect a change in my way of life, which I confess has become inexpressibly wearisome to me. Silly officers, silly conversations, nothing else. If there were only one man with whom one might have a talk from one's soul! Turgenef is right in speaking of the 'irony of solitude,' when by oneself one becomes perceptibly stupid. Though Nicolenka took away with him —God knows why—the greyhounds (we, Epishka and I, often call him a pig for this), still, during whole days from morning till night, I go out shooting alone with a dog. And this is my only pleasure; indeed, not a pleasure, but a means of stupefaction. You get tired and hungry, and fall dead asleep, and the day is passed. If you have an opportunity, or should be in Moscow, buy for me Dickens' *David Copperfield* in English, and send me Saddler's English Dictionary, which is among my books."

During this time Tolstoy was writing his *Boyhood*, and had finished a tale called *The Recollections of a Billiard-Marker*, which was sent to the editor of *The Contemporary*, expressing at the same time his dissatisfaction with his work, and the hurry in which it was done.

About the same time one of his occupations was reading Schiller's biography.

After having returned from a short journey to the village of Khassaf-Yurt, Tolstoy puts down in his diary:

" For all the prayers I have invented I substitute a single one, ' Our Father.' All the petitions I am able to address to God are expressed in a way much more elevated and much worthier of Him in the words: ' Thy will be done on earth as it is in heaven.' "

In her Memoirs the Countess S. A. Tolstoy describes another interesting incident of his Caucasian life—the attitude of Tolstoy to the St. George's Cross.

Readers are already aware that Tolstoy had distinguished himself several times in military exploits, and that he coveted the reward of the soldier's St. George's Cross. The commander of his battery, Colonel Alexeyef, was very fond of Tolstoy. After one of the engagements, several St. George's Crosses had been sent to the battery. These crosses were to be distributed next day, but on the eve of this day Tolstoy had to be on duty on the island where the guns were placed.

With his usual inclination to be carried away by everything, he, instead of going, played chess till late at night, and was not on duty. The commander of the division, Olifer, not finding him on duty, was very angry, reprimanded him severely, and put him under arrest.

The following day the crosses were distributed in the regiment, and the bands played. Tolstoy knew that he was to have had one, but, instead of enjoying the grand event, he was in prison and in despair at the time.

Another opportunity presented itself for receiving the cross, but it again proved a failure, the reason of the failure being, however, more to his credit.

Crosses were sent to the battery for good conduct in a certain engagement with mountaineers. This time Tolstoy knew beforehand that he was to get one.

But just before the distribution Colonel Alexeyef spoke

to him in the following terms: " You know that St. George's Crosses are mostly given to old, deserving soldiers, to whom they give a right to life pensions in proportions to the salary they have been receiving during service. On the other hand, crosses are given to those non-commissioned officers who are in favor with their superiors. The more crosses that are received by the non-commissioned officers, the more are taken away from the old, deserving soldiers. I will give you one if you like, but, if you are willing to decline it, it will be given to an old and very worthy soldier who deserves such a cross and who is looking forward to it as a means of livelihood." Notwithstanding his passionate desire to own the cross, Tolstoy immediately gave up his claim, and after this he had no further opportunity of getting it.

To conclude our description of Tolstoy's life in the Caucasus, we will quote a few lines from the reminiscences of an officer, M. A. Yanzhul, who served in the seventies in the village Starogladovsk, and came across traces of Tolstoy's sojourn there.

"In 1871 I was made officer of the 20th Artillery Brigade, of the same brigade and village of Starogladovsk in which seventeen years before Count L. N. Tolstoy had lived and served in the army. The village of Starogladosk with its handsome women of the striking local type, its valiant Grebensky Cossacks, and 'the commander's house surrounded by high old poplars,' described by Tolstoy in his well-known story, *The Cossacks*, had been familiar to me for more than twenty years. At my time the memory of Lyof Nicolayevich, as they called him there, was still fresh in the village. They used to point out to me the old Maryana, the heroine of the story, and several old Cossack sportsmen, who knew Tolstoy personally and had with him shot pheasants, and hunted wild boars. One of these Cossacks, as all know, went on horseback in the eighties from the village to Yasnaya Polyana to pay Tolstoy a visit. At the battery I met Captain Trolof (now deceased), who had known Tolstoy as a quarter-gunner, and related incidentally that even then the Count possessed the marvellous capacity of a story-teller who carried away the listeners by his interesting conversation."[1]

[1] "Notices of L. N. Tolstoy," by M. A. Yanzhul. *Russian Olden Times*, February 1890, p. 335.

Further on Yanzhul gives a short sketch of the character of Tolstoy's superior, the commander of his battery:

"Nikita Petrovich Alexeyef, the commander of the battery in which Count Tolstoy served, was loved and respected by all for his kindness. He enjoyed the reputation of a scholarly *artillerist*, a universalist, was distinguished for his extreme piety, and was particularly fond of going to church, where he spent hours kneeling and making bows. To this is to be added, that he had lost one ear, which a horse had bitten off. One of his peculiarities was this: he could not bear to see officers drinking, especially young ones. In accordance with the customs of the good old times, all officers dined with their commander. And here Tolstoy, by way of a joke, often pretended to want some drink. On these occasions Petrovich, in a solemn fashion, persuaded him not to take any, and used to offer some sweets instead of spirits."

The description of Tolstoy's life in the Caucasus would not be complete if we omitted his two comrades, the dogs Bulka and Milton. He tells their history in his *Books for Reading*, in a series of charming idyllic pictures of Caucasian life with which almost all Russian school-children are familiar.

At last there arrived the long-expected order, promoting Tolstoy to the rank of an officer.

January 13, 1854, he passed his officer's examination, which at that time was a meaningless formality, and began to prepare for his departure.

January 19th he started for Russia. February 2d he arrived in Yasnaya Polyana. On the journey, which took in those days about a fortnight, he met with a very violent snowstorm that probably gave him the subject for his tale of that name. The short time of his stay in Russia he spent with his brothers, his aunt, and his friend Perfillief.

An order to join the Danube army was already awaiting him, and he accordingly arrived in Bucharest, March 14, 1854.

Having finished the description of the Caucasian period of Tolstoy's life, I think it will interest the reader if I give his own opinion of that period such as it is at the present time. Tolstoy looks back upon that time with pleasure, considering it one of the best periods of his life, notwithstanding all his lapses from his then vaguely realized ideal. He thinks that his subsequent military service, and especially his literary activity, were injurious to his character, and that it was only his return to the country and his work at school with the peasant children that helped him to feel as if he were born again and renewed his spirit within him.

CHAPTER VIII

THE DANUBE AND SEBASTOPOL

A short review of political events: Their reflection on Tolstoy's works. *His arrival in the Danube army:* A letter to Tatiana concerning the journey and his first impressions—Another to her on Silistria—An entry in the diary about himself—A picture of his Roumanian recollections. *Departure to the Crimean army:* Arrival at Sebastopol—New and powerful impressions. *A letter to his brother Sergey:* Patriotic mood—Project for a popular military review. *The fourth bastion:* The verses—Departure to Simferopol—A letter to Tatiana—A letter to his brother Sergey concerning life at the front. *Prophecy about himself:* Literary works—The battle at the Black River—A letter to Nekrassof about war—Correspondents for *The Contemporary*—Impression made on Alexander II by the *Sebastopol Tales*—Panayef's letter to Tolstoy concerning the attacks of the censor upon his story—Nekrassof's letter to Tolstoy concerning the monstrosities of the censorship and the importance of his talent—Opinion of a comrade in service. *The military career before him and its obstacles:* "The Sebastopol Song"—Remarks upon it by Venyukof—Reminiscences of one of the writers of song—The second song—The music—Impression made by the *Sebastopol Tales* on the literary circle—Opinions of Turgenef and Pissemsky—Surrender of Sebastopol—Writing of the report—Transferred to St. Petersburg—Tolstoy's attitude to his military duties—Reminiscences of N. A. Krylof.

BEFORE entering upon the narrative of this period, I must say a few words concerning the chain of political events which brought about the changes in Tolstoy's life.

The reign of Nicholas was approaching its end. Despotism was at its height, and the oppression of both the higher classes and the masses provoked a desire to revolt. As always happens, the Government, instinctively feeling the threatening storm, turned recklessly to adventures abroad. The potentially accumulated energy of violence is thus discharged in the bloody slaughter of an obedient herd of soldiers, trained for the purpose of making them able and willing to come to the rescue of governments in the difficult moments of their criminal existence. The populace and the higher classes also half consciously participate in such massacres, just as a man in misery seeks to stay his anguish by drinking.

Thus, ruined and demoralized by the tyranny of Nicholas I, on November 4, 1853, Russia declared war with Turkey. At first the Russian army scored successes, entering the Turkish dominion and occupying Moldavia, and the Russian Black Sea fleet, under the command of the celebrated Nakhimof, destroyed the Turkish fleet at Synope.

At this juncture two European powers, France and England, interfered, and then began the well-known Crimean campaign, which was marked by the heroic defence of Sebastopol, a feat unprecedented in history. As is usual in such a crisis, along with the noisy movements of outward life, the inner life ran its course in the hearts of the best men, both of the people and of the higher classes, and took shape in new ideals—in liberal social reforms of a certain kind, which, however, so far only faintly reflected the needs of the people. These two agencies, the direction of the energy of the people into heroic military exploits and the fact of the national spiritual life being stirred by the new ideals, gave a character to the creative activity of Tolstoy during this period.

Almost from the first these two great phenomena came into opposition one with the other, and consequently Tolstoy's works took that form of high poetic tragedy which is so marked in his tales of Sebastopol.

Tolstoy, as has been stated above, was sent out to the army of the Danube, after having seen his relations.

On reaching Bucharest, he writes a letter to his aunt Tatiana, in the shape of a diary, describing in a concise way the journey and first impressions on arriving.

"From Kursk I have made about 2,000 versts instead of the 1,000 I intended, and I went through Poltava, Balta, Kishineff, and not by Kief, which would have been out of the way. As far as the province of Cherson I had excellent sleighing, but there I was obliged to give up sleighing, and to do a thousand versts in a perekladnaya,[1] over dreadful roads, as far as the frontier, and from the frontier to Bucharest it is impossible to describe the state of the roads; in

---

[1] Term indicating a travelling vehicle, without springs, which was ordinarily used for travelling in Russia, and is somewhat similar to a small working-cart.—*Trans.*

order to understand it, one must have tasted the pleasure of doing a thousand versts in a cart smaller and worse than those in which we transport manure. Not understanding a word in Moldavian, and finding no one who understood Russian, and moreover paying for eight horses instead of two, although my journey lasted only nine days, I spent more than 200 roubles, and arrived almost sick from fatigue.

"*19th March.*—The prince was not here, but he arrived yesterday, and I have just seen him. He received me better than I expected, really as a relation. He embraced me; he has invited me to come to dine with him every day, and he wants to keep me attached to his person, but that is not yet decided.

"Pardon me, dear aunt, for writing so little—I have not yet collected my ideas—this big and beautiful town, all these introductions, the Italian opera, the French theatre, the two young Gorchakofs, who are very nice fellows . . . so that I have not remained for two hours at home, and I have not thought of my occupations.

"*22d March.*—Yesterday I learned that I am not to remain with the prince, but am going to Oltenitsa to rejoin my battery."

Two months later he again writes, but now in another frame of mind:

"While you imagine me exposed to all the dangers of war, I have not yet smelled Turkish powder, and I am staying very quietly at Bucharest, walking about, enjoying music, and taking ices. Indeed all this time, with the exception of two weeks I passed at Oltenitsa, where I was attached to a battery, and a week I passed journeying about Moldavia, Wallachia, and Bessarabia by order of the General Serzhputovsky, to whom I am now attached for special commissions, I have remained at Bucharest, and, to speak the truth, the kind of life which I lead here, being, as it is, somewhat dissipated, quite idle, and very expensive, displeases me infinitely. Before this it was the service which kept me here, but now I have remained for three weeks owing to a fever I contracted during my journey, but from which, thank God, I am now sufficiently recovered to join—in two or three days' time—my general, who is in camp near Silistria. Speaking of my general, he appears to be a very good fellow, and, although we know each other very little, to be well disposed toward me. What is, moreover, pleasant is that his staff is composed for the most part of gentlemen. The two sons of the Prince Serge, whom I have found here, are nice fellows, especially the younger, who, although not particularly clever, has much nobility of character and a very kind heart. I like him very much."

We next quote from a letter which refers to events on the Danube, though written from Sebastopol. As the reader will notice, Tolstoy first addresses his aunt Tatiana, and then his brother Nicolas. To our mind, this letter should form a page in a history of Russia.

"I will speak to you of the past, of my memories of Silistria. I saw there so much that was interesting, poetic, and touching that the time I passed there will never be effaced from my memory. Our camp was stationed on the other side of the Danube, *i. e.*, on the right bank, on very elevated ground among beautiful gardens belonging to Mustafa Pasha, the governor of Silistria. The view from this place is not only magnificent but of the greatest interest for all of us; not to mention the Danube, its isles and its shores, some occupied by us, others by the Turks, one saw the town, the fortress, and the little forts of Silistria as it were on the palm of one's hand. One heard the booming of cannon and guns unceasingly, day and night, and with a glass one could distinguish the Turkish soldiers. It is true, it is a curious kind of pleasure to see people killing each other, nevertheless every evening and every morning I got on to my cart and remained for whole hours observing, and I was not the only person who did. The spectacle was really fine, especially at night. During the night my soldiers generally undertook trench work, and the Turks threw themselves at them in order to hinder them, then you should have seen and heard the fusillade. The first night I passed in the camp this terrible noise awoke and frightened me; I thought an assault had commenced, and I got my horse ready very quickly; but those who had already passed some time in the camp told me that I had only to keep quiet, that this cannonade and fusillade were ordinary things, and that they jokingly called them 'Allah.' Then I lay down again, but being unable to sleep I amused myself by counting, watch in hand, the number of discharges of cannon I heard, and I counted 110 explosions in the space of one minute. Yet all this at close quarters had not the frightful character it would appear to have. At night, when nothing could be seen, it was a question of who could burn most powder, and, with these thousands of cannon-shots, a score and a half of men at most were killed on both sides. You will allow me, dear aunt, to address myself in this letter to Nicolay, for since I have begun to give details of war, I should like to continue and address myself to a man who understands and can give you explanations of what may be obscure to you. Well, this was an ordinary spectacle which we had every day, and in which, when I was sent with orders into the trenches, I took my share; but we also had extraordinary spectacles such as the one the day before the assault, when a mine of 240 lbs. of powder was exploded under one of the enemy's forts. On the morning of this day the prince had been to the trenches with all his staff (as the general I am attached to belongs to it, I was there too) in order to give definite instructions in view of the assault of the next day. The plan, too long for me to be able to explain it here, was so well combined, and everything had been so well anticipated, that no one doubted as to its success. By the bye, I ought, besides, to tell you that I am beginning to feel admiration for the prince (you ought to hear what is said about him among the officers and the men; not only have I never heard any evil spoken of him, but he is universally worshipped). I saw him under fire for the first time that morning.

"You should see his figure, somewhat ridiculous with his high stature, his hands behind his back, his cap on the back of his head, his spectacles, and the way he has of speaking like a turkey cock. One could see he was so absorbed in the general progress of affairs that the shells and bullets did not exist for him; he exposed himself to danger with such simplicity that one would have thought he was unconscious of it, and involuntarily one was more afraid for him than for oneself; and then he gave his orders with such clearness and precision, and at the same time was always affable with every one. He is a great, *i. e.,* a capable and honest man, as I understand the words; a man who has devoted all his life to the service of his country, and not through ambition, but as a duty. I will tell you a feature of his connected with the history of this assault

Tolstoy, 1854.

I had begun to describe. In the afternoon of the same day that they exploded the mine, about 600 pieces of artillery opened fire on the fort which they wished to take, and this was continued all night. It was one of those sights, and it caused one of those emotions which one never forgets. In the evening again the prince, amid all the commotion, went to sleep in the trenches, in order himself to direct the assault which was to commence at three o'clock of the same night. We were all there, and, as is always the case on the eve of a battle, we all pretended to be no more concerned with the morrow than with any ordinary day, and I am certain that all, in the depth of their hearts, felt a little nervous, and not even a little but very much so, at the idea of this assault. As you are aware, Nicolas, the time which precedes an engagement is the most unpleasant—it is only then that one has time for fear, and fear is one of the most disagreeable of feelings. Toward the morning, the nearer the moment approached the more did this feeling diminish, and toward three o'clock, when we were all waiting to see fired the batch of rockets which were to be the signal for the attack—I was in such good spirits that, had they come to tell me the assault would not take place, it would have greatly grieved me. And lo and behold, exactly an hour before the time fixed for the assault, an aide-de-camp arrived from the Field-Marshal with the order to raise the siege of Silistria! I may say, without fear of being mistaken, that this news was received by all, men, officers, and soldiers, as a veritable misfortune, the more so that it was known through spies who often came to us from Silistria and with whom I myself often had opportunity to talk—it was known that, if once this fort were captured—an event which no one doubted—Silistria could not hold out for more than two or three days. Do not you think that if this news was calculated to pain any one it must have been the prince, who throughout all this campaign had done everything for the best, yet saw in the very middle of the action the Field-Marshal arrive on top of him and spoil the whole thing? And then, having in this assault his only chance of repairing our reverses, he receives a counter order from the Field-Marshal at the instant of commencing. Well, the prince had not a moment's ill-feeling, he who is so impressionable; on the contrary, he was glad to be able to avoid the slaughter, for which he would have had to accept the responsibility, and during all the time of the retreat, which he himself directed, though he did not go back till the last soldier was through it, and which was accomplished with remarkable order and precision, he was in better spirits than he had ever been before. What greatly contributed to his good humor was the emigration of about 7,000 families of Bulgarians whom we took with us, mindful of the ferocity of the Turks—a ferocity in which, notwithstanding my incredulity, I was compelled to believe. The moment we had abandoned the various Bulgarian villages we had occupied, the Turks made away with every one who remained with the exception of women young enough for their harems. There was a village to which I had gone from the camp to get milk and fruit, in which the population had been exterminated in the way I have described. But no sooner did the prince communicate to the Bulgarians that those who desired could cross the Danube with the army and become Russian subjects, than all the country rose, and all, with their women, children, horses, and cattle approached the bridge; but as it was impossible to take them all, the prince was compelled to refuse those who came the last, and you should have seen their sorrow. He received all the deputations which came from these poor people, he talked with each of them, he endeavored to explain to them the impossibility of the thing, he offered to let them cross without their wagons and their cattle, undertaking to maintain the people themselves until they should reach Russia, and to pay out of his own pocket for private ships to transport them; in a word, doing all he possibly could to give help to these people.

"Yes, dear aunt, I would greatly desire the realization of your prophecy. The thing which I most crave is to be the aide-de-camp of a man like him, whom I love and whom I esteem from the depth of my heart. Good-by, and, dear aunt, I kiss your hands."

In the midst of these strong and new sensations, Tolstoy does not forsake his regular habit, that of self-reproach; this is reflected in the entries of his diary.

"*7th July.*—I have no modesty. This is my great deficiency. What am I? One of the four sons of a retired lieutenant-colonel, left from the age of seven without parents, and who, under the guardianship of women and strangers, received neither a worldly nor scientific education, and then became emancipated at seventeen; a man without any great wealth, without any social position, and, above all, without principle, who has let his affairs get out of order to the last extremity, who has passed the best years of his life without aim or pleasure; who has finally banished himself to the Caucasus in order to run away from his debts, and, above all, from his habits, and who, having taken advantage of some connection or other which had existed between his father and a commander-in-chief, has got himself transferred, at the age of twenty-six, to the Army of the Danube as lieutenant, with hardly any means but his pay (having to use such means as he possesses for the payment of his remaining debts), without patrons, without knowledge of worldly manners, without knowledge of the service, without practical capacities, but with enormous vanity. Yes, such is my social position. Let us see what is my personality.

"I am ugly, awkward, uncleanly, and, in the worldly sense, uneducated; I am irritable, a bore to others, rude, intolerant, and as bashful as a child. I am almost completely ignorant. What I do know I have learned anyhow, independently, by snatches, incoherently, in a disorderly way, and all comes to—so little. I am self-indulgent, irresolute, inconstant, stupidly vain and hot-headed, as are all people with a weak character. I am not brave, I am not methodical in my life, and am so lazy that for me idleness has become almost a necessary habit.

"I am intelligent, but my intelligence has not yet been thoroughly tried on anything. I have neither a practical nor a worldly nor a business intelligence.

"I am honest, *i. e.*, I love what is right, have got myself into the habit of loving it; and when I deviate from it I am dissatisfied with myself, and return to it with pleasure; but there are things I like more than what is right—fame. I am so vain, and so little has this feeling been gratified that often I am afraid lest, between fame and virtue, I might, if the choice were given me, choose the former.

"Yes, I am arrogant, because I am inwardly proud, though I am shy in society."

At times a softened mood would come over him, and he would write with some poetic feeling, as the following entry in his diary shows:

"After dinner I leaned upon the balcony and looked at my favorite lamp which gleams so nicely through the foliage. Just then, after a few storm-clouds which have to-day passed and moistened the ground, there lingered one big cloud covering the whole of the southern portion of the sky, and there was a peculiar pleasant lightness and humidity in the air. The landlady's pretty daughter, like myself, was reclining in the window leaning on her elbows. A barrel-organ came along the street, and when the sounds of a good ancient waltz, after gradually retreating, completely vanished, the girl gave a sigh from the depths of her soul, rose quickly, and left the window. I felt so happy that I could not help smiling, and continued a long time gazing at my lamp—the light of which was ever and anon hidden as the wind moved the branches of the tree—gazing at the tree, at the fence, at the sky; and everything assumed a beauty such as I had never seen it wear before.

The unsuccessful campaign of the Army of the Danube, the dull life of the staff, all this was unsatisfactory to Tolstoy. He wanted more vigorous activity, greater excitement, and he begged to be sent to join the army in the Crimea.

After the retreat from Silistria (July 20th) he went to the Crimea. His journey lay through the towns of Tekuchi, Berlad, Yassi, Kherson, and Odessa. He reached Sebastopol November 7, 1854. On his way he fell ill and was in a hospital, which explains the length of time he spent on the journey.

On his arrival he was attached to the 3d Light Battery of the 14th Artillery Brigade.

Here he was overwhelmed with such a flood of new impressions that for some time he could not master them. At the end of a fortnight, on November 20th, he writes to his brother Seryozha:

"DEAR FRIEND SERYOZHA: I have behaved very ill to you all ever since my leave began, and how this happened I myself do not know; at one time a distracted life, at another the dulness of my life and disposition, at another war, at another some one in the way, and so on; but the chief reason has been a distracted life, full of outside interferences. So much have I learned, experienced, and felt during this year that one positively does not know what to begin to describe, or whether one will be able to describe it as one would like. To Aunty I wrote about Silistria, but to you and Nicolenka I will not write like that—I would like to communicate with you so that you may understand me as I wish. Silistria is now an old song; now it is all Sebastopol, about which I dare say you have yourself read with a beating heart, such as I had four days ago. Well, how can I tell you all that I saw there, and where I went, and what I did, and what the French and English say—the wounded prisoners—*and whether they suffer and suffer much,* and what heroes our foes are, especially the English. We can talk over all this some day at Yasnaya or Pirigovo; and about much of it you will learn from myself through the press. I will explain later what I mean, but now I will give you an idea of the position of our affairs at Sebastopol. The town is besieged from one side only—from the south side—on which, when the enemy approached, we had no fortifications. Now we have on this side more than 500 guns of enormous calibre, and several lines of earthworks, positively impregnable.

"I passed a week in the fortress, and up to the last day kept losing my way among these labyrinths of batteries as in a forest. The enemy has for more than three weeks in one place been only 180 yards off, and does not advance; at his slightest forward movement he is covered with a hail of shot.

"The spirit of the troops is beyond description. There was not so much heroism in the time of ancient Greece. Kornilof, when making the round of the troops, instead of, 'I greet you, boys!' said: 'One must die, boys; will you die?' and the troops shouted, 'We will die, your Excellency! Hurrah!' And this was not mere show, but on the face of each one could see that it was not in jest but *in earnest,* and 22,000 men have already fulfilled this promise.

"A wounded and almost dying soldier told me how they attacked the 24th French Battery and were not reinforced; he wept aloud. A company of marines almost revolted because they wanted to relieve them from a battery on which they had remained thirty days under shell fire. Soldiers snatch the fuses out of the shells. Women carry water to the bastion for the soldiers, and many of them are killed and wounded. Priests with crosses go to the bastions and read prayers under fire. In one brigade, the 24th, there were 160 men wounded who would not leave the ranks. Wonderful time! Now, however, after the 24th, we have somewhat quieted down, and it has become splendid at Sebastopol. The enemy has almost ceased to fire, and all are convinced that he will not take the town; indeed, it would be impossible. There are three possible events: either he will make a general attack, or else he is diverting us with false works, or else fortifying himself in order to winter. The first is the least and the second the most probable. I did not succeed in being even once in action; but I thank God that I have seen these men and live in this glorious time. The bombardment of the 5th will remain the most brilliant and glorious exploit, not only of Russian but of universal history. More than 1,500 guns for two days played upon the town, and they not only did not force it to surrender, but they did not even silence one gun in two hundred of our batteries. It seems to me that if this campaign is not favorably looked upon in Russia, posterity will place it higher than all others. Do not forget that with equal, even inferior forces, with bayonets alone, and with the worst troops of the Russian army (such is the 6th Corps), we are fighting with a more numerous foe, possessing a fleet and armed with 3,000 guns, excellently made rifles, and with his best troops. I do not mention the superiority of the enemy's generals.

"Our army alone can stand and conquer under these conditions, and conquer shall yet, this I am convinced of. You should see the French and English prisoners (especially the latter): each one is better than the last, I mean morally and physically; they are a *splendid people*. The Cossacks say that even they feel pity in sabring them, and by their side you should see any one of our riflemen: small, lousy, and shrivelled up, in a way.

"Now I will tell you how it is that you will learn from me through the press about the exploits of these lousy and shrivelled up heroes. In our artillery staff office, consisting, as I think I wrote to you, of very good and honorable men, the idea has been started of publishing a military periodical for the purpose of maintaining a good spirit in the troops, a cheap review (at three roubles), and in popular language, so that the soldiers could read it. We have written a prospectus of the paper and presented it to the Prince. The idea pleased him very much, and he submitted the prospectus and a specimen number, which we had composed, to the Emperor for sanction. The money for the publication has been advanced by myself and Stolipin. They have made me editor, together with a certain Mr. Constantinovich, who has published *The Caucasus,* and is an experienced man in this line. In the review will be published descriptions of battles, not so dry and untruthful as in other papers, exploits of bravery, biographies and obituaries of good men, and particularly of the rank and file; military stories, soldiers' songs, popular articles about engineering and artillery, arts, etc. This thing pleases me very much; first, I like this occupation, and, secondly, I hope that the periodical will be useful and not at all bad. All this remains presumptive until we get the Emperor's answer, and I confess I am anxious about it. In the trial copy we sent to St. Petersburg we carelessly inserted two articles, one by myself and the other by Rostovtsef, which are not quite orthodox. For this business I shall require 1,500 roubles, which are lying in the office, and which I have asked Valeryan to send me. As I have already gossipped this to you, tell it to him too. Thank God I am well, and I have been living happily and pleasantly from the very time I returned from abroad. In general, my life in the army is divided into two periods: abroad a bad one, where I was ill and poor and lonely, and at home a pleasant one. Now I am well and have got good comrades, but I am still poor, for money is soon gone.

"I do not write, but I instinctively feel how Aunty is bantering me. One thing troubles me: this is the fourth year of my life without female society; I may become quite uncouth and unfit for family life, which I so enjoy.

"Well, good-by. God knows when we shall see each other, unless you and Nicolenka take it into your heads some day, when out hunting, to look in from Tambof at our headquarters."

I have given the whole of this remarkable letter, because it shows how young in his spirit Tolstoy was at that time, how liable to be carried away by his feelings, and how this stood in the way of any clear understanding of what was going on round him. But glimpses of vivid consciousness and prophetic inspiration appear with all the greater force in the background.

However, these powerful outward impressions did not occupy the whole of Tolstoy's soul, and while alone, writing his diary, possibly in the tents of the 4th battalion, he was still the same as he had always been and as he is now, ever seeking for and striving after the ideal. His frame of mind at that time found vent in the following poetical form:

"When, oh when, shall I at last cease to pass my time without aim or enthusiasm, and to feel a deep wound in my heart without knowing how to heal it? Who made this wound? God alone knows, but from birth I have been bitterly tormented by a sense of the insignificance which threatened my future and by painful sadness and doubt." [1]

He moved to Simferopol on November 23d.

January 6, 1855, he writes a pacifying letter to his aunt Tatiana:

"I have not taken part in the two bloody battles which have taken place in the Crimea, but I went to Sebastopol immediately after the battle of the 24th, and I passed a month there. They no longer fight—they devastate the country because of the winter, which is exceptionally severe, especially at the present moment; but the siege goes on. What will be the issue of this campaign? God only knows; but, in any case, the Crimean campaign must come to an end in three or four months one way or another. But, alas! the end of the Crimean campaign does not mean the end of the war, which, on the contrary, it appears will last very long. I had mentioned in my letters to Serge, and, I think, to Valerian, an occupation which I had in view, and which greatly attracted me; now that there is an end of the notion, I may explain it. I had the idea of founding a military journal. This plan, at which I had worked with the coöperation of many very distinguished persons, was approved by the Prince and sent to the Emperor for confirmation; but, as in

[1] We translate the verses in prose.—*Trans.*

our country there are intrigues against everything, people were found who were afraid of the competition of this journal; and perhaps, too, the idea did not fall in with the views of the Government. The Emperor has refused.

"I confess this disappointment gave me infinite pain, and has greatly altered my plans. If God will that the Crimean campaign should terminate in our favor, and I do not receive an appointment with which I can be satisfied, and if there be no war in Russia, I shall leave the army and go to St. Petersburg to the Military Academy. This plan occurred to me, first, because I should not like to abandon literature, with which it is impossible for me to occupy myself in this camp life; and, secondly, because it seems to me I am beginning to become ambitious, or rather, not ambitious, but I should like to do some good, and, in order to do that, it is necessary to be something more than a sublieutenant; thirdly, because I should like to see you all and all my friends. Nicolas writes that Turgenef has made the acquaintance of Marie. I am very glad of it; if you see him, tell Varinka that I beg him to embrace him on my behalf, and to tell him that, although I know him only by correspondence, I should have had a lot of things to say to him."

The life which followed is very well pictured in his letter to his brother, written in May, 1855. In it he gives a chronological summary of the events of his military life during the preceding winter of 1854-55.

"Although you probably know through our folks where I am and what I have been doing, I will repeat to you my adventures since Kishinef, the more so that my story may be interesting to you, and you will learn from it in what phase I now am—for it seems that my fate is always in some phase or other. From Kishinef I petitioned to be transferred to the Crimea, partly for the purpose of seeing this war, and partly in order to tear myself away from the staff of Serzhputovski, which I did not like, but chiefly from patriotism, which at that time I confess took hold of me strongly. I did not request to be sent to any particular point, but left the authorities to dispose of my fate. In the Crimea I was attached to a battery in Sebastopol itself, where I passed a month very pleasantly in the circle of simple and kind comrades, who are especially engaging during real war and danger. In December our battery was removed to Simferopol, and there I lived six weeks in the comfortable home of a landowner, going to Simferopol to dance and play the piano with young ladies, and, with the Government officials, to shoot deer on the Chaterdag. In January there was another redistribution of officers, and I was transferred to a battery encamped at ten versts from Sebastopol. There *j'ai fait la connaissance de la mère de Kousma*,[1]—the nasty circle of officers in the battery, the commander, though a kind creature, yet harsh and coarse; no comfort, cold earth huts; not one book, not one man with whom one could speak. Here I received 1,500 roubles for the periodical, the sanction of which had already been refused; and here I lost 2,500 roubles, thus proving to the whole world that I am still a *frivolous fellow*, although the above circumstances may be accepted *comme circonstances atténuantes*.[2] But still it was very, very disgraceful. In March it became warmer, and a good fellow and most excellent man arrived and joined the battery, one Brenefski; so I began to recover myself, and on the first of April my battery, during the actual bombardment, went to Sebastopol, where I quite recovered myself. There, until May 15th, although in serious danger, having been on duty four successive days in a battery of the 4th bastion, yet we had the spring and excellent weather, a mass of impressions and of people, all the conveniences of life, and the company of well-bred men like ourselves, so that these six weeks will remain one of my pleasantest recollections. On May 15th Gorchakof, or the commander of the artillery, was pleased to intrust me with the formation and command of a mountain detachment at Belbek, twenty versts from Sebastopol, with which I am up to now very well satisfied in many respects.

"This is a general description. In the next letter I will write about the present more in detail."

To this short description we may add that its jocular tone does not harmonize with the serious thoughts and feelings which beset him at the time.

In his diary of March 5, 1855, he puts down the following prophecy about himself:

"A conversation about divinity and faith suggested to

---

[1] A jocular translation into French of a Russian slang byword "Kousma's Mother," popularly used to indicate a difficult plight.—*Trans.*
[2] French for extenuating circumstances.—*Trans.*

me a great, a stupendous idea, to the realization of which I feel myself capable of devoting my life. This idea is the foundation of a new religion corresponding to the present state of mankind—the religion of Jesus but purified from dogma and mysticism, a practical religion, not promising future bliss, but giving bliss upon earth. I feel that this idea can be realized only by generations consciously looking toward it as a goal. One generation will hand on the idea to the next and, some day, enthusiasm or reason will bring it into being. To act with a deliberate view to the religious union of mankind, this is the leading principle of the idea which I hope will command my enthusiasm."

Of course when a man first writes the above words, and after that is engaged for fifty years, with the resolution and ability shown by Tolstoy, in elaborating the means of realizing his idea, we may be sure his place was not in the artillery.

He had a vague consciousness of this, and from time to time the idea struck him that he was born not for a military career, but for a literary life.

Moreover, he never wholly forsook his literary activity.

On his way from Roumania to Sebastopol he went on with *The Wood-Cutting Expedition;* in Sebastopol he began to write *Youth* and *Tales from Sebastopol.*

From the 11th to the 14th of April he remained in bastion No. 4. The sense of danger was a spiritual awakening to him, and he addresses God with the following prayer:

"Lord, I thank thee for Thy continual protection. How surely Thou leadest me to that which is right! And what an insignificant creature should I be wert Thou to abandon me! Leave me not, Lord; direct me, and not for the satisfaction of my poor desires, but for the attainment of the eternal and mighty object of existence, unknown to me and yet recognized by me."

On August 4, 1855, Tolstoy took a part, although indirectly, in the battle of the Black River. He hastens to reassure his relatives, and in a letter to his brother, of August 7, 1855, says, by the way:

"I am writing you a few lines to reassure you about myself with reference to the battle on the 4th, in which I took part and was not hurt; but I did not do anything, because my mountain artillery had no occasion to fire."

At the same time, as is seen from Tolstoy's correspondence with Nekrassof, he kept his eye on Russian literature, and actively supported the editors of *The Contemporary;* in fact he got together at Sebastopol a group of contributors. This is what he wrote to Nekrassof:

"RESPECTED NICOLAY ALEXEYEVICH—You must have already received my article, *Sebastopol in December,* and the promise of Stolypin's article. Here it is, notwithstanding the wild orthography of this manuscript, which you will yourself get corrected, if it is to be published without erasures by the censor, which the author has tried his best to avoid. You will, I hope, agree that such military articles are unfortunately very scarce with us or else do not get published. Perhaps, by this same courier, an article by Saken may be sent, of which I say nothing, and which I hope you will not print. The corrections in Stolypin's article in black ink are made by Horulef with his left hand, his right hand being wounded. Stolypin requests that they should be put in footnotes. Please insert, if possible, mine as well as Stolypin's in the June issue. Now we are all together, and the literary society of the fallen Journal is beginning to be organized, and, as I told you, you will receive from me every month two, three, or four articles of a contemporary military character. The best contributors, Bakunin and Rostovtsef, have not yet had time to finish their articles. Be so kind as to direct your answer to me, and in general write by this courier, an adjutant of Gorchakof's, and by the others who are continually going to and fro between you and us."[1]

SEBASTOPOL, *April* 30, 1855.

On June 15th, in Bakhtchisarai, he received a letter from Panayef and a copy of *The Contemporary,* with his printed tale, *Sebastopol in December.* From this letter he learned that the tale had been read by the Emperor Alexander II.

Evidently it had made a deep impression on the Emperor, for he ordered it to be translated into French. In the same month of June Tolstoy finished the tale *The Wood-Cutting Expedition,* and sent it to *The Contemporary.*

In July he completed and sent to the editors his new tale, *Sebastopol in May.*

[1] The Literary Reminiscences of J. Panayef.

In his letter from St. Petersburg, dated August 28, 1858, Panayef relates the following incident in connection with this story:

"In my letter, delivered to you by Stolypin, I wrote you that your article had been passed by the censorship with a few slight changes, and begged you not to be angry with me, because it was necessary to add a few words at the end so as to mollify an expression. Nearly 3,000 copies of the article, *Night in Sebastopol*,[1] were printed, when the censor prevented publication of the number by ordering a copy to be brought him from the printing-office; hence the August issue appeared on the 18th January, and during my absence—I went to Moscow for a few days—it was presented to the president of the Committee of Censors, Pushkin, whom you should know in connection with Kazan. If you know Pushkin, you may imagine what followed. Pushkin became wild; he was very angry with the censor as well as with me for presenting such articles to the censorship, and he made corrections in it himself. In the meantime I returned to St. Petersburg, and was horror-struck when I saw the changes made. I did not want to print the article at all, but Pushkin, in an interview with me, said that I *must* publish it in its transformed shape. Nothing could be done, and your mutilated article will appear in the September number, omitting the letters L. N. T., which I should hate to see at the bottom of it after that. But the article was so good that even after it was completely destroyed by the censor I gave it to Milutin, Krasnokutsky, and others to read. Everybody likes it very much, and Milutin wrote me that I should commit a sin by depriving readers of this article and by not publishing it even in its present form.

"At any rate, do not blame me because your article has been published in such a shape. I was forced to do it. If it is God's will that we should meet some day, for which I long, I will clear up the matter to you. Now I will say a few words in regard to the impression generally made on us, and on everybody else to whom I have read it, by your story, *Night*, in its original shape . . . Censorship is out of the question here.

"Everybody thinks this story more forcible than the first one, owing to the minute and profound analysis of the

---

[1] *Sebastopol in May* was thus called then.

emotions and feelings of men who are constantly in the face of death, owing to the accuracy with which army officers are depicted, their intercourse with members of the nobility, and their mutual relations. In short, everything is perfect—described in a masterly way; but the whole thing is so full of bitterness, everything is so keen and biting, merciless and cheerless, that at this moment, when the scene of this story is held almost sacred, it hurts those that are far from it. The very events of the story might make a disagreeable impression.

"*The Wood-Cutting Expedition*, with its dedication to Turgenef, will also appear in September (Turgenef begged me to thank you very much for your remembering him and being so attentive). . . . Even in this story, which passed three censors—the Caucasian censor (Secretary of State Butkof), the military censor (Major-General Stefen), and one civil censor (consisting of Pushkin and us)—the types of officers have been tampered with, and unfortunately some parts have been struck out."

In September Nekrassof wrote Tolstoy:

"DEAR SIR LYOF NICOLAYEVICH—I arrived in Petersburg in the middle of August to find *The Contemporary* in a very sad plight.

"The shocking state to which your article [1] was brought turned my last drop of blood. At this moment I cannot think of it without pain and indignation. Your work, to be sure, will not be lost. . . . It will always bear witness to the power capable of such deep and sober truth in circumstances in which it is not everybody who could have kept it unimpaired. I need not say how highly I value this article and the trend of your talent in general as well as its power and freshness as a whole. It is just what the Russian public needs; the truth—the truth, of which so little remains in Russian literature since the death of Gogol. You are quite right in caring most of all for this side of your capacity. Truth in the form presented by you in our literature is something quite new to us. I do not know of any author at the present moment who could make one love and sympathize with him so deeply as the one to whom I now write. But I have one dread—lest the course of time, the abomina-

[1] Evidently he means Tolstoy's tale *Sebastopol in May*, 1855.

tions of real life, and the deaf and dumb environment should affect you in the same way as they have affected most of us, and destroy that energy which is indispensable to an author, at least to those authors who are necessary for Russia at present. You are young; certain changes are taking place; they may—let us hope—end in good, and then a wide arena may be opened before you. Your beginning is such that the least sanguine persons are carried far away in their hopes. But I have turned from the purpose of my letter. I shall not console you by telling you, true as it is, that the printed fragments of your article are very much appreciated by many; for to those who know the article in its real shape they are nothing but a string of phrases without sense or inner meaning. But it cannot be helped. I must say one thing, the article would not have been printed in this shape were it not necessary. But it is not signed by your name. *Felling Wood* passed the censorship fairly well, though a few precious criticisms are lost. My opinion of the work is this: in form it may resemble Turgeneff, but the resemblance ends there; the rest belongs to you and could be written by no one but you. In this sketch there are many wonderfully striking observations and it is entirely new, interesting, and judicious. Don't disdain this type of sketches: in our literature hitherto nothing but trivialities have appeared about the soldier. You are only opening the subject, and, in whatever way you choose to tell us what you know of it, all will be exceedingly interesting and useful. Panayef handed me your letter in which you promise soon to send us *Youth*. Please do. Setting aside the review, I am personally interested in the continuation of your first production. We will keep space for *Youth* in the tenth or eleventh number, according to the time it arrives.

"The money will be forwarded to you one of these days. I have settled for the winter in Petersburg, and shall be glad to hear from you occasionally. Accept my sincere respect,

"N. NEKRASSOF."[1]

But, needless to say, literary work was not Tolstoy's chief occupation at that time. He was leading the conven-

[1] Four letters by N. A. Nekrassof to Count L. N. Tolstoy. *Niva Monthly Literary Supplement*, No. 2, 1898.

tional life of an officer, and was "a good comrade," as is certified by his contemporaries and fellow-officers.

Nazaryef quotes in his reminiscences the narrative of a former comrade of Tolstoy, who evidently recalled with delight the time he had spent together with Count Tolstoy in the battery. He even recognized himself as one of the characters in the *Sebastopol Tales*. "I may say," related the old man, with a smile of pleasure on his face, "Tolstoy, with his stories and his impromptu verses, encouraged us all in the direst moments of our military life. In the full meaning of the word he was the soul of our battery. When we were in his company, we did not notice how time flew, and there was no end to the general good spirits. When the Count was not there—he had left for Simferopol—all were downcast. No news of him for a day, two, three . . . At last he came back . . . looking exactly like the prodigal son—gloomy, worn out, dissatisfied with himself. He would take me aside out of the way, and begin to do penace. He would tell everything about his carousing, playing cards, as to where he spent the days and nights, and, would you believe it? his repentance and sufferings were as deep as if he had been a great culprit. It was pitiful to see him, so great was his distress. . . . This is the kind of man he was. He was, in a word, peculiar, and, to tell you the truth, not quite comprehensible to me; but, on the other hand, he was a rare comrade, an honest soul, and to forget him is quite impossible."

Tolstoy's conduct as a brave officer, and his familiarity with higher circles, could readily have secured for him an advantageous military career. The publication of his Sebastopol sketches, which had attracted the attention of Nicholas, and of the Empress Alexandra Feodorovna—who, it was said, shed tears while reading the first tale—would have contributed to the same end. But his very gifts put an end to his military advancement. The obstacle to a brilliant military career proved to be "The Sebastopol Song."

This is the history of this song:

The version we quote is from the *Olden Times,* where it appeared in full. The well-known author and scholar, M. T. Venyukof, wrote with the text of the song the following note:

"In the years from 1854 to 1856 I was studying military science in the Academy of the general staff, and there I received from the Crimea—the theatre of war—through one of my comrades of the battery, Iv. Vas. Anossof, an officer in the 14th Artillery Brigade, a copy of the following song:

THE SEBASTOPOL SONG.

The fourth day,[1] we were gone
To fight them on the mountain,
    The devil drove us on,
    The devil drove us on.

    It was old General Vrevsky,[2]
He used to say to Gortchakof,
    When he had had his whiskey:

    "Prince, we must have that hill;
I'll tell a tale about it,
    If I don't have my will."

    The grandees, great and small,
They've put their heads together,
    The place Bécoque and all;

    But Bécoque had some doubt,
And what it was he'd better say
    He wouldn't quite make out.

    As they made up their mind,
The topographers were spoiling
    The best paper they could find;

    At last they got it right;
But there were three ravines to pass,
    And they forgot that quite.

    Well, Prince and Count rode out;
The topographers were left behind
    Upon the great redoubt.

    The Prince said, "Now, Liprandi!"
Said he, "I can't go on just yet,
    Hold hard a bit, *attendez;*

    "You don't want clever men,
You'd better send a man like Read,
    I'll have a look again."

[1] August 4, 1855. The Battle of the Black River.
[2] Baron P. A. Vrevsky, late Chief of the Chancery of the Minister of War, while in the Crimea, urged Gortchakof to give a decisive battle to the allied Powers.

>   Read's not a man who fears;
> He led us to the bridge at once,
>   "So here you go, three cheers!"
>
>   But Martineau cried "Stop!
> Let's wait till the reserves are here."
>   "No, make the men come up."
>
>   Hurrah! we made a noise,
> But there must have been some mistake,
>   For we never saw the boys.
>
>   Upon Fedyukhin's height
> Only three companies arrived,
>   But the whole did start all right.
>
>   Our host was very small!
> The French were four to one,
>   Besides the thousands within call.
>
>   The garrison, we said,
> Must surely come and help us
>   When they heard the shouts we made.
>
>   But General Sacken hied
> To praise the Holy Mother
>   At the very time we cried!
>
>   General Belevkof shook
> The flag quite fiercely; but that face,
>   You should have seen his look.
>
>   So it was "Right about!"
> But oh! the men who sent us out,
>   The men who sent us out!

"As to the authorship of this witty, farcical song," continued Venyukof, "Anossof, in his letter, informed me that the general opinion of the army ascribed it to our gifted author, Count L. N. Tolstoy, 'but you understand,' wrote Anossof, 'one cannot exactly assert it, were it only for fear of injuring Tolstoy, supposing him to be really the author.'"

Later on the same version of the song was again printed in the *Olden Times* under the signature of "One of the authors of 'The Sebastopol Song.'"

This is how the part author relates the history of the song:

"Count L. N. Tolstoy no doubt took part in the compilation of this song, but he did not compose all its verses.

THE SEBASTOPOL SONG

It would not be fair to ascribe to him the whole of this witty production.

"Therefore, in the interest of historical truth, I will tell you, as a witness, how it originated:

"During the Crimean War, very often—almost every evening—the members of the artillery staff and some other officers used to meet at Krizhanovsky's, who commanded the artillery staff.

"Lieutenant-Colonel Balyuzek usually sat at the piano, all the rest standing round and improvising verses. Each introduced his thought and word. Count L. N. Tolstoy introduced his own too, but not all. One may say therefore that this improvisation was a common act, which expressed the mood of the military circle."

Here follow the names of the authors of "The Sebastopol Song": Lieutenant-Colonel Balyuzek (afterward governor of Turgai, now deceased), who used to sit at the piano; Captain A. Y. Friede, at present commander of the Caucasian Artillery; Lieutenant-Captain Count L. N. Tolstoy; Lieutenant V. Lughinin; Lieutenant Shulein; Lieutenant-Captain Serzhputovsky; Lieutenant Shklyarsky, an officer of the Uhlan Regiment; N. F. Koslyoninof, No. 2, and an officer of the Hussar regiment, N. S. Mussin-Pushkin.

"We received a copy of a similar song written probably under the same circumstances, but somewhat later. The music of it was given us by Sergey Tolstoy from memory. This song contains many popular expressions not fit for print. Where a change was possible, we replaced them, without changing rhythm or meaning, by more polite language. Where this was impossible, dots were put in place of the expressions.

> September, the eighth day,
> For the faith and for the Czar
> Before the French we ran away,
> Before the French we ran away.
>
> And our Prince Alexander
> Let all the fleet sink out at sea,
> Our admiral and commander.
>
> And then he said "Good-by;
> Go on all you and fight your best,
> I'm for Bakhtchisarai."

In our rear St. Arnault lay;
He was kind enough to wait a bit,
   And then he blazed away.

We were obliged to call
For help on Tuesday's holy Saint,
   Or he'd have caught us all.

What was Liprandi at?
He captured all the forts he could,
   But what's the use of that?

From Kishinef was passed
The word, an army would come up,
   And in they marched at last.

'Twas Danneberg that led:
They told him, "Never spare your men,
   You've got to go ahead."

Pavlof marched off uphill,
And Soymonof went to meet him,
   But they may be climbing still.

Liprandi, when he knew
The French had got the upper hand,
   Was puzzled what to do.

No doubt the grand dukes came,
But the French, instead of being afraid,
   Kept firing all the same.

Ten thousand men there fell:
What the Czar ever did for them
   Is more than I can tell.

The prince, he did complain;
He said the soldiers were no good,
   And faced about again.

And on that fatal day
Of heroes there were only two,
   And the grand dukes were they.

They had their St. George too,
And were taken to St. Petersburg
   For all the world to view.

And the priests, as they were bound,
Prayed that a hurricane might come
   And all the French be drowned.

The wind was very rough,
But the Frenchmen stayed and faced it out,
   They were of better stuff.

In winter they made sorties—
And many a man they killed of us—
From up there where the fort is.

Let Khrulef come and lead,
And drive the Turk from Kozlof, as
We never could succeed.

"More soldiers," Menschik prayed:
Till the Czar, to keep his spirits up,
Sent Saken to his aid.

Menschik was great at sea,
And he wrote bluntly to the Czar,
"Father, our Czar," said he,

"Your Yerofeyich was never
Much more use than your youngsters,
And I'm sure they're none whatever!"

The Czar upon this flew
Into a rage, and so fell ill,
When holding a review.

He went to heaven, we know,
Most likely he was wanted there;
'Twas well he had to go.

But, when on his deathbed,
"You'd better just be on your guard,"
Unto his son he said.

The son was not too kind;
"Dear Menschik," he wrote, "you can go
To the devil if you don't mind.

"I know who'll do the work:
The man I mean's Prince Gortchakof,
The same as fought the Turk.

He won't much beg for men;
I'll send for him promotion,
And he won't ask again."[1]

If one thinks of the circumstances in which these songs were written, of all the horrors of death, groans of the wounded, bloodshed, fires, murders, filling the atmosphere

---

[1] This soldier's song, as well as the first one, a few pages back, has been translated very freely, as it would have been impossible to render in English the peculiar vernacular of Russian soldiers.—*Trans.*

in Sebastopol, one cannot help being struck with admiration of the moral strength of those men who could indulge in good-natured jests at their own cost in the face of constant threat of sufferings and death.

Meanwhile in literary circles in St. Petersburg Tolstoy became more and more known. He conquered his first severe critic, Turgenef. Readers will remember the account of Mme. Golovachof-Panayef, which we quote at the beginning of this chapter, how Turgenef checked Panayef's enthusiasm by his reasonings.

In 1854 Turgenef wrote from his estate, Spasskoye, to E. Y. Kolbassin, a collaborator of *The Contemporary:*

"I am very glad to hear of the success of *Boyhood*. Let Tolstoy only survive, and I hope he will yet astonish us all—his is a first-rate gift. I met his sister (she is married to a Count Tolstoy, too)—a very charming woman. . . ."[1]

When the *Sebastopol Tales* were printed Turgenef became most enthusiastic, and thus expressed his enthusiasm in a letter to Panayef:

"Tolstoy's article on Sebastopol is a gem. Tears came into my eyes when I read it, and I shouted hurrah! I am much flattered by his desire to dedicate his new tale to me. I saw in the *Moscow News* the advertisement of *The Contemporary*. Very good; God grant you may keep your promises, that is to say, that articles may safely pass the censorship, that Tolstoy may not be killed, and so on. It will help you greatly. Tolstoy's article made a great sensation here. . . . Spasskoye, July 10, 1855."[2]

One may say that after the appearance of the *Sebastopol Tales* Tolstoy had risen to the rank of a foremost author. A. E. Kony, in his biography of T. F. Gorbunof, quotes the following interesting opinion of Pissemsky concerning these tales:

"About this time," said Kony, "Pissemsky—who was then writing his remarkable novel, *The Thousand Souls*—after having listened to some passages out of the *Sebastopol Tales* by the then 'only promising great writer of the Russian Land,' gruffly said to Gorbunof: 'This young

[1] The First Collection of T. S. Turgenef's Letters, p. 9. Published by the Society of Help to Authors, 1885. St. Petersburg.
[2] Literary Reminiscences by Paneyef, 1888.

officer will eclipse us all—one might as well give up writing. . . .' "[1]

After the fall of Sebastopol, Tolstoy was sent as a courier to St. Petersburg, and was attached to a rocket battery.

Before leaving Sebastopol, Tolstoy had applied his literary abilities to making a report of the last battle. Of this report, in his article, "A few words concerning *War and Peace*," he himself says:

"After the loss of Sebastopol, the commander of the artillery, Krizhanovsky, sent me the reports of the artillery officers from all the bastions, and requested me to compose an account from more than twenty of these reports. I regret that I did not copy them. They were the best specimen of the kind of naïve, unfailing military falsehood which always furnishes the material for descriptions. I believe that many of these comrades of mine who composed these reports, if they read these lines, will laugh as they call to mind how, by the orders of the authorities, they wrote of matters which they could not know anything about."[2]

During his military service Tolstoy had disagreements with his superior officers and comrades owing to his love for justice.

In accordance with the custom of those days, commanders of different parts of the battery, as well as the commander of the whole battery, used to save up part of the money given them from the treasury to spend on keeping the battery. The money thus saved they generally kept for themselves, getting a certain regular income which led to many abuses.

Tolstoy, on making his accounts, found a surplus over the expenses; he added it to the sum allotted for the battery instead of appropriating it. This practice was viewed with great disfavor by other commanders, and General Krizhanovsky reproved him for it. N. A. Krilof bears testimony to this in his reminiscences. In 1856 he was transferred to the 14th Battery, which Tolstoy had recently quitted. Tolstoy is remembered in the brigade as a good

---

[1] A Biographical Sketch of I. F. Gorbunof, by A. E. Kony. (Preface and Works, p. 115.)
[2] "A few words about the book *War and Peace*." *The Russian Archives*, 1868.

horseman, a genial companion, and an athlete. He would lie on the floor, a man weighing 5 poods would be placed on his hands, and he would lift him up by straightening his arms; in tugging a stick nobody could beat him. A great many witty anecdotes are attributed to him, which he used to tell in a masterly way. The Count was accused of preaching to the officers to refund to the Government the excess of forage money in case an officer's horse does not consume the quantity of fodder it is supposed to eat.[1]

In St. Petersburg quite a different life awaited Tolstoy, into which he plunged with his unfailing youthful energy.

[1] *Russkiya Vedomosti*, p. 136, 1900.

CHAPTER IX

ST. PETERSBURG

Arrival at St. Petersburg: Attached to the rocket battery—Note from *My Confession* relating to this period—*The Contemporary*—The circle of writers—The association—Quarrel between Turgenef and Katkof—Interference of Tolstoy—Belinsky and Tolstoy—The cause of Tolstoy's indifference to Belinsky. *Literary education of Tolstoy:* Rousseau—Stendhal—List of books read by him—Fet's acquaintance with Tolstoy at Turgenef's—Encounter of Turgenef with Tolstoy at Nekrassof's—Grigorovich's recollections of Tolstoy—Dinners at *The Contemporary's* office—Danilevsky's reminiscences of Tolstoy—Tolstoy's attitude to Herzen—Turgenef's opinion of Tolstoy quoted by Garshin—The narrative of Mme. Golovachof-Panayef of Turgenef's attacks on Tolstoy. *Turgenef's letters to Tolstoy from Paris:* Their mutual relations—About the articles of Tchernishevsky—Tolstoy's opinion of Turgenef's *Faust*—The affairs of *The Contemporary*—Letter from Botkin to Druzhinin about *King Lear*—Tolstoy's opinion—Turgenef's letter to Druzhinin on Tolstoy—Druzhinin's opinion of *Childhood*. *Death of his brother Dmitry:* Tolstoy's recollections of the death—Literary works—Contributing articles to three reviews—Tolstoy's intention to go abroad—The toils of love. *Affairs of "The Contemporary":* Project of a new review—Removal to Moscow—A visit to the family Bers. *Yasnaya Polyana:* Tolstoy's illness—His retirement from service—Tolstoy's intercession in favor of a fellow-officer—Entrance into a new period of activity. *Dissatisfaction with his literary environment:* Recollections of this in *Confession*—Foundation of a literary fund—Pushkin's works—The state of Tolstoy's mind according to *Confession*—Striving after personal happiness.

TOLSTOY was sent to St. Petersburg as a despatch bearer. There he was attached to a rocket battery under General Konstantinof, and returned to the front no more.

In St. Petersburg, where he arrived November 21, 1855, he found himself at once in the circle of *The Contemporary*, and was received there with open arms.

In his *Confession*, Tolstoy thus speaks of that period:

"During that time I began to write, out of vanity, love of gain, and pride. I followed as a writer the same path which I had chosen as a man. In order to obtain the fame and the money for which I wrote, I was obliged to hide what was good, and bow down before what was evil. How often while writing have I cudgelled my brains to conceal, under the mask of indifference or pleasantry, those yearnings for something better which formed the real problem of my life! I succeeded in my object, and was praised. At twenty-six years of age, on the close of the war, I came to St. Petersburg, and made the acquaintance of the authors of the day.

"I met with a hearty reception and much flattery." [1]

Naturally, during the twenty years before he wrote those lines, Tolstoy was beset by various feelings, though even then his unsparing self-analysis and scepticism were pushed so far as to astonish his companions.

The Contemporary was a review founded by A. S. Pushkin and Pletnyof. Its first number was issued in 1836. After Pushkin's death, the review was published from 1838 to 1846 by Pletnyof alone, and lost all its importance. In 1847 N. A. Nekrassof and T. T. Panayef became the proprietors of the review. In collaboration with the well-known literary critic Belinsky, they managed in a short time to attract the best authors, and, until its suppression by the authorities in 1866, this review was the chief organ of progressive Russian art, criticism, and sociology.

At the time of Tolstoy's appearance in Petersburg, the more intimate members of this literary circle are to be seen in the two well-known photo-groups of authors—Panayef, Nekrassof, Turgenef, Tolstoy, Druzhinin, Ostrovsky, Goncharof, and Grigorovich and Sollogulo. One may add to the circle V. P. Botkin, Fet, and others not included in the two groups.

Members of the staff of *The Contemporary* were bound by certain obligations as to honoraria as well as the contribution of articles. These obligations were sometimes found too burdensome, and caused many unpleasant frictions among literary men. Publishers and editors of other reviews would, by urgent entreaties, obtain "copy" from the celebrated authors belonging to the personnel of *The Contemporary*. The administration of that review resented such proceedings very much, a feeling which was reciprocated by the rival publishers. Tolstoy's German biog-

[1] *How I Came to Believe* published by *Free Age Press*.

rapher, Loewenfeld, gives a description of one such incident as follows:

"Turgenef and Katkof had a quarrel in which Tolstoy was involved, partly by his own fault. Turgenef had been for some time an assiduous contributor of Katkof's, and the latter was naturally loath to part with such an author. He commissioned his brother to call daily on both the young authors, and solicit from them articles for his review. Turgenef, growing tired of these endless petitions, on a sudden impulse promised to write something for Katkof, but could not keep his promise. Katkof was furious, and attacked Turgenef in public, arguing that, since Turgenef promised to write for him, he could not at the same time give his services 'exclusively' to *The Contemporary*." On the other hand, as a member of *The Contemporary* staff, he was precluded from contributing to Katkof's review. His gentle and compliant nature played him a bad turn this time.

Tolstoy took the part of his friend. He wrote a long letter to Katkof in defence of Turgenef. "The gentle nature of Turgenef, as well as his politeness, had induced him to make promises to both parties. Tolstoy requested Katkof to publish his letter. Katkof agreed, on the condition that his answer should be printed as well, and he therewith sent a rough sketch of it. But it was of such a character that Tolstoy thought it wiser to give up his part of mediator."[1]

The association of *The Contemporary* ceased long before, and it became an ordinary publishing concern.

Tolstoy did not meet Belinsky in the circle of *The Contemporary*. The latter died in 1848, after having worked hard to put the *Review* on a satisfactory footing. His enthusiasm breathed new life into the dying periodical, and made its existence secure for a long while to come. But Tolstoy was not influenced directly by Belinsky. The reason for this was, in the first place, the different character of their respective times. Belinsky was a man of the forties, in the full sense of the word, whereas Tolstoy entered upon his literary career in the fifties, and moved among Belinsky's followers, who lacked his attractive power; though, on the other hand, the social surroundings in which Tolstoy had

---

[1] Loewenfeld, *Count L. N. Tolstoy*, p. 125 Moscow.

TOLSTOY GRIGOROVICH
GONCHAROF TURGENEF DRUZHININ OSTROVSKY

Group of contributors to the "Sovremennik" (The Contemporary Magazine).

been reared could not be favorable to his intimacy with these representatives of the republic of letters—*raznotchintsy*, as they called themselves, all sorts and conditions of men. He kept company with men of his own standard of breeding, and even with them was always reserved, independent, mostly in opposition, and trying to influence others, while himself little responsive to outside influence. One may point out a more serious cause, that underlying difference in general views. Though Tolstoy had not yet definitely formed his views of life, still the tendency of *The Contemporary* had never attracted him.

Moreover, as Tolstoy has acknowledged in his literary work, he was more attracted by talent that was simply artistic than by that of a social tendency.

In his youth he had been under the sway of Rousseau's philosophical teaching.

Discussing the subject of French literature with Professor Boyer from Paris, who paid him a visit in the spring of 1901, Tolstoy thus expressed his opinion of his two teachers—Rousseau and Stendhal:

"People have been unjust to Rousseau, the greatness of his thought was not recognized, and he was calumniated. I have read the whole of Rousseau, all the twenty volumes, including the dictionary of music. I admired him with more than enthusiasm, I worshipped him. At fifteen I wore on my neck, instead of the usual cross, a medallion with his portrait. With some of his pages I am so familiar that I feel as if I had written them myself. As to Stendhal," continues Tolstoy, "I will speak of him only as the author of *Chartreuse de Parme* and *Rouge et Noir*. These are two great, inimitable works of art. I am, more than any one else, indebted for much to Stendhal. He taught me to understand war. Read once more *Chartreuse de Parme*, his account of the Battle of Waterloo. Who before him had so described war—*i. e.*, as it is in reality? Do you remember Fabracius crossing the battlefield and 'understanding nothing,' and how the hussars threw him with ease over the back of his horse, his splendid general's horse?

"Subsequently my brother, who had served in the Caucasus before me, confirmed the faithfulness of Stendhal's descriptions. He enjoyed war very much, but did not belong to those who believed in the Bridge of Arcole. He used to say to me, 'All that is embellishment, and in war there is no embellishment.' Soon afterward in the Crimea I easily verified all this with my own eyes. I repeat, all I know about war I learned first of all from Stendhal." [1]

We will now give the titles of the literary works which influenced Tolstoy at this period. We take them from the list of names which we have already partly quoted.

From twenty to thirty-five years of age Tolstoy was chiefly influenced by the following works:

TITLES.	DEGREE OF INFLUENCE.
Goethe, *Hermann und Dorothea*	Very great.
V. Hugo, *Notre Dame de Paris*	Very great.
Tyuchef, *Verses*	Great.
Koltsof, *Verses*	Great.
Fet, *Verses*	Great.
Plato, *Phædo and the Symposium* (Gotsin's translation)	Very great.
Odyssey and *Iliad*	Very great.

Thus we have the more or less complete list of Tolstoy's literary guides.

Tolstoy entered the circle of St. Petersburg authors, his powerful artistic personality and obstinate, often aggressive, temperament creating a storm in their hitherto quiet and peaceful atmosphere.

The following is from Fet's reminiscences of Tolstoy's first appearance in St. Petersburg:

"Turgenef used to get up and take his tea in the St. Petersburg fashion, very early, and during my short stay in town I called every morning about ten to have a quiet talk with him. On the second morning when Zakhar opened the door I saw in the hall a dress sword with a ribbon of St. Anne.

"'Whose sword is this?' I inquired, as I proceeded to the drawing-room.

"'If you please, come this way,' said Zakhar in a low voice, pointing to the left of the corridor. 'This is Count Tolstoy's sword, and his excellency is asleep in the drawing-room. Ivan Sergeyevich is drinking tea in the study.'

"During the hour I spent with Turgenef we conversed in a low voice, being afraid to awaken Tolstoy, who was asleep in the next room.

[1] Paul Boyer, *Le Temps*, 28th August, 1901

"'He is like this all the time,' said Turgenef, smiling. 'He came from Sebastopol, straight from the battery, stopped here at my place, and then and there plunged into dissipation. Carousals, gypsies, and card-playing all night; and afterward he sleeps like a top till two in the afternoon. At first I tried to restrain him, but after a while I gave it up.'

"About this time I was introduced to Tolstoy, but our acquaintance was a formal one, I not having yet read a single line of his nor even heard of him as an author, although Turgenef mentioned to me his tale of *Childhood*. But from the first I noticed in young Tolstoy a kind of unconscious antagonism to all accepted rules in the domain of reasoning. During this short period I saw him only once at Nekrassof's, at our bachelor's literary party. There I witnessed how Turgenef, eager and breathless in discussion, was driven to despair by the apparently calm, but all the more sarcastic, replies of Tolstoy.

"'I cannot accept,' said Tolstoy, 'what you said just now as your conviction. I stand at the door with a dagger or sword in hand, and say, "While I am alive, no one shall enter this door." That is conviction. But you two are trying to conceal the real meaning of your thoughts from each other, and you call this conviction.'

"'Then why do you come here?' said Turgenef, panting and in a thin falsetto, his voice during warm discussions always reaching this high pitch. 'Ours is not your banner! Go to Princess B-e-b-e.'

"'Why should I ask you where I am to go?' returned Tolstoy. 'Besides, idle talk will by no means beget convictions, wherever I go.'

"As far as I can remember, this was the only encounter between Turgenef and Tolstoy at which I was present, and I cannot help saying that, although I understood that the controversy related to politics, I took too little interest in the subject to pay attention to it. I must add that, from what I heard in our circle, Tolstoy was in the right, and, if indeed men suffering from the *régime* then in force were to try to describe their ideal, they would find the greatest difficulty in formulating their wants.

"Who of us at that time did not know the boon-companion, the partner in all sorts of frolics, and the capital fellow at telling amusing anecdotes, Dmitri Vassilyevich

Grigorovich, celebrated for his novels and stories? This is how he, by the way, told me of the encounters between Turgenef and Tolstoy in the same house of Nekrassof: 'My dear boy, my dear boy,' said Grigorovich, choking with laughter till tears came to his eyes, and stroking me on the shoulder, ' you cannot imagine what scenes we had here. Mercy on us! Turgenef speaks shriller and shriller, then pressing his hand to his throat, and with a look of a dying gazelle, whispers: " I cannot talk any longer! It will give me bronchitis!" and with enormous strides begins to walk up and down the three rooms. "Bronchitis!" sneers Tolstoy, " it's an imaginary illness. Bronchitis is a metal!" Of course the host Nekrassof is trembling heart and soul: he is afraid to lose both Turgenef and Tolstoy, in whom he foresees a powerful support for *The Contemporary*, so he is bound to manœuvre. We are all upset and at a loss what to say. Tolstoy is lying down in the middle of the room on a leather sofa and sulks; Turgenef, with the lappets of his jacket asunder and his hands in his pockets, continues to walk up and down all the three rooms. To prevent a catastrophe, I approached the sofa and said: " My dear Tolstoy, don't get excited! You have no idea how he appreciates and loves you!" " I will not allow him," says Tolstoy, his nostrils dilating, " to be spiteful to me. And now he walks up and down the room on purpose, crossing his democratic legs close to me." ' "[1]

D. V. Grigorovich, in his *Literary Reminiscences,* tells a similar story of the earlier period of Tolstoy's acquaintance with St. Petersburg authors:

" On my return from Marynsky to St. Petersburg, I met Count Tolstoy. I was first introduced to him in Moscow at the house of the Sushkof family, where he still wore his military uniform. He lived in St. Petersburg, in Ofitzersky Street, on the lower floor of a small set of chambers next the lodgings of M. L. Mikhailof, the author. It seems they were not acquainted. His keeping permanent rooms in St. Petersburg was incomprehensible to me, for from the very first he not only disliked St. Petersburg itself, but was irritated with everything connected with it.

" Having learned from him during our interview that he was invited to dine that very day with the editorial staff

[1] A. Fet, *My Reminiscences*, Part I, p. 105.

TURGENEF

GRIGOROVICH

NEKRASSOF

SOLLOGUB

PANAYEF

Another group of contributors to the "Sovremennik."

of *The Contemporary*, and that, though he had already written for that review, he yet knew very little the members of its staff, I agreed to go with him. On the way I warned him to be careful and not touch certain subjects, and in particular not to attack Georges Sand, who at that time was the idol of most of the members. The dinner went off quietly. Tolstoy was rather taciturn, but toward the end he could no longer control himself. Hearing praise bestowed on a new novel by Georges Sand, he abruptly declared his hatred of her, adding that her heroines, if they existed in reality, ought to be tied to the hangman's cart and driven through the streets of St. Petersburg as an example. Even at that time he had formed that personal standpoint about women and the woman question which he so forcibly expressed in his novel *Anna Karenina*.

"The incident at that dinner party may have been caused by his dissatisfaction with everything that bore the *cachet* of St. Petersburg, but more probably by his tendency to contradiction. Whatever judgment might have been passed, and the greater the authority of his interlocutor, the more he would insist on asserting an opposite view and in retorting sharply. Watching how he listened to his interlocutor, how he scrutinized him, how sarcastically he screwed up his lips, one would have thought he was thinking not so much how to answer a question as how to express an opinion which should be a puzzle and surprise to the questioner. This is how Tolstoy impressed me in his youth. In discussion he pushed his arguments to the furthest extreme. I happened once to be in the next room when he and Turgenef were having a discussion; hearing their loud voices I went into the room. Turgenef was pacing up and down showing signs of great embarrassment; he profited by the door I opened and went out immediately. Tolstoy was lying on the sofa, and his excitement was so great that it was only with great difficulty that I managed to calm him and take him home. The subject of their discussion remains unknown to me to the present moment."[1]

This tendency of Tolstoy to contradiction is also illustrated in the following episode related in the reminiscences of G. P. Danilevsky:

"At the end of the fifties I met Tolstoy in St. Petersburg

---

[1] Complete edition of the Works of D. V. Grigorovich, vol. xii, p. 326.

in the family of a well-known sculptor and painter. The author of the *Sebastopol Tales* had just arrived in St. Petersburg; he was a young, stately artillery officer. A very good likeness of him at that time is to be found in the well-known group of photographs by Levitsky, where he is taken together with Turgenef, Goncharof, Ostrovsky, and Druzhinin. I remember well how Count Tolstoy entered the drawing-room of the lady of the house during the reading aloud of a new work of Herzen's. Quietly standing behind the reader's chair, and waiting till the end of the reading, he began at first softly and shyly, but then boldly and hotly to attack Herzen and the enthusiasm with which his writings were accepted. He spoke with such sincerity and force, that in this family I did not come across Herzen's publications any more."[1]

We know that Tolstoy changed his opinion of Herzen later on, and this will be mentioned in due place.

E. Garshin, in his reminiscences of Turgenef, gives the following interesting account of Turgenef's opinion of Tolstoy. It shows the early element of mutual incompatibility which almost brought their relations to a fatal end.

" 'Tolstoy,' said Turgenef, 'developed early a trait of character which, as the foundation of his gloomy view on life, causes in the first place much suffering to himself. He never believed in the sincerity of men. Any kind of emotion seemed false to him, and he had the habit, by the extraordinary penetrating glance of his eyes, of piercing through the man who struck him as false.'

"Turgenef told me that never in his life had he experienced anything more depressing than the effect of that penetrating glance, which, combined with two or three venomous remarks, could exasperate one who had no great self-control to the verge of madness. This subject of Tolstoy's casual experiments, and almost the exclusive subject, was his friend Turgenef. He was, so the latter said, greatly annoyed by Turgenef's self-possession and his serenely calm attitude at that period of brilliant literary achievement, and Count Tolstoy seemed to have made up his mind to exasperate this quiet, kind-hearted man, who was working with full conviction of doing the right thing. The worst of it

---

[1] "A Visit to Yasnaya Polyana," by G. P. Danilevsky. *Historical Review*, March, 1886, p. 529.

was that Tolstoy did not believe this, he thought that the men whom we consider good are only hypocrites or try to display their goodness, and that they affect to be convinced that they are doing their work for a good cause.

"Turgenef recognized Count Tolstoy's attitude, but resolved by all means to keep his own ground and remain self-possessed. He tried to avoid Tolstoy, and with this object went to Moscow, then went to his country place, but Count Tolstoy followed him step by step, 'like a woman in love,' to use Turgenef's words as he told the story."[1]

All these facts as to the mutual relations of the two authors show that any real spiritual intimacy between them was impossible. But the liberal movement carried both of them in the same direction, and they considered themselves fellow-workers for the same cause. Besides, their aristocratic origin, their education, their prominent position in the literary circle—all this, though against their will, was bringing them, outwardly at any rate, together. But, as readers will see from the following incident, whenever they tried to be more than simple companions, a conflict was the result, and this sometimes exposed their priceless lives to danger. To do them justice, they both clearly realized the distance dividing them, they owned it openly to each other and to others, and, what is more important, they made great moral efforts to keep up, if not cordial, at least amicable relations based on mutual respect. On this ground they present a suggestive example to following generations.

We may insert here the account given by Mme. Golovachof-Panayef of the early days of the acquaintance of Turgenef and Tolstoy, which confirms our assertion.

"I must go back and tell of the appearance of Count Tolstoy in the circle of *The Contemporary*. He was then still an officer, and the only collaborator of *The Contemporary* who wore a military uniform. His literary talent had by this time made such a mark that all the leaders in literature had to accept him as their equal. Besides, Count Tolstoy was not a shy man, he was aware of his talent, and behaved, as I thought, with a certain more or less ease of manner or nonchalance.

"I never entered into conversation with the authors

---

[1] E. Garshin, "Reminiscences of I. S. Turgenef." *Historical Review*, November, 1883.

when they met at our house, I only listened in silence and observed them. I was particularly interested in watching Turgenef and Tolstoy, when they happened to be together and had a discussion or made remarks to one another, for they were both very clever and observant.

"I never heard Tolstoy express his opinion of Turgenef, and as a rule he said nothing of any of the authors, at least before me. Turgenef, on the other hand, seemed impelled to pour out observations about everybody.

"When Turgenef made Tolstoy's acquaintance, he said of him:

"'There is not a word, not a movement, which is natural in him. He is constantly posing, and I am at a loss to understand in so intelligent a man this foolish pride in his wretched title of Count!'

"'I did not notice it in Tolstoy,' said Panayef.

"'But there are many things you don't notice,' said Turgenef.

"After a time Turgenef came to the conclusion that Tolstoy had the ambition to be considered a Don Juan. Count Tolstoy one day related to us certain interesting episodes which had happened to him during the war. When he went away Turgenef said:

"'You may boil a Russian officer for three days in strong suds and you won't succeed in getting rid of the braggadocio of a Junker; you may cover him with a thick veneer of education, still his brutality will shine through.'

"And Turgenef began to criticise every sentence of Tolstoy's, the tone of his voice, the expression of his face, and finally said:

"'And only to think that at the bottom of all this brutality lies merely the desire to get promoted.'

"'Look here, Turgenef,' remarked Panayef, 'if I did not know you so well, I should think, when I listen to your abuse of Tolstoy, that you are jealous of him.'

"'On what grounds can I be jealous of him? Of what, tell me!' cried Turgenef.

"'Oh, no doubt, you have no reason; your talent is equal to his. . . . But people may think. . . .'

"Turgenef laughed, and with a kind of pity in his voice remarked:

"'Panayef, you are a good observer when it concerns

NEKRASSOF (co-editor)   TURGENEF   LEO TOLSTOY
PANAYEF (editor)   GRIGOROVICH   OSTROVSKY

Caricature of the "Inevitable Contributors" of the "Sovremennik."

coxcombs, but I don't advise you to go beyond the proper sphere of your observations.'

"Panayef was hurt.

"'It's for your own good that I said that,' he added, and went out of the room.

"Turgenef was very much excited, and repeated with vexation:

"'Only Panayef's head could entertain such nonsense—that I am jealous of Tolstoy! Is it his title that I am jealous of?'

"Nekrassof spoke very little all this time, suffering as he was from a sore throat. He merely said to Turgenef:

"'Do leave it alone, whatever Panayef may have said; as if indeed any one would suspect you of such an absurdity.'"[1]

Turgenef, with his honest, truthful nature, had many times publicly declared his great admiration of Tolstoy's talent, and more than that, he once said to a French publisher, using the expression of John the Baptist in relation to Jesus Christ: "I am unworthy to untie his shoe." Their relations nevertheless were never cordial.

Only on his death-bed, in his last letter to Tolstoy, while with touching tenderness imploring him to return to literary activity, he gave him the name with which no Russian author had been hitherto honored, the name of "the great writer of the Russian land." And this glorious name will follow him into eternity.

To give the reader an idea of the relations between Tolstoy and Turgenef at the early period of their acquaintance, we will interrupt the chronological order of our work and quote several letters of Turgenef to Tolstoy, written in the same year.

To Leo Tolstoy.

"Paris, *November* 16, 1856.

"My dear Tolstoy—Your letter of October 15th was crawling toward me for a whole month. I received it only yesterday. I have thought it well over what you write to me, and I believe you are mistaken. It is a fact that I cannot be quite straightforward with you, because I cannot be quite

[1] *Reminiscences of Mme. A. Golovachof-Panayef*, p. 279.

frank with you. It seems to me that we became acquainted in an awkward way, and at an evil moment, but, when we meet again, all will be much easier and smoother. I feel I love you as a man (as to my love for the author—needless to mention it); yet many things in you jar upon me, and in the end I have found out that it is better for me to keep aloof from you. At our next meeting let us try again to go hand in hand—perhaps it will come off better. But at a distance, however strange it sounds, my heart is disposed to you as to a brother, and I feel a tenderness for you. In a word, I love you—there is no doubt about it; let us hope that in time something good will come of it.

"I have heard of your illness and I was grieved, and now I beg you to dismiss the thought of it from your mind. You are imagining things yourself, and probably think of consumption, but I can assure you, you have not got it.

"I am very sorry for your sister; she is one who ought to enjoy good health; I mean, if there is anybody who deserves to be quite well, it is she; instead, she is a constant sufferer. Let us hope the Moscow treatment may help her. Why don't you recall your brother? Why should he stay in the Caucasus? Does he intend to become a great warrior? My uncle informed me that you have all of you gone off to Moscow, and I therefore forward this letter to Botkin, Moscow.

"French conversation is as distasteful to me as it is to you, and never did Paris appear to me so flatly prosaic. Contentment does not suit it; I saw this city in other days, and then I liked it better. I am kept here by an old indissoluble tie with a particular family, and by my daughter, of whom I am very fond; she is a good, intelligent girl. Were it not for this, I would have long ago joined Nekrassof in Rome. I have received from him two letters—he is a little bored in Rome, and no wonder—all that is great in Rome only surrounds him; he does not share in it. And one cannot exist for long on a diet of sympathy and admiration, when those feelings occur involuntarily only at rare intervals. Yet he is better off there than in St. Petersburg, and his health is improving. For the present Fet is staying in Rome with him. He had written a few graceful verses, and a detailed account of his travels containing much that is childish, but also many clever, sensible sayings—and a kind of touching simplicity and sincerity of impression. He is, in fact, a darling, as you call him.

"Now as to Tchernishevsky's articles. I don't like their arrogant, dry tone, the expression of a harsh nature. But I rejoice at their being printed, rejoice over the reminiscences of B., and the quotations from his articles; I rejoice that at last his name is uttered with respect. However, you cannot sympathize with me in this joy. Annenkof assures me that I derive these impressions from living abroad; that with them this is already a thing of the past, they now want something else. Perhaps he is a better judge, as he is on the spot; still I am pleased.

"You have finished the first part of *Youth*—that is glorious. What a pity I cannot hear you read it! If you don't turn aside from your path (and there is no reason why you should), you will go far ahead. I wish you health, activity, and freedom—spiritual freedom.

"As to my *Faust*, I don't suppose you will like it very much. My writings might have pleased you and perhaps influenced you in some way, but only up to the time when you became quite independent. There is no need for you to study me now, you will only see my difference of manner, my faults and omissions. It remains for you to study man, your own heart, and the really great authors. I am a writer of a transition period, and am of use only to men who are in a transitory state. Well, good-by and be well. Write to me. My present address: Rue de Rivoli, No. 206.

"Thanks to your sister for the two added words; remember me to her and her husband. I am grateful to Varenka for remembering me.

"I intended to tell you something of the authors here, but keep this for the next letter. I shake your hand warmly.

"I do not stamp my letter, do the same with yours." [1]

December 8, 1856, he wrote to Tolstoy:

"DEAR TOLSTOY—Yesterday my good fairy took me past the post-office, and it occurred to me to inquire about letters at the *post-restante* for me, though by this time all my friends ought to know of my Parisian address. There I found your letter, in which you speak of my *Faust;* you can easily imagine what a pleasant reading I had. Your

[1] *Letters of I. S. Turgenef* (First Collection), p. 27.

sympathy caused me great and sincere delight. And besides, the whole of your letter breathed gentleness and frankness and a kind of friendly serenity. It remains for me to hold out my hand across the 'ravine' which long ago turned into a hardly perceptible chink; we won't mention it, it is not worth it.

"I dare not speak to you on a subject which you mention; these are delicate things; they are killed with a word before they are ripe, but when they are ripe a hammer cannot break them. God grant everything may come off successfully and well. It may bring you that spiritual equilibrium you needed so much when I first knew you. I see you are very friendly with Druzhinin and under his influence. This is well, only mind not to feast on him too much. When I was at your age I was more influenced by enthusiastic natures, but you are a different man from me; moreover, perhaps, the times are now different. I am eagerly looking forward to get the *Reading Library*. I am anxious to read the article on Belinsky, although I don't expect to derive much pleasure from it. As to *The Contemporary* being in bad hands, that is beyond doubt. At first Panayef used to write very often and assure me he would not act 'heedlessly,' underlining this word, but he is subdued now and keeps silent like a child who has misbehaved at mealtime. I have written to Nekrassof with full details about it, and this will very likely induce him to leave Rome and return earlier than he intended. Please let me know in what number of *The Contemporary* your *Youth* will appear, and, by the way, give me your final impression of *Lear*, which you have probably read if only for the sake of Druzhinin."[1]

We do not possess exact information as to Tolstoy's opinion of *King Lear* in Druzhinin's translation, but from the letter of Botkin to Druzhinin quoted below, one can see that Tolstoy liked Druzhinin's translation.

Here is the letter:

"What a success your *Lear* proves," writes Botkin. "To me it was certain; still, how the pleasure increases when the inner conviction becomes a reality. There it is, the well-known antipathy of Tolstoy to Shakespeare which Turgenef so much fought against! I must do myself the

[1] *Letters of I. S. Turgenef* (First Collection), p. 33.

justice to state that I was convinced that at the first opportunity this antipathy would disappear; but I am glad that your excellent translation brought that opportunity."[1]

It seems the joy of Botkin was premature, for Tolstoy persisted in his dislike to Shakespeare, but on this we shall have occasion to remark in one of the following chapters.

On the 5th December, 1856, Turgenef wrote to Druzhinin from Paris: "By the way, I am told you are very intimate with Tolstoy, and he is now so nice and open. I am very glad. When this new wine has been through the fermenting process it will turn out a beverage worthy of the gods. What about his *Youth,* which was submitted to your judgment? I wrote to him twice, the second time c/o Vassenka (Botkin)."[2]

Youth really was forwarded to Druzhinin to be criticised by him; he read it, and wrote the following interesting letter in answer:

"Twenty sheets should be written about *Youth.* I read it with wrath, shouting and swearing; not on account of its want of literary worth, but owing to the copy and the handwriting. This mixing together of two different handwritings distracted my attention and prevented an intelligent perusal; it was just as if two voices were shouting in my ear and purposely confusing me, and I know that the impression was not as complete as it should have been. However, I will say to you what I can. Your task was awful, but you have accomplished it well. None of the present-day writers could have grasped the unintelligible, fleeting period of youth and depicted it in such a manner. Cultured people will derive great enjoyment from your *Youth*; if anybody tells you that this work is inferior to *Childhood* and *Boyhood,* you may spit in his face. There are depths of poetry in your work; all the first chapters are excellent, only, until the description of spring and the removal of double windows, the introduction is rather dry. After that the arrival at the village is fine, just before that the description of the Nekhludof family, the father's explanation of his reasons for marrying, the chapters 'New Comrades' and 'I am falling through.' Many chapters

---

[1] From Drushinin's papers, *Twenty-five Years,* a volume published by the Society of Assistance to Authors and Scholars, St. Petersburg, 1884.
[2] *Letters of I. S. Turgenef* (First Collection), p. 32.

breathe the poetry of ancient Moscow, which nobody had observed in the proper way. Baron Z.'s coachman is admirable (I speak as one who understands). Some chapters are prosy and dry, as, for instance, all about the stipulations with Dmitri Nekhludof, the descriptions of his relations to Varenka, and the chapter on family understanding. The feast at Yar's is also rather long, as well as the Count's visit with Ilinka, which comes before it. The recruiting of Semyonof will not pass the censor. You must not be afraid of arguing; it's all clever and original. You are apt to analyze too minutely, which might become a great defect. Sometimes you are ready to say, ' Such and such a fellow's thigh indicated that he desired to travel in India.' You must curb this inclination, but on no account should it be suppressed. All your analytic work should be conducted in this way. Every one of your defects has elements of force and beauty; nearly all your merits contain grains of defect.

"Your style is in harmony with your matter. You are illiterate in a marked degree. Sometimes your illiteracy is that of a neologist or a great poet who is perpetually reconstructing a language in his own manner, or that of an officer who sits in his tent and writes to a friend. It may be said for certain that all the pages written by you in a kindly mood are excellent, but as soon as you grow cold, your style gets confused and diabolical forms of speech bubble up. Therefore passages written unsympathetically should be looked through and corrected. I tried to make corrections at times, but I gave up the idea; you alone can do this task and you should do it. It is of importance that you should avoid long sentences. Chop them into two or three . . . don't be afraid to use full-stops . . . use with scant ceremony words like *that, which,* and *this;* they should be struck out by tens. If you are in a difficulty, take a sentence and imagine that you want to communicate it to somebody in a fluent, familiar way.

"It is time to close, but there are still a good many things to be said. The bulk of the less educated readers will like *Youth* less than *Childhood* and *Boyhood.* The small size of these two works, and some episodes, such as the tale of Karl Ivanovich, are in their favor. The dullest man cherishes a few childish memories and rejoices when their poetry is made clear to him, but the period of youth (of that confused and disconnected youth which is full of hard knocks and humiliation which you unveil for us) is usually buried in the soul, and hence it loses its vividness and becomes obliterated.

"It would mean much labor to make your work reach the understanding of the masses, by inserting two or three amusing incidents, etc., but hardly anybody could make it suit the taste of the majority.

"The plot and the framework of your *Youth* will provide a feast for thinking people who understand poetry.

"Let me know if I should forward the MS. to you or hand it over to Panayef. You have not made a large stride in a new direction with this work, but you have shown what there is in you, and what can be effected by you."

The fact that Druzhinin could have written to Tolstoy in such a manner shows that they really were on familiar terms, and that Druzhinin could influence him.

Tolstoy's stay in St. Petersburg—from November till May—was interrupted by a short visit to Orel, on business connected with family affairs.

February 2d Tolstoy received the news of his brother Dmitri's death; he drew a vivid picture of the latter's personality in his Reminiscences, quoted by us in the chapter on *Youth*. Here we quote the second part of those Reminiscences, referring to his brother's subsequent life, illness, and death:

"When we made a partition of our property the estate Yasnaya Polyana, on which we lived, fell to my lot. Seryozha was a lover of horses, and, as there was a stud at Pirogovo, he received that estate, which was what he desired. To Mitenka and Nicolenka were given the other two estates—to Nicolenka, Nicolskoye; to Mitenka, the Kursk of Scherbachovka, which came to us from Perovskaya. I have kept a statement from Mitenka explaining what were his views as to the possession of serfs. The idea that this sort of thing ought not to be, but that serfs should be set free, was quite unknown in our circle in the forties; the possession of serfs by inheritance appeared a necessary condition of life, and it was thought that the only thing that could be done to prevent this possession from being an evil was that the landowner should concern himself with the moral welfare of the peasants as well as their material condition. From this point of view Mitenka explained his project very seriously, naïvely, and sincerely. He, a lad of twenty when he left the university, took upon himself the duties—thinking that he could not do otherwise—of directing the morality of hundreds of peasant families, and thought to do this by threats of punishments and punishments, as is recommended by Gogol in his letters to a landowner. I think I remember that Mitenka had these letters, which had been pointed out to him by the prudent priest— thus did Mitenka commence his landlord's duties. But besides these duties toward the serfs there was at that time another duty which it was deemed impossible to neglect— that was military or civil service, and Mitenka, having finished with the university, decided to enter the civil service. In order to decide which branch to select, he purchased an almanac, and, having examined into all the branches of civil service, he came to the conclusion that the most important one was legislation, whereupon he went to St. Petersburg and there applied to the officials at the head of that department. I can imagine Taneyef's astonishment when, on giving his reception, he stopped in front of a high, round-shouldered, badly dressed man among the supplicants (Mitenka always dressed merely for the purpose of covering his body), a man with quiet, fine eyes; and on inquiring what he wanted, received for answer that he was a Russian nobleman who had gone through the university, and, being desirous of being useful to his country, had chosen legislation as his province.

" ' Your name?'

" ' Count Tolstoy.'

" ' You have not yet served anywhere?'

" ' I have only just finished my university course, and my desire is merely to be useful.'

" ' Then what post do you desire to have?'

" ' It is all the same; any one in which I can be useful.'

" His gravity and sincerity so struck Taneyef that he drove Mitenka to the department of legislation and there handed him over to an official.

" Probably the official's attitude toward him, and above all toward the work, repelled Mitenka, for he did not enter that department. He had no acquaintance in St. Petersburg except the student Obolensky, whom he had known at Kazan. Mitenka called on him at his summer residence. Obolensky told me about it laughing.

"Obolensky was a very worldly, ambitious man, but gifted with tact. He related how on that occasion he had guests (probably of the aristocracy, with whom Obolensky associated), and Mitenka came to him through the garden in a nankeen coat. 'At first I did not recognize him, but, when I did, I tried to put him at his ease. I introduced him to my guests and asked him to take his coat off, but it turned out that there was nothing under the coat; he did not think anything necessary.' He sat down, and immediately, without being disconcerted by the presence of the guests, he turned to Obolensky with the same question he had put to Taneyef: Where was it best to serve in order to be useful?

"To Obolensky, with his views on service as merely a means of satisfying ambition, such a question had probably never occurred. But with the tact which he possessed and with external good nature he answered, mentioning various posts, and offered his assistance. Mitenka was evidently dissatisfied both with Obolensky and Taneyef, and left St. Petersburg without entering the civil service. He went to his country place, and at Soudja, I think it was, he accepted some local post and busied himself with rural work, especially among the peasants.

"After we had both left the university, I lost sight of him. I know that he lived the same severe, abstemious life, knowing neither wine, tobacco, nor, above all, women, up to twenty-six years of age, which was very rare at that time. I know that he associated with monks and pilgrims, and became very intimate with an extremely singular man —our guardian—who lived at Voyekof's place, a man whose origin no one knew. This man was called Father Luke. He walked about in a cassock, was very ugly, small of stature, one-eyed, but cleanly in his person and exceptionally strong. When he shook hands, he gripped your hand as if with pincers, and always spoke very solemnly and mysteriously. He lived at Voyekof's, near the mill, where he had built himself a little house, and cultivated a remarkable flower-garden. It is this Father Luke whom Mitenka used to take about with him. I heard also that he associated with an old-fashioned old man, a miserly neighboring landowner, one Samoyloy.

"I think I was already in the Caucasus when an extraordinary alteration took place in Mitenka. He suddenly took to drinking, smoking, wasting money, and going with women. How this came to pass with him I do not know; I did not see him at the time. I only know that his seducer was a deeply immoral man, very attractive externally, the youngest son of Islenyef. I will tell about him later. In this life Mitenka remained the same serious, religious man he was in everything. A prostitute named Masha, who was the first woman he knew, he ransomed from her abode and took into his house. But this life did not last long. I believe it was not so much the vicious and unhealthy life which he led for some months in Moscow as the internal struggle and the qualms of conscience which suddenly destroyed his powerful organization. He contracted consumption, went to the country, was treated in towns, and took to his bed at Orel, where I saw him for the last time, immediately after the Crimean War. He was in a dreadful state: the enormous palm of his hand appeared visibly attached to the two bones of the lower arm, his face was all eyes, and they were the same beautiful, serious eyes, with a penetrating expression of inquiry in them. He was constantly coughing and spitting, but he was loath to die, did not wish to believe he was dying. Poor pox-marked Masha, whom he had rescued, wearing a kerchief round her head, was with him and nursed him. In my presence, at his own wish, a miraculous icon was brought. I remember the expression of his face when he prayed to it.

"At that time I was particularly odious. I had arrived at Orel from St. Petersburg, in which city I was moving in society, and I was full of vanity. I was sorry for Mitenka, but not much. I just looked about me in Orel and went away again; he died a few days later.

"I really think that what troubled me most in his death was that it prevented me from taking part in some private theatricals which were then being organized at court, and to which I had been invited."[1]

Peace was concluded on March 12th, and this circumstance made it easier for Tolstoy to get his leave.

[1] From Tolstoy's *Personal Reminiscences*.

During the winter he finished *Lost on the Seppe; or, The Snowstorm; Two Hussars, An Old Acquaintance,* and *A Russian Proprietor.* Tolstoy had to distribute his works among three periodicals; thus the first two novels appeared in *The Contemporary,* the third in the *Reading Library,* and the fourth in *Memoirs of the Fatherland.*

Among other things Tolstoy wrote to his aunt Tatiana at this period:

"I have finished my *Hussars* (a novel), and have not taken up anything else; besides, Turgenef, whom I have begun to love (I realize it now), notwithstanding that we always quarrelled, is gone. Hence I feel terribly lonely."

This letter shows that Tolstoy's relation to Turgenef varied from time to time.

St. Petersburg life was evidently not to Tolstoy's liking. Soon after his arrival he did his best to get away, and prepared to go abroad.

In the letter to his brother of March 25, 1856, he says incidentally:

"I shall start for abroad in eight months; if I can get leave I shall go. I have already written about this to Nicolenka and asked him to come with me. If we were all three to arrange to go together, that would be excellent. If we each take 1,000 roubles, we could do the trip very well. Please write. How did you like *The Snowstorm?* I am dissatisfied with it, seriously, and now there is much I should like to write, but there is really no time in this accursed St. Petersburg. At all events, whether I am allowed or not to go abroad in April, I intend to take leave of absence and stay in the country."

On the 12th of May, while yet in St. Petersburg, he put down in his diary:

"A powerful means to secure true happiness in life is —without any rules—to spin in all directions, like a spider, a whole web of love and catch in it all that one can—old women, children, women, and constables."

. . . .

It may be supposed that *The Contemporary's* business as well as literary affairs gave little satisfaction to its chief supporters; this was perhaps due to the individual diversity of convictions, views, habits, education, and surroundings of the contributors, as this always hinders any common work devised by educated people. In every circle composed of "intellectuals," division into groups very soon takes place: a tolerant attitude is very soon replaced by indifference; after that rivalry asserts itself, culminating in open enmity. That was the case with *The Contemporary*.

As far back as the beginning of 1856 the idea struck some of the contributors of separating and founding a new magazine. Druzhinin's letter to Tolstoy bears testimony to this. In it he says, among other things:

"Availing myself of some surplus energy, I hasten to have a talk with you concerning a matter which occupied us at our last meeting and which is now being favorably considered by many of our comrades in St. Petersburg. The want of a journal which should be purely literary and critical, and counteract all the frenzies and indecencies of the present time, is felt in a marked degree. Goncharof, Yermin, Turgenef, Annenkof, Maikof, Mikhailof, Avdeyef, and many others back up this idea with their hearty approval. If you, Ostrovsky, Turgenef, and perhaps our half-insane Grigorovich (though we could get along without him), would join this group, it may be taken for granted that the whole of the belles-lettres will be concentrated in one journal. What this organ shall be, whether a new journal, or a reading library on premises hired by the company, as to all this, you might devise some scheme and let us know what it is. Here the majority is bent on taking a lease on moderate terms, and the publisher consents. For my part, I have nothing to say either for or against, but offer my services to a purely literary journal, on whatever principles it is got up.

"As to the department of science, the following professors could be regarded as willing contributors: Gorlof, Oostryalof, Blagoveschensky, Berezin, Zernin, as well as those who contribute now—I am naming the most talented—Lavrof, Lkhovsky, Kenevich, Vodovozof, Dumilin. Although Turgenef is a hopeless worker, he will be a valuable man, considering his activity, as well as his position in literature. However, the details have to be left in the background now; we must agree as to the whole and decide the main points.

"Judging by the interest you have manifested in this matter, I count on your support. By the way, I have a request to make of you, as I am still following my old occupation, and starting a new journal might take up a good deal of time, I beg your permission to have you in the meantime included in the number of contributors to the *Reading Library*. Do not dispose of all your articles, but leave some work for me toward the autumn, making your own choice and stipulating for your own conditions. I won't worry you about this, being aware that without my entreaties you will do everything for me that you can.

"Write me a few lines about all this and about your life in general, your anticipations, and Marie's health; give her my best and sincere regards. Also let me know your address. We must keep up correspondence about the new journal; I am afraid that our forces will get scattered, we have only enough for one edition. It is immaterial what was the idea of the undertaking, as long as we all unite in working at it. So, in summer, as you often go to see Turgenef, try to influence him and direct this delightful but unreliable . . . toward our common goal. Judging by what he has said to me a hundred times, the idea of such a journal should please him; but how can one rely on anything he says? Let him consider to what a low stage our journals have been reduced by the splitting of forces; *Russky Vestnik* alone has kept its ground well, but it has a jaded appearance now owing to the falling off of 'Ateney'; 'Ateney,' however, is very dull. There is nothing to say about St. Petersburg."

On May 17th Tolstoy set off for Moscow.

May 26th he spent in the house of Dr. Bers, married to a friend of Tolstoy's childhood, Mademoiselle Islenef; they were then living at Pokrovskoye, not far from Moscow. In Tolstoy's diary there are a few words about this visit.

"The children were all there. What jolly, charming little girls!" One of them, the youngest, became Tolstoy's wife six years later.

After that he proceeded on his journey, and on May 28th arrived at Yasnaya Polyana.

Next day he wrote a letter to his brother Sergey, in which, among other things, he remarked:

"In Moscow I passed ten days . . . exceedingly pleasantly, without champagne and gypsies, but a little in love —with whom I will tell you later."

On his arrival in Yasnaya, he naturally goes to greet his neighbors, his sister Marie, Turgenef, and others.

From the two following letters to his brother, we see that at the end of the summer he was seriously ill. Thus at the beginning of September, 1856, he writes:

"Only now, at nine o'clock in the evening, Monday, can I give you a good answer; before this I kept getting worse and worse. Two doctors have been called, forty leeches have been applied, but it is only a little while ago that I fell asleep, and I have awakened feeling considerably better. Still for five or six days I cannot think of going. So *au revoir*. Please let me know when you start, and whether there really are great arrears in the farming work of your estate, and do not devastate the sporting places too much without me; the dogs I may perhaps send to-morrow."

In his letter of September 15th he says:

"MY DEAR FRIEND SERYOZHA: My health has improved and it has not. The pains and the inflammation have passed, but there remains some kind of oppression in the chest. I feel shooting sensations and, toward the evening, pains. Perhaps it will pass off gradually of itself, but I shall not soon make up my mind to go to Kursk, and, if not soon, then it is no good going at all. If I am not better in a fortnight or so, I would rather go to Moscow."

Soon after he again removed to St. Petersburg, whence he wrote to his brother the 10th of November, 1856:

"Excuse me, dear friend Seryozha, for writing only two words. I have no time. Since my departure ill luck pursues me. Of those I love not one is here. In the *Otechestvenniya Zapiski* they say I have been abused for the *Military Stories*. I have not yet read it, but Konstantinof made a point of informing me the moment I arrived that the Grand Duke Michael,[1] having learned that I was reported to have composed a song, is displeased, especially for my having, as it was said, taught it to the soldiers. This is too bad. I have had an explanation upon the subject with the Chief of the Staff. There is only one thing as it should be—my health is all right, and Shipulinski says my lungs are in perfect order."

[1] Brother of the Emperor Nicholas I.

Tolstoy at the time of his retirement from military service, 1856.

On November 26, 1856, Tolstoy retired from military service. We may mention a good act done by him at the close of his service.

The commander of the battery where Tolstoy served, Captain-Lieutenant Korenitsky, was to be tried by court-martial after the war, but thanks to Tolstoy's influence and exertions he was spared.

With the retirement of Tolstoy from service begins a new period of his life, full of social and literary interests, with strivings after personal happiness.

Notwithstanding his uncompromising views and his rejection of literary authorities, Tolstoy was a welcome guest and a valued member of the literary circle of *The Contemporary.*

But Tolstoy himself was far from pleased with that circle. It could not be otherwise. One need only read the reminiscences of authors belonging to that period, for example, Herzen, Panayef, Fet, and others, men of different schools, to come to very sad conclusions as to the moral weakness of those men, though they pretended to be leaders of humanity. When we think of the dinner parties of Nekrassof, the carousals of Herzen, Ketcher, and Ogarel, Turgenef's love for the culinary art, all those friendly parties, incomplete without a great deal of champagne, hunting, card-playing, etc.—we are pained to think of the idleness, the mental blindness of these men, who could not see the evil of their revels, with all the love for democracy and progress which they mixed up with them. In the midst of this shamelessness, which is perhaps still going on in some shape or other even at the present day, only one voice of accusation and self-correction resounded—the voice of a man whose soul could not endure that self-deception. That voice was Tolstoy's.

In his *Confession* he gives the following picture of the manners of the literary people, *i. e.,* of society, at the end of the fifties and beginning of the sixties:

"Before I had time to look round, the prejudices and views of life common to the writers of the class with which I associated became my own, and completely put an end to all my former struggles after a better life. These views, under the influence of the dissipation into which I plunged, issued in a theory of life which justified it. The view taken by my fellow-writers was, that life is a development, and the principal part in that development is played by ourselves, the thinkers, while, among the thinkers, the chief influence is again due to ourselves, the poets. Our vocation is to teach mankind.

"In order to avoid answering the very natural question, 'What do I know, and what can I teach?' the theory in question is made to contain this formula, that the answer is not required, but that the thinker and the poet teach unconsciously. I was myself considered a marvellous *littérateur* and poet, and I therefore very naturally adopted this theory. Meanwhile, thinker and poet though I was, I wrote and taught I knew not what. For doing this I received large sums of money; I kept a splendid table, had an excellent lodging, associated with loose women, and received my friends handsomely; moreover, I had fame. It would seem, then, that what I taught must have been good, the faith in poetry and the development of life was a true faith, and I was one of its high priests, a post of great importance and of profit. I long remained in this belief, and for a year never once doubted its truth.

"In the second year, however, and especially in the third of this way of life, I began to doubt the absolute truth of the doctrine, and to examine it more closely. The first suspicious fact which attracted my attention was, that the apostles of this belief did not agree among themselves. Some proclaimed that they were the only good and useful teachers, and all others worthless; while those opposed to them said the same of themselves. They disputed, quarrelled, abused, deceived, and cheated one another.

"Moreover, there were many among us who, quite indifferent to right or wrong, only cared for their own private interests. All this forced on me doubts as to the truth of our belief. Again, when I doubted this faith in the influence of literary men, I began to examine more closely into the character and conduct of its chief professors, and I convinced myself that they were men who led immoral lives, and were most of them worthless and insignificant individuals, and far beneath the moral level of those with whom I had associated during my former dissipated and military career; these men, however, had none the less an amount of self-confidence only to be expected in those who are conscious of being saints, or for whom holiness is an empty name.

"I grew disgusted with mankind and with myself, and discovered that the belief which I had accepted was a delusion. The strangest thing of all was that, though I soon saw the falseness of the belief and renounced it, I did not renounce the position I had gained by it; I still called myself a thinker, a poet, and a teacher. I was simple enough to imagine that I, the poet and thinker, was able to teach other men without knowing myself what it was I attempted to teach. I had only gained a new vice by my companionship; it had developed pride in me to a morbid extreme, and the self-confidence with which I taught what I did not know amounted almost to insanity."

However, while living in the same circle with these men, Tolstoy had taken part in all their affairs, and was one of the most active members in their common enterprises. Thus one of the most important schemes of the Society of Assistance to Authors and Scholars, the so-called "Literary Fund," is in many respects indebted to him for its foundation. Druzhinin is generally considered the founder of the society. But in Tolstoy's diary there is the following note:

"*Jan.* 2, 1857.—I wrote a project of the fund at Druzhinin's."

The name of Tolstoy must therefore be added to the list of the founders of the "Literary Fund."

To this period belong his more thorough study and admiration of Pushkin's works.

According to Tolstoy, he seriously appreciated Pushkin after having read Merimée's French translation of his *Gypsies*.

The reading of this work, thus expounded in prose form, gave Tolstoy a very strong impression of the greatness of Pushkin's poetical genius.

In Tolstoy's diary, of the date January 4, 1857, there is the following remark:

"I dined at Botkin's house alone with Panayef; he read Pushkin to me. I went into Botkin's study, and there wrote a letter to Turgenef; then I sat down on a couch and wept with joyful tears. I am of late decidedly happy, rejoicing in the advance of my moral development."

The advance of moral development to which he refers

did not allow Tolstoy to find satisfaction in that society and in its work, and he eagerly looked for another outlet. As a restless spirit usually manifests its uneasiness in action, so Tolstoy showed restless activity, and one way in which his impatience found vent was foreign travel, apparently without a fixed plan. This is what he says about the matter in his *Confession*, judging himself and those surrounding him with his characteristic plainness of speech:

"I lived in this senseless manner another six years, up to the time of my marriage. During this time I was abroad. My life in Europe, and my acquaintance with many eminent and learned foreigners, confirmed my belief in the doctrine of general perfectibility, and I found the same theory prevailed among them. This belief took the form which is common among most of the cultivated men of the day. It may be summed up in the word 'progress.' I believed at that time that this word had a real meaning. I did not understand that, when, on being tormented like other men by the question how I was to better my life, I answered that I must live for progress, I was only repeating the reply of one who is carried away in a boat by the waves and the wind, and who, to the one important question, 'Where are we to steer?' should answer, 'We are being carried somewhere or other.'"

But, before going abroad, Tolstoy gave up a great deal of time to the search for personal and family happiness.

CHAPTER X

ROMANCE

The importance of this romantic experience in Tolstoy's life—A short summary of similar facts in his earlier life—His acquaintance with the family A.—Departure of A. for the coronation fêtes—Letter of V. A. to Tolstoy's aunt about the coronation—The indignation of Tolstoy—His answer—Tolstoy's journey to St. Petersburg for two months in order to test the depth of his feelings—The resumption of good relations—Tolstoy's letters evince doubt concerning stability and wisdom of their sentiment—Tolstoy's letter to his aunt Tatiana asking for advice—A letter concerning true love—Correspondence interrupted for three weeks by V. A. forbidding him to write to her—Last letter of Tolstoy to V. A. from Russia—Tolstoy's letter to his aunt from Moscow—Tolstoy's final letter to V. A. from Paris—Tolstoy's letters to Tatiana concerning his former love—The connection of this love affair with *Family Happiness*.

I HAVE now to relate one of the most important passages of Tolstoy's life, embracing the history of his falling in love. It did not lead to marriage, still, in my opinion, it must have had a very great influence on his life. Like many other episodes it brings out very clearly certain traits of his character, such as, in the first place, his ardent, impulsive nature, and next the power exercised by his supreme guide, reason, which keeps the passions under control and directs them to a good end; lastly, the simplicity, sincerity, and chivalry of his character. We see this both where his actions are determined by the highest principles, and also in connection with the petty details of everyday life. The story is interesting in itself as dealing with the relations between a man and a woman, and giving in connection therewith a grave and instructive experience, by attention to which young people might be saved from a great deal of unhappiness.

In Tolstoy's life up to this time there had already been a few incipient love affairs, but they had led to nothing. The strongest case was that of his boyish affection for Sonitchka Kaloshin. This was followed by the affair of Z. N. while he was at the University; but the love really only existed in his own imagination, Z. N. herself hardly knew anything about it. The Cossack girl has been mentioned already. After this there was a kind of a society love affair with Madame S., of which she herself probably was scarcely conscious; Tolstoy was always shy and reserved in connection with such matters.

However, his love for V. A. was a more powerful and serious feeling. Their relations had become thoroughly understood and avowed, and had been declared to a circle of relatives and acquaintances as those of lovers.

Unfortunately, Tolstoy's extensive and interesting correspondence with this girl cannot yet be published owing to circumstances beyond my control, and I have to confine myself to a short summary of its contents.

Let us remember how, in a letter from Sebastopol, Tolstoy complained of the want of female society and expressed his fear of becoming incapacitated for it, and thus depriving himself of the possibility of married life, which he held in high honor.

Thoughts of women and family life were constantly in his mind after he returned from the campaign, and on his way through Moscow he was struck by a good-looking girl, the daughter of a landowner of the neighborhood, the result being, in no long time, a romantic mutual attachment.

The first letter is written by Tolstoy from Yasnaya Polyana to Moscow, where the young lady was staying. The family she lived in comprised an aunt, a fashionable lady who was fond of court life, and three sisters; besides this lady's nieces and Zh., and also a French governess. After spending the summer in Sudakovo, a country place not far from Yasnaya Polyana, they moved to Moscow in August to be present at the coronation festivities of Alexander II, in August 26, 1856.

The young lady enjoyed herself very much during the festivities, and, in a letter to Tolstoy's aunt, she described them in enthusiastic language. This letter was the first disappointment to Tolstoy. As he was attracted by the girl, he could not help looking upon her as his possible life-companion, and he thought he ought to explain to her his views of social and family life; but he was disagreeably surprised by finding himself completely misunderstood, the lady's attitude toward sundry questions of the highest importance being one of absolute indifference. However, he still hoped to influence her in the right direction, in reliance on her young and susceptible nature, and, finding her by no means unsympathetic, he used all his eloquence to make her take a serious view of their relations. Consequently his letters breathe the most tender solicitude for her, are full of precepts relating to trifles, but leading incidentally to general questions of philosophy. Now and then in distress at her lack of comprehension he would write in a bitter sarcastic tone; then, again, he would soften down to a tender caress as from a father to his child.

In one letter he expresses his horror and despair at the discovery how unworthy of her, as he held, were the objects in which she took an interest. In fact, he mercilessly jeers at the young lady's passion for coronation festivities, balls, parades, and flirtations with aides-de-camp, and ends his letter with a portentously affected sentence.

For a long time he got no answer. He was agitated, wrote again, begged for forgiveness, and at last succeeded in eliciting a good-humored reply.

It appears from his letters that, after the coronation, the family returned to Sudakovo, where Tolstoy was often in their house, and that the mutual inclination grew and strengthened.

But Tolstoy was not the man to be carried away blindly and heedlessly by his feelings. He resolved to submit their attachment to the test of time and distance, and went to stay at St. Petersburg for two months.

From Moscow he wrote a letter in which he attempted a sort of education of the young lady, which letter makes it plain that what is called the passion of love did not exist between them.

He goes very fully into the question of mutual attraction and insists upon the very great significance of marriage, and finally he explains his determination to put their friendship to the test of a temporary separation. Though this did not appeal to the young lady, whose affections were strongly engaged, yet she agreed, and they kept up a correspondence.

Before long, Tolstoy had to go through a new trial not imposed by himself, but coming from without. While in St. Petersburg, he learned from a trustworthy source that this "charming girl" allowed her pianoforte teacher, Mortier, to make love to her, and that, in fact, she fell in love with him. And all this took place during those unfortunate coronation fêtes. It is true she tried hard to counteract this feeling, and even broke off all relations with Mortier, but the very fact of this sudden love affair was a frightful shock to Tolstoy. Under the impulse of the bitter feeling called forth by this discovery he wrote to her a letter full of reproaches, but, evidently relenting, he never posted it. Then he wrote another, which was posted. In this he also referred somewhat severely to the flirtation with Mortier.

One can, of course, easily notice that the discovery made by Tolstoy of the continued relations of the lady with Mortier caused an incurable wound to his developing love, and that he did not cut short his relations with her only because he thought nature and time would fulfil the operation better. From that time they became more of comrades, and only at rare intervals, and then, I presume, more in imagination, did the flame of love show itself.

Getting no answer to his letter, and having very probably satisfied himself with the argument that "*pas de nouvelles—bonnes nouvelles,*" he continued to influence her life rather as her teacher than as her lover, and wrote her a detailed letter concerning their possible relations in the future, setting forth for her a minute plan of their duties, surroundings, circle of acquaintances, and apportionment of time, and trying to get his future life-companion interested in serious and vital questions.

He did not receive any answer to his letters for a long time, and remained somewhat in doubt.

At last he was rewarded for his patience by receiving several belated letters all at once, and the relations between the two friends became again very loving.

He initiates her in his literary plans, describes his life in St. Petersburg, and continues to develop his pure and high ideals of family life to her.

However, the beginning of doubt which had crept into Tolstoy's mind is more evident in these last letters. Through the expressions of love a kind of oppressive feeling betrays itself, as the outcome of their somewhat artificial relations. This false note becomes obvious also to her, the intensity of their mutual feeling grew less, and both were on the lookout for an honorable escape.

In a letter to his aunt Tatiana, Tolstoy confessed the cooling down of his love, and asked her advice in this difficulty. The letter was written in Moscow, to which place he went early in December and remained till the end of the month.

Moscow, Dec. 5, 1856.

"You again write to me about V. in the same tone in which you have always spoken to me about her, and I again answer in the way in which I have always answered. Just as I had left, and for a week later, it appeared to me that I was in love, as it is called, but, with my imagination, that is not difficult. At present, and especially since I have strenuously taken to work, I would like, and very much like, to say that I am in love with or simply love her, but this is not the case. The one feeling I have toward her is gratitude for her love, and also the thought that of all the girls I have known and do know she would have been the best for my wife, as I understand married life. It is in this that I would like to know your candid opinion as to whether I am mistaken or not, and I desire your advice, firstly, because you know both her and me, and, above all, because you love me, and those who love are never mistaken. It is true that I have tested myself very unsatisfactorily, for since I left I have been leading a solitary life, rather than a dissipated one, and have seen very little of women, but, notwithstanding this, I have often had minutes of vexation with myself for having so closely approached her, and have repented of it. Still, I say that, were I once convinced of the constancy of her nature, and sure that she would always love me, if not as much as she does now, at least more than she does any one else, I would not hesitate a minute to marry her. I am sure that in that case my love toward her would continually increase, and that by means of this feeling she could become a noble woman."

His letters to the young lady had now become cool and argumentative. He still used the words "in love," but, it seemed, only playfully, without the former enthusiasm. He addressed his letters to St. Petersburg, where she went to spend the winter season—an ambition she had cherished for a long time.

The coldness in the tone of his letters did not escape her, and she wrote to him with loving reproach. Two kind letters from her resulted in some return of love on his part; he sent her a letter written in a soft tone, and with some warmth of expression. In a subsequent letter Tolstoy confesses that he is "losing his head," and tries to define "love" by reference to the mutual education that comes of it. However, as may be seen, they could never agree as to what love precisely was, and the more sincerely and cordially Tolstoy expressed his thoughts and his feeling for her, the less they penetrated her soul and the more resistance she offered. This same resistance his last letter failed to overcome, and her reply made him change his tone, and friendship took the place of love.

After this there followed an interruption of three weeks. Very evidently their relations had changed and turned into friendship. Tolstoy meanwhile settled in St. Petersburg in order to prosecute his literary work. They exchanged letters once more; however, nothing was arranged, and she forbade him to write to her. But he continued to write, confessing his guilt toward her and himself.

He further tells her that he is going abroad, and gives her his address in Paris, begging her to write to him there, were it even for the last time.

Finally, before he left Moscow for abroad, he wrote to his aunt about the whole matter.

"DEAR AUNT—I have received my passport for abroad and have come to Moscow, intending to pass a few days with Marie, and then go to Yasnaya to arrange my affairs and take leave of you.

"But I have now changed my mind, chiefly on Mashinka's advice, and have decided to remain with her here a week or two, and then go direct by Warsaw to Paris. You probably understand, dear Aunt, why I do not wish to come to Yasnaya now, or rather to Sudakovo, and even ought not to do so. I think I have behaved very badly in relation to V., but, by seeing her now, I should behave yet worse still. As I have written you I am more than indifferent to her, and fear I can no longer deceive either myself or her. Whereas, if I came, I might perhaps, owing to weakness of character, again deceive myself.

"Do you remember, dear Aunt, how you laughed at me when I told you that I was leaving for St. Petersburg that I might test myself, yet it is to this idea that I owe the fact of not having made the unhappiness of this young lady and myself, for do not think that it was inconstancy or infidelity. No one has taken my fancy during these two months, but I have simply come to see that I was deceiving myself, and that I have not only never had, but never shall have, the slightest feeling of true love for V. The only thing which greatly pains me is that I have injured the young lady, and that I shall not be able to take leave of you before my departure. I intend returning to Russia in July, but, should you desire it, I will come to Yasnaya to embrace you, for I shall have time to get your answer at Moscow."

After this Tolstoy really got away, and from Paris, in reply to a letter from his old sweetheart, which he received there, he wrote her his last friendly letter, in which he speaks of his feeling as of a mistake belonging to the past, thanks her for her friendship, and wishes her happiness.

Tolstoy's aunt evidently did not approve of this rupture, as she was desirous to see her nephew married, and before long she reproached him for his inconstancy, even accusing him of having acted dishonorably toward the girl who had been tormented with doubts and expectations on his account. In reply to this Tolstoy wrote the following interesting letter:

"By your letter, dear Aunt, I see that we do not at all understand each other in regard to this affair. Although I confess that I was to blame, in having been inconstant, and that everything might have happened quite differently, yet I think I have acted quite honestly. I have never ceased to say that I did not know the feeling that I had for the young lady, but that it was not love, and that I was anxious to test myself. The experience showed me that I was mistaken in my feeling, and I wrote about it to V. as plainly as I could.

"After this, my relations with her have been so sincere that I am sure the memory of them will never be disagreeable, were she to marry, and it is for this reason that I wrote to her, saying that I would like to hear from her. I do not see why a young man should necessarily either be in love with a girl and marry her, or have no friendly relation with her at all, for as to friendship and sympathy for her, I have always retained a great deal. Mademoiselle Vorgani, who wrote me such a ridiculous letter, should have realized all my conduct in regard to V., how I endeavored to come as seldom as possible, how it was she who engaged me to come oftener and to enter into nearer relations. I understand her being vexed that a thing she had greatly desired did not take place (I am perhaps more vexed than she), but that is no reason for telling a man who has endeavored to act in the best way possible, and who had made sacrifices for fear of rendering others unhappy, that he is a brute, and making every one else think so. I am sure Tula is convinced I am the greatest monster."

Judging by this letter one can imagine what impression the rupture made on the lady and her friends.

A short time afterward, having learned from his aunt's letter that his old sweetheart's sister was getting married, his former feeling reawoke, and he wrote as follows:

"As to V., I never loved her with a real love, but I allowed myself to be drawn into tasting the evil pleasure of inspiring love, which afforded me an enjoyment which I had never known before.

"But the time I have passed away from her has proved to me that I have no longing to see her again, much less to marry her. I feel only fear at the thought of the duties I should be obliged to fulfil toward her without loving her, and it is for this reason that I made up my mind to go away sooner than I intended. I have behaved very ill; I have asked pardon of God, and I ask it of all those I have grieved, but it is impossible to repair matters, and now nothing in the world could make the thing begin anew. I desire all happiness to Olga; I am enchanted with her marriage, but to you, my aunt, I confess that, of all things in this world, that which would give me the greatest pleasure would be to learn that V. was going to marry a man whom she loved, and who was worthy of her; for although I have not got in the depth of my heart the slightest atom of love for her, I still regard her as a good and honorable girl."

Thus ended this short but pathetic affair, a most interesting passage in Tolstoy's life. Having known a period of strong agitation and outlived it, he, so to speak, turned to account this episode of his life, with the sensations which he experienced, by describing them in his novel *Family Happiness,* in an artistic form, as any one can see who compares the work of art with the author's actual life. We may in fact say that what is represented as taking place in the novel is the course of events which might have occurred in his real life, and the real romance was the commencement or prologue of the fiction.

After this unsuccessful affair Tolstoy resumed his literary and social activity.

PART IV

TRAVELS, LITERARY AND SOCIAL
ACTIVITY

PART IV

TRAVELS, LITERARY AND SOCIAL ACTIVITY

CHAPTER XI

THE FIRST JOURNEY ABROAD—LIFE IN MOSCOW—BEAR-HUNTING

Departure abroad by post-chaise: A letter from Turgenef—A letter from Botkin—Relations between Turgenef and Tolstoy—Journey to Dijon—Albert—While in Paris Tolstoy is present at an execution—Tolstoy's thoughts on this, from his diary and *Confession*—Journey to Piedmont—Departure to Clarens—A letter to Tatiana—The Countess A. A.—In Boccage—Journey on foot to Chateau d'Oex—Swiss pictures of nature. *Journey to Lucerne:* A letter to Tatiana—Incident with a musician—Protest and profession of faith by Tolstoy. *Return to Russia:* Visit to Nekrassof—Reading of the tale *Lucerne*. *Return to Yasnaya Polyana:* The programme of life—What is self-sacrifice—The *Iliad* and the New Testament—Silence of critics—Tolstoy's opinion of it. *Departure from Moscow:* Visit to Fet—Society life, gymnastics—Arrival in Moscow of the Countess A. A. Tolstoy—Tolstoy's journey to the Princess Volkonsky—Three deaths. *The return to Yasnaya Polyana:* The formation of a musical society in Moscow—Letter about spring to the Countess A. A. Tolstoy—Visit to Yasnaya Polyana by the Fets. *T. A. Yergolsky:* Her recollections of Tolstoy—His attraction for the duties of his estate—Tolstoy's letter to Fet—Views of the nobility of Tula upon the emancipation of the serfs—Tolstoy's letter about authorship to Fet. *The bear hunt:* Fet's narrative—Tolstoy's letter to Tatiana—A great desire is worse than slavery—A short trip to St. Petersburg—Verses of Turgenef—Tolstoy at Turgenef's in Spassky—Unhappy mood—The work at school—Recollection of it in *Confession*. *The election of Tolstoy as a member of the Moscow Society of Admirers of Russian Literature:* Tolstoy's speech and the reply of Khomyakof—The fulfilled prophecy.

JANUARY 29th Tolstoy left Moscow and travelled by mail post to Warsaw, and from Warsaw by rail to Paris, where he arrived on February 21st.

There Turgenef awaited him. As early as January 23d the latter wrote to Druzhinin:

"Tolstoy writes that he intends coming over here, and

then going in the spring from here to Italy. Tell him to make haste, if he wishes to find me. Anyhow, I will write to him myself. Judging from his letters, I see that he is going through most beneficial changes, and I am rejoicing at it like an 'old nurse.' I have read his *A Russian Proprietor*, which pleased me very much by its frankness and almost full freedom of conviction; I say 'almost,' because in the way he states the problem to himself lies (perhaps unknown to him) a certain prejudice. The essential moral impression of the tale (I don't speak of the artistic one) is this, that until serfdom ceases to exist, there would be no possibility of *rapprochement* and mutual understanding in spite of the most disinterested, honest desire to meet, and this impression is good and true; but side by side with it runs another secondary impression—namely, that, on the whole, teaching the peasant or improving his position is useless, and this impression I cannot agree with. But his mastery of the language, of the tale, of characteristics is very great."

After meeting Tolstoy, Turgenef wrote to Polonsky:

"Tolstoy is here. A change for the better has taken place in him, and a very considerable one.

"This man will go far and will leave a deep trail after him."

In a letter to Kalbassin, of March 8th, from Paris, Turgenef said:

"I very often see Tolstoy here, and I had the other day a very nice letter from Nekrassof, dated from Rome.

"But I cannot become intimate with Tolstoy, we take such different views."

This is Tolstoy's estimate at that time of Turgenef and Nekrassof, whom Tolstoy found in Paris, as quoted by Botkin in his letter to Druzhinin of March 8, 1857.

Tolstoy writes thus about his interview with him:

"They are both roaming in a sort of darkness, they are dejected and complain of life, do nothing, and apparently both feel the weight of their mutual relations."

Turgenef writes that Nekrassof suddenly went away again to Rome. Tolstoy's letter is only a page, but full of vitality and freshness. Germany interests him very much, and he intends to study that country more fully by-and-by. In a month's time he starts for Rome.[1]

---

[1] From papers by **Druzhinin**, *Twenty-five Years' Manual*. St. Petersburg, 1884.

FIRST JOURNEY ABROAD

This correspondence shows that the relations between Tolstoy and Turgenef were always unsatisfactory, and that with all their efforts, they could not become cordial friends.

In March Tolstoy and Turgenef made a journey to Dijon and spent a few days together there. While there, Tolstoy wrote the tale about the musician Albert. Then they came back to Paris, where Tolstoy witnessed an execution which he described in his *Confession,* and which made an indelible impression upon him, of which he made a brief entry in his diary:

"*6th April,* 1857.—I rose before seven and went to see an execution. A stout, white, healthy neck and breast: he kissed the Gospel and then—death. What a senseless thing! It made a strong impression, which has not been in vain. I am not a political man. Morality and Art I know that I love and can . . . The guillotine for a long time prevented me from sleeping, forcing me to look round."

This is what he says on the subject in *How I Came to Believe:*

"Thus, during my stay in Paris, the sight of a public execution revealed to me the weakness of my superstitious belief in progress. When I saw the head divided from the body, and heard the sound with which they fell separately into the box, I understood, not with my reason, but with my whole being, that no theory of the wisdom of all established things, nor of progress, could justify such an act; and that if all the men in the world from the day of creation, by whatever theory, had found this thing necessary, it was not so, it was an evil thing. And that, therefore, I must judge of what was right and necessary, not by what men said and did, not by progress, but what I felt to be true in my heart."

Tolstoy put off his journey to Rome till the autumn, and in the spring set out from Paris for Geneva, from which place he writes to his aunt Tatiana:

"I have passed a month and a half in Paris, and so pleasantly that I say to myself every day that I did well to come abroad. I have gone very little either into society or the literary world, or the world of cafés and public entertainments, but, nevertheless, I have found so much here that is new and interesting to me that every day, when I go to bed, I say to myself: 'What a pity it is the day has passed so quickly!' I have not even had time to work as I intended.

"Poor Turgenef is very ill physically, and still more so morally. His unfortunate connection with Madame V. and her daughter keeps him here in a climate which is very bad for him, and it is piteous to see him. I should never have thought he could so love!"

From Geneva Tolstoy went on foot to Piedmont with Botkin and Druzhinin, who had come there; after that he settled down on the banks of Lake Geneva, at the little village of Clarens, from which he wrote an enthusiastic letter to his aunt Tatiana:

"18th May, 1857.

"I have just received your letter, dear Aunt, which has found me, as you must know by my last letter, in the neighborhood of Geneva, at Clarens, in the same village as that in which Rousseau's Julie lived. . . . I will not attempt to describe the beauty of the country, especially at the present time, when all is in leaf and flower; I will merely tell you that it is literally impossible to tear oneself away from this lake and these shores, and that I pass most of my time in gazing and admiring as I walk about, or else merely as I sit by the window in my room. I do not cease to congratulate myself on the idea I had of leaving Paris and coming to pass the spring here, although it brought upon me your reproach of inconsistency. I am really happy, and I begin to feel the advantages of having been born with a silver spoon in my mouth.

"There is here a charming society of Russians—Pushkins, Karamzins, and Mescherskys; and all, God knows why, have taken affectionately to me. I feel this and the month I have passed here so pleasantly, and am so well and hearty that I am quite in low spirits at the thought of leaving."

Besides these friends in the neighborhood of Geneva, there lived at that time in the village Baucage, near the lake, Tolstoy's friend, the Countess A. A. Tolstoy, who was maid of honor to the grand duchess Marya Nicolayevna,

FIRST JOURNEY ABROAD

who there gave birth to a son, Count Stroganof. It was a very great pleasure to Tolstoy to visit them.

He spent about two months at Clarens and resolved to continue his journey on foot. Having made the acquaintance of a Russian family there, he invited one of them, a boy named Sasha, of the age of ten, to go up the mountains with him. At first they were to have walked to Friburg, crossing the gorge Jaman, but, after having crossed it, they changed their minds and turned in the direction of the Château d'Oex, from which they proceeded to Thun by the mail post.

Among the unpublished manuscripts of Tolstoy are his notes of this journey, from which a few descriptions of Swiss landscape may be quoted. He first of all went by steamer from Clarens to Montreux.

"*15th May*, 1857.—The weather was clear, the light blue and brilliantly dark blue Leman, spotted white and black with sails and boats, shone before our eyes almost on three sides of us; behind Geneva, some way from the bright lake, the hot atmosphere trembled and darkened; on the opposite shore the green Savoy mountains rose abruptly, with little white houses at their base and with jagged rocks, one of which looked like an enormous white woman in an ancient costume. To the left, near the red vines in the dark-green thicket of fruit trees, was distinctly seen Montreux with its graceful church standing half-way down the slope, Villeneuve on the Vevey shore with the iron roofs of its houses brightly shining in the midday sun, the mysterious cleft of the Vallais with its mountains heaped one upon another, the white Col de Chillon over the water near Vevey, and the much-belauded little island artificially yet beautifully placed in front of Villeneuve. The lake was slightly rippled, the sun beat down perpendicularly upon its blue surface, and the sails, scattered about the lake, appeared motionless.

"It is wonderful how, having lived in Clarens two months, still each time, when in the morning and still more in the evening after dinner I open the shutters of the windows already in the shade and look out on the lake and the distant blue mountains reflected in it, their beauty blinds me and startles me with a thrill. I immediately wish to love and even feel the love of others for myself, and regret the past, hope for the future, and feel it become a joy to be alive. I desire to live long, very long, and the thought of death fills me with a childish, poetic awe. Sometimes, sitting alone in the shady little garden and gazing, as I constantly do, on these shores and this lake, I even feel, as it were, the physical impression of their beauty pouring into my soul through my eyes."

Again, as they climbed up the mountains:

"Above us the wood birds were pouring out their songs such as are not heard on the lake. Here one feels the smell of the damp of the forest and of felled pine trees. The walk was so pleasant that we were loath to hurry on. Suddenly we were struck by a curious, delightful spring smell. Sasha ran into the wood and gathered some cherry blossom, but it was almost scentless. On both sides were seen green trees and shrubs without bloom. The sweet overpowering odor kept on increasing. After we had advanced a hundred yards the shrubs opened to the right, and an immense sloping valley, flecked with white and green, with a few cottages over it, was disclosed before our eyes. Sasha ran to the meadow to gather white narcissus with both hands, and brought me an enormous bouquet, with a very strong scent, but, with the love of destruction natural to children, he ran back to trample and tear the tender and beautiful young succulent flowers which gave him so much pleasure."

At Avants they passed the night. After the ascent Tolstoy wrote the following reflections:

"16/28 *May.*—What I was told is true—the higher you ascend the mountains the easier it is to advance. We had already been walking more than an hour and neither of us felt either the weight of his bags or any fatigue. Although we did not yet see the sun, it threw its rays over us on to the opposite height, touching on its way a few peaks and pines on the horizon. The torrents beneath were all audible where we stood, close to us only snow water soaked through the soil, and, at a turning of the road, we again saw the Lake Vallé at an appalling depth beneath us. The base of the Savoy mountains was completely blue, like the lake, only darker; the summits, lighted by the sun, were throughout of a pale pink. There were more snow-clad peaks, which seemed higher and of a more varied shape. Sails and boats like scarcely visible spots were seen on the lake. It was a beautiful sight, beautiful beyond measure, but this is not

Nature, although it is something good. I do not like what are called glorious and magnificent views—somehow they are cold.

" . . . I like Nature when it surrounds me on all sides, and then unfolds in infinite distance—but still when I am myself in it. I like it when the warm air is first all about me and then recedes in volume into infinite distance; when those same tender leaves of grass which I crush as I sit on them give their greenness to boundless meadows; when those same leaves which, stirred by the wind, move the shadows about my face, give their hue to the distant wood; when the very air you breathe makes the dark blue of the limitless sky; when you are not rejoicing and revelling in inanimate Nature alone; when round about you buzz and dance myriads of insects, lady-birds crawl, and birds are pouring out their songs.

" But this is a bare, cold, desolate, gray little plateau, and somewhere there something veiled with the mist of distance. But this something is so far off that I do not feel the chief delight of Nature—do not feel myself a part of this infinite and beautiful distance. I have nothing to do with this distance."

Continuing his journey, Tolstoy, in July, reached Lucerne, from which he wrote to his aunt:

"LUCERNE, 8*th July.*

" I think I have told you, dear Aunt, that I have left Clarens with the intention of undertaking rather a long journey through the north of Switzerland, along the Rhine, and from Holland to England. From there I intend again passing through France and Paris, and in August making a short stay at Rome and Naples. If I can stand the sea crossings which I shall encounter in going from The Hague to London, I think of returning by the Mediterranean, Constantinople, the Black Sea, and Odessa. But all these are plans which I shall perhaps not carry out owing to my changeable disposition, with which you, my dear Aunt, justly reproach me. I have arrived at Lucerne. It is a town in the north of Switzerland, not far from the Rhine, and I am already postponing my departure, so as to remain a few days in this delicious little town. . . . I am again all alone, and I will confess to you that very often this solitude is painful to me, as the acquaintances one makes in hotels and trains are not a resource; yet this isolation has at least the advantage of prompting me to work. I am working a little, but it advances badly, as it usually does in summer."

During his stay at Lucerne he had an adventure, which he describes in *The Memoirs of Prince Nekhludof*. The tale referred to the year 1857, and is therefore connected with his own journey.

In this tale, as we know, the lovely description of Swiss Nature is interrupted by expressions of indignation at the way in which its harmony is spoiled in order to please the well-to-do tourists, chiefly English.

What strikes him especially is the contrast between the dull respectability of the *table d'hôte* and the wild, but soft and exhilarating beauty of the lake. The feeling is intensified in him when he hears the song of a street singer with a harp. As if by magic, this song attracts general attention, and strikes a chord in his soul to which he is unable to give tone.

"All the confused and involuntary impressions of life suddenly received meaning and charm for me, as though a fresh and fragrant flower had bloomed in my soul. Instead of the fatigue, distraction, and indifference for everything in the world which I had felt but a minute before, I suddenly was conscious of a need of love, a fulness of hope, and a joy of life, which I could not account for. 'What is there to wish, what to desire?' I uttered involuntarily. 'Here it is—you are on all sides surrounded by beauty and poetry. Inhale it in broad, full draughts with all the strength you have! Enjoy yourself! What else do you require? All is yours, all the bliss.'"

The same dull, respectable English surround this beautiful flower of poetry like a black frame.

The singer finished, and held out his hat beneath the windows of a grand hotel, on the veranda of which stood a crowd of smartly dressed listeners, who none of them gave him anything.

Amazed at the stony indifference of these people, Tolstoy ran after the musician, and invited him to the hotel to partake of a bottle of wine. This defiant action created a sensation in the hotel, but that was precisely what he wanted. His object was to wound those self-satisfied tourists; he wanted to express his indignation at their heartlessness. However, the sensation passed away, and was almost forgotten, leaving the author with a bitter feeling against the injustice of men and their incapacity to understand the highest happiness, the simple, humane, and at the same time sympathetic attitude toward Nature.

"How could you, children of a free, humane nation, you Christians, you, simply men, even, answer with coldness and ridicule to a pure enjoyment afforded you by an unfortunate mendicant? But no; there are refuges for beggars in your country. There are no beggars, there must not be, and there must not be the feeling of compassion upon which beggars depend.

"But he labored, gave you pleasure; he implored you to give him something of your superabundance for his labor, which you made use of, and then you looked down at him with a cold smile from your high, shining palaces, as at a curiosity, and among hundreds of you, happy and rich people, there was not found one man or woman to throw anything to him! Put to shame, he walked away from you —and the senseless crowd pursued and insulted with its laughter, not you, but him, because you are cold, cruel, and dishonest; because you stole enjoyment from him, which he had afforded you, they offended *him*.

"*On the 7th of July, 1857, an itinerant singer for half an hour sang songs and played the guitar in Lucerne in front of the Schweizerhof, where the richest people stop. About one hundred persons listened to him. The singer three times asked all to give him something. Not one person gave him anything, and a great many laughed at him.*

"This is not fiction but a positive fact, which those who wish may find out from the permanent inmates of the Schweizerhof, and by looking up in the newspapers who the foreigners were who on the 7th of July stopped at the Schweizerhof.

"This is an occurrence which the historians of our time ought to note down with fiery, indelible letters."

An outcry of astonishment broke forth from his heart in the presence of the riddle of the tangled chain of men's relations to each other and their petty feelings as compared with the harmonious grandeur of sovereign nature. The author expressed his feelings in a pathetic artistic form and thus finished his tale:

"What an unfortunate, miserable being is man with his need of positive solutions, cast into this eternally moving, endless ocean of good and evil, of facts, of reflections and contradictions! Men have been struggling and laboring for ages to put the good all on one side, and the evil on the other. Ages pass, and no matter what the unprejudiced mind may have added to the scales of good and evil, there is always the same equilibrium, and on each side there is just as much good as evil.

"If man could only learn not to judge, not to conclude sharply and positively, and not to give answers to questions put before him only that they might always remain questions! If he only understood that every idea is both just and false! False—on account of its one-sidedness, on account of the impossibility of man's embracing the whole truth; and just—as an expression of one side of human tendencies. They have made subdivisions for themselves in this eternally moving, endless, endlessly mixed chaos of good and evil; they have drawn imaginary lines on this sea, and now they are waiting for this sea to be parted asunder, as though there were not millions of other subdivisions from an entirely different point of view in another plane. It is true—these new subdivisions are worked out by the ages, but millions of these ages have passed and will pass yet.

"Civilization is good, barbarism evil; freedom is good, enslavement evil. It is this imaginary knowledge which destroys the instinctive, most blissful primitive demands of good in human nature. And who will define to me what freedom is, what despotism, what civilization, what barbarism? And where are the limits of the one and of the other? In whose soul is this measure of good and evil so imperturbable that he can measure with it this fleeting medley of facts? Whose mind is so large as to embrace and weigh all the facts even of the immovable past? And who has seen a condition such that good and evil did not exist side by side in it? And how do I know but what I see more of the one than of the other only because I do not stand in the proper place? And who is able so completely to tear his mind away from life, even for a moment, as to take an independent bird's-eye view of it?

"There is one, but one sinless leader, the Universal Spirit, who penetrates us all as he does one and each separately, who imparts to each the tendency toward that which is right; that same Spirit who orders the tree to grow toward the sun, orders the flower to cast seeds in the autumn, and orders us to hold together unconsciously.

"This one, sinless, blissful voice is drowned by the boisterous hurry of growing civilization. Who is the greater man and the greater barbarian—the lord, who upon seeing the singer's soiled garment angrily rushed away from the table, who did not give him for his labor one-millionth of his worldly goods, and who now, well-fed and sitting in a lighted, comfortable room, calmly judges of the affairs of China, finding all the murders committed there justified, or the little singer, who, risking imprisonment, with a franc in his pocket, has for twenty years harmlessly wandered through mountains and valleys, bringing consolation to people with his singing, who has been insulted, who to-day was almost kicked out, and who then, tired, hungry, humiliated, went away to sleep somewhere on rotting straw?

"Just then I heard in the town, amid the dead silence of the night, far, far away, the guitar and the voice of the little man.

"No, I involuntarily said to myself, you have no right to pity him and to be indignant at the lord's well-being. Who has weighed the internal happiness which lies in the soul of each of these men? He is sitting somewhere on a dirty threshold, looking into the gleaming, moonlit heaven, and joyfully singing in the soft, fragrant night; in his heart there is no reproach, no malice, no regret. And who knows what is going on now in the souls of all these people, behind these rich, high walls? Who knows whether there is in all of them as much careless, humble joy of life and harmony with the world as lives in the soul of this little man?

"Endless is the mercy and all-wisdom of Him who has permitted and has commanded all these contradictions to exist. Only to you, insignificant worm, who are boldly, unlawfully trying to penetrate His laws, His intentions, only to you do they appear as contradictions. He looks calmly down from His bright, immeasurable height and enjoys the endless harmony in which you all with your contradictions are endlessly moving. In your pride you thought you could tear yourself away from the universal law. No, even you, with your petty little indignation at the waiters, even you have responded to the harmonious necessity of the endless and the eternal."

From Lucerne Tolstoy continued his journey up the Rhine, Schaffhausen, Baden, Stuttgart, Frankfort, and Berlin.

On August 8th he was in Stettin, and therefrom arrived in St. Petersburg by boat, August 11th. (July 30th, O. S.)

He remained in St. Petersburg a week, visited the circle of *The Contemporary*, called on Nekrassof and read to him his tale *Lucerne*, which was printed in the September number of *The Contemporary*, in 1857. On August 6th he left for Moscow, and then went straight on to Tula.

Soon after his arrival at Yasnaya Polyana he plunged into business in connection with his estate.

In his diary of that period the following entry is found:

"This is how, during my journey, I divided my day: I put, first of all, literary work, then family duties, then the estates; but the estates I must leave in the hands of the steward as much as possible; but I must educate and improve him, and I must only spend two thousand roubles, the rest should be used in the interests of the peasants. My great stumbling-block is the vanity of Liberalism. One should live for oneself, and a good deed a day is sufficient."

A little later he wrote:

"Self-abnegation does not consist in saying, 'Take from me what you like'; but in laboring and thinking in concert with others, so as to give oneself to them."

August he devoted to reading, and studied two remarkable subjects, Homer's *Iliad* and the Gospels. Both produced a strong impression upon him.

"I have finished reading the inexpressibly beautiful conclusion of the *Iliad*." Thus he expresses himself, and the beauty of both these subjects makes him regret that there is no connection between them. "How could Homer fail to know that the only good is love?" he exclaims, mentally comparing these two books. And he himself answers: "He knew of no revelation—there is no better explanation."

In the middle of October Tolstoy moved to Moscow, together with his eldest brother Nicolay and his sister Marie.

His diary shows that he arrived there on the 17th. On October the 23d he left that city for St. Petersburg, intending to stay there a few days.

His tale *Lucerne* (Memoirs of Prince Nekhludof), printed, as above mentioned, in *The Contemporary*, was not appreciated by the critics, and therefore made no impression.

The silence of the critics gives striking and obvious proof how narrow-minded, short-sighted, and incapable they were. On the whole, from 1857 up to 1861, according to the opinion of Zelinsky, who published a collection of critical essays on Tolstoy, there were no criticisms on Tolstoy's works in spite of the fact that during that time he printed such remarkable works as *Youth, Lucerne, Albert, Three Deaths,* and *Family Happiness*.

Tolstoy was aware of the indifference of the critics, and after his return from St. Petersburg in October, 1857, he wrote in his diary:

"St. Petersburg at first grieved, and then put me right. My reputation has fallen or just lingers, and I have been much grieved inwardly; but now I am at peace. I know that I have got something to say, and the power of saying it strongly; as for the rest, the public may say what it likes. But it is necessary to work conscientiously, to lay out all one's power, then . . . let them spit on the altar."

Tolstoy returned to Moscow on October 30th. During his stay there he very often saw Fet, who, in his Reminiscences, thus described his visits:

"One evening, while we were taking tea, Tolstoy appeared quite unexpectedly and informed us that they, the Tolstoys, *i. e.*, his elder brother Nicolay and his sister Countess Marie, had all three settled in the furnished rooms of Verighin, in the Piatnitsky Street. Before long we all became intimate.

"I don't know how the Tolstoy brothers, Nicolay and Lyof, became acquainted with S. Gromeka; it occurred probably in our house. All three very soon became great friends, being all of them enthusiastic sportsmen."[1]

The Moscow life of Tolstoy at this period (the end of the fifties) had no remarkable feature. At this time his physical nature was in full glow and strength, and drew him

[1] A. Fet, *My Reminiscences*, 1848–1889, Part I, p. 214.

in the direction of ambitious enterprises, amusements, and society life in general.

Fet relates that sometimes in the evening they had concerts in which Countess Marie N. Tolstoy joined, herself a pianoforte-player and a lover of music. Sometimes she would arrive accompanied by Lyof and Nicolay, sometimes by the latter only, who would say:

"Lyof has put on his evening suit again and gone to a ball." [1]

Fet gives the following account of these recreations:

"I. P. Borisof had known Tolstoy in the Caucasus, and being himself far superior to the average man, he could not, from their first meeting in our house, resist the influence of that giant. But at that time Tolstoy's love for gayety was more striking, and when he saw him going out for a walk in his new coat, with gray beaver collar, his dark curly hair showing under a fashionable hat worn on one side, with a smart cane in hand, Borisof quoted these words from a popular song: 'He leans on his stick, and he boasts that it is made of hazel.'

"Gymnastics were very popular with the fashionable young people at that time, the favorite exercise being that of jumping over a wooden horse.

"If any one desired to get hold of Tolstoy between one and two in the afternoon, he had to go to the gymnasium hall at the Great Dmitrovka. It was interesting to watch how Tolstoy, in his tights, eagerly tried to jump over the horse without catching the leather cone stuffed with wool, and placed on the horse's back. No wonder that the active, energetic nature of a young man of twenty-nine demanded such violent exercise, but it was strange to see next to him old men with bald heads and protruding stomachs. One young man would wait for his turn, and every time run and touch the back of the horse with his chest, then quietly go aside, giving way to the next one." [2]

In the beginning of January, 1858, Countess Alexandra Andreyevna Tolstoy, a friend of Tolstoy in his youth, paid a visit to Moscow. He saw her off to Klin by the Nicolayevsky railway, and then went to stay at the house of the Princess Volkonsky, whose name was introduced in the chapter

[1] A. Fet, *My Reminiscences*, 1848-1889, Part I, p. 216.
[2] *Ibidem.*

of Tolstoy's forefathers on his mother's side. This Princess Volkonsky was the cousin of Tolstoy's mother; she used to pay long occasional visits at Yasnaya Polyana, and she was able to tell Tolstoy many things of great interest about his father and mother.

Tolstoy cherished a most pleasant remembrance of this visit; it was during his stay that he wrote the tale *Three Deaths*.

The idea of death began seriously to absorb his attention, and, as usual, his desire was to make the solution of the great problem consist in a harmony of the human soul with nature. Any divergence from this solution involves unutterable suffering; its attainment, eternal good; "the sting" of death therefore then disappears.

He returned to Yasnaya Polyana in February. Then he went again to Moscow, and in March to St. Petersburg for a fortnight. In April he again returned to Yasnaya Polyana, and remained there the whole summer. During this period Tolstoy devoted much of his time to music, and in Moscow, in association with Botkin, Perfilyef, Mortier, and others, founded a Musical Association. Madame Kareyevsky lent her hall for the concerts got up by this association, which eventually resolved itself into the Conservatoire of Moscow. In the same year, while in Moscow, Tolstoy became very intimate with the family of S. T. Aksakof, the elder.

Springtime generally exhilarated Tolstoy. The influx of energy which he experienced is well described in a letter to his aunt, A. A. Tolstoy, written in 1858.

"Auntie, it is spring, ... For good people it is very good to be alive on earth; even for such as me it is sometimes good. In nature, in the air, in everything—hope, future, and exquisite future ... sometimes one is mistaken and thinks that it is not only for nature that a future and happiness wait, but also for oneself, and then one feels happy. I am now in *such* a state, and with the egotism peculiar to me I hasten to write to you about things interesting only to myself. I very well know when I bethink myself that I am an old frozen-out potato, boiled with sauce into the bargain; but spring so acts upon me that I sometimes catch myself in the full swing of visions that I am a plant which, together with others, has only just opened, and will peacefully, simply, and joyously grow in God's world. Accordingly at these times there takes place such an inner elaboration—a purifying and an ordering of which no one who has not experienced this feeling can form any idea. All the old—away! All worldly conventionalities, all laziness, all egotism, all vices, all confused, indefinite attachments, all regrets, even repentance—all this, away! . . . give place to a wonderful little flower which is budding and growing along with spring . . ." and so on.

This letter is rather long but very interesting. It would, in fact, be interesting for its close alone, at which Tolstoy makes the following request:

"Good-by, dear Auntie, do not be angry with me for this nonsense, and answer me with wise words imbued with kindness—and Christian kindness. I have long ago wished to write to you that it is more convenient for you to write in French, and for me feminine thought is more comprehensible in French."

During this spring Fet and his wife, while on their way through Moscow to their country abode, paid a visit to Tolstoy in Yasnaya Polyana.

In his Reminiscences Fet thus described this visit, giving at the same time an interesting notice of Tolstoy's aunt, Tatiana Alexandrovna Yergolsky:

"Having bought a warm and comfortable kibitka [1] covered with matting, we started, in company with Mariushka (idealized by Tolstoy in his *Family Happiness*), by mail post for Mtsensk. Nobody dreamed of a railway at that time; as to the bare telegraph-posts along the roads, people said the wire would be first attached, and after that freedom for the serfs will be sent down the wire from St. Petersburg. By this time we were on such good terms with Tolstoy that it would have been a great deprivation to us not to call on him and stay for a day in Yasnaya Polyana to rest a little. There we were introduced to the charming old lady, Tolstoy's aunt, Tatiana Alexandrovna Yergolsky, who received us with that old-fashioned hospitality which at once makes the entrance under a new roof so pleasant. Tatiana Alexandrovna was not absorbed in the things of the past, but fully shared the life of the present.

"She mentioned that 'Seryozhenka Tolstoy had gone to

[1] Kirghiz tent.

his house at Pirogovo, and Nicolenka might yet stay on for a while in Moscow with Mashenka, but Lyovochka's friend D., she said, came in the other day and complained of his wife's neuralgia.' In any difficulties she always used to consult Lyovochka, and was quite satisfied with his explanations. Thus, driving in the autumn with him to Tula, looking out of the carriage window, she suddenly asked, '*Mon cher* Leon, how is it people write their letters by telegraph?' 'I had,' said Tolstoy, ' to explain as simply as possible the action of a telegraph instrument similarly arranged at both ends of the wire, and as I was concluding I heard her say, "*Oui, oui, je comprends, mon cher.*"'

"Having kept her eyes fixed on the wire for more than half an hour, she at last asked, '*Mon cher* Leon, how can this be? For a whole half-hour I have not seen a single letter pass along the telegraph?'

"Sometimes," relates Tolstoy, "we used to sit at home with my aunt for a whole month without seeing any one, and suddenly, while serving the soup, she would begin, 'But do you know, dear Leo, they say——'

"The long autumn and winter evenings have remained for me as a wonderful recollection. To these evenings I owe my best thoughts, the best impulses of my soul. I sit in an arm-chair reading, thinking, and at times listening to her conversation with Natalya Petrovna, or Dunechka the maid, which was always good and kind; I exchange a few words with her and again sit and read and think. This wonderful arm-chair still stands in my home, though it is not what it was, and another couch on which slept the kind old woman Natalya Petrovna, who lived with her, not for her sake, but because she had nowhere else to live. Between the windows under the looking-glass was her small writing-table, with little china jars and a small vase, in which were held the sweets, cakes, and dates, to which she treated me. By the window two arm-chairs, and to the right of the door a comfortable embroidered arm-chair, on which she liked me to sit of an evening.[1]

"The chief delight of this life was the absence of material worry, the affectionate terms on which we all were, in the strong mutual attachment free from all doubt and mis-

---

[1] "Then one could say, '*Wer darauf sitzt, der ist glücklich, und der Glückliche bin ich*' ('Whoever sits thereon is happy, and I am the happy one')."

giving by which close kinsfolk and household were bound together, and the consciousness of the flight of time.

"Indeed, I was truly happy when seated in that arm-chair. After leading a bad life at Tula, playing cards with the neighbors, after the gypsy singers, as well as my shooting and hunting—silly vanity—I would return home, go to her (my aunt) by old habit and we would kiss each other's hands, I—her dear, energetic hand; she—my impure, vicious hand; and having greeted each one in French, also by old habit, one would exchange a joke with Natalya Petrovna and seat oneself in the cosy arm-chair. She (my aunt) knows all I have been doing, regrets it, but never reproaches me, always treats me with the same love and affection. Seated in my arm-chair, I read and meditate, and I listen to her conversation with Natalya Petrovna. They either recall old times, or play at 'Patience,' or make prognostics, or joke about something, and both old ladies laugh—especially auntie, with her dear, childlike laugh, which I can hear at this moment. I tell them how the wife of an acquaintance has been unfaithful to her husband, adding that the husband must have been glad to have got rid of her. And suddenly auntie, who has just been talking with Natalya Petrovna about an excrescence of wax droppings on a candle foreshadowing a guest, raises her eyebrows and says, as a thing long settled in her soul, that a husband should not feel thus, because he would quite ruin his wife. Then she tells me about a drama among the servants, of which Dunechka has told her. Then she reads out a letter from my sister Mashenka, whom she loves, if not more, at least as much as myself, and speaks about her husband, her own nephew, without condemnation, yet grieving over the suffering he has caused Mashenka. Then I again read, and she examines her little collection of sundries—all souvenirs.

"But the chief feature of her life which involuntarily insinuated itself into me was her wonderful, universal kindness to every one without exception. I try to recall any one case when she got angry, or said a rough word, or condemned anybody, and I am unable to do so. I cannot call to mind one such word during thirty years. She spoke well of another aunt of ours who had cruelly hurt her feelings by taking us away from her; and she did not condemn my sister's husband, who had acted so badly. As to what her goodness was to the servants, it goes without saying. She grew up with the knowledge that there are masters and servants, but she used her own position only to serve others. She never reproached me directly for my bad life, although she was pained at it. Neither did she reproach my brother Sergey, whom she also warmly loved, when he formed a connection with a gypsy girl. The only indication of anxiety which she gave on occasions when he was very late in coming home, was that she used to say, 'What's the matter with our Sergey?' Instead of Seryozha, merely Sergey. She never in words taught how one should live; she never moralized. All her moral work was worked out within her, and externally appeared only deeds—indeed, not deeds—there were none of these, but all her peaceful, humble, submissive life of love, not an agitated self-admiring passion, but a quiet, unobtrusive love.

"She fulfilled the inner work of love, and therefore she had no cause to hurry anywhere. And these two features, love and repose, imperceptibly attracted one into her society, and gave a special delight to intimacy with her.

"And, as I know no case when she hurt any one, so also I know no one who did not love her. She never spoke about herself; never about religion, as to what one should believe, or what she herself believed and prayed for. She believed all, save that she repudiated one single dogma—that of eternal punishment. '*Dieu, qui est la bonté même, ne peut pas vouloir nos souffrances.*'

"Except at Te Deums and Requiems I never saw her pray. Only through a special affability with which she sometimes met me when I, occasionally late at night, after having said good-by, returned to her, did I guess that I had interrupted her prayer. 'Come in, come in!' she used to say. 'And I had just been saying to Natalya Petrovna that Nicolas would look in again.' She often called me by my father's name, and this was specially pleasant to me, as it showed that her conceptions of me and of my father were blended in one love of both. At this late time of the evening she was already in her nightdress, with a shawl thrown over her shoulders, with little spindle-like legs, in her slippers—Natalya Petrovna was in a similar *négligé*.

"'Sit down, sit down,' she used to say when she saw that I could not sleep, or was suffering from solitude. And the memory of these irregular late sittings-up are especially dear to me. It often happened that Natalya Petrovna, or else myself, would say something funny, and she would laugh good-naturedly, and immediately Natalya Petrovna would laugh too, and both old ladies would laugh for a long time, themselves not knowing at what, but like children, merely because they loved every one and felt happy.

"It was not only the love for me which was joyous. The atmosphere was joyous, an atmosphere of love to all present, absent, living and dead, and even to animals.

"I will, if I have occasion to dig up my past life, say a good deal more about her. Now I will mention only the attitude of the poor, of the peasants of Yasnaya Polyana toward her, as manifested at her funeral; when we carried her through the village there was not one homestead among the sixty from which the dwellers did not come out and demand a halt and a requiem. 'She was a good lady, she did no one any harm,' said all. And for this she was loved, and greatly loved. Laotze says that things are valuable through what is absent from them. So also with life—the best feature it can have is that it should not contain evil. In the life of my aunt Tatiana Alexandrovna there was no evil. This is easy to say, but the character is difficult to exemplify. And I have known only one individual who exemplified it.

"She died quietly, gradually falling asleep, and died as she wished to die, not in the room where she lived, so as not to sadden it for us.

"In her last moments she recognized scarcely any one. Me she always recognized, smiling, and her face glowing like a lamp when the button is pressed, and sometimes she moved her lips endeavoring to pronounce the name 'Nicholas,' thus, just before her death, quite inseparably uniting me with the one she had loved all her life.

"And it was to her—to her—that I refused that little joy which dates and chocolates afforded her, and that not so much on her own account as for the pleasure she took in treating me to them—and refused her the possibility of giving a little money to those who asked from her. I cannot recall this without an acute pang of conscience. Dear, dear Auntie, pardon me. '*Si jeunesse savait, si viellesse pouvait*'—not in regard of the welfare which one has missed for oneself in youth, but of the welfare one has not given —of the evil one has done to those that are no more.'"[1]

The scanty but valuable information which Tolstoy gives about the servants who surrounded him during his childhood is exceedingly interesting. This information may serve as a supplement to what is described in his published story *Childhood*. We find this description in his Reminiscences as well.

Though Tolstoy did not spend the whole of the summer 1858 in Yasnaya Polyana, being often away in Moscow, yet peasant life interested him more and more, and he made an effort to get in touch with " common " people.

In his Reminiscences Fet quotes the words of Tolstoy's brother Nicolay, full of fine humor concerning those efforts:

" In answer to our inquiries the Count gave with undisguised delight the following account of his beloved brother: ' Lyovochka,' he said, ' tries hard to become better acquainted with the life of the peasant, and his way of managing his land, of which we all know very little. However, I really cannot tell how far the acquaintance will go. Lyovochka desires to take in all, not to miss anything, not even gymnastics. That is why there is a bar placed under the window of his study. To be sure, setting aside prejudices with which he is so much at war, he is right; the gymnastics don't interfere with his estate affairs, but his bailiff views the matter somewhat differently. ' I would come,' he said, ' for orders, but the master had got hold of a perch with one knee, and was hanging in his red tights with his head downward swinging, his hair falling down dishevelled, and his red face bursting. I did not know whether to listen to his orders or to stand and wonder at him.' Lyovochka was pleased to see how Yufan would spread wide his arms when he was ploughing. And now Yufan became the emblem of the country's power, something like Mikula Selyaninovich. Spreading out his elbows, he too stuck to the plough and tried to imitate Yufan."

In May of the same year Tolstoy wrote to Fet from Yasnaya Polyana:

" DEAREST OLD FELLOW—I am writing two words only to say that I embrace you with all my might, that I have received your letter, that I kiss Maria Petrovna's hands,

[1] From Tolstoy's Manuscript Memoirs.

send a greeting to all yours. Auntie is very thankful for your remembering her, and greets you; and so does my sister. What a splendid spring it has been and is still. In my solitude I have enjoyed it immensely. My brother Nicolas must be at Nikolskoye; catch him there and do not let him go. This month I intend coming to see you. Turgenef has gone to Winzig until August to treat himself. The deuce take him! I am tired of loving him. He will not cure himself, but us he will deprive of his company. With this, good-by, dear friend. If before my arrival you will write no verses, I will manage to squeeze them out of you. Yours, COUNT L. TOLSTOY.

"What a Whitsuntide we had yesterday! What a service at church, with fading wild-cherry blossom, white hair, bright red cretonne, and a hot sun!"

And then another:
"Hallo, old man! Hallo! First, you yourself give no sign of life, when it is spring and you know that we are thinking of you, and that I am chained, like Prometheus, to a rock, and nevertheless thirst to see and hear you. You should either come or write, decidedly. Secondly, you have appropriated my brother, and a very good one. The chief culprit, I think, is Maria Petrovna, to whom I send my best greetings, and whom I beg to return my own brother. Joking apart, he sent to say he was coming back next week. And Druzhinin will also be here, so do come too, dear old fellow."

After discharging his summer duties at the estate, Tolstoy would take his share in works of public interest.

A meeting of noblemen of the Tula province was held in the autumn of 1858, from September 1 to September 4, for the election of representatives to the Tula Committee for the Improvement of the Status of the Peasantry. At that meeting, in virtue of the statute regulating elections, by which the nobles have a right to express their opinion on the wants of their province and on provincial affairs generally, a hundred and five noblemen handed over to the Tula Marshal of nobility the following resolution, to be presented to the Provincial Committee:

"Having in view the improvement of the status of the

peasant, the security of the landowner's position in respect of his property, and the safety of both peasants and landowners, we, the undersigned, are of opinion that the peasants ought to be liberated and a certain amount of land allotted to them and their descendants, and that the landowners should be compensated fully and fairly in money by means of some financial operation which will not result in compulsory relations between landowner and peasant; all such relations the nobility consider should be abolished." (There follow the signatures of a hundred and five noblemen of Tula Province, among them was of course the name of the Krapovna landowner, Count L. N. Tolstoy.)[1]

We must return to Fet's Reminiscences.

"Since my wife and I left Moscow in the autumn of 1858, Tolstoy contrived, as may be seen from the following letter to me forwarded from Novosyolki to Moscow, to go out hunting with Borisof, who lent Tolstoy his whipper-in, together with a horse and dogs.

"October 24th he wrote from Moscow:

"'DEAREST OLD CHAP, FETINKA—Indeed you are a dear fellow, and I love you dreadfully. That's all. To write stories is silly—a shame. To write verses . . . well, you may do so; but to love a good man is very pleasant. And yet perhaps against my will and consciousness, it is not myself but an unripe story working in me, that makes me love. I sometimes think so. However one may avoid it, still from time to time between manure and this Kapoemon, one finds oneself writing a story. I am glad, however, that I have not yet allowed myself to write, and will not. Thank you most heartily for your trouble about the veterinary, etc. I have found the Tula one, and he has begun the treatment. What will come of it I don't know. And the deuce take them all. Druzhinin requests me to write a story for him like a friend. And I really intend to compose one. I will compose such a one that there will be nothing in it: The Shah of Persia is smoking a pipe, and I love you. That will be a poser. Joking apart, how is your "Hafiz"? Whatever may be said, the height of wisdom and firmness for me is to rejoice at other people's writing, but not to let one's own out into the world in an

[1] *The Contemporary*, 1858, vol. lxxii, p. 300.

ugly garb, but to consume it oneself with one's daily bread. Yet sometimes one suddenly feels such a desire to be a great man, and so annoyed that hitherto this has not been realized. One even hurries to get up, or finish one's dinner in order to begin. One couldn't express all one's frivolous thoughts, but it is pleasant to communicate at least one to such a dear old fellow as you are, who lives entirely in such frivolity; send me one of the longest pieces of poetry by "Hafiz" you have translated, *me faire venir l'eau à la bouche,* and I will send you a sample of wheat. Sport has bored me to death. The weather is excellent, but I do not go hunting alone.'"

In December, 1858, during a hunting expedition, Tolstoy met with an accident which nearly cost him his life. Fet describes it in this way:

"Gromeka wrote on December 15, 1858:

"'As you desired me, I hasten to inform you, dear Afanasy Afanasyevich, that one of these days, about the 18th or 20th, I mean to go out bear-hunting. Tell Tolstoy that I have bought a she-bear with two young ones, and that if he cares to take part in the hunt, he must come to Volochok about the 18th or 19th, straight on to my place, without ceremony, and that I will meet him with open arms, and a room will be ready for him. If he is not coming, please let me know at once.

"'I think the hunt will certainly take place on the 19th. It will be best, therefore, indeed necessary, to come on the 18th.

"'If Tolstoy would like to put it off to the 21st, then let me know; it would be impossible to wait longer.'

"For greater inducement the well-known leader in bear hunts, Ostashkof, paid Tolstoy a visit. On his appearance in the hunting-field, the scene can only be compared to the plunging of a red-hot iron into cold water. Wild excitement and uproar followed. Seeing that each bear-hunter must possess two guns, Tolstoy borrowed my German double-barrelled gun, intended for small shot. At the appointed day our hunter, Lyof Nicolay, started for the Nicolayevsky railway station. I will try to repeat correctly all I heard from Tolstoy and his companions in the bear hunt.

"When the hunters, each carrying two loaded guns,

took their places along the meadow running through the wood, which looked like a chess-board from its openings, they were advised to tread the deep snow as wide as possible round them, so as to get more freedom of movement. But Tolstoy remained at his post in snow almost up to his waist, declaring that there was no need to tread the snow at all, as they were going to shoot the bear and not to fight her. Accordingly the Count placed one of the guns against the trunk of a tree, so that when he had fired off the two charges of his gun he could throw it away and, holding out his hand, catch mine. Presently the she-bear was startled out of her den by Ostashkof, and made her appearance. She rushed out down the valley along which the hunters were placed in a direction at right angles to it, by one of the openings. This alley opened on to the spot where was standing the hunter nearest to Tolstoy, so that the latter could not even see the approach of the bear. But she, probably scenting the hunter she was after all the time, swiftly rushed to the cross opening and suddenly appeared at a very short distance from Tolstoy and quickly flew at him. Tolstoy deliberately aimed and pulled the trigger, but probably missed, for in the cloud of smoke he saw something huge approaching. He gave another shot almost face to face, and the bullet hit the bear's jaw, where it stuck between the teeth. The Count could not move aside, the untrodden snow giving him no room, and he had no time to snatch my gun, for he was knocked down and fell with his face in the snow. At a run the bear crossed over him. 'There,' thought the Count, ' all is over with me. I missed now, and shall have no time to shoot at her again!'

"At this moment he saw something dark over his head. It was the she-bear, who had instantly returned, and who tried to bite the head of the hunter who had wounded her. Lying with his face downward in the thick snow, Tolstoy could only offer passive resistance, trying as much as he could to draw his head between his shoulders, and expose his thick fur cap to the beast's mouth. Perhaps in consequence of these instinctive manœuvres, the bear, being twice unsuccessful, managed to give only one considerable bite, with her upper teeth tearing the cheek under his left eye, and with the lower the whole skin of the left part of his forehead. At that moment Ostashkof arrived near, and, running up with his small switch in his hand, he approached the bear with his usual 'Where are you getting to? Where are you getting to?' At the sound of this exclamation the bear ran away as quickly as she could. It seems the next day she was surrounded and killed.

"The first words of Tolstoy, when he got up with the skin hanging down his face, which had to be bandaged with handkerchiefs on the spot, were: 'What will Fet say?' I am proud of it still."[1]

Having got over the shock, Tolstoy hastened to inform his aunt of the incident, and, in his letter of December 25th, thus described what had happened:

"First of all I congratulate you, secondly I am afraid that news of an adventure I have had may in some way reach you in an exaggerated form, and therefore I make haste to inform you of it myself.

"I have been hunting bears with Nicolas. On the 21st I shot a bear; on the 22d, when we again went out, an extraordinary thing happened to me. The bear, without seeing me, charged me; I shot at it at a distance of six yards, missed it the first time, the second mortally wounded it; but it rushed at me, knocked me down, and, while my companions were running up, it bit me twice, in the forehead over the eye and under the eye. Fortunately this lasted only ten or fifteen seconds; the bear made its escape, and I rose up with a slight injury which neither disfigures me nor causes pain; neither the skull nor the eye is injured, so that I have escaped with merely a little scar, which will remain on my forehead. I am now in Moscow and feel perfectly well. I am writing you the whole truth without concealing anything, so that you may not be anxious. Everything is now over, and it only remains to thank God, who has saved me in such an extraordinary way."

This episode served as a subject for his tale, *The Wish is Stronger than Bondage,* published in the *Books to Read.* There are many artistic details left out by Fet with which the fancy of the artist adorned the real facts of the incident. That is why, in relating it, we preferred to use the reminiscences of Tolstoy's friend and his own letter, as better serving our purpose.

[1] A. Fet, *My Reminiscences,* Part I, p. 226.

The early months of 1859 Tolstoy spent in Moscow, and in April he went to St. Petersburg, where he spent ten days in the company of his friend A. A. Tolstoy. He cherished the most grateful memories of this visit.

At the end of April Tolstoy was again in Yasnaya Polyana, and there he remained for the whole summer.

During the summer Tolstoy paid a visit to Turgenef at his house at Spasskoye.

In verses sent to Fet on July 16, 1859, Turgenef wrote thus:

> "Embrace, please, Nicolay Tolstoy,
> And give to Lyof Tolstoy my compliments, and to his sister too.
> He rightly says in his postscriptum:
> I have 'no cause' to write to him. I know
> He loves me slightly and I love him slightly—
> Too different in us are our elements,
> But many are the roads across this world,
> We need not stand in one another's way.'"[1]

These lines show that their relations continued mutually respectful and amiably cold.

However, the visit went off smoothly. In his letter to Fet of October 9th of the same year, Turgenef thus speaks of their meeting:

"Our ladies send their best greetings to all of you. I had a quiet talk with Tolstoy, and we parted on friendly terms. It seems there can be no misunderstanding between us, because we know each other too well, and we understand that it is impossible for us to become intimate. We are modelled in different clay."

In August Tolstoy is again at Moscow, where he spent the autumn.

The year 1860 found him again in a perturbed mood.

Yet during the winter of '59–'60 he enjoyed rest and pleasure in his schools. In his *Confession* he speaks of that time in the following terms:

"On my return from abroad I settled in the country and occupied myself with the organization of schools for the peasantry. This occupation was especially grateful to me, because it was free from the spirit of imposture which so strikes me in the career of a literary teacher.

---

[1] A. Fet, *My Reminiscences*, Part I, p. 305.

"Here again I acted in the name of progress, but this time I brought a spirit of critical inquiry to bear on the system on which the progress rested. I said to myself that progress was often attempted in an irrational manner, and that it was necessary to leave a primitive people and the children of peasants perfectly free to choose the way of progress which they thought best. In reality I was still bent on the solution of the same impossible problem, how to teach without knowing what it was I had to teach. In the highest sphere of literature I had understood that it was impossible to do this, because I had seen that everybody had his own way of teaching, and that the teachers quarrelled among themselves, and scarcely succeeded in concealing their ignorance. Having now to deal with peasant children, I thought I could get over this difficulty by allowing the children to learn whatever they liked. It seems now absurd, when I remember the experiments by which I carried out this whim of mine as to teaching, though I knew in my heart that I could teach nothing useful, because I myself did not know what it was necessary to teach."

This constant feeling of dissatisfaction with himself, this searching for the meaning of life, was a permanently active force, leading him forward on the path of his moral progress.

In February Tolstoy was admitted a member of the Moscow Society of Admirers of Russian Literature.

On February 4, 1859, a meeting of the Society was held, under the presidency of A. S. Khomyakof.

At this meeting Tolstoy was present, and was one of the newly elected members; and, in accordance with the rules of the Society, he had to make an inaugural address. In it, as stated in the records of the Society, he mentioned the advantage of the purely artistic element in literature over all temporary tendencies. Unfortunately, this speech has never been preserved. In the minutes of the sitting it is stated that at first it was resolved to have the address printed, together with the works of the Society, but afterward, the works not being published, the speech was returned to the author, who has probably mislaid it along with useless papers.[1]

---

[1] The Moscow Society of Admirers of Russian Literature. *The Collection of Minutes.* One of the few remaining copies is in the British Museum.

We can get some idea of this speech from the excellent reply made by A. S. Khomyakof, which we quote *in toto:*

"The Society of the Admirers of Russian Literature, in adding you, Count Tolstoy, to the number of its members, bids you welcome as a worker in the field of pure art. In your address you defend the tendency of pure art, placing it above all other temporary and casual tendencies of literary activity. It would be strange if the Society did not sympathize with you, but I beg leave to say that the justice of your views, so skilfully expounded by you, does not exclude the rights of the contemporary and the casual in the domain of letters. That which is always just, that which is always beautiful, that which is unchangeable like the fundamental laws of the soul—that undoubtedly occupies, and must occupy, the foremost place in the thoughts, in the impulses, and therefore in the words of man. That, and that alone, is handed down from generation to generation, from nation to nation, as a precious inheritance, always being multiplied and never forgotten. But, on the other hand, there exists in the nature of man, and in the nature of society, as I had the honor to state, a constant demand for self-exposure; there are moments, important moments, in history when this self-denunciation acquires special decisive rights, and comes forward in the domain of letters with greater precision and greater sharpness.

"In the historic process of the life of a nation, the temporary and the casual acquire the significance of the universal, of the all-human, if only for the reason that all generations, all people, can and do understand the painful cries and the painful confessions peculiar to a particular generation or a particular people. The rights of literature, as subordinate to eternal beauty, do not annihilate the rights of literature as the instrument of criticism and of the disclosure of human defects, while at the same time they help to heal social sores. There is boundless beauty in the serene truth and harmony of the soul; but there is also true and high beauty in the penitence which restores truth and guides men or communities to moral perfection. Let me add that I cannot share the one-sided views (as they seem to me) of German æsthetics.

"Of course, art is quite free: in itself it finds its justification and its aim. But freedom of art, abstractedly understood, has nothing to do with the inner life of the artist.

"The artist is not the theory, not the domain of thought and intellectual activity: he is a man, and always a man of his time, usually its best representative, steeped in its spirit, and that both in its established and its still developing tendencies.

"By the very sensitiveness of his organization, without which he could not be an artist, he, more than others, enters into all the painful as well as joyful sensations of the world which surrounds him.

"By always devoting himself to the true and the beautiful, he involuntarily reflects in word, thought, and imagination the contemporary epoch in its mixture of truth, which gladdens a pure heart, and falsehood, which perturbs its harmonious repose.

"Thus flow together the two streams of literature of which we spoke; thus a writer, a servant of pure art, becomes at times a trenchant social critic, and that unwittingly and sometimes even against his will. I beg leave, Count, to take you as an example. You are treading the particular path of literary art unflinchingly and rightly, but are you really quite alien to the tendency which you call denunciatory literature?

"Now, in the picture of the consumptive driver dying on the stove in the midst of a group of comrades, who are evidently indifferent to his sufferings, is it not possible that you revealed some social disease, some kind of vice? In describing this death, did you not feel pain at the callous indifference of those good-natured but unawakened human souls? Yes, and therefore you were and must be an involuntary teacher. I wish you good speed on the grand path you have chosen.

"Success be with you in the future as it has been hitherto, or let it be still greater, for your gift is not a transitory gift, not one to be soon exhausted. But, believe me, in letters the eternal and artistic constantly absorb the temporary and transient, developing and ennobling them, and all the various streams of the domain of human letters constantly flow together, forming one harmonious current."[1]

[1] *Russian Archive*, 1896, No. 11, p. 491. Article of V. N. Lyaskovsky, "A. S. Khomyakof: his Biography and his Teaching."

The prophecy of Khomyakof was fulfilled. Apart from the denunciatory element of all Tolstoy's work of the first period, twenty years later Tolstoy came forward with his own penitence, and then with his denunciation of contemporary evils. And in this cause he has concentrated all his powerful artistic gifts.

CHAPTER XII

THE SECOND JOURNEY ABROAD—HIS BROTHER'S DEATH

Tolstoy's letter to Fet about Turgenef's and Ostrovsky's works—Reading and thinking about progress—Lull in Tolstoy's literary activity—Attitude of his friends—Visit to Yasnaya Polyana by Fet and his wife—Characteristic of N. N. Tolstoy described by Fet—Turgenef's opinion of N. N. Tolstoy. *Foreign journey of N. N. Tolstoy*: Turgenef's counsels—Tolstoy's letter to Fet about the management of the estate—Attitude of Druzhinin toward the interruption of literary activity in Fet and Tolstoy—Letter to N. N. Tolstoy from St. Petersburg—His letter from Sodene—Tolstoy's resolution to go abroad. *Departure of Tolstoy and his sister with her children in a steamer from St. Petersburg to Stettin*: Tolstoy's attitude toward this journey in *Confession*—His sojourn in Berlin—The university, the meeting of artisans, the Moabit Prison—The continuance of his journey—Saxon Switzerland—Dresden—Meeting with Auerbach described from the reminiscences by Schuyler—The Saxon schools—Kissingen—Letter to Tatiana—Study of works on philosophy—His opinion of Herzen—Acquaintance with Julius Froebel—Study of the works of Riehl—Walks in the outskirts—Harz, Thüringen, Wartburg—Tolstoy on Luther—Illness of N. N. Tolstoy—N. N. Tolstoy's letters to Fet—N. N.'s letters to Diakof—His journey to Kissingen—The meeting there of the three brothers: Sergey, Nicolay, and Lyof—Arrival of L. N. Tolstoy in Sodene and departure of the whole Tolstoy family to Frankfort—Reminiscences of Countess A. A. Tolstoy. *The arrival of the Tolstoy family at Hyères*: Tolstoy's letter to Tatiana—Hope for N. N.'s recovery—N. N.'s letter to Diakof. *Death of N. N. Tolstoy*: Tolstoy's letter to his aunt Tatiana—Tolstoy's letter to his brother Sergey—Impression made upon L. N. Tolstoy by death of his brother—Letter of Tolstoy to Fet about his brother's death and about the absurdity of life—Reflections on the death of a boy—The comparison of these thoughts with the latest conclusion—Reminiscences of Plaksin about life in Hyères with L. N. Tolstoy—Continuation of the journey—Visit to Marseilles by L. N. Tolstoy and his opinion of the local popular education—Tolstoy in Paris—Schuyler's narrative about Tolstoy—His opinion of contemporary French writers—A journey to London: *Acquaintance with Herzen.* Reminiscences of Mme. Tuchkof-Ogaref—Account by Herzen's daughter—Palmerston's speech—Emancipation of the serfs—Tolstoy's appointment as Peace Mediator—Departure from London to Brussels—Acquaintance with Proudhon and Lelewel—Tolstoy at Weimar—Goethe's house—The

Froebel gardens—Recollections of a schoolmaster—Jena, Dresden—Second visit of Auerbach—Entry in diary concerning Auerbach—Letter to Tatiana—*Berlin,* acquaintance with Diesterweg—Discussion of Tolstoy with Diesterweg about education and instruction. *Return to Russia*: Tolstoy's attitude to German theories on education.

IN February, 1860, Fet wrote to Tolstoy to consult him as to an intention which he had of buying some land and devoting himself to agriculture. Tolstoy's answer was very sympathetic, he approved of Fet's plans, offered his help, mentioning certain lands for sale, and after this business-like part of the letter, of no general interest, he expressed the following important thoughts about some works of Turgenef and Ostrovsky:

" I have read *On the Eve*. This is my opinion. To write stories is in general a mistake, and especially so on the part of those who feel unhappy and do not exactly know what they desire from life. However, *On the Eve* is much better than *A Nest of Nobles*, and there are in it excellent negative characters: the artist and the father. The other characters not only fail to be types, but their conception, their situation, is not typical, or else they are quite trivial. However, this is Turgenef's usual mistake. The young lady is wretchedly drawn: 'Oh, how I love you . . . she had long eyelashes. . . .' In general it always astonishes me in Turgenef that with his intelligence and poetic sensitiveness he is not able to avoid insipidity, and that even in his methods. There is more of this insipidity in his negative methods, reminding one of Gogol. There is no humanity, no sympathy with the characters, but monsters are represented whom he abuses but does not pity. This painfully jars with the liberal tone and bearing of all the rest. This method may have been good in times gone by and in those of Gogol. Besides, one must add that if one does not pity one's most insignificant characters, then one should cut them up like mincemeat, or else laugh them down till one's sides ache; but not treat them as Turgenef does filled with spleen and dyspepsia. In general, however, no one else now could write such a story, although it will not meet with success.

" *The Tempest*, by Ostrovsky, is to my mind a pitiful work, but it will succeed. Neither Ostrovsky nor Turgenef is to blame, but the times. . . . Another thing is now required. It is not for us to learn, but to teach Tommy and

Mary at least a little of what we know. Good-by, dear friend."

Tolstoy had arrived at the conclusion that a man endowed with brains and enriched with knowledge must, before deriving pleasure from them for himself, give a share in the benefit of them to those who are deprived of both. Accordingly, he had devoted to the school the time he had free from his work on the estate. In these occupations he passed the winter of 1859–60. At the same time, while doing reading, serious reading, he had come to the following conclusions:

"*1st February.*—I have read *La dégénérescence de l'esprit humain,* and about there being physically a higher degree of intellectual development. In this state I mechanically thought of prayer. Prayer to whom? What! is God conceived so clearly that one can beseech and communicate with Him? If I do conceive such a one He loses all majesty for me. A God whom one can beseech and serve is the expression of the weakness of one's mind. God is God precisely because I cannot imagine the whole of His being. Besides, He is not a being, but a Law and a Power.

"Let these lines remain as an indication of my conviction of the power of the mind."

Then he reads Auerbach's stories, *Reynard the Fox* by Goethe, and finally about the same time he jots down the following thought:

"A strange religion is mine and that of our time, the religion of progress. Who said that progress was good? It is merely the absence of faith and the striving after lines of activity—represented as faith. Man requires an impulse—*Schwung*—Yes, that is it."

These thoughts were fully developed in his educational works, as we shall see later on, and also in the self-analysis contained in his confession quoted above.

Tolstoy's friends were watching his literary career with intense interest, treating condescendingly and half-jokingly "the foolishness and eccentricity," as they called them, of those manifestations of the deep inner growth in Tolstoy, which most of them wholly failed to understand.

Thus Botkin casually wrote to Fet on March 6, 1860:

"I learned with joy from Turgenef's letter, that Tolstoy has again set to work at his Caucasian novel. He may play

SECOND JOURNEY ABROAD

the fool as long as he likes, still I maintain he is a man with great gifts. Any portion of his foolishness is of more value to me than the wisest acts of others."[1]

Turgenef's attitude was the same: here is part of his letter to Fet of the same year:

"But Lyof Tolstoy still goes on in his queer way. Such is evidently his destiny. When will he make his last somersault and stand on his feet?"[2]

In the spring of 1860, Fet and his wife paid their usual visit at Yasnaya Polyana on their way from town to the country. Fet made a short note of his stay there on this occasion.

"Of course, we could not refuse ourselves the pleasure of spending a couple of days in Yasnaya Polyana, where, to add to our joy, we found dear N. N. Tolstoy, who for his original Oriental wisdom has earned the nickname of Firdusi. How many delightful plans of staying in the gable in Yasnaya Polyana were discussed in great detail by us during those two days! It did not occur to any one of us how unsound all those plans were."

Further on Fet tells of the coming of Nicolay Tolstoy to their place:

"Once Nicolay Tolstoy arrived here in the middle of May and told us that his sister Marie Tolstoy and his brothers had persuaded him to go abroad on account of his unbearable fits of coughing. He was very thin at this time, apart from his usual slimness. From time to time in his good-natured laughter could be heard that note of irritability which is habitual with consumptive people. I remember how he once got angry and pulled his hand from the coachman, who had tried to kiss it. True, he said nothing in the presence of the serf, but when the latter went out to see to the horses, he began to complain with annoyance in his voice to me and Borisof: 'What made the idiot kiss my hand? It never happened before.'"[3]

Since we have to speak of Tolstoy's relations to his brother during his life and at his death, it may be well to quote Fet's character-sketch of this remarkable man:

"Count N. N. Tolstoy, who called on us almost every

---

[1] A. Fet, *My Reminiscences*, Part I, p. 324.
[2] A. Fet, *My Reminiscences*, Part I, p. 325.
[3] *Ibid.*, p. 326.

evening, used to bring with him a moral interest and vivacity, which it is difficult to describe in a few words. At that time he was still wearing his uniform as an artillery officer, and it was sufficient to give a glance at his thin hands, his great thoughtful eyes, and hollow cheeks to be convinced that cruel consumption had laid its merciless hold on this good-natured and kindly humorous man. Unfortunately, this remarkable man, of whom to say that he was loved by those who knew him is not enough, for they simply worshipped him, this man, while in the Caucasus, had acquired that habit of indulgence in alcoholic liquors which at that time was common among officers. Though I afterward knew N. Tolstoy intimately, and spent with him much time in far-off hunting-fields, where it would have been easier to drink than at evening parties, yet during our three years' friendship I never noticed the slightest symptom of his being overcome by wine or spirits. He would sit in an arm-chair close to the table and sip his tea with some cognac added to it. Being of a very modest disposition, he needed a great deal of questioning to make him talk. But once launched on any subject, he would reveal all the acuteness and mirth of his kind-hearted sense of humor. He evidently adored his youngest brother Lyof. But one had to hear how ironically he described his society adventures. He could so definitely separate what is the real substance of life from its gauzy outer seeming, that he treated with equal irony the higher and lower strata of Caucasian life. The celebrated hunter, of the sect of old believers, uncle Epishka (in Tolstoy's *Cossacks*, Yeroshka), was evidently discovered and defined with the mastery of an artist by N. Tolstoy."[1]

N. N. Tolstoy wrote very little. We only know of his *Memoirs of a Sportsman.*

E. Garshin in his "Reminiscences of Turgenef" quotes the following opinion of his concerning N. Tolstoy:

"The humility of life," said Turgenef, "which was theoretically worked out by Lyof Tolstoy, was really practised by his brother. He always lived somewhere in the outskirts of Moscow, in poor lodgings which were more like a hut, and gladly shared what he had with the poorest man. He was a delightful character and a good story-teller, but

---

[1] A. Fet, *My Reminiscences*, Part I, p. 217.

writing was almost physically impossible for him. The very process of writing was a difficulty with him, just as it is with a laborer whose hands are so roughened by work that he can scarcely hold the pen between his fingers." [1]

To the general joy of his friends, N. Tolstoy's journey abroad was actually settled. This joy, however, was of short duration.

He left Russia *via* St. Petersburg with his brother Sergey.

Turgenef, who had a strong regard for him, felt very anxious, and wrote to Fet from Sodene on June 1, 1860:

"What you tell me of Nicolay Tolstoy's illness grieves me deeply. Is it possible that this dear, good fellow must perish? How could any one neglect such an illness? Is it possible that he did not try to overcome his indolence and go abroad for his health? He used to travel to the Caucasus in most infernally uncomfortable vehicles. Why not make him come to Sodene? One meets here dozens of sufferers from chest complaints: the Sodene waters are almost the best, if not *the* best for such cases. I say all this to you at a distance of two thousand versts, as if my words were of some help. . . . If Tolstoy has not yet started, he will not go. . . . This is how fate plays with us all." [2]

He repeats the same in the postscript of the same letter:

"If N. Tolstoy has not yet gone, throw yourself at his feet and implore him, then drive him by force abroad. The air here, for instance, is so mild, nothing of the kind exists in Russia." [3]

Of course Tolstoy was very much alarmed by his brother's illness. Here is a letter written about that time by him to Fet, in which, besides his anxiety about his brother, he expressed certain views on agricultural work:

". . . That besides your literary work you wish to find a place on the earth and burrow about in it like an ant—such an idea was not only bound to suggest itself to you, but you are sure to realize it better than myself, being, as you are, a good man with a healthy outlook on life. However, it is not for me at the present moment to partronizingly approve or disapprove of you, for I am burdened with a sense of

---

[1] E. Garshin, "Reminiscences of Turgenef." *Historical Review*, November, 1883.
[2] A. Fet, *My Reminiscences*, Part I, pp. 328, 329.
[3] *Ibidem.*

great inconsistency. Farming in the big way I am doing, oppresses me; personal labor on the land I can only as yet contemplate at a distance. On the other hand, I am oppressed by family worries, the illness of Nikolenka, of whom there is yet no news from abroad, and the departure of my sister in three days' time depress me. In general I feel undone. Owing to my sister's helplessness and the desire to see Nicolas, I will to-morrow procure a passport for abroad and will perhaps accompany them, especially if I do not get any news or get bad news from Nicolas."

At that time a pause ensued in the literary activity of both Tolstoy and his friend Fet, who, though feebly, yet accurately reflected the inner process going on in Tolstoy's life.

The following are examples of the well-reasoned letters written by Druzhinin to Tolstoy and Fet, inciting them to literary work. His letter to Tolstoy is particularly interesting:

"I hasten, my amiable friend Tolstoy, to answer your letter concerning your attitude to literature. As you will probably understand, every writer is attacked by moments of doubt and dissatisfaction with himself; it does not matter how strong and natural this feeling is, nobody relinquishes literature in consequence, but all write on till the end of life. But all your good and evil impulses stick to you with peculiar tenacity, and therefore you are more bound to think over it than anybody else, and you should consider the whole matter in a genial manner.

"In the first place, remember that, compared with the labor of poetry and thought, all other labors seem trivial. *Qui a bu, boira*, and for a writer to give up his activity at the age of thirty means depriving himself of one-half of all the interests of life. And this is only one of the difficulties of the matter; there is much of wider significance.

"On all of us there rests a responsibility attached to the extreme importance of literature to Russian society. An Englishman or an American would laugh, if told that in Russia not only men who are thirty years old, but gray-haired landowners possessing two thousand serfs, pore over a novelette of a hundred pages which has appeared in a magazine, is being devoured by everybody, and provokes talk in society for a whole day. It does not matter by what art you try to explain this matter, it is not to be explained by means of art. What in other countries is only talk of careless dilettantism, in ours takes a different shape. In our country things have come to this, that a novelette—a diversion and the lowest kind of literature—becomes either useless trash or the voice of a new mind for the whole Empire. For instance, we all know Turgenef's weakness, but a whole ocean separates his poorest novelette from the very best novels of Mrs. Eugénie Toor's with her half-talent. The Russian public, having a peculiar taste, has from a crowd of writers chosen four or five as superior to the rest, and values them as new minds, disregarding all considerations and inferences. Partly through your talents, partly owing to the bright traits of your spirit, and partly to the lucky concurrence of circumstances, you are placed in a favorable position for influencing the public; consequently it is impossible to retire and hide oneself, one must work on till one's strength and means are exhausted. This is one side of the matter, but there is another. You are a member of a literary circle, which is honest, independent, and influential, as far as possible, and which, during ten years of persecution and reverses, still, in spite of its own shortcomings, firmly upholds the banner of everything that makes for Liberalism and enlightenment, and bares all the pressure of the ironies of life without ever committing a mean action.

"In spite of all the coldness of society, its want of enlightenment, and its tendency to treat literature with mere condescension, this circle has gained respect and moral force, and even if, as no doubt is the case, there are shallow, not to say foolish and insignificant people in it, still they add something to the whole, and are not quite useless. Notwithstanding the short time it is since you arrived, you have a place and a voice in this circle, such as, for instance, Ostrovsky does not possess, though he has great talent, and is as much respected for his moral attitude as you are for yours. It would take too long to find out how this has come about, but that is not the chief thing. Once having cut yourself off from the literary circle and surrendered yourself to inactivity, you will feel lonely, and will deprive yourself of an important *rôle* in society. Here I finish my dissertation owing to lack of space in the letter; if these suggestions prove of interest to you, you will develop and complete them yourself."

With the same friendly advice he addresses Fet:

"Dear Fet—What I said to Tolstoy I repeat to you, as to your intention to write no more. Stick to your resolution till you are ready to write something good; but when you are able to write, then you will change your mind without outside influence.

"To keep good poetry and a good book unpublished is impossible, had you sworn a thousand oaths to do so; so you need not trouble. For these last two or three years you and Tolstoy have been in an uninspired mood, and you act wisely in keeping silent; but as soon as the soul is stirred and something good is created, you will both break silence. Therefore don't bind yourselves with promises, the more so because nobody expects any from either of you. What is not right in Tolstoy's resolution and yours is this—they have originated under the influence of a certain grudge against literature and the public. But if an author is to be offended at every manifestation of indifference and every piece of harsh criticism, there will be no one left to do any writing except Turgenef, who manages somehow to be everybody's friend. To take to heart literary squabbles is, in my opinion, the same thing as to get angry with the horse you are riding for misbehaving while you are in a poetic mood. I may tell you that I have been abused and offended to a degree, yet this has not deprived me of a particle of my appetite; on the contrary, I have found a peculiar pleasure in my determination to sit firmly and move forward, and I shall certainly not stop writing till I have said all I think necessary to say."[1]

Druzhinin was certainly mistaken in thus attributing his friends' silence to irritation against the public. If such an irritation existed, it was but the outcome of the same cause which kept them from writing, the conviction that neither the reader nor the author had any firm moral basis and bond of union for mutual understanding.

The authors did not know what to write; the readers, as represented by the critics, did not know what to demand

[1] A. Fet, *My Reminiscences*, Part I, p. 334.

from the authors. This would continue to be the case till some great event of life or history would stir the brain and feeling of the author and incite him to activity.

Let us return to N. Tolstoy's illness.

On his way abroad he wrote to Fet from St. Petersburg:

"My dear friends, Fet and Ivan Petrovich, I keep my promise even before I gave it. I intended to write from abroad, and now I write from St. Petersburg. We are off on Saturday—*i. e.*, to-morrow. I consulted Zdekauer, he is a St. Petersburg doctor, and not a Berlin man, as I made out from Turgenef's letter. The watering-place Turgenef is staying at, Sodene, is the same that we are sent to, consequently my address, too, is Francfort on Main."

Following this, Fet received his second letter sent from Sodene itself:

"Not having heard from you, I write to inform you that I reached Sodene safely; however, they did not fire any cannon at my arrival. In Sodene we found Turgenef, who is alive and well, so well that he himself owns he is 'perfectly' well. He has discovered a certain German girl, and is very enthusiastic about her. We (it refers to dear old Turgenef) play at chess, but somehow it does not work: he is thinking about his German girl, and I about getting well. As I have sacrificed this autumn, I must become a giant by next autumn. Sodene is an excellent place. I have been scarcely a week here, and feel already a great deal better. We are, my brother and I, in lodgings. For three rooms we pay twenty guldens a week, table d'hôte = one gulden, wine forbidden. From this you can infer what an unpretending place Sodene is, but I like it. Facing my windows grows a not exactly beautiful tree, still a bird has made its home there and sings on it every evening; it reminds me of the wing of the building at Novosyolky.

"Give my regards to Marya Petrovna and be well, my friends, and write to me often. I believe I shall stay a long time at Sodene, about six weeks at least. I do not describe the journey, because I was ill all the time. Once more, good-by."[1]

On July 3d Tolstoy, with his sister and her children, took the steamer at St. Petersburg to go to Stettin for Berlin.

[1] A. Fet, *My Reminiscences*, Part I, p. 332.

The illness of his brother was the reason which hastened Tolstoy's departure abroad, though he had been ready long before. His purpose was to get acquainted with what had been done in Europe for popular education.

"After a year spent by me in work among the schools (in Russia)," says Tolstoy in his *Confession*, "I went abroad for the second time in order there to find out how I could manage to learn to teach others without knowing anything myself."

But Tolstoy could thus severely criticise the object of his journey only twenty years later, when he gave himself up to the study of this subject with all the passionate fervor of his temperament.

The illness and death of his brother did not stop this work, it only divided the journey in two parts.

We will try to describe more fully what took place.

From Stettin Tolstoy arrived in Berlin with his sister, who continued her journey to join her brother at Sodene, while Tolstoy remained for a few days in Berlin.[1]

He attended the university, and was present at the lectures given by Droysen, the Professor of History, and also at those of Dubois-Raymond, the Professor of Physics and Physiology. Besides this, Tolstoy went to the evening classes for artisans—Handwerksverein—and got very much interested in the popular lectures of one prominent professor, especially in the system of "query-boxes."[2] This method of national education was till then unknown to Tolstoy, and it struck him by its animation and the freedom of intercourse which it encouraged between the representatives of science and the people at large. Unfortunately, forty years have since gone by, but Russia has not yet reached this simple method of educating the people. The police censorship, theological and lay, makes the application of the system impossible.

After this Tolstoy visited the Moabit Prison, with its newly introduced method of scientific torture, known by the name of solitary confinement. Needless to say, this new invention did not produce a favorable impression on him.

[1] The interesting details of the second journey abroad we borrow from the book of Loewenfeld, *Count L. N. Tolstoy: His Life and Works*, in which this journey is minutely described. We have only corrected a few mistakes with the help of Tolstoy's letters to his relations.

[2] A system of putting written questions in a box, to be answered later by the speaker.—*Trans.*

SECOND JOURNEY ABROAD

He left Berlin on July 14th.

He stopped for a day in Leipsic to examine the schools, and, having crossed the so-called "Swiss-Saxony," which impressed him very much by its beauty, he paused at Dresden, where he met the well-known popular writer Berthold Auerbach.

The American writer, Schuyler, in his Reminiscences, gives Tolstoy's account of this interview, amplifying it by a few details collected afterward:

"In helping Tolstoy to arrange his library, I noticed that the works of Auerbach occupied the honored place on the first shelf. He took the two volumes of *Ein Neues Leben,* and told me to read that very remarkable book when I went to bed, adding:

"To this author I was indebted for the opening of a school for my peasants, and for so becoming interested in national education. When I went abroad for the second time, I visited Auerbach without naming myself. When he came into the room I only said, 'I am Eugene Baumann,'[1] and when he showed astonishment I made haste to add, 'not actually by name, but by character.' And then I told him who I was, how his writings had compelled me to think, and what a good effect they had upon me.

"In the following winter," continues Schuyler, "I had an opportunity of spending a few days in Berlin. While there, under the hospitable roof of the American ambassador, Mr. Bancroft, I had the pleasure of meeting Auerbach, with whom I got very well acquainted during that time. In speaking of Russia, we turned to Tolstoy, and I reminded him of the incident.

"'Yes,' he said, 'I remember how I was taken aback by the odd-looking gentleman, when he told me he was Eugene Baumann, for I was afraid he would threaten me with prosecution for defamation or libel.'"

The examination of the schools in Saxony did not satisfy Tolstoy.

In his travelling notes we find the following short description of these schools:

"I visited a school. It was dreadful. Prayers for the King, whippings, everything learned by heart, frightened, mentally distorted children."

[1] The hero of a story by Auerbach.

On July 19th he continued his journey, and arrived at Kissingen, where he was near his brother.

In Kissingen he continued to read a great deal; on natural science he read Bacon; on religion, Luther; on politics, Riehl. He probably read Herzen at the same time, for there is a short entry about him in his diary.

"Herzen—a scattered intellect, sick with vanity, but broad, agile and kind, distinguished, purely Russian."

In Kissingen Tolstoy made the acquaintance of Julius Froebel, the German sociologist, author of *The System of National Politics,* and nephew of the educationist Froebel, the founder of the Kindergarten.

According to Froebel, Tolstoy astonished him by his strong views, which were quite new to the German scholar, and seemed not to harmonize with his "system."

"Progress in Russia," Tolstoy said, "must emanate from national education, which will give better results in our country than in Germany, because the Russian people are not yet perverted, whereas the Germans resemble a child who has been for several years undergoing a wrong education."

Popular instruction must not be compulsory, such was his idea. If it is good, he said, then the need of it must be born of itself, just as the desire of nutrition is created by hunger.

He expressed with great animation his views upon communal peasant ownership of land, and saw in the "artel" the future of social organization. Froebel often smiled as he listened to similar views expressed by Tolstoy with reference to the German people. Tolstoy was struck by not finding in a single German peasant household either *Village Tales* or the works of Goebel. Russian peasants, he declared, would have shed tears over such books.

The impressions received by him from Berthold Auerbach in Dresden, and from Froebel during their walks together, confirmed him in a task the outline of which had only existed vaguely in his mind. The author of *The System of Social Politics* pointed out to him that the works of Riehl were more in sympathy with his (Tolstoy's) views, and Tolstoy, with all the ardor of youth, began to study *The Natural History of the People as the Foundation of German Social Policy.*

The nephew of Frederic Froebel was also by vocation an educationist. He made Tolstoy acquainted with the ideas of the founder of the Kindergarten system.

In Kissingen Tolstoy visited all the suburbs, which are rich in natural beauty and historical reminiscences. He crossed the Harz, stopped at some towns in Thuringia, and from Eisenach went on to Wartburg.

The personality of the German reformer, whose hard struggle is recalled by Wartburg, interested Tolstoy very much. Luther's rupture with the old traditions, his bold and upright progressive activity, and the ideas of which he was a representative, carried Tolstoy completely away, and after a visit to the room in which were written the first words of the Bible in German, he wrote down in his diary this short sentence: "Luther is great."

Meanwhile the invalid N. Tolstoy wrote to Fet on July 19th:

"I would have written long ago, my dear friends, only I wanted to give you the news of all our Tolstoy household, but a great muddle ensued some time ago, which at last cleared up in this way: my sister and her children arrived at Sodene, where she will stay and pursue her cure; Uncle Lyovochka remains at Kissingen, five hours distant from Sodene, and is not coming to Sodene, so that I shall not see him. Your letter I have sent to Lyovochka, by my brother Sergey, who will call at Kissingen on his way to Russia. He will call on you soon, and tell you everything in detail. Forgive me, dear Afanasy Afanasyevich, I have read your letter to my brother. There is much truth in it, when you speak of things in general; but when you mention yourself, you are not right; there is always the same defect of being unbusinesslike; you do not know yourself, and you know nothing of what is around you. But pots are not boiled by the gods; now, be practical, go unhesitatingly into business, and I am sure it will drive the babbler out of you; besides, it will probably squeeze out of you some lyrical verses, which Turgenef and I and a few more fellows would read with pleasure. As to the rest of the world—forget it. What I love you for, my dear Afanasy Afanasyevich, is this, that you are all truth; what comes out of you is in you, and is not mere words, as is the case with dear old Ivan Sergeyevich. Yet I feel quite lonely without him in Sodene, apart from the fact that our chess club has come to grief. Even my appetite is not the same, since I have ceased to sit beside his stout and healthy figure, asking either for carrots to add to the meat, or meat to add to the carrots. I have often talked with him of you, especially lately. 'Now Fet is starting, now Fet is coming, now Fet is shooting at last.' Ivan Sergeyevich has bought a dog—a black pointer—half-breed. I have finished my water cure and intend to undertake a few excursions. Yet my chief quarters will be Sodene and the address the same."

Nicolay Tolstoy left so few literary works that we quote below some of his letters to the common friend of the Tolstoy brothers, Dmitri Alexeyevich Diakof. Although their contents are not very rich, still they reflect his kindheartedness.

He wrote to Diakof twice from Sodene:

1. "DEAR DIAKOF—Did you get my letter from St. Petersburg? If you did, you are committing a crime by not answering. What is the matter with you? I hope all your folks are well—for Christ's sake answer me if Darya Alexandrovna is going abroad. When, to what place, or is she gone already? If I knew all this I would go to meet her straight off. I have done taking mineral waters and now I am resting. My sister is at Sodene too, she will stay four weeks. My address is: Sodene, near Francfort-on-Main, Landlust House, etc.

"My health has improved, but I am not well yet; I dare say I could say the same about your people. For Christ's sake, let me know how you are managing your household, what plans you have made, etc. Lyovochka is in Kissingen; Seryozha was with me in Sodene; he got stumped by playing roulette and went back to Russia; he will probably call at your place. Yours,   COUNT N. TOLSTOY."

"*July* 19*th*.

2. "I don't know how to thank you, Darya Alexandrovna, for your postscript; it means that you have not forgotten your neighbor. How is your health? How is Masha? I expect we shall meet this year, and I look forward to it with delight; only let me know where you are,

and I will look you up at once. My sister is at Sodene with me, and begs me to remember her to you. We are both of us cursing the weather—just fancy, we had no summer here. The wind blows and it rains all the time, not only in Sodene but all over Europe. Do not let this frighten you; do come and bring us some nice weather. With esteem and respect, your faithfully,

"Count N. Tolstoy."

"I am afraid, dear Dmitri, that this letter will not reach you in time; if you get it, let me know immediately where you are going. Where will you pass the autumn? That's the chief point. My address is the same as before—Sodene—as I don't know myself where I shall go after this. I have been prescribed grapes and a good climate; however, neither of them can be found in Europe this year. My sister's regards to you. Yours, N. Tolstoy.

"*August 28th.*"

After this, very unsatisfactory news began to arrive from Sodene. N. Tolstoy had enjoyed a few weeks in a beautiful spot, in company with his sister and her children and his brother Sergey, but his health did not improve. The doctors advised him to move to Italy.

On August 6th Sergey Nicolayevich Tolstoy returned home. Naturally, he took the opportunity to stop at Kissingen, which takes a five hours' journey, to see his brother Lyof and inform him of the serious fears they entertained concerning the health of Nicolay. Three days after, on the very date when Sergey Nicolayevich had to start for Russia, his brother Nicolay arrived at Kissingen. Their sister and her children remained at Sodene to finish their cure.

Nicolay Tolstoy stayed a short time in Kissingen and went back to Sodene, but Lyof Tolstoy remained for some time on the Garz, enjoying nature and devoting his leisure to reading.

At last he came to Sodene on August 26th. There everything was ready for departure, and on August 29th Tolstoy with his brother went to Freiburg.

Evidently powerful idiosyncrasies had made Tolstoy very original even in appearance. We have heard how he frightened Auerbach. In Francfort a similar incident happened. His aunt A. A. Tolstoy speaks of it thus:

"We arrived at Francfort. One day Prince Alexander of Hessen and his wife called on me, and during their visit the door suddenly opened and Tolstoy appeared in a most singular dress, reminding one of Spanish robbers as seen in pictures. I simply gasped, so great was my astonishment. . . . Tolstoy was not pleased with my visitors and soon went away.

"'*Qui est donc ce singulier personnage?*' asked my astonished guests.

"'*Mais c'est Léon Tolstoy.*'

"'*Ah, mon Dieu, pourquoi ne l'avez vous pas nommé? Après avoir lu ses admirables écrits nous mourions d'envie de le voir,*' they reproached me."[1]

From Francfort all the Tolstoy family, by advice of their doctors, moved to Hyères on the Mediterranean. But poor Nicolay Tolstoy did not benefit by it and died shortly afterward.

A few days after his arrival Tolstoy wrote his aunt Tatiana a letter in which the hope that his brother would recover is still perceptible.

"The state of Nicolay's health is still the same, but it is only here that we can expect any improvement, for the kind of life he led in Sodene, the journey, and the bad weather were on the contrary sure to injure him. Here the weather has been splendid these three days, and they say it has been fine all along. There is here a certain Princess Galitzin who has been living in the country for nine years. Marie has made her acquaintance, and this princess says she arrived here in a much worse state than that of Nicolay, and now she is a sturdy woman in perfectly good health."

But Nicolay was getting worse and worse. A few days before his death he wrote to Diakof in Paris; his handwriting had become faint and straggling, and he himself confessed that his strength was failing him.

"I write you a few lines to let you know where I am. I and my sister are passing the winter at Hyères. Here is

---

[1] Iv. Zakharin (Takunin). "Countess Alexandra Andreyevna Tolstoy." *The Messenger of Europe*, June, 1904.

Tolstoy during his second stay abroad, 1860.

my address and that of Lyovochka as well—Mme. Senequier's House, Rue du Midi, Hyères. Alas! I could not go to Paris, such a journey is beyond my strength, I am too weak. As soon as you arrive and find my letter, let me know where you stopped, how you completed the journey, etc. If we cannot see each other, let us keep up correspondence. Yours entirely, N. TOLSTOY."

September 20, 1860 (N. S.), he died, and Tolstoy thus informs his aunt Tatiana of it:

"DEAR AUNT—The black seal will tell you all that I have been expecting from hour to hour for a fortnight has happened to-day at nine in the morning. Only yesterday evening did he for the first time allow me to help him to undress; this morning for the first time he returned to bed and asked for a nurse. He was conscious the whole time. A quarter of an hour before his death he drank some milk and told me he felt well. This morning he even joked and showed interest in my plans of education. Only a few minutes before death he murmured several times, 'My God, my God!' I think he felt his position, but deceived us and himself. . . . I have only just closed his eyes. I shall now soon be with you and personally relate everything to you. I do not think of bringing back his body. The Princess Galitzin has undertaken to arrange everything concerning the burial.

"Good-by, dear Aunt. I cannot console you. It is the will of God, that is all. I am not now writing to Sergey. He is probably out hunting—you know where. So inform him or send him this letter."

On the day following the funeral he also writes to his brother Sergey concerning it:

"You have, I presume, heard of Nicolenka's death. I am sorry for you that you were not here. However painful it is, I am glad all this took place in my presence, and that it has affected me as it should have done. Not like the death of Mitenka, of which I learned when I was not thinking at all about him. However, this is quite a different thing. With Mitenka were associated memories of childhood and family feeling and no more; but this was, for you and for me, a man whom we loved and *respected* positively more than any one on earth. You know the selfish feeling which used latterly to take hold of us—'the sooner it is finished the better'; but now it is dreadful to write and to recall those thoughts. Till the last day, with his extraordinary force of character and concentration of mind, he did everything to avoid being a burden to me. On the day of his death he dressed and washed himself, and in the morning I found him dressed in his arm-chair. It was only about nine hours before his death that he surrendered to his illness and requested to be undressed. The first time was in the lavatory. I had gone downstairs when I heard his door open; I returned, he was nowhere to be found. At first I was afraid of entering the lavatory; he did not like it, but I heard him cry out, ' Help me!'

"And on that day he gave himself up and became subdued and submissive; he did not groan, did not criticise any one, praised all, and kept saying to me: 'Thank you, *my friend.*' You understand what this means in our relations. I told him I had heard how he was coughing in the morning, but I shrank from coming in from a foolish kind of shyness. 'I am sorry, it would have *consoled* me.' He did suffer, but only once, two days before his death, he said: 'What dreadful, sleepless nights! Toward the morning the cough chokes one, a whole month! and what visions one had—God only knows. Again two nights more like this—it is awful.' Never once did he clearly say he felt the approach of death. But I only mean he did not express it. On the day of his death he ordered an indoor suit; yet, at the same time, when I said that, if he did not get better, Mashenka and myself would not go to Switzerland, he replied, 'Do you really imagine I shall get better?' And that in such a tone that it was evident he felt his position, but did not speak of it for my sake, and I did not show what I thought for his. Yet, when that day came, I seemed to know, and I was with him all the time. He died without any suffering, at least so far as we could see. His breath became slower and slower and all was over. The next day I went into his room and was afraid to uncover the face. I thought it would show still greater marks of suffering and fill me with more awe than during his illness, but you cannot imagine what a beautiful face it was, with his best expression of happiness and peace.

"Yesterday he was buried here. At one moment I thought of removing him and of telegraphing to you, but changed my mind. There is no use irritating the wound. I am sorry for you that the news will reach you while at sport and entirely taken up with your usual distraction, and will not affect you as it did us. It is well that it should be so. I now feel what I have often heard, that when one loses such a one as he was, it becomes much less painful to think of one's own death.

"Your letter came at the very moment of the funeral service. No, you will not water the garden with him any more.

"Two days before his death he read to me his memoirs about sport and spoke much about you. He said that God had made you a happy man in every way, and yet you torment yourself. Only on the second day did I bethink myself of getting his portrait taken and a mould of his face. The portrait does not catch now his remarkable expression, but the mould is beautiful."

This death produced a strong impression on Tolstoy, and at first repelled him from life and shook his faith in good. This is the entry he makes in his diary:

"*13th Oct., 1860.*—It will soon be a month since Nicolenka died. Dreadfully has this event torn me away from life. Again the question: Why? I am not far from going there. Where? Nowhere. I am trying to write, compelling myself, but unsuccessfully, for the sole reason that I cannot attribute to my work that significance which is necessary to have the power and the patience to work. During the funeral itself the thought came to me to write a materialistic gospel, the life of Christ—a Materialist."

In a letter to Fet of the 17th October, 1860, when the first impressions of the bereavement had already settled down and his inert consciousness again took the ascendency, Tolstoy thus describes his brother's death:

"I presume you already know what has happened. On the 20th of September he died, literally in my arms. Nothing in life has ever produced such an impression upon me. He spoke the truth when he used to say there is nothing worse than death. And when one clearly realizes that it is the end of all, then there is nothing worse than life either. What should one worry about or strive for, if of that which was Nicolas Tolstoy nothing has remained? He did not say that he felt the approach of death, but I know that he followed its every step and knew for certain how much yet remained. A few minutes before death he fell into a doze and suddenly awoke and murmured with horror: 'But what is this?' He had seen it, this absorption of oneself in nothing. And if he found nothing to catch hold of, what can I find? Still less. And it is certain that neither myself nor any one will so struggle with it to the last moment as he did. Two days before his death I offered to place a convenience in his room. 'No,' he said, 'I am weak, but not so weak as that; we will yet struggle on.'

"Until the last moment he did not surrender to death, he did everything himself, kept endeavoring to work, wrote, questioned me about my writings, gave advice. But all this, as it appeared to me, he did, not from inner impulse, but on principle. One thing, Nature—that remained until the last. The day before his death he was in his room and fell exhausted on his bed by the open window. I came in. He said with tears in his eyes:

"'How I have been enjoying this view for the last hour. "From dust thou art and to dust thou shalt return." Only one thing remains—the vague hope that there is in Nature, of which in the earth one will become a part, something which will abide and will be found.'

"All who knew him and saw his last moments say: How wonderfully, peacefully, and quietly he died. But I know how dreadfully painful his end was, for not a single feeling of his escaped me. A thousand times did I say to myself, 'Let the dead bury their dead,' but let us use to some purpose our remaining strength. One cannot attempt to persuade a stone to fall upward instead of downward, as attraction takes it. One cannot laugh at a joke one is tired of. One cannot eat when one has no appetite. Of what avail is anything when to-morrow will begin the agonies of death with all the abomination of falsehood and self-delusion, and when all will end in nothing, in absolute nought for oneself. An amusing situation indeed. 'Be useful, be virtuous, be happy while you are alive,' people say to each other; but thyself and happiness and virtue and

[A facsimile of a letter written by Tolstoy in 1860.]

utility consist in truth. And the truth I have gathered out of a life of thirty-two years is that the position we are placed in is dreadful. 'Take life as it is,' they continue, 'you have yourselves put yourselves in this position.' Quite right! I do take life as it is. As soon as men reach the highest degree of development, they clearly see that all is bunkum, deceit; and that truth, which after all they value most—that this truth is awful, that when you see it well and distinctly you awake with horror and say as my brother did: 'But what is this?' But, of course, so long as there is a desire to know and express the truth, one endeavors to know and express it. This is all that has remained for me out of the moral world, and higher than which I cannot place myself. And this only shall I do, but not in the form of your art. Art is a lie, and I can no longer love a beautiful lie.

"I shall pass the winter here for the reason that it matters not where one lives. Please write to me. I love you as my brother did. He remembered you until the last moment."[1]

Tolstoy, who had witnessed thousands of deaths at Sebastopol, had noted them then only with his "bodily" eyes. But here the death of a beloved brother made him see death for the first time with his "spiritual" eyes, and he felt quite overcome. Being a sincere man, he frankly acknowledged that he was quite crushed by it, and was helpless before its power. This truthfulness saved him. From that moment one may say the idea of death never left him. It led him to the inevitable spiritual crisis and to final victory.

A month later he wrote the following in relation to another death:

"A boy of thirteen has had a painful death from consumption. What for? The only explanation is given by belief in restitution in the hereafter. If that does not exist, then neither does justice, and justice is not necessary, and the desire of it is a superstition.

"Justice answers to the most essential demand in man's relation to man. The same also does man search for in his relation to the universe. Without future life this does not exist. The adaptation of the means to the end is the only irrefragable law of nature, naturalists will say. But this does not exist in the sphere of the human soul—love, poetry;

[1] Fet, *My Reminiscences*.

in the best spheres this law does not apply. All these features have been and have gone without finding expression. Nature has far overreached her end in giving man his aspiration toward poetry and love, if her one law is the adaptation of the means to the end."

Twenty-seven years later he wrote a book, *Life*, which he concluded with these words:

"The life of man is an aspiration toward welfare; what he aspires to is given to him; a life which cannot be death, and a welfare that cannot be evil."

Interesting facts of Tolstoy's life in his sister's house at Hyères after the death of their brother are given by Sergey Plaksin, then a little boy living in the same boarding-house with his mother. He thus relates the settlement and life of the Tolstoys in the Villa Tosh:

"The Count's family occupied the upper floor of the villa, and Tolstoy had his writing-table in the glass-house, with a view over the sea. During his stay in Hyères, Tolstoy often visited his sister at her summer residence, spending many days there.

"Being an indefatigable walker, Tolstoy would make out our itinerary, always discovering new places for our rambles. One day we would go to see the boiling of salt on the peninsula Porquerolle; another day we would climb up the S. M. to a small chapel with a statue of the Blessed Virgin, or we marched off to see the ruins of a castle called, nobody knew why, 'Trou des fées.'

"On the way Tolstoy used to tell us children all kinds of tales. I remember one about a golden horse, and a gigantic tree from the top of which could be seen all seas and towns. Being aware of my weak chest, he often put me on his shoulders, and went on with his tales as he walked. Need I add that we simply worshipped him?

"At dinner in the evening Tolstoy used to relate to our good-natured hosts all sorts of amusing nonsense about Russia, which they did not know whether to believe or not, unless the Countess or my mother sifted the truth from the fiction.

"Directly after dinner we used to collect, according to the weather, either on the wide terrace or in the drawing-room, and the bustle would begin. We presented a ballet and opera, with a piano mercilessly torturing the ears of our audience; 'we' being the mothers, Count Tolstoy, and my nurse Liza. The ballet and opera were replaced by gymnastics, when Tolstoy himself appeared as our professor, and insisted chiefly on the development of muscle.

"He would lie stretched on the floor and make us do the same, and then we had to get up without using our arms. He arranged a certain construction made of strings, and to our greatest delight and joy himself took part in the exercise.

"Whenever we made too much noise, and the mothers appealed to Tolstoy to keep us quiet, he would place us all round the table, and order us to bring ink and pens.

"Here is a sample of our work with Tolstoy.

"'Look here,' he said to us once, 'I will teach you.'

"'Teach us what?' inquired the bright-eyed Lizanka, the lady of my heart.

"Giving no answer to his niece, Tolstoy continued:

"'Write!'

"'What about, uncle?' insisted Lizanka.

"'Listen, I will give you a theme.'

"'What will you give us?' went on Lizanka.

"'A theme!' repeated Tolstoy firmly. 'Write an answer to the question: What is the difference between Russia and other countries? Write here, in my presence, and nobody is to copy from anybody else! Do you hear?' he added sternly.

"So writing began, as they say, *à qui mieux mieux*. However much Kolia would bend his head on one side, the lines always crawled to the right upper corner of the sheet. He panted and puffed, producing strange sounds through his nose, but it was of no use for the poor fellow; yet Tolstoy had strictly forbidden us to write on lined paper, declaring it was nonsense. 'You must write without lines.' While we were engaged in writing our essays, the Countess and my mother would sit down on the sofa and read in a low voice some new French book, while Count Tolstoy walked up and down the room, sometimes making the nervous Countess exclaim:

"'Why, Lyovochka, you are moving about like a pendulum! I wish you would sit down!'

"In half an hour our 'essays' were ready, and mine happened to be the first that our mentor got hold of. He tried to read it; but it was hopeless trying to make out anything in the lines, all running, as they did, up to the top of the page, so he returned me the manuscript, saying:

"'Read aloud yourself'; and I loudly proclaimed that Russia differs from other countries in this, that at Shrovetide people eat pancakes and go out toboganning, and at Easter they like to color eggs.

"'Bravo,' exclaimed Tolstoy, and began to decipher the manuscript of Kolya, who asserted that Russia's distinction consists in 'snow.' With Liza it was the 'troika'—a team of three horses.

"The best definition was given by Varia, the eldest of us.

"As a reward for our evening studies Tolstoy brought us water-colors from Marseilles, where he used to go very often from Hyères, and he taught us to paint.

"Tolstoy used to spend nearly the whole day with us. He taught us, joined in our games, took interest in our squabbles, discussed them, and decided who was right and who was wrong."[1]

Here we shall quote a story about Tolstoy's life in Hyères, as related by his sister Marie:

"Tolstoy was always distinguished by his originality, which often amounted to extravagance.

"We lived on in Hyères after our brother's death. Tolstoy was already well known there, and the Russian community at Hyères and in its neighborhood sought his acquaintance. Once we were invited to an evening party at the house of the Princess Dandakof-Rorsakof. All those of any distinction were assembled there, and Tolstoy should have been the 'lion' of the evening, but, just as if it were intentional, he did not arrive till very late. The guests were getting low-spirited, the hostess had exhausted her powers of entertainment, and she thought with grief of her spoiled soirée. However, at last, at a very late hour, the arrival of the Count Tolstoy was announced. The hostess and the guests cheered up, but one may imagine their surprise when Tolstoy entered the drawing-room in his travelling dress and wooden shoes. He had just been for a long walk; after the walk he came to the party without calling at his own house, and tried to assure everybody that wooden shoes were the best and most convenient covering for the feet, and ad-

[1] S. Plaksin, *Count L. Tolstoy among Children*, pp. 15-25. Moscow, 1903.

vised everybody to get a pair. Even then everything was forgiven him, and the evening party was the more interesting. Tolstoy was in excellent spirits. There was much singing at the party and Tolstoy had to play the accompaniment."

In Hyères Tolstoy gave himself up greatly at times to literary work. He wrote there *The Cossacks*, and an article *On National Education*. He remained in Hyères till the beginning of December, and then went *via* Marseilles to Geneva; there he parted from his sister, who had moved there also with her children. From there he started once more on his travels, first visiting Italy, Nice, Leghorn, Florence, Rome, Naples—these were the principal points of his journey. In Italy, according to his own words, he experienced his first lively impressions of antiquity. He went to Paris, again *via* Marseilles, in fact he visited this last city several times during his foreign travel. The life of the great French industrial town seems to have attracted and interested him.

This is how Tolstoy, in one of his articles upon education, describes his stay at Marseilles:

" Last year I was in Marseilles, where I visited all the schools for the working people of that city. The proportion of the pupils to the population is very great, and the children, with few exceptions, attend school three, four, and even six years.

" The school programme consists in learning by heart the catechism, biblical and universal history, the four operations of arithmetic, French orthography, and book-keeping. In what way book-keeping could form the subject of instruction I was unable to comprehend, and not one teacher could explain it to me. The only explanation I was able to make to myself, when I examined the books kept by the students who had finished the course, was that they did not know even three rules of arithmetic, but that they had learned by heart to operate with figures, and that, therefore, they had also learned by rote how to keep books. (It seems to me that there is no need of proving that the *tenue des livres, Buchhaltung,* as it is taught in Germany and England, is a science which only requires about four hours of explanation in the case of a pupil who knows the four operations in arithmetic.)

"Not one boy in these schools was able to solve the simplest problem in addition and subtraction. And yet they operated with abstract numbers, multiplying thousands with ease and rapidity. To questions from the history of France they answered well by rote, but if I asked anything at haphazard, I received such answers as that Henry IV had been killed by Julius Cæsar. . . .

"In Marseilles I also visited a lay school, and also a monastic school for grown persons. Out of 250,000 inhabitants, less than one thousand, of these only two hundred men, attend these schools. The instruction is the same: mechanical reading, which is acquired in a year or in a longer time, book-keeping without the knowledge of arithmetic, religious instruction, and so forth. After the lay school I saw the daily instruction offered in the churches; I saw the *salles d'asile*, in which four-year-old children, at a given whistle, like soldiers, made evolutions around the benches, at a given command lifted and folded their hands, and with strange, quivering voice sang laudatory hymns to God and to their benefactors, and I convinced myself that the educational institutions of the city of Marseilles were exceedingly bad.

"If, by some miracle, a person should visit all these establishments, without having seen the people in the streets, in their shops, in the cafés, in their home surroundings, what opinion would he form of a nation which was educated in such a manner? He certainly would conclude that that nation was ignorant, rude, hypocritical, full of prejudices, and almost barbarous. But it is enough to enter into relations with, and talk to a common man, to be convinced that the French nation is, on the contrary, almost such as it regards itself to be: intelligent, clever, affable, free from prejudices, and really civilized. Look at a city workman of about thirty years of age: he will write a letter without such mistakes as are made at school, often without any mistakes at all; he has an idea of politics, consequently of modern history and geography; he knows more or less history from novels; he has some knowledge of the natural sciences. He frequently draws and applies mathematical formulæ to his trade. Where did he learn all this?

"I found an answer to it in Marseilles without any trouble when, after the schools, I began to stroll down the streets to frequent the dram-shops, *cafés chantants*, museums, workshops, quays, and bookstalls. The very boy who told me that Henry IV had been killed by Julius Cæsar knew very well the story of the *Three Musketeers* and of *Monte Cristo*. I found twenty-eight illustrated editions of these in Marseilles, costing from five to ten centimes. To a population of 250,000 they sell 30,000 of them; consequently, if we suppose that ten people read or listen to one copy, we find that all have read them. In addition there are the museum, the public libraries, and the theatres. Then the cafés, two large *cafés chantants*, where any one may enter for fifty centimes worth of food or drink, and where there are daily as many as 25,000 people, not counting the smaller cafés, which hold as many more: in each of these cafés they give little comedies and scenes, and recite verses. Taking the lowest calculation, we get one-fifth of the population who get their daily oral instruction, just as the Greeks and Romans were instructed, in their amphitheatres.

"Whether this education is good or bad is another matter; but here it is, this unconscious education, which is so much more powerful than the one by compulsion; here is the unconscious school which has undermined the compulsory school, and has made its significance dwindle down almost to nothing. There is left of the latter only the despotic form with hardly any inner significance. I say with 'hardly any,' because I exclude the mere mechanical ability of putting letters together and writing down words—the only knowledge which is carried away after five or six years' study."

In January, 1861, Tolstoy was in Paris. As in every place, he here tried to observe the ways of the people.

"When I was in Paris," he said to Schuyler, "I generally passed half my time in omnibuses, simply to amuse myself in observing the people; and I can assure you that in every passenger I recognized one of the characters in Paul de Kock."

In his conversation with Schuyler, Tolstoy entirely denied Paul de Kock's alleged immorality.

"In French literature," he said to Schuyler, "I highly value the novels of Alexandre Dumas and Paul de Kock."

Upon Schuyler expressing his consternation, Tolstoy continued:

"No," he added, "don't tell me any of that nonsense about Paul de Kock being immoral. He is somewhat improper according to English ideas; he is more or less what the French call *leste* and *gaulois,* but never immoral. Whatever he may say in his writings, and notwithstanding his slight jocose liberties, his tendency is completely moral. He is a French Dickens; his characters are all taken from life, and are as perfect as Dickens's.

"As for Dumas, every novelist must understand him. His plots are splendid, not to speak of their finish. I can read them over and over again, but plots and intrigues are his principal aim."

In Paris Tolstoy saw Turgenef, and their interview brought them somewhat nearer together.

After this Tolstoy went to London, and there met Herzen. He remained in London for six weeks, and saw Herzen almost every day. They had long talks, and discussed the most interesting subjects. Unfortunately neither Herzen nor Tolstoy made notes of these conversations.

A few lines describing their first meeting appear in the reminiscences of Mme. Tuchkof-Ogaref:

"Herzen was also visited by L. N. Tolstoy, whose *Childhood, Boyhood,* and *Youth* were well known all over the reading world. Herzen was delighted with them. He particularly admired the boldness of Tolstoy in treating of delicate, deeply seated feelings, experienced perhaps by many, but expressed by none. As to his philosophic views, Herzen considered them weak, hazy, and often unconvincing."[1]

More is told by Herzen's daughter, Natalya Alexandrovna, who has a vague recollection of this meeting. She was then a little girl, but had already read Tolstoy's works, and was enthusiastic about them. Hearing from her father that Tolstoy was coming, she asked permission to be present at the interview. At the appointed day and hour she entered her father's study and sat in a chair at the farthest corner, so as not to be noticed. Soon after the man-servant announced the arrival of Count Tolstoy. With a sinking heart she waited for his appearance, but great was her disappointment when she beheld a man dressed in the latest fashion, of society manners, and who began to talk enthusiastically about cock-fights and prize-fights, of which he had

[1] *The Olden Times,* 1894.

seen a good deal in London. Not one word from the heart, not one word which came up to her expectations did she hear during the only meeting at which she was present.

However, we may surmise that the intercourse of the two great Russian writers was not limited to the subject of sport, considering that at their farewell meeting Herzen gave Tolstoy a letter of introduction to Proudhon.

While in England, Tolstoy, as always, visited schools; he went, too, to the House of Commons, where he listened to a speech of three hours' duration from Palmerston.

In England he learned of his being appointed a Peace Mediator,[1] and on February 19, 1861, the day of the abolition of serfdom, he started for home *via* Brussels, where he visited Proudhon. This energetic, independent thinker, himself made from the ranks of the people, made a powerful impression on Tolstoy, and probably influenced his views. One day during a conversation Tolstoy said that Proudhon gave him the impression of a strong man who has *le courage de son opinion*. The well-known aphorism of Proudhon, *La propriété c'est le vol*, might well have been used as an epigram in any of Tolstoy's essays of economics.

While in Brussels, Tolstoy also visited the Polish historian and politician Lelewel, who lived there in old age and great poverty. In the same city Tolstoy wrote the story *Polikushka*. On April 13th Tolstoy left Brussels and went to Russia *via* Germany.

In Germany the first town which he visited was Weimar. There he was a guest of von Maltitz, the Russian ambassador, who introduced him to the Knight-Marshal Bolisy-Morconet, and the latter in his turn presented him to the Grand Duke, Charles Alexander. On April 16th Maltitz also furnished him with the means of visiting Goethe's dwelling-place, which was then closed to the public. But Tolstoy took more interest in Froebel's Kindergartens, which were conducted under the management of Minna Schelholm, who was a direct pupil of Froebel's; she gladly gave the Russian Count, who was so fond of knowledge, information about her teaching and showed him how children played and studied.

Dr. Von Bode recently inserted an interesting article,

---

[1] Mediators were appointed by the Imperial Government at the emancipation of the serfs, to arbitrate between the peasants and landowners.—*Trans.*

entitled "Tolstoy in Weimar," in a Weimar educational journal named *Der Saemann* (The Sower), in which, besides generally known facts, he relates a story by Julius Stoetrer, who knew Tolstoy personally, and who died only this year. Tolstoy visited his school at Weimar. Here is the story:

"On Good Friday, just as lessons began, at one o'clock, I was in the second class and was about to commence teaching, when a pupil of the seminary opened the door and said, peeping in, 'A gentleman wants to see you.'

"A gentleman followed without giving his name, and I took him for a German, as he spoke as good German as any of us. 'What lesson are you going to have this afternoon?' he asked. 'History first, then German,' I replied.

"'I am very glad to hear it! I have visited schools of Southern Germany, France, and England; and should like to get acquainted with those of North Germany too. How many grades are there in your school?'

"'Seven. This is the second. However, I do not know my pupils yet, as I am just commencing, so that I cannot gratify your curiosity.'

"'That makes no difference to me. The plan and the method of instruction are what I care about. Please tell me what plan you follow in teaching history?'

"I had worked out my own plan of teaching history and explained it to the schoolmaster, which was what I believed my guest to be.

"He produced his memorandum-book from his pocket and began hurriedly making notes. Suddenly he said:

"'It looks as if one thing had been left out in this rather elaborate plan. Native history.'

"'No, it is not omitted. The next grade is devoted to the history of the Fatherland.'

"I had to begin the lesson, so I started with telling about the four degrees of culture. The foreigner went on making notes. When the lesson was over he asked: 'What comes next?'

"'I really intended beginning to read German, but if you prefer something else it can be changed.'

"'I am glad of this. You see, I've pondered a good deal how to make thoughts flow fluently.'

"This expression of his I shall never forget. I tried to

gratify him, and asked the children to write a short composition. I named a subject, and the children had to write a letter on it in their copy-books. This seemed to interest the stranger very much; he walked between the benches, took up the pupils' copy-books by turns and tried to make out how they wrote and what about.

"Not to distract the children I kept my seat. When the work was coming to an end, the foreigner said: 'Can I take these compositions with me? They are of the utmost interest to me?'

"'Thats' a little too much,' thought I, but told him politely that it was impossible. 'The children,' I said, 'have purchased their copy-books, and the price of each is six groschen; Weimar is a poor town, and their parents will be angry if they have to get new copy-books.'

"'That can be overcome,' he said, and stepped outside.

"I felt uneasy, so I sent a pupil to ask Herr Monhaupt, the headmaster, and a friend of mine, to come to our class, as something unusual was taking place. Monhaupt came.

"'You have played a nice trick on me,' said I; 'you have sent a queer fellow to me who wants to deprive the scholars of their copy-books.' 'I never did such a thing,' said Monhaupt. 'But,' I replied, 'you are the director of the seminary, and he was brought to me by one of your pupils.'

"Monhaupt recollected then that during his absence an official of importance had called at his place and told his wife that the gentleman who was accompanying him should be assisted in every way and shown everything.

"In the meantime the stranger came back carrying a large package of writing paper in his hands, which he had bought in the nearest shop. When he came I had to introduce him to the director, and they exchanged credentials.

"'Monhaupt, the director,' said the one.

"'The Count Tolstoy, from Russia,' said the other.

"So this was a Count and not a schoolmaster—a Russian who spoke German quite fluently.

"We bade the children rewrite their compositions on the sheets of paper that had been bought. Tolstoy collected all the sheets, rolled them up, and gave them to his servant, who was waiting outside.

"From my place he went to the director of the professional school, Trebsti, whom he knew and who had been in Russia."

Dr. Bode finished his article with the following words, dedicated to the memory of his old teacher:

"One more word concerning Julius Stoetrer. On Easter Sunday, 1905, he died, at the age of nearly ninety-three. I considered him a remarkable man because he was acquainted with the two people whose books have taught me the very best I know. He knew Tolstoy and Goethe. It is a fact that Stoetrer had conversed with Goethe himself. In 1828 he was attending a gymnasium at Weimar, and lived with a school friend of his and Eckermann in the same house, within a few steps of Goethe's home. Both boys often saw the old man sitting by the window. But they wanted to get a closer look at him, so they asked Eckermann, who was good enough to give them an opportunity.

"One summer day in 1828 Eckermann admitted both boys to Goethe's garden by the back door. The poet was taking a stroll in the garden, dressed in a light, home-made coat; having noticed the scholars, he came up to them, asked what their names were and what they wanted; told them to be diligent in their studies, and walked on.

"There was nothing striking about this conversation, but though Stoetrer, being a splendid schoolmaster and an agreeable man, had been received with respect all his life, yet he had never encountered anything which gave him such lasting joy as this talk with his greatest contemporary."

While continuing his journey through Germany Tolstoy visited Gotha, saw the Froebel Kindergartens, and made acquaintance with prominent educationists. In Jena he made the acquaintance of the young mathematician, Keller, and persuaded him to go to Russia to help him in his educational work. He stopped for a short time at Dresden, where he again saw Auerbach. He makes the following short, fragmentary description of him in his diary:

"*Dresden, April 21st.*—Auerbach is a most delightful man. *Ein Licht mir eingefangen.* His stories: *A Juryman; On the First Impression of Nature; Versoehnung; Abend; The Pastor Klauser.*

"Christianity he called the spirit of mankind, higher than which there is nothing. He reads verse exquisitely. About music as *Pflichtloser Genuss.* A turning point, according to his opinion, toward depravity. The story from *Schatzkaestlein.* He is forty-nine years old. He is straightforward, young, believing, free from the spirit of negation."

From Dresden he wrote to his aunt Tatiana the following lines:

"I am well and burning with a desire to return to Russia. Being in Europe, and not knowing when I can return, you will understand that I wish to get as much good as possible from my stay abroad. And this time I think I have succeeded. I am bringing back so many impressions, so much information, that I shall have to work a long time before I can put them all in order in my head. I intend to remain at Dresden until the 10/22, and, for Easter, I intend at all events being at Yasnaya. From here—should navigation not be resumed by the 25th—I shall go by Warsaw to St. Petersburg, where I must get the necessary sanction for a periodical I intend editing at Yasnaya Polyana. I am bringing with me a German from the university who is a teacher and clerk—a very agreeable and well-educated man, but still quite young and inexperienced."

On April 22d he was in Berlin, and there met the son of the celebrated educationist Diesterweg, the head of the Teachers' Institute. He expected to find him a man of enlightenment and free from prejudice, with original views on the subject of education, but he proved, to use Tolstoy's expression, to be a cold, heartless prig, who thought it possible to develop and guide children's souls by means of rules and regulations.

During the hour they spent in discussing schools and educational matters the chief subject of their conversation was the difference in the conception of the words: education, instruction, and teaching.

"Diesterweg spoke with malicious sarcasm of people who made such subdivisions, as, according to him, all these ran together. And yet we spoke of *education, culture,* and *instruction,* and we clearly understood each other."

As we advance we shall see that Tolstoy was dissatisfied not only with the views of this educationist, but with all the methods he studied in the schools of Western Europe, and that he made use of the experience gained in France, England, and Germany for his teaching at Yasnaya Polyana only in the sense that he worked on still more independent lines than before.

Berlin was the last foreign town in which Tolstoy stayed. On April 23, 1861, after a nine months' absence, he recrossed the Russian frontier.

As one might expect, the heavy German *Wissenschaft* did not satisfy Tolstoy, though he applied his best gifts and all his soul to the study of it—theoretical as well as practical—enlarging and clearing up all, whatever was not evident, by means of conversations with its most prominent representatives and by watching the application of its methods in the schools.

The study of this department of learning strengthened Tolstoy's idea that it was necessary to begin anew from the beginning, *i. e.*, that he must, quite independently, start the work of educating the people on lines of his own, and he plunged into it heart and soul.

The German theories did not help Tolstoy, because they did not satisfy his demands, which were too high, and, with his uncompromising character, he could not lower them, and could not condescend to any hypocritical, half-hearted acceptance.

Notwithstanding the rare scrupulousness of German scholars, their methods were not based on truth.

At the foundation of their science, as indeed would be the case with any other European science, lies the desire, however rarely openly avowed, of acquiring a privileged position for themselves and consequent leisure, to be used, no doubt, in the interests of the people. But while they are in process of acquiring this leisure, the people have to bear deep and unmeasured suffering, and the result, genuine intercourse, becomes impossible. The people, exasperated, or at the best, suffering in silence, keep aloof from those benefactors who, without understanding them, offend them with their condescension, and the best these latter can do is to patch up by some palliatives the cruel physical and moral wounds they have caused to the people.

What new impulse Tolstoy gave to the science of education we shall try to explain in one of the following chapters.

CHAPTER XIII

TOLSTOY AND TURGENEF—EMANCIPATION OF THE SERFS—PEACE MEDIATOR

Emancipation of the peasants—Correspondence of Tolstoy with Turgenef and Fet—Visit to Fet by Turgenef and Tolstoy. *Quarrel at the breakfast table*: Conversation about Turgenef's daughter and her governess—The altercation—The parting of the visitors—Tolstoy's letter to Turgenef demanding satisfaction—Turgenef's reply—Tolstoy's letter with the challenge—Turgenef's answer—Tolstoy's letter to Fet—Tolstoy's breaking off relations with Fet—Reconciliatory letter of Tolstoy to Turgenef—Absurd rumors about Tolstoy—Turgenef's letter to him containing a challenge—Tolstoy's answer—Turgenef's letter to Fet—Distorted account of the event in Garshin's reminiscences. *Appointment of Tolstoy as a Peace Mediator*: Confidential correspondence between the marshal of nobility, the minister and governor of the province—Confirmation of Tolstoy's appointment—Case of Mme. Artyukhof—Case of Mikhailovsky—Affair of Mme. Zaslonin—Affair of Ossipovich—Conflict with the Assembly of Justices—Attitude of other landowners toward Tolstoy—Tolstoy's dissatisfaction with his work—Petition for leave to resign—The discharge—The bailiff's account of Tolstoy's attitude to his duties—Recollections of Prince D. Obolensky about the elections of 1861—Dinner and toasts—Tolstoy's carelessness in connection with the formalities of office work.

AFTER his return from abroad Tolstoy passed through St. Petersburg. In the beginning of May he was in Moscow, and soon afterward in Yasnaya Polyana.

Russia was then celebrating the coming of a new era, the liberation of the peasantry from serfdom.

All those who were honest, educated, and of progressive opinions turned their energy in the direction of social reform. One of the first among them was Lyof Tolstoy.

With the beginning of social work his life became so many-sided, that one must turn away from the strict chronology of the story and give a parallel description of his principal kinds of contemporary activity. Every direction that his labors took was connected with facts of his personal and family life.

At the beginning of the sixties the social activity of Tolstoy manifested itself chiefly in two spheres: in the administrative as a peace mediator, and in the educational as a teacher, organizer of peasant schools, and educational writer.

We intend to give a description of both branches of activity, but before that it is necessary to narrate some facts of Tolstoy's personal life.

On his return home he hastened to call on his good neighbors, Fet and Turgenef. A correspondence ensued between them. Turgenef wrote to Fet from Spasskoye:

"*Fetti carissime!* I send you a note from Tolstoy, to whom I wrote to-day asking him to come at the beginning of next week without fail, so that we might together invade you in your Stepanovka while the nightingales are still singing and the spring smiles 'bright, beatific—impartial.' Expect me at the end of next week in any case, and till then be quite well, don't worry, remembering the words of Goethe: '*Ohne Hast, ohne Rast,*' and throw, if only a one-eyed glance, at your orphan muse."

The letter contained the following note from Tolstoy:

"I embrace you from all my heart, dear friend, for your letter and your friendship, and for your being Fet. Turgenef I would like to see, but you ten times more. It is so long since we have seen each other, and so much has happened to both of us since. I am very glad about your farming operations when I hear and think of them, and I am a little proud that I have, in at least a small measure, contributed toward them. We both of us are in a position to understand the advantage. A friend is a good thing to have; yet he may die, may for one reason or other go away, or one many be unable to keep up with him. But nature is still better . . . she is cold and difficult to deal with, and important and exacting, but then she is such a friend! One cannot lose her until death, and when one dies one is absorbed in her. I now, however, associate less with this friend, I have other interests which engage me; and yet, without the consciousness that this friend is here at hand, and that were one to stumble one could catch hold of her —life would be a sad thing. . . ."

"In spite of these kind promises," writes Fet in his Reminiscences, "a carriage appearing at the coppice and turning from the crossing to our porch was a surprise to us, and we were delighted to embrace Turgenef and Tolstoy. The few buildings on our estate at the time made Turgenef exclaim in wonder, spreading out his large hands: 'We look and look, where is Stepanovka, but in reality we see a greasy pancake and on it a lump, and this is Stepanovka.'

"When the visitors had rested a little from their journey, and the hostess had made use of the two hours before dinner to give it a more substantial and cheering appearance, we plunged into a most lively conversation, such as can be held only among men not wearied by life."[1]

During this visit an unfortunate event occurred—the quarrel between Turgenef and Tolstoy. It is very fully described by Fet, from whom we borrow the greater part of the description, adding a few corrections and filling some gaps, in accordance with new materials at our disposal.

"In the morning at the usual time," says Fet, *i. e.*, about eight o'clock, our visitors came down to the dining-room, in which my wife was sitting at the samovar at one end of the table and I at the other, waiting for my coffee, Turgenef at the right and Tolstoy at the left of the hostess.

"Being aware of the importance which Turgenef attached to his daughter's education, my wife inquired whether he was pleased with his English governess.

"Turgenef showered praises on the governess, and among other things related that the governess, with truly English practicality, asked Turgenef to fix a sum of money which his daughter could use for charitable purposes. 'Now,' said Turgenef, 'the governess requests my daughter to take the old clothes of the poor and, after mending them herself, to return them to the owners.'

"'And do you consider this right?' asked Tolstoy.

"'Of course I do; it brings the charitable person nearer to real want.'

"'And I think that a richly dressed girl who manipulates dirty, ill-smelling rags is acting a false and theatrical farce.'

"'I beg you not to say this,' exclaimed Turgenef, his nostrils dilating.

"'Why should not I say what I am convinced of?' answered Tolstoy.

[1] A. Fet, *My Reminiscences*, Part I, p. 368.

"Turgenef said: 'Then you think that I do not bring up my daughter properly?'

"Tolstoy's answer to this was that he thought what he said, and without venturing upon personalities, expressed his thoughts."[1]

Fet had no time to cry out to Turgenef to desist when, pale with wrath, the latter said: "If you persist in speaking in this way, I will box your ears." With these words he left the table, and, catching hold of his head in great excitement, stepped into the next room. He came back a second after and said, turning to Fet's wife: "For God's sake forgive my hasty action, which I deeply repent."

He then left the room again. After this the visitors took their leave.

At the first halting-place from Novosyolky, the property of P. N. Borisof, Tolstoy sent a letter to Turgenef with a demand for satisfaction. Then he went on further to Boguslav, the halting-place half-way between Fet's estate and his own estate, Nicolskoye. He sent for pistols and bullets to Nicolskoye and, without waiting for an answer to his first letter, sent a second one with a challenge.

In this letter to Turgenef he said that he did not care to fight in a vulgar manner, that is to say, when two authors come with a third one, with pistols, and the duel ends in champagne-drinking—he wanted to fight in real earnest, and asked Turgenef to come to the frontier with pistols.

Tolstoy spent a sleepless night waiting for an answer.

At last came a letter—Turgenef's answer to the first letter. Turgenef wrote:

"L. N. TOLSTOY. DEAR SIR—In answer to yours I can only repeat what I considered it my duty to declare at Fet's house. Being carried away by a feeling of animosity which I could not help, and the causes of which it is useless to enter into, I offended you without any positive provocation on your part, and I asked pardon for it. What happened this morning shows clearly that all attempts at *rapprochement* between such different natures as mine and yours will lead to no good, and I do my duty to you the more willingly as this letter will probably be the last sign of any relations between us. With all my heart I trust it will satisfy you,

[1] *Memoirs of Countess S. A. Tolstoy.*

and I give my consent beforehand to any use you may care to make of it.

"With my respects, I have the honor to remain your faithful servant,   Iv. TURGENEF.

"SPASSKOYE, *May* 27, 1861."

A postscript followed the same day.

"10 o'clock, P.M.

"Ivan Petrovich has just brought me back my letter, which my servant sent by mistake to Novosyolky instead of forwarding it to Boguslav. I earnestly beg you to forgive this unexpected and disagreeable misadventure. I hope my messenger will still find you in Boguslav."

Tolstoy wrote to Fet probably on the same day:

"I could not refrain from opening yet another letter from Turgenef in answer to mine. I wish you all that is good in your relations with this man, but I despise him. I have written to him, and now have nothing more to do with him, except so far as, should he desire it, to give him satisfaction. Notwithstanding all my apparent indifference, I did not feel at my ease, and I felt that I ought to demand from Turgenef a more positive apology, which I did in my letter from Novosyolky. Here is his answer, which I accepted as satisfactory, merely answering that the grounds upon which I excuse him are not opposite features in our characters, but—such as he can himself understand.

"Besides this, owing to his delay, I have sent another letter in rather harsher terms and with a challenge: to this I have received no answer, but, if I do receive one, I will send it to you unopened. So this is the end of an unfortunate business; if it gets beyond the threshold of your house, please let it pass with this accompaniment."

Meanwhile Turgenef thus answered his challenge:

"Your servant says that you desire to receive an answer to your letter, but I don't see what I can add to what I have said already. Maybe, when I acknowledge your right to demand satisfaction by arms, you will prefer to be satisfied with my expressed and repeated apology. As to that, it is for you to choose. I can say without affectation that I would willingly face your fire in order to wipe out the effect of my really insane words. The fact of my saying what I did is so foreign to the habits of all my life that I can ascribe it to nothing but the irritation caused by the extreme and constant antagonism of our views. This is not an apology, I mean, not a justification, but an explanation. Such incidents being ineffaceable and irreparable, I consider it my duty, in parting from you forever, to repeat once more that in this affair you were right and I was wrong. Let me add, that it is no question of my willingness or unwillingness to show myself a brave man simply, but whether I acknowledge your right to challenge me to a duel—according to usual formalities, of course, *i. e.*, with seconds—as well as to forgive me. You have chosen what you prefer, and to me remains to abide by your decision.

"Again allow me to assure you of my respect.
"Iv. Turgenef."

In his desire to reconcile his friends, Fet very likely attempted something of the kind, judging by the following extract from his memoirs:

"L. Tolstoy has sent me the following note:

"'Turgenef . . . which I beg you to transmit to him as accurately as you transmit to me his nice utterances, notwithstanding my repeated requests not to speak of him.
"'Count L. Tolstoy.

"'And I beg you yourself not to write to me any more, as I will not open your letters, any more than those of Turgenef.'

"I need not say," remarks Fet, "that I did my best to bring the affair, which unfortunately occurred in my house, to a clear issue. For this purpose I went to Spasskoye.

"I remember the indescribably sarcastic mood of the immortal Turgenef. 'What an unheard-of idea,' he exclaimed, ' to demand that all shall be of our opinion, and, if that cannot be, to demand a formal apology and conclude the matter with pistols.' So said the uncle to me, but what he said to Ivan Sergeyich I don't know. As to my efforts to patch up the affair, they ended, as one sees, in a formal rupture with

Tolstoy, and at the present moment I cannot remember how our friendly relations were renewed."[1]

Some time elapsed, says the Countess S. A. Tolstoy, and, while in Moscow, Tolstoy was one day in one of those charming moods which sometimes came over him, full of humility and love, and wishing and striving for the good and great. While in this mood he could not bear to have an enemy. Therefore he wrote a letter to Turgenef on September 25th, in which he expressed his regret that their relations were hostile. "If I offended you," he wrote, "forgive me; I am very unhappy to know I have an enemy."

This letter was sent to the bookseller Davidof, who had business transactions with Turgenef. For some reason it was not delivered to Turgenef in time, and meanwhile he was alarmed by certain silly rumors, which he thus related to Fet in his letter of November 8th from Paris:

"'By the by,' one more tale, 'the last one,' concerning the unfortunate affair with Tolstoy. On my way through St. Petersburg I heard from 'reliable people' (Oh, those reliable people!) that copies of the last letter of Tolstoy to me, the one in which he 'despises' me, are circulating all over Moscow, and that these copies are spread about by Tolstoy himself. This made me very angry, and I have sent him a challenge from here for the time of my return to Russia. Tolstoy replied that the circulation of copies is a sheer fiction, and at the same time enclosed a letter in which he *asked forgiveness and renounced his challenge.* Of course this must put an end to the affair, and I only ask you to inform him (for he writes that my address to him on my part he would consider an offence) that I renounce my challenge and so on, and I hope that all this is buried forever. His letter (the apologetic one) I destroyed, but the other one, which, according to him, had been sent through the bookseller Davidof, I have not received at all. And now to all this affair *de profundis.*"[2]

Of this letter to Tolstoy, mentioned in the letter to Fet, we find the following note in Tolstoy's diary:

"*October.*—Yesterday I received a letter from Turgenef in which he accuses me of telling people that he is a coward, and says that I distribute copies of my letter. I wrote to him

[1] A. Fet. *My Reminiscences*, vol. i, p. 368.
[2] *Ibid.*, p. 381.

that this was nonsense, and also sent him a letter saying, 'You call my action dishonorable, and desire to give me a regular slap in the face, but I regard myself as to blame, beg your pardon, and retract my challenge.'"

"This letter was written," adds Countess Tolstoy in her memoirs, "under the impulse of the idea that, if Turgenef is devoid of the sense of personal honor, and needs honor before the public, he may use this letter; but that he (Tolstoy) is above it, and despises public opinion. Turgenef was weak enough to agree to it, and replied that he considered himself satisfied."

In another letter to Fet of January 7, 1862, Turgenef writes about the same:

"And now, to ask a plain question: have you seen Tolstoy? Only to-day have I got the letter he sent me in September through the bookstores of Davidof (the punctuality of Russian tradesmen is remarkable indeed!). In this letter he speaks of his intention to offend me, apologizes, etc. But almost at the same time, in consequence of different gossip, of which, I believe, I informed you, I had sent him my challenge, etc. All this drives one to the conclusion that our constellations move discordantly in the ether, and it would be best for us, as he proposes, not to meet. But you may write, or tell him (when you see him) that, without phrases and witticisms, I like him very much at a distance, I respect him and watch his career with sympathy, but when we come together everything takes a different aspect. It cannot be helped! We must go on living as if we existed on different planets or in different ages." [1]

Probably Fet said something to Tolstoy in the way of a message from Turgenef, and again caused irritation against himself, of which he informed Turgenef, for the latter wrote to him, among other things, the following:

"PARIS, *January* 14, 1862.

"DEAREST AFANASI AFANASYEVICH—In the first place I feel it necessary to apologize to you for the utterly unexpected tile (*tuile*, as the French have it) which fell on your head because of my letter. It is a slight consolation to me that I could not foresee such a sally from Tolstoy, but in-

[1] A. Fet, *My Reminiscences*, p. 384.

tended it all for the best. It proves, however, that it is a wound not to be touched at all. Once more please forgive my involuntary sin." [1]

With this we may wind up the narrative of a deplorable incident, which like a clap of thunder discharged the tension of the atmosphere between the two great men, and perhaps helped afterward to bring them together on a more sincere and sounder basis.

We must add that the description of this matter in Garshin's " Reminiscences of Turgenef," printed in the *Historical Review* for November, 1883, is full of misstatements as to place and time, and was probably not gathered from firsthand sources.

In 1861 and 1862 Tolstoy occupied the post of a Peace Mediator of the fourth section of the Krapivensky District. His employment in this capacity is hardly known in literature—fortunately its memory is still green among some contemporaries, who were at that time intimate with him. Their remarks are undoubtedly of great interest.

The reputation which Tolstoy won as a manager of his own estate on new principles, *i. e.*, those of one who does not oppress and sweat his peasants, had almost proved an obstacle to his getting the above-mentioned appointment. Correspondence passed and information was given in a sense unfavorable to him in reference to the post. We give here the more important extracts from the material in our possession concerning this affair. The Marshal of Nobility of the province, V. P. Minin, wrote to the Minister of the Interior, Valuyef, complaining of the Governor of the Tula province Lunskoy for having appointed Tolstoy Peace Mediator. These are his words:

" Being aware of a hostile attitude to him on the part of the Krapivensky Nobility, due to his management of his own estate, the Marshal is afraid lest, with the Count's appointment to the post, some unpleasant conflicts may take place, which may hinder the peaceful settlement of such an important matter."

Then the Marshal pointed out the transgression by the Governor of certain formalities as regards the appointment, hoping that these might serve to annul it.

The Minister of the Interior replied to the Marshal of

---

[1] A. Fet, *My Reminiscences*, p. 284.

the Nobility that there must be some misunderstanding, and that he would write about it to the Governor.

In reply to the Minister's inquiry the Governor sent the following interesting confidential report, which shows that at that time the high official spheres marched in advance of Russian society, which had not yet awakened to the situation:

(*Confidential.*)

"To this I have the honor to add, that what gave rise to the present correspondence may be the appointment of Count L. Tolstoy as a Peace Mediator of the Krapivensky district, contrary to the opinion of the Marshals of Nobility, both of the province and the district, who object to his election on the alleged ground that he is disliked by the local nobility.

"Being acquainted with Count Tolstoy, and knowing him for a well-educated man, and one in great sympathy with the present reform, and taking also into consideration the expressed desire of some landowners of the Krapivensky district to have him as their Peace Mediator, I cannot replace him by another person quite unknown to me. The more so as Count Tolstoy was pointed out to me by your Excellency's predecessor,[1] among other persons, as one enjoying the best reputation.

"Lieutenant-General Darogan."

After this followed the confirmation of the appointment as Peace Mediator by the Senate.

Interesting papers have lately appeared relating to Tolstoy's activity as Peace Mediator.

These materials throw a new light on his personal character, as in all the suits of which records are produced he appears as a true champion of the peasants against the harsh tyranny of the landowners and police-officers, and one may easily believe that the fears of the Marshal of the Nobility were not without foundation.

Out of the fifteen suits, quoted in those papers, we will choose the most characteristic.

In one case, the landowner, one Mme. Artyukhof, com-

[1] Lanskoy.

plained of her late house servant, Mark Grigoryef, that he had left her, considering himself a " free man."

On this Tolstoy wrote:

" Mark can go away immediately with his wife wherever he likes, in virtue of my orders. I beg you (1) to compensate him for the three months and a half he has worked for you illegally since the announcement of the Act, and (2) to compensate his wife for the assault upon her, which was still more illegal. If you are dissatisfied with my resolution, you have a right to lodge a complaint with the Assembly of the Justices of the Peace, and with the Council of the Province. I can give you no further explanations. With my best respects, I remain, yours faithfully,

"Count L. Tolstoy."

Mme. Artyukhof lodged a complaint before the Assembly of Peace Mediators. As the Assembly consisted of Peace Mediators who disapproved of Tolstoy's proceedings, they set aside his decision in this case, as in many others, and forwarded the case to the Provincial Court. Fortunately his course was there viewed with sympathy, and his decision in this case, as in many others, was confirmed.

So Mark Grigoryef was set free, and his wife was compensated for the assault committed by Mme. Artyukhof.

An interesting affair is the case of the damage done by peasants to a field belonging to one Mikhailovsky.

The peasants tilled the landowner's field, and during their rest allowed the horses to graze in the meadow of a neighboring landowner. The latter complained to Tolstoy. Tolstoy first asked the landowner to forgive the peasants this trespass, hoping probably thus to improve the relations between the landowner and the peasants, who had cause to complain of him. The landowner refused to overlook the damage done, and requested an assessment of it to be made and the fine to be paid to him, claiming that it should be eighty roubles.

A long correspondence arose out of this case. The landowner Mikhailovsky, in complaining to the Assembly of Peace Mediators, described Tolstoy's action in this way:

" Hereupon Count Tolstoy arrived at the village Panino,

invited three peasants of the nearest village, Borodino, as referees, and they went together to the damaged meadow. The referees to whom he proposed to assess the damages due for the meadow declared that about three *dessyatins*[1] of the meadow had been damaged, and the fine they considered right would be ten roubles per dessyatin. To this Count Tolstoy did not agree, and proposed to them to make it only five roubles. The referees did not contradict Count Tolstoy; and so the case of the Panino peasants damaging the landowner's meadows was settled by Tolstoy in this way, that the peasants had to pay the landowner Mikhailovsky for the three dessyatins five roubles each."

Considering this and other proceedings of Count Tolstoy to be illegal, Mikhailovsky said: "I am firmly convinced that a just Government, in its solicitude for the improvement of the status of the peasants, would not allow that such improvement and enrichment of the peasants should be carried out in the manner put in practice by the Peace Mediator, Count Tolstoy."

The District Assembly of the Justices, in view of Mikhailovsky's petition, requested an explanation from Tolstoy, but in a paper under No. 323, of September 16, 1861, he replied that " he did not think it necessary to give any information as regards the petition of Mikhailovsky, in virtue of paragraphs 29, 31, and 32 of the regulation Act in connection with the courts of peasants' affairs. The resolution passed in this case by the District Assembly, and presented to the Provincial Assembly, was dismissed by the latter without any written report, with the following remark: " To be added to the case."

Another case, slight as it is, shows us clearly how far Tolstoy was from having selfish aims in all these proceedings, and how ready he was to acknowledge a mistake of his own, being guided in his actions only by a sincere wish for justice.

A certain Mme. Zaslonin, a landowner, complained of Tolstoy to the Assembly for having issued a leave-of-absence passport to her house serf. Tolstoy was present at the examination into the affair, and owned that he committed a blunder, and offered to compensate the lady for the loss she had suffered.

---

[1] A dessyatin is about three acres.

However, these affairs did not all end in such a satisfactory manner for Tolstoy, as, in making himself the champion of the people's right, he had to face a whole party of serf-owners, who firmly stuck to their old customs and privileges. Thus the landowner Ossipovich and his former serfs had a dispute as follows: Part of the village had been burned, and the landowner would not allow the peasants to build on the same spot, but requested them to move their homesteads, refusing at the same time to give them proper allowance for new buildings, and to free them from obligatory work, and give them the time necessary for restoring their ruined homes.

Tolstoy could see that on the one hand the demands of the peasants were reasonable, but on the other he knew the pitiful situation of the ruined small landowner, and did not think him able to satisfy the demands of the peasants. He appealed therefore to the nobles of the district to help their colleague to extricate his needy peasants out of the difficulty, or simply to help the peasants directly. Both his proposals were dismissed, and the peasants were urged to comply with all the demands of their landowner.

The suit dragged on for some time, going from one court of justice to another. Tolstoy saw that the case would be decided against the peasants, and that his opinion would be disregarded. He then protested again, and when, during the hearing of the case before the Assembly, he saw that the members of the tribunal intentionally misrepresented the affair, he left the Assembly without signing the resolutions relating to cases which had been heard in his presence, being determined to exhaust all means to procure a decision in the peasants' favor. The Assembly lodged a complaint against him with the Provincial Assembly, but this complaint met with no attention.

Again we see how Kostomarof got possession of the peasants holdings by declaring them to be his house servants; that is to say, to belong to a section of the peasants whom the new law did not provide with land. Tolstoy took their part, and after many trials he succeeded in securing their holdings for them.

The poorer landowners resorted to all sorts of subterfuges in order to give to the peasants the smaller allotments of land, and that of the worst quality. As soon as Tolstoy noticed this tendency, he refused to confirm the charters regulating the mutual relations of landowners and peasants, and tried his best to annul them.

We need hardly say that Tolstoy's sympathy for the peasants was exceedingly distasteful to the landowners. They proclaimed that Tolstoy had thrown a seed of discord between the landowners and the peasantry, and had finally destroyed the patriarchal relations between them; that he was provoking rebellion among the peasants, who were encouraged by him to commit many unlawful acts; that even the officials of the peasants' administrations, in order to ingratiate themselves with Tolstoy, did not perform the duties imposed upon them by the law, so that the result was perfect anarchy in the villages, and innumerable irregularities such as stealing, lawlessness, and so forth.

Of course, Tolstoy's proceedings as Peace Mediator made the peasants put implicit confidence in him, and this annoyed the landowners still more, so that he was faced with growing difficulties in his task, and had soon to cease his efforts in the hard struggle.

He felt, in fact, very much dissatisfied. As early as July, 1861, he wrote in his diary:

"The post of arbitrator has given me little material for observation, and has definitely spoiled my relations with the landowners, besides upsetting my health."

On February 12, 1862, Tolstoy wrote to the Provincial Court of Justice on peasants' affairs:

"As the appeals against my decisions which have been made to the Provincial Court have no valid ground, and yet these cases and many others have been and are still being decided against my opinion, so that almost every judgment pronounced in the district under my charge is set aside, and even the Starshinas[1] are removed by the Court of Arbitrators, under such circumstances, giving rise to a want of confidence in the arbitrator on the part of both peasants and landowners, it becomes not only useless but impossible for the arbitrator to continue to act. I respectfully request the Provincial Court to have the above-mentioned appeals investigated by one of its members, and at the same time I find myself obliged to inform the Provincial Court that until such investigation takes place I do

[1] Elected peasant officials over groups of villages.

not think it convenient to carry on my duties, and have therefore transferred them to a deputy."

It was on March 9th that Tolstoy had accepted the office of Peace Mediator, but he only performed his duties up to April 30th, when, under the pretext of illness, he handed them over to the eldest candidate for that post in the 4th Division. The Senate at last informed the Governor of Tula on May 26th, in a document No. 24,124, that a resolution had been passed to discharge the artillery lieutenant, Count Lyof Tolstoy, on the ground of ill health from the duties of Peace Mediator of the Krapivensky District, and that this had been confirmed by the Imperial Senate.[1]

The following story, taken from the biography of Loewenfeld, shows how groundless were the assertions of the landowners as to Tolstoy's favoritism toward the peasants. One can see from it that Tolstoy had defended the demands of the landowners with equal fairness when he considered them just.

"A witness of Tolstoy's proceedings as a Peace Mediator, a German from the Baltic Provinces and bailiff of a landowner in the Tula Province, had occasion to call upon him on a matter of business at Yasnan Polyana on his patron's behalf. What gave occasion to the visit was a disagreement on certain points relating to peasant allotments. This could only be settled on the spot, and the Peace Mediator therefore went in April to the estate of his neighbor, accompanied by a peasant boy of twelve years of age—his little land surveyor, as the Count jokingly called him, because he always carried with him the measuring-chain. Tolstoy received a peasant deputation, consisting of two elders and one member of the village council, who came to see him to talk over the matter.

"'Well, friends, what do you want?' said Tolstoy.

"The delegates stated the request of the village. Instead of the pasture ground appointed to them, they wanted another piece of land so as to increase their allotment.

"'I am very sorry, but I cannot do as you wish,' said the Count. 'If I did so, I should cause a great loss to your landlord,' and he proceeded to explain quietly the position of the matter.

[1] D. T. Oospensky, "Archive Materials for the Biography of Count L. N. Tolstoy." *Russian Thought*, 1903, vol. ix.

"'Well, arrange it somehow, little father,' said one of the delegates.

"'No, I can do nothing,' repeated the Count.

"The peasants exchanged glances, scratched their heads, and persisted, saying: 'Do it, somehow, little father.'

"'If you only would, little father,' continued the spokesman, 'you are sure to be able to manage it.'

"The other two delegates nodded their heads approvingly.

"The Count crossed himself and said: 'In the name of holy God, I swear that I cannot help you.'

"But when even after this the peasants still repeated, 'Do it somehow, little father, be so kind,' the Count turned in vexation to the bailiff and said: 'One may be an Amphion and move mountains and forests sooner than convince these peasants.'

"During the whole interview, which lasted about an hour, says our authority, the Count was the personification of patience and friendliness. The obstinacy of the peasants did not draw a harsh word from him."[1]

The memoirs of a friend and relative of Tolstoy, Prince Dmitry Dmitrievich Obolensky, refer to the same period:

"In 1861 new elections took place in Tula, and there was to be a dinner in honor of those Peace Mediators who took part in the elections. In the very same reception hall where Volotsky and Prince Cherkassky had quarrelled and were on the point of fighting a duel about something connected with the peasant question, Volotsky first expressed his sympathy with Cherkassky as his colleague, also a Peace Mediator. . . . This dinner was memorable to me. My uncle, T. A. Rayevsky, as the oldest man present, was chairman. Some of the landowners subscribed to the dinner, and, of course, I was one of the company. I had to sit next to Count L. N. Tolstoy, a Peace Mediator at the time, whom I then knew very well.

"The first toast was naturally the Czar-Liberator, and it was received with great enthusiasm.

"'I drink to it with particular pleasure,' said Count Tolstoy to me. 'No other toasts are needed, for in truth it is to the Emperor only that we owe the emancipation.'

"However, other toasts followed. Especially success-

[1] G. Loewenfeld, *Count Tolstoy, his Life and Works*, p. 228.

ful was the toast, proposed by P. F. Samarin, to the Russian people—a very awkward subject at the time. But Peter Feodorovich had cleverly pointed out in his speech that almost everywhere in the Tula Province the relations with the peasants were on a very good footing, because, the landowners having used their power moderately, the relations in question always had been good, and at present were still better than before. And this was true: the reform went off peacefully in our province, as compared with others.

"In the year of the abolition of serfdom," continued Obolensky, "Count Tolstoy started his school in Yasnaya Polyana, in which I took great interest. I was in the habit of visiting the Count pretty often, and sometimes in the winter would go out hunting with him, stopping for rest in places a long way off. I have had delightful times with him. Who would recognize in the present venerable philosopher the reckless sportsman who used to leap ditches and ravines with great agility, and to spend days at a distance? It is difficult to imagine a better companion. But I believe the Count was a poor Peace Mediator, because of his absence of mind. I very well remember the first charter of regulations coming from him. It had been subscribed in this way:

"At the request of So-and-so, because of their illiteracy, the house-serf So-and-so signed the charter of regulations. No name was added. Just as the Count dictated: 'Write, I have signed for So-and-so,' the house-serf had written word by word, not mentioning the name either of the peasant or his owner. And the Count, without reading what the house-serf had written, sent off the charter, duly sealed, to the Provincial Court. My stepfather, who was then a member of the Court, and at whose house I lived, received this charter. He only shrugged his shoulders over such a document."[1]

Tolstoy proved incapable in chancellor's office work, but his heart and brain worked well as Peace Mediator, and he has left kind memories of his activity in this direction. But he had greater success, though he met with no fewer obstacles, in the matter of education, of which we treat in the following chapters.

[1] Prince Obolensky, *Reminiscences*. The Russian Archive, 1894.

CHAPTER XIV

EDUCATIONAL ACTIVITY OF TOLSTOY—FOUNDATION OF THE SCHOOL—THEORIES

First attempt at founding a school in 1849: Return to school work in 1859-60—Tolstoy's preparation for the work—Search for answer to the questions what to teach and how to teach—Indifference of educationists—Number of schools opened—Conditions of their opening—List of teachers—Attitude of the children toward the rules of the school. *Theories*: About instruction of the people—The people's resistance—To use compulsion or to change the system?—Possible reasons for using compulsion—Reasons: religious, philosophic, experimental, and historic—The instability of all of them—Appeal to Russian educationists—Criterion of education—Freedom—Method of instruction, experiment. *Aims of the review "Yasnaya Polyana"*: Appeal to the public—Contents of the review—Its epigraph. *On methods of teaching to read and write*: Reading not the first step of education—Reading and writing, a craft—General method—Striving after improvement. *Education and instruction*: Definitions: education is compulsory, instruction free—Causes of compulsion: family, religion, state, society—Admissibility of the first three causes—Weakness of the fourth—Causes of the error, the people's silence—Means of educational compulsion, the schools—True meaning of a university—Criticism of existing universities—What is to be done?—Pessimistic assertion. *Attitude of critics*: Refutation by Markof and Tolstoy's reply. *Progress, and definition of the word instruction*: There is no progress. *Criticism of official project*: Its unsuitability to the needs of the Russian people—Restraint of natural developments of instruction—Conclusion adverse to the conclusion of Markof.

TOLSTOY had several times started on educational work.

As far back as 1849, when he returned to Yasnaya Polyana from St. Petersburg, along with other institutions and reforms by means of which he tried to approach the people, he established a school for peasant children. From his *A Russian Proprietor* we know how unsuccessful these first attempts were. With his departure for the Caucasus the school was closed. He reopened it on his return to Yasnaya Polyana after his resignation and his first journey abroad, as was mentioned in the proper place.

On recommencing his school work, Tolstoy soon realized his lack of theoretical knowledge, and hastened to fill the void in his education by reading, foreign travel, personal relations with prominent educationists, and practical work in different schools. Feeling himself thus restored, he for the third time and with better zeal turned to his school, and carried it up to a remarkably high level.

In one of his educational articles he thus relates his endeavors and preparations to found a school:

"Fifteen years ago, when I took up the matter of popular education without any preconceived theories or views on the subject, with the one desire to advance the matter in a direct and straightforward manner, I, as a teacher in my school, was at once confronted with two questions: (1) What must I teach? and (2) How must I teach it? . . .

"In the whole mass of people who are interested in education, there exists, as there has existed before, the greatest diversity of opinions. Formerly, just as now, some in reply to the question of what ought to be taught, said that, outside the rudiments, the most useful information to give in a primary school is taken from the natural sciences; others, even as now, that this was not necessary, and was even injurious; while some, as now, proposed history, or geography, and others denied their necessity; some proposed the Ecclesiastic-Slavonic language and grammar, to be taken in connection with religion; others found that, too, superfluous, and ascribed a prime importance to 'development.' On the question of how to teach, there has always been a still greater diversity of answers. The most diversified methods of instructing in reading and arithmetic have been proposed. . . .

"When I encountered these questions and found no answer for them in Russian literature, I turned to the literature of Europe. After having read what had been written on the subject, and having made the personal acquaintance of the so-called best representatives of the science of education in Europe, I not only failed to find anywhere an answer to the question I was interested in, but I convinced myself that this question does not even exist in connection with any science of Education as such; as every educationist of every given school firmly believed that the methods he used were the best, because they were founded on absolute truth, and that it would be useless for him to look at them with a critical eye.

"However, because, as I said, I took up the matter of popular education without any preconceived notions, or else because I took up the matter without getting hold of laws from a distance as to how I ought to teach, but became a schoolmaster in a village popular school in the backwoods —I could not reject the idea that there must of necessity exist some criterion by means of which I could solve the question what to teach and how to teach it. Should I teach, by heart, the psalter or the classification of the organisms? Should I teach according to the sound-alphabet, taken from the Germans, or simply use the prayer-book? In the solution of this question I was aided by a certain tact in teaching, with which I am gifted, and especially by that close and passionate interest which I took in the subject.

"When I entered at once into the close and direct relations with those forty tiny peasants that formed my school (I call them tiny peasants because I found in them the same characteristics of perspicacity, the same immense store of information from practical life, of jocularity, simplicity, and loathing for everything false, which distinguishes the Russian peasant), when I saw their susceptibility, their readiness to acquire the information which they needed, I felt at once that the antiquated church method of instruction had outlived its usefulness, and was of no use to them. I began to experiment on other proposed methods of instruction; but, because compulsion in education, both by my conviction and my character, are repulsive to me, I did not exercise any pressure, and, the moment I noticed that something was not readily received, I did not put any compulsion on the pupils, but looked for something else. From these experiments it appeared to me, and to those teachers who gave instruction with me at Yasnaya Polyana and in other schools on the same principles of freedom, that nearly everything which in the educational world was written about schools was separated by an immeasurable abyss from the truth, and that many of the proposed methods, such as object-lessons, the teaching of natural sciences, the sound method, and others, called forth contempt and ridicule, and were not accepted by the pupils. We began to look for those contents and those methods which were readily taken up by the pupils, and hit upon that which forms my method of instruction.

"But this method stood in a line with all other methods, and the question why it was better than the rest remained unsolved as before. . . .

"At that time I found no sympathy in all the educational literature, indeed not even any contradiction, but simply complete indifference in regard to the question which I put. There were some favorable criticisms of certain trifling details, but the question itself evidently did not interest any one. I was young then, and this indifference grieved me. I did not understand that with my question, 'How do you know what to teach and how to teach?' I was like a man who, let us say, in a gathering of Turkish pashas, who were discussing the question in what manner they could collect the greatest amount of revenue from the people, should make them the following proposition: 'Gentlemen, before considering how much revenue to collect from each, we must first analyze the question on what your right to exact that revenue is based.' Obviously all the pashas would continue their discussion of the measures of extortion, and would reply only with silence to his irrelevant remark."

Tolstoy's letters from abroad show the interest which he took in the school while he was away. During the whole of the time the teaching in the school went on without ceasing. It continued with greater regularity after his return to Yasnaya Polyana in the spring of 1861, and in 1862, as Tolstoy says in his article on Education:

"Fourteen schools were opened in a district containing ten thousand souls when I was a rural judge, besides which there existed about ten schools in the district among the clericals and on the manors among the servants. In the three remaining districts of the county there were fifteen large and thirty small schools among the clericals and manorial servants. . . .

"Everybody will agree that, leaving aside the question of the quality of instruction, such a relation of the teacher to the parents and peasants is most just, natural, and desirable."

Incidentally we may mention the names of the teachers of the ten schools under Tolstoy's jurisdiction where his views on the education of the people were supported. In the Golovenkovsky school the teacher was one Alexander Serdobolsky, a pupil of the Kazan gymnasium; in the Trasnensky school, Ivan Aksentyef, a pupil of the Penza gymnasium; in Lomintsevok, Alexey Shumilin, a pupil of the Kaluga gymnasium; in the Bagucharof school, Boris Golovin, a pupil of the Tula theological seminary; in the Baburino school, Alfonse Erlenwein, a pupil of the Kishinef gymnasium; and in Yassenki, Mitrofan Butovich, a pupil of the Kishinef gymnasium; in the Kolpeno school, Anatoly Tomashevsky, who finished his studies in the Saratof gymnasium; in Gorodnya, Vladimir Tokaschevich, who finished his studies in the Penza gymnasium; in the Plekhanovo school, Nicolay Peterson, who finished his studies in the Penza gymnasium for the nobles; the Bogucharof village community chose Sergey Gudim, an ex-student of the Kazan University, in the place of its former teacher, Morozof.[1]

Perhaps some of these men may come across this biography, and its perusal may induce them to write down memories of their collaboration with the great teacher.

In one of his articles on education, Tolstoy himself sets forth in detail the organization of the school at Yasnaya Polyana:

"The school is held in a two-storied stone building. Two rooms are given up to the school, one is a cabinet of physical curiosities, and two are occupied by the teachers. Under the roof of the porch hangs a bell with a rope attached to the clapper; in the vestibule downstairs stand parallel and horizontal bars, while in the vestibule upstairs there is a joiner's bench. The staircase and the floor of the vestibule are covered with snow or mud; here also hangs the programme.

"The order of instruction is as follows: at about eight o'clock, the teacher living in the school, a lover of external order and the administrator of the school, sends one of the boys, who nearly always stay overnight with him, to ring the bell.

---

[1] D. T. Oospensky, "Archive Materials for Tolstoy's Biography." *Russian Thought*, 1903, vol. ix.

The house at Yasnaya Polyana used by Tolstoy as a school, 1860-62.

"In the village people rise with the fires. From the school the fires have long been observed in the windows, and, half an hour after the ringing of the bell, there appear in the mist, in the rain, or in the oblique rays of the autumnal sun, dark figures, by twos, by threes, or singly, on the mounds (the village is separated from the school by a ravine). The necessity of herding together has long disappeared for the pupils. A pupil no longer requires to wait and shout: 'O boys, let's go to school! She has begun.' He knows by this time that 'school' is neuter, and he knows a few other things, and strange to say, for that very reason, has no longer any need of a crowd. . . .

"The children have nothing with them—neither reading-books nor copy-books. No lessons are given to take home.

"Not only do they carry nothing in their hands, but they have nothing to carry even in their heads. They are not obliged to remember any lesson, or anything that they were doing the day before. They are not vexed by the thought of the impending lesson. They bring with them nothing but their impressionable natures and their convictions that to-day it will be as jolly in school as it was yesterday. They do not think of their classes until they have begun.

"No one is ever rebuked for being late, and they never are late, except in the case of some of the older ones, whose fathers now and then keep them back to do some work. In such cases they come running to school at full speed, and all out of breath.

"So long as the teacher has not yet arrived, they gather near the porch, pushing each other off the steps, or sliding on the frozen crust of the smooth road, while some go to the school-rooms. If it is cold, they read, write, or play, waiting for the teacher.

"The girls do not mix with the boys. When the boys have anything to do with the girls, they never address any one in particular, but always all collectively: 'O girls, why don't you skate?' or, 'I guess the girls are frozen,' or, 'Now, girls, all of you against me!' There is only one girl, from the manor, with very great general ability, about ten years of age, who is beginning to make herself conspicuous among the herd. This girl alone the boys treat as their equal and as a boy, except for a delicate shade of politeness, condescension, and reserve.

"Popular education has always and everywhere been to me an incomprehensible phenomenon. The people want education, and every separate individual unconsciously seeks education. The more highly cultured class of people —society, the officers of the Government—strive to transmit their knowledge and to educate the less educated masses. One would think that such a coincidence of necessities would lead to satisfaction being given to both the class which furnishes the education and the one that receives it. But the very opposite takes place. The masses continually counteract the efforts made for their education by society or by the Government, as the representatives of a more highly cultured class, so that these efforts are frequently frustrated."

As with every conflict, so also here, it was necessary to solve the question: Which is more lawful, the resistance or the action itself? Must the resistance be broken, or the action be changed?

The question has been somehow always settled in favor of violence. But some sound reasons ought to be produced for the use of such violence. What are they? To this question Tolstoy gives the following answer. The arguments may be religious, philosophical, experimental, and historical, and then he discusses each of these kinds of arguments separately:

"But in our time, when religious education forms but a small part of education, the question what good ground the school has for compelling the young generation to receive religious instruction in a certain fashion remains unanswered from the religious point of view."

"The philosophical arguments cannot afford a reason for coercion.

"All the philosophers, beginning with Plato and ending with Kant, tend to this one thing, the liberation of the school from the traditional fetters which weigh heavily upon it. They wish to discover what it is that man needs, and on these more or less correctly divined needs they build up their new school.

"Luther wants people to study Holy Writ in the original, and not according to the commentaries of the holy fathers. Bacon enjoins the study of Nature from Nature, and not from the books of Aristotle. Rousseau wants to teach life from life itself, as he understands it, and not from previous experiments. Every step forward taken by the philosophy of history consists only in freeing the school from the idea of instructing the younger generation in that which the elder generations considered to be science, in favor of the idea of instructing them in what they themselves need. This one common and, at the same time, self-contradictory idea is felt in the whole history of educational theories: it is common, because all demand a greater measure of freedom for the school; contradictory, because everybody prescribes laws based on his own theory, and by that very act that freedom is curtailed.

"The educational experiments tend still less to convince us of the lawfulness of compulsory education. Not only is the experiment sad in itself, but the school stupefies the children by distorting their mental faculties; it tears them away from the family during the most precious time of their development, deprives them of the happiness of freedom, and converts the child into a jaded, crushed being, wearing an expression of fatigue, fear, and ennui, repeating with its lips strange words in a strange language; and in reality the experience of school-work gives nothing besides these, for it takes place amid conditions destroying any possible value in the experiments.

"School, so it would appear to us, ought to be a means of education and, at the same time, an experiment on the young generation, constantly giving new results. Only when experiment is at the foundation of school-work, and every school is, so to speak, an educational laboratory, will the school keep pace with the universal progress, and experiment will be able to lay firm foundations for the science of education.

"The historical arguments are as feeble as the philosophical. The progress of life, of techincal knowledge, of science, proceeds faster than the progress of the school, and the school therefore remains more and more behind the social life, and becomes ever worse and worse."

The argument that as schools have existed and are existing, therefore they are good, Tolstoy meets by describing his personal experience of schools in Marseilles,

Paris, and other towns in Western Europe, which brought him to the conclusion that the greater part of the people's education is acquired not at school, but in life, and that free, open instruction by means of public lectures, sights, meetings, books, exhibitions, and so on, quite surpasses all school tuition.

Finally Tolstoy addresses himself especially to Russian educationists, saying that if we are, for example, to acknowledge the existence of German schools as desirable, in spite of their defects, on the ground of historic experiment, still the question remains: On what grounds are we Russians to defend the school for the people, when no such schools yet exist with us? What historic reasons have we to declare that our schools must be the same as those of the rest of Europe?

"What are we Russians to do at the present moment? Shall we all come to some agreement and take as our basis the English, French, German, or North American view of education and any one of their methods? Or shall we, by closely examining philosophy and psychology, discover what in general is necessary for the development of a human soul, and for making out of the younger generation the best men possible according to our conception? Or shall we make use of the experience of history—not in imitating those forms which history has evolved, but in comprehending those laws which humanity has worked out through suffering? Shall we say frankly and honestly to ourselves that we do not know and cannot know what future generations may need, but that we feel ourselves obliged to study this need, and that we wish to do so; that we do not wish to accuse the people of ignorance for not accepting our education, but that we shall accuse ourselves of ignorance and self-conceit if we persist in educating the people according to our ideas?

" Let us cease looking upon the people's resistance to our education as upon a hostile element, but let us rather see in it an expression of the people's will, which alone ought to guide us. Let us finally adopt the view which we are so plainly told, both by the history of educational methods and the whole history of education, that if the educating class is to know what is good and what is bad, the classes which receive the education must have full power to express their dissatisfaction, or, at least, to swerve from the education which instinctively does not satisfy them—that the only criterion of educational methods is liberty."

The article ends in the following avowal:

"We know that our arguments will not convince many. We know that our fundamental convictions that the only method of education is experiment, and its only criterion freedom, will sound to some like trite commonplace, to some like an indistinct abstraction, to others again like a visionary dream. We should not have dared to disturb the repose of the theoretical pedagogues and to express these convictions, which are contrary to all experience, if we had to confine ourselves to the reflections made in this article; but we feel ourselves able to prove step by step, and taking one fact after another, the applicability and propriety of our convictions however wild they may appear, and to this end alone do we devote the publication of the periodical *Yasnaya Polyana*."

The magazine *Yasnaya Polyana*, which was in fact itself an interesting educational experiment, lasted for one year. Twelve numbers were issued.

The first number began with the following appeal to the public:

"Entering on a new work, I am under some fear, both for myself and for those thoughts which have been for years developing in me, and which I regard as true. I am certain beforehand that many of these thoughts will turn out to be mistaken. However carefully I have endeavored to study the subject, and have involuntarily looked upon it from one side, I hope that my thoughts will call forth the expression of a contrary opinion. I shall be glad to afford room for all opinions in my magazine. Of one thing only am I afraid —that these opinions may be expressed with acridity, and that the discussion of a subject so dear and important to all as that of national education may degenerate into sarcasms, personalities, and journalistic polemics; and I will not say that sarcasms and personalities could not affect me, or that I hope to be above them. On the contrary, I confess that I fear as much for myself as for the cause itself; I fear being carried away by personal polemics instead of quietly and persistently working at my subject.

"I therefore beg all future opponents of my views to express their thoughts so that I may explain myself, and substantiate my statements in those cases in which our disagreement is caused by our not understanding one another, and might agree with my opponents when the error of my view is proved. COUNT L. N. TOLSTOY."

Each number contained one or two theoretical articles, then reports of the progress of the schools under the management of Tolstoy, bibliography, description of school libraries, accounts of donations, and a supplement in the shape of a book for reading.

The motto of the magazine was the saying: *Glaubst zu schieben und wirst geschoben,* that is to say, " You mean to push, but in reality it is you who are pushed."

This magazine has become a bibliographical rarity. True, Tolstoy's own principal articles have been included in the fourth volume of the full edition of his works, but, besides those articles, there appeared in the magazine many different short notices, descriptions and reports of great interest for teachers in a theoretical as well as in a practical sense.

In his article " On methods of teaching to read and write," Tolstoy tries in the first place to prove that *reading* is not the *first* step in instruction, but only an intervening one.

" Since it is not the *first*, then it is not the principal one.

" If we want to find the foundation, the first step in education, why should we look for it perforce in the rudiments, instead of much deeper? Why should we stop at one of the endless number of the instruments of education and see in it the alpha and omega of education, when it is only one of the incidental, unimportant circumstances of education?

" By ' Education ' we do not mean merely a knowledge of ' Reading and Writing.'

"We see people who are well acquainted with all the facts necessary to know for the purpose of farming, and with a large number of interrelations of these facts, though they can neither read nor write; or excellent military commanders, excellent merchants, managers, superintendents of work, master mechanics, artisans, contractors, and people simply educated by life, who possess a great store of information and of sound reasoning based on that information, who can neither read nor write. On the other hand we see those who can read and write, and who have acquired no new information by means of those accomplishments."

Among the reasons which cause a contradiction between the real needs of the people and the tuition imposed upon the people by the cultured classes, Tolstoy points out certain features in the historic development of educational institutions.

"First were founded, not the lower, but the higher schools: at first the monastic, then the secondary, then the primary schools. . . . The rudiments are in this organized hierarchy of institutions the last step, or the first from the end, and therefore the lower school is to respond only to the exigencies of the higher schools.

"But there is also another point of view, from which the popular school appears as an independent institution, which is not obliged to perpetuate the imperfections of the higher institution of learning, but which has an aim of its own, viz., that of supplying popular education."

"The school for reading and writing exists among the people in the shape of the workshop, and, as such, satisfies the need for those accomplishments, and reading and writing are for the people a certain kind of art or craft."

Having made clear the gist of this matter of writing and reading, and pointed out its place in the life of the people, Tolstoy goes on further to investigate different methods of teaching to read and write.

After having examined the defects and merits of the old-fashioned methods of teaching to read letter by letter, and the method of learning by sound; after having further discussed the comical and pedantic German Lautieranschauungsunterrichtsmethode, he came to the conclusion that all methods are good and all are bad, that the talent and ability of the teacher are at the foundation of any method, and he finally addresses to the teacher the following advice:

"Every teacher of reading must be well grounded in the one method which has been evolved by the people, and must further verify it by his own experience; he must endeavor to find out the greatest number of methods, employing them as auxiliary means; must, by regarding every imperfection in the pupil's comprehension, not as showing a defect in the pupil, but a defect in his own instruction, endeavor to develop in himself the ability of discovering new methods. Every teacher must know that every method invented is only a step, on which he must stand in order to go farther; he must know that if he himself will not do it, another will adopt that method, and will, on its basis, go farther, and that, as the business of teaching is an art, completeness and perfection are not obtainable, while development and improvement are endless."

With still greater detail and clearness does Tolstoy present his educational ideas in his article "Education and Instruction."

In the first place, he states the fact that the majority of educationists, Russian and European, confuse these two ideas. Then he tries to restate the distinction between these conceptions, giving his own definitions to the three principal educational terms—Education, Training, and Instruction.

"*Education* in the broad sense of the term is, according to our conviction, the sum total of all those influences which develop man, give him a broader outlook and new knowledge, children's games and their sufferings, punishments inflicted by their parents, books, work, study, whether compulsory or free, art, science, life—all these educate.

"*Training* is the influence exercised by one man on another for the purpose of making him adopt certain moral habits.

"*Instruction* is the transmission of knowledge from one man to another (one can be instructed in chess, or history, or boot-making). Teaching, an aspect of instruction, is the influence exercised by one man upon another for the purpose of leading him to acquire certain accomplishments (to sing, to do carpentering, to dance, to row, to recite). Instruction and teaching are means of education when they are exercised without compulsion, and means of training when teaching is compulsory, and when instruction is directed in an exclusive way, *i. e.*, when only those subjects are given which the teacher regards as necessary.

"There are no rights of education. I do not acknowledge such, nor have they been acknowledged, nor will they ever be, by the young generation under education, which always and everywhere is set against compulsion in education."

"Education is compulsory, instruction is free. Where lies the right to compulsion?

"Where do we find the justification of any compulsion by humanity?" To this question Tolstoy gives the following answer:

"If such an abnormal condition as the use of force in culture—education—has existed for ages, the causes of this phenomenon must be rooted in human nature. I see these causes—(1) in the family, (2) in religion, (3) in the State, and (4) in society (in the narrower sense, which in our country embraces only the official circles and the gentry)."

While not approving of the influence of the first three sources of compulsion, Tolstoy admitted that it was intelligible.

"It is difficult to hinder parents from bringing up their children to be different from what they are themselves; it is difficult for a believer not to strive to bring up his child in his own faith; finally, it is difficult to claim that Governments should not educate the officials whom they require.

"But by what right does the privileged, progressive society educate by its own standard the people alien to itself? This can be explained by nothing but gross egotistical error.

"What is the reason of this error?

"I think it is that we do not hear the voice of those who attack us; we do not hear it, because it does not speak in print or down from the professor's chair. But it is the mighty voice of the people, which one must listen to carefully in order to hear it."

Tolstoy then began the examination of the methods of this educational compulsion, *i. e.*, those practised in the schools from the lowest to the highest, and he found nothing cheering in them. He criticised especially the organization of our universities.

Without rejecting university instruction on principle, Tolstoy declared:

"I can understand a university, corresponding to its name and its fundamental idea, as a collection of men for the purpose of their mutual culture. Such universities, unknown to us, spring up and exist in various corners of Russia; in the universities themselves, in the students' clubs, people come together, read and discuss, until at last rules establish themselves when to meet and how to discuss. There you have real universities! But our universities, in spite of all the empty talk about the seeming freedom of their structure, are institutions which, by their organization, in no way differ from female boarding-schools and cadet academies."

"Besides the absence of freedom, of independence, one of the chief defects of our university life is its aloofness from real life.

"See how the son of a peasant learns to become a farmer; how the sexton's son, reading in the choir, learns to be a sexton; how the son of a Kirgiz cattle-dealer becomes a herder: he enters very early into direct relations with life, with Nature, and with men; he learns early, while working, to make his work productive; and he learns, being secure on the material side of life, that is, so far as to be sure of a piece of bread, of clothes to wear, and of a lodging. Now look at a student, who is torn away from home, from the family, cast into a strange city, full of temptations for his youth, without means of support (because the parents provide means only for bare necessities, while all is spent on frivolity), in a circle of companions who by their society only intensify his defects; without guides, without an aim, having pushed off from the old and having not yet landed at the new. Such, with rare exceptions, is the position of a student. From this results that which alone can result; you have officials who are fit only for Government posts; or professional officials, fit for society, or people aimlessly torn away from their former surroundings, with a spoiled youth, and finding no place for themselves in life, so-called people with *university culture*—advanced, that is, irritable, sickly Liberals.

"The university is our first and our chief educational institution. It is the first to arrogate to itself the right of education, and it is the first, so far as the results which it obtains indicate, to prove the impropriety and impossibility of university education. Only from the social point of view is it possible to justify the fruits of the university. The university trains not such men as humanity needs, but such as corrupt society needs."

Tolstoy foresaw the timid objections to his radical solution of the question on the part of those fearing a change. and answered these at once, concluding his answer with the following reply:

"'What are we to do, then? Shall there, really, be no county schools, no gymnasia, no chairs of the history of Roman law? What will become of humanity?' I hear.

"There certainly shall be none, if the pupils do not need them, and you are not able to make them good.

"'But children do not always know what they need; children are mistaken,' and so forth, I hear.

"I will not enter into this discussion. This discussion would lead us to the question: Can man's nature be judged by a tribunal of men? and so forth. I do not know that, and do not take that stand; all I can say is that if we know what to teach, you must not keep me from teaching Russian children by force, French, mediæval genealogy, and the art of stealing. I can prove everything as you do.

"'So there will be no gymnasia and no Latin? Then, what am I going to do?' I again hear.

"Don't be afraid! There will be Latin and rhetoric, and they will exist another hundred years, simply because the medicine is bought, so we must drink it (as a patient said). I doubt whether the thought, which I have expressed, perhaps indistinctly, awkwardly, inconclusively, will become a common possession in another hundred years; it is not likely that within a hundred years will die those ready-made institutions, schools, gymnasia, universities, and that within that time will grow up freely formed institutions, having for their basis the freedom of the learning generation."

Of course such audacious ideas could not be accepted by educationists, who during the sixties have been at the head of national instruction in Russia. Offended science did not even deign to take such ideas seriously. In *The Collection of Criticisms upon Tolstoy*, by Zelinsky, a book very carefully composed, there are only two serious articles devoted to the magazine *Yasnaya Polyana*, and to the school of the same name. They are printed in *The Contemporary* of 1862.

To one of these, the article of E. Markof, Tolstoy replied in his magazine by an article, "The Progress and Definition of Instruction."

The gist of Markof's argument, given in a *résumé* at

the end of his article, consists in an open acknowledgment of the right of compulsory education on the part of society, and its right of rejecting free instruction, after making which he proceeds to express his approval of contemporary systems of instruction. As to the school in Yasnaya Polyana, he speaks with enthusiasm of its practice, but holds that it is inconsistent with the theories of its founder and guide, L. N. Tolstoy.

In his reply to Markof, Tolstoy repeats and explains what has been said by him in his preceding articles, and comes to the conclusion that their principal difference is the fact that Markof believes in progress and he does not.

In explanation of his want of belief in progress he says:

"The process of progress has taken place in all humanity from time immemorial, says the historian who believes in progress, and he proves this assertion by comparing, let us say, the England of the year 1685 with the England of our time. Even if it were possible to prove, by comparing Russia, France, and Italy of our time with ancient Rome, Greece, Carthage, and so forth, that the prosperity of the modern nations is greater than that of antiquity, I am still struck by one incomprehensible phenomenon; they deduce a general law for all humanity from the comparison of one small part of European humanity in the present and the past. Progress is a common law of humanity, they say, except for Asia, Africa, America, and Australia, except for one thousand million people.

"We have noticed the law of progress in the dukedom of Hohenzollern-Sigmaringen, with its three thousand inhabitants. We know China, with its two hundred millions of inhabitants, which overthrows our whole theory of progress, and we do not for a moment doubt that progress is the common law of all humanity, and that we, the believers in that progress, are right, and those who do not believe in it are wrong, and so we go with cannons and guns to impress the idea of progress upon the Chinese. Common-sense, however, tells us that if the history of the greater part of humanity, the whole so-called East, does not confirm the law of progress, but, on the contrary, overthrows it, that law does not exist for all humanity, but only as an article of faith for a certain part of it.

"I, like all people who are free from the superstition of

progress, observe only that humanity lives, that the memories of the past augment as much as they disappear; the labors of the past frequently serve as a basis for the labors of the present, and just as frequently as an impediment; that the well-being of people now increases in one place, in one stratum, and in one sense, and now diminishes; that, no matter how desirable it would be, I cannot find any common law in the life of humanity; and that it is as easy to subordinate history to the idea of progress as to any other idea or to any imaginable historical fancy.

"I will say even more; I see no necessity for finding common laws for history, independently of the impossibility of finding them. The common eternal law is written in the soul of each man. The law of progress, or perfectibility, is written in the soul of each man, and is transferred to history only through error. As long as it remains personal, this law is fruitful and accessible to all; when it is transferred to history, it becomes an idle, empty prattle, leading to the justification of every insipidity and to fatalism. Progress in general in all humanity is an unproved fact, and does not exist for all the Eastern nations; therefore, it is as unfounded to say that progress is the law of humanity as it is to say that all people are fair except the dark-complexioned ones."

The propositions stated are developed in detail by Tolstoy in his article, but as this subject oversteps the limits of our narrative, we will conclude by mentioning one more paper, entitled "A Project for a General Plan of People's Schools Organization." This article contains some witty criticisms, and a readable review of the Government regulation concerning schools in 1862.

Tolstoy's general critical remarks on the regulation can be summed up thus: (1) The regulation is based upon the American system; the people are to pay school rates, and the schools are to be maintained by the Government with the sum collected. But what is good in a democratic republic may turn out very bad in a despotic state, where the law expressing the so-called "will of the people" becomes a gross invasion of the rights of the people. (2) The general inefficiency of the project follows from its inadaptability to the needs of the people, owing to entire ignorance of Russian life on the part of the author. (3) The control of popular education sanctioned by this regulation will prove an obstacle to the popular education already existing, which is freely spreading.

After having finished this brief summary of Tolstoy's opinions on education, we must give our own conclusion, which is in opposition to the conclusion of M. Markof, and is this, that the practice of the school at Yasnaya Polyana does not in the least contradict Tolstoy's views, but, on the contrary, amounts to their direct application, which is accomplished with unique success.

CHAPTER XV

THE WORK OF THE YASNAYA POLYANA SCHOOL

The evening walk—Fédka, Sémka, and Prónka: Tolstoy's tales—The turning to discourse on art. *A lesson in authorship:* "Feeding with the spoon, poking the eye with the handle"—Process of creation—Sémka and Fédka—Artistic details—The truthfulness of the description—Literary ambitions—Tolstoy's excitement. *The first history lesson:* The Tula province, Russia, the law, the classes, the frontier—Weakness of this method. *The second history lesson:* Tolstoy's account of the year 1812 and the events preceding it—Powerful impression—Rousing of patriotism—Unsoundness of this method—The teaching of music and drawing. *His departure for Samara:* On board steamer—Letter from Samara to Tatiana—Letter from the sanatorium. *Search by the police in Yasnaya Polyana:* Account by Markof—Recollections of Prince Obolensky—Description of it by Tolstoy to the Countess A. A. Tolstoy—Tolstoy's demand for satisfaction—A letter by Tolstoy to the Countess A. A. Tolstoy—Petition handed to the Emperor—His reply—Correspondence of two ministers about the pernicious tendency of the review *Yāsnaya Polyāna*.

IN his educational articles of practical interest Tolstoy gives an artistic description of several incidents in school life, a subject in which he took a warm and sincere interest, not like a stern pedant demanding obedience, but like a boy joining in the joys and sorrows of his school companions, giving them his whole soul, and sharing his great spiritual riches with them.

By putting together the incidents thus described, one sees the gigantic figure of the great educationist in all its grandeur.

1. THE WORKING OF THE SCHOOL.

"It was not cold outside—a moonless winter night with clouds in the sky. We stopped at the cross-roads; the older, third-year pupils stopped near me, asking me to accompany them farther; the younger ones looked awhile at me and then ran off down hill. The young ones had begun to study with a new teacher, and they no longer had that confidence in me that the older boys had.

"'Come, let us go to the preserve' (a small forest within two hundred steps of the house), said one of them. Fédka, a small boy of ten, of a tender, impressionable, poetical, and impetuous nature, was the most persistent in his demands. Danger seemed to form his chief condition for enjoyment. . . .

"He knew that there were wolves in the forest then, and so he wanted to go to the preserve. The rest joined in, so we went, all four of us, into the wood. Another boy, I shall call him Sémka, a physically and morally sound lad of about twelve, nicknamed Vavílo, walked ahead and kept exchanging calls with somebody in his ringing voice. Prónka, a sickly, meek, but uncommonly talented boy, the son of a poor family—sickly, I think, mainly on account of insufficient food—was walking by my side.

"Fédka was walking between me and Sémka, talking all the time in his extremely soft voice, telling us how he had herded horses here in the summer, or saying that he was not afraid of anything, or asking, 'Suppose some one were to jump out at us!' and insisting on my answering him. We did not go into the forest itself—that would have been too terrible—but even near the forest it was getting darker; we could hardly see the path, and the fires of the village were hidden from view.

"Sémka stopped and began to listen.

"'Stop, boys! What is that?' he suddenly said.

"We held our tongues, but we could hear nothing; still it added terror to our fear.

"'Well, what should we do if one should jump out and make straight for us?' Fédka asked.

"We began to talk about robbers in the Caucasus. They recalled a story of the Caucasus I had told them long ago, and I told them more stories about abréks, Cossacks, and Khádzhi-Murát. Sémka was strutting ahead of us, stepping broadly in his big boots, and evenly swaying his strong back. Prónka tried to walk by my side, but Fédka pushed him off the path, and Prónka, who apparently always submitted to such treatment on account of his poverty, still rushed up to my side during the most interesting passages, though sinking knee-deep in the snow.

Tolstoy during his educational activity.

"Everybody who knows anything about peasant children has noticed that they are not accustomed to any kind of caresses—tender words, kisses, being fondly touched with the hand, and so forth. . . . It was for this reason that I was startled when Fédka, who was walking by my side, in the most terrible part of the story suddenly touched me lightly with his sleeve, and then grasped two of my fingers with his whole hand, and did not let them go.

"The moment I was silent, Fédka begged me to proceed, and that in such an imploring tone and with so much agitation that I could not refuse.

"'Don't get in my way!' he once angrily called out to Prónka, who had run on in front; he was really quite savage with him—he had such a mingled feeling of terror and joy, as he was holding on to my finger, that he could not bear any one daring to interrupt his pleasure.

"'More, more! That's fine!'

"We passed the forest and were approaching the village from the other end.

"'Let us go back again,' all cried, when the lights became visible. 'Let us take another walk!'

"We walked in silence, now and then sinking in the loose, untrodden snow; the white darkness seemed to be swaying before our eyes; the clouds hung low, and seemed to be piled over us—there was no end to that whiteness over which we alone crunched through the snow; the wind rustled through the bare tops of the aspens, but we were protected from the wind behind the forest.

"I finished my story by telling them that the abrék, being surrounded, began to sing songs, and then threw himself on his dagger. All were silent.

"'Why did he sing a song when he was surrounded?' asked Sémka.

"'Didn't you hear? He was getting ready to die!' Fédka replied sorrowfully.

"'I think he sang a prayer,' added Prónka.

"All agreed. . . .

"We stopped in the grove, beyond the threshing-floors, at the very end of the village. Sémka picked up a stick from the snow and began to strike the frozen trunk of a lime tree. The hoar frost fell from the branches upon his cap, and the lonely sound of his beating was borne through the forest.

"'Lyof Nikolayevich,' Fédka said (I thought he wanted to say something again about the countess), 'why do people learn singing? I often wonder why they really do?'..

"It feels strange to me to repeat what we spoke on that evening, but I remember we said everything, I think, that there was to be said on utility and on plastic and moral beauty."

A rare happiness fell to the writer of these lines, as to Fédka, who held Tolstoy by his fingers and was rapt in ecstasy. I more than once walked with Tolstoy on the same spot (Zakas). Listening to his tales I have experienced the same feeling, which cannot be expressed in better words than those used by Fédka: "Go on, go on! ah, how nice!"

2. The Lesson in Composition.

"Once, last winter," Tolstoy goes on, "I forgot everything after dinner as I read Snegiref's book, and even returned to the school with the book in my hands. It was a lesson in the Russian language.

"'Well, write something on a proverb!' I said.

"The best pupils, Fédka, Sémka, and a few others, pricked up their ears.

"'What do you mean by "on a proverb"? What is it? Tell us!' the questions ran.

"I happened to open the book at the proverb: 'He feeds with the spoon, and pricks his eye with the handle.'

"'Now, imagine,' I said, 'that a peasant has taken a beggar to his house, and then begins to rebuke him for the good he has done him, and you will see that "he feeds with the spoon, and pricks his eye with the handle."'

"'But how are you going to write it?' said Fédka and all the rest, who had pricked up their ears. They retreated, having convinced themselves that this matter was beyond their strength, and betook themselves to the work which they had begun.

"'Will you write it yourself?' one of them said to me.

"Everybody was busy with his work; I took a pen and ink and began to write.

"'Well,' said I, 'who will write it best? I am with you.'

"I began the story, printed in the fourth number of the *Yásnaya Polyána,* and wrote down the first page. Every unbiassed man who has the artistic sense and feels with the poorer classes will, upon reading this first page, written by me, and the following pages of the story, written by the pupils themselves, separate this page from the rest, as if he were taking a fly out of the milk; it is so false, so artificial, and so badly expressed. I must remark that in the original form it was more monstrous still, as much has been corrected, thanks to the hints given by the pupils.

"Fédka kept looking up from his copy-book to me, and upon meeting my eyes, smiled, winked, and repeated: 'Write, write, or I'll give it to you!' He was evidently amused to see a grown person write a theme.

"Having finished his theme worse and faster than usual, he climbed on the back of my chair and began to read over my shoulders. I could not proceed; others came up to us, and I read out to them what I had written.

"They did not like it, and none of them praised it. I felt ashamed, and, to soothe my literary vanity, I began to tell them the plan of what was to follow. The further I got in my story, the more enthusiastic I became; I often corrected myself, and they kept helping me out. One would say that the old man should be a magician; another would remark: 'No, that won't do, he must be just a soldier; the best thing will be if he steals from him; no, that won't go with the proverb,' and so forth.

"All were exceedingly interested. It was evidently a new and exciting sensation for them to be present at the process of creation and to take part in it. Their judgments were all, for the most part, to the same effect, and they were just, whether they spoke of the very structure of the story or of the incidents and the characters given to the personages. Nearly all of them took part in the composition; but, from the outset, those who distinguished themselves were the positive Sémka, by his marked artistic power of description, and Fédka, by the correctness of his poetical conception, and especially by the glow and rapidity of his imagination.

"Their demands had so little of the accidental in them and were so definite, that more than once, after beginning a discussion, I had to give way to them. I was strongly possessed by the demands of a regular structure and of an exact correspondence of the idea of the proverb to the story; while they, on the contrary, were only concerned about the demands of artistic truth. I, for example, wanted that the peasant, who had taken the old man to his house, should himself repent of his good deed, while they regarded this as impossible, and introduced a cross old woman.

"I said: 'The peasant was at first sorry for the old man and afterward did not like giving away the bread.'

"Fédka replied that that would make the story improbable. 'From the first he did not obey the old woman, and would not submit later on.'

"'What kind of a man is he, according to you?' I asked.

"'He is like Uncle Timoféy,' said Fédka, smiling. 'He has a scanty beard, goes to church, and he has bees.'

"'Is he good but stubborn?' I asked.

"'Yes,' said Fédka, 'he will not obey the old woman.'

"From the time that the old man was brought into the hut, the work became animated. They evidently for the first time felt the charm of clothing artistic incidents in words. Sémka distinguished himself more than the rest in this respect; the correctest details were poured forth one after the other. The only fault that could be found with him was that these details sketched only the actual moment, without connection with the general feeling of the story. I hardly could write their descriptions as fast as they gave them, and only asked them to wait and not forget what they had told me.

"Sémka seemed to see and describe that which was before his eyes; the stiff, frozen bast shoes, with the dirt oozing from them as they thawed, and the half-burned scraps into which they were shrivelled when the old woman threw them into the oven.

"Fédka, on the contrary, saw only such details as brought out for him the particular feeling which he had for particular individuals. Fédka saw the snow drifting behind the peasant's leg-rags, and the expression of compassion with which the peasant said, 'Lord, how it snows!' (Fédka's face even showed how the peasant said it, and besides this he swung his hands and shook his head.) He saw the cloak, all rags and patches, and the torn shirt, under which could be seen the shrunken body of the old man, wet from the melting snow. He created the old woman, who growled, as, at the command of her husband, she took off his bast shoes, and the pitiful groan of the old man as he muttered through his teeth, ' Softly, motherkin, I have sores here.'

"Sémka needed mainly objective pictures; bast shoes, a cloak, an old man, a woman, all almost independent of one another; but Fédka had to make others feel the pity with which he was filled himself. He ran ahead of the story, telling how he would feed the old man, how the latter would fall down at night, and would later teach a boy in the field to read, so that I was obliged to ask him not to be in such a hurry and not to forget what he had said. His eyes sparkled with positive tears; his swarthy, thin little hands were clasped convulsively; he was angry with me, and kept urging me on: ' Have you written it, have you written it?' he kept asking me.

"He treated all the rest despotically; he wanted to talk all the time, giving the story not as a story is told, but as it is written, that is, artistically clothing in words the sensuous pictures. Thus, for example, he would not allow words to be transposed; if he once said, ' I have sores on my feet,' he would not permit me to say, ' On my feet I have sores.' His soul, now softened and irritated by the sentiment of pity, that is, of love, clothed every image in an artistic form, and denied everything that did not correspond to the idea of eternal beauty and harmony.

"The moment Sémka was carried away into giving disproportionate details about the lambs in the inclosure, and so forth, Fédka grew angry and said, ' What a lot of bosh!' I only needed to suggest what the peasant was doing, while his wife went to the gossip, to call forth at once in Fédka's imagination a picture with lambs bleating at the inclosure, with the sighs of the old man and the delirium of the boy Serézhka; I only needed to suggest an artificial and false picture, to make him immediately remark angrily that that was not necessary.

"For example, I suggested the description of the peasant's looks, to which he agreed; but to my proposition to describe what the peasant was thinking when his wife had run over to the gossip, there immediately rose before him this very way of expressing his thought, 'If you got in the way of Savóska, the corpse, he would pull all your locks out!' He said this, leaning his head on his hand the while, with such a tone of fatigue and quiet gravity—although in his usual good-natured voice—that the boys shook with laughter.

"The chief quality in every art, the feeling of measure, was developed in him to an extraordinary degree. He writhed at the suggestion of any superfluous feature, made by some one of the boys.

"He directed the structure of the story so despotically, and with such right to this despotism, that the boys soon went home, and only he and Sémka, who would not give in to him, though working in another direction, were left. We worked from seven to eleven o'clock; they felt neither hunger nor fatigue, and even got angry at me when I stopped writing; they undertook to relieve me in writing, but they soon gave that up, as matters would not go well.

"It was then for the first time that Fédka asked my name. We laughed because he did not know.

"'I know,' he said, 'how to call you; but how do they call you in the manor? We have such names as Fokanychef, Zyabref, Ermílin.'

"I told him.

"'Are we going to print it?' he asked.

"'Yes.'

"'Then we shall have to print work by Makárov, Morózov, and Tolstóy.'

"He was agitated for a long time and could not sleep, and I cannot express the feeling of agitation, joy, fear, and almost regret, which I experienced during that evening. I felt that with that day a new world of enjoyment and suffering was opened up to him—the world of art; I thought that I had received an insight into what no one has a right to see—the germination of the mysterious flower of poetry.

"I felt both dread and joy, like the seeker after the treasure who suddenly sees the flower of the fern—I felt joy, because suddenly and quite unexpectedly there was revealed to me that stone of the philosophers which I had vainly been trying to find for two years—the art of teaching the expression of thought; and dread, because this art made new demands—brought with it a whole world of desires, which stood in no relation to the surroundings of the pupils, as I thought in the first moment. There was no mistaking. It was not an accident, but a conscious creation. . . .

"I gave up the lesson, because I was too much agitated.

"'What is the matter with you? You are so pale—are you ill?' my companion asked me. Indeed, only two or three times in my life have I experienced such a strong sensation as on that evening, and for a long time I was unable to render an account to myself of what I was experiencing. I distinctly felt that I had criminally looked through a glass hive at the work of the bees, concealed from the gaze of mortal man; it seemed to me that I had debauched the pure, primitive soul of a peasant boy. I vaguely felt something like repentance for an act of sacrilege, . . . and at the same time I was happy as a man must be happy who beholds that which no one has beheld before."

3. THE FIRST LESSON IN HISTORY.

Tolstoy narrates: "I had intended to explain in the first lesson in what way Russia differed from other countries, where its frontiers were, the nature of the structure of its government, then to say who was the present ruler, and how and when the Emperor ascended the throne.

"*Teacher.* Where do we live, in what country?

"*A pupil.* In Yásnaya Polyána.

"*Another pupil.* In the field.

"*Teacher.* No, in what country is Yásnaya Polyána, and the Government of Túla?

"*Pupil.* The Government of Túla is seventeen versts from us. Where is it? The Government is a Government, and that is all there is to say about it.

"*Teacher.* No. Túla is the capital of the Government, but a Government is something different. Well, what country is it?

"*Pupil (who has learned some geography before).* The earth is round like a ball.

"By means of questions as to what country a German, whom they knew, had lived in before, and where they would get if they were to keep travelling all the time in one direction, the pupils were led up to answer that they lived in Russia. Some, however, replied to the question where we should get if we travelled all the time in one direction, that we should get nowhere. Others said that we should get to the end of the world.

"*Teacher (repeating the pupil's answer).* You said that we should come to some other countries; where will Russia end and other countries begin?

"*Pupil.* Where the Germans begin.

"*Teacher.* So, if you meet Gústav Ivánovich and Karl Feodorovich in Túla, you will say that the Germans have begun and that there is a new country?

"*Pupil.* No, when the Germans begin thick.

"*Teacher.* No, there are places in Russia where the Germans are thick. Ivan Fómich is from one of them, and yet that is still Russia. Why is it so?

"Silence.

"*Teacher.* Because they obey the same laws with the Russians.

"*Pupil.* One law? How so? The Germans don't come to our church and they eat meat on fast-days.

"*Teacher.* I do not mean that kind of law, but they obey one Czar.

"*Pupil (sceptical Sémka).* That is funny. Why have they a different law, and yet obey the Czar?

"The teacher feels the need of explaining what a law is, and so he asks what is meant by ' obeying a law,' or ' being under one law.'

"*Girl (independent manorial girl, hurriedly and timidly).* To accept the law means ' to get married.'

"The pupils look inquiringly at the teacher. The teacher begins to explain that the law consists in putting a man in jail and in punishing him for stealing or killing.

"*Sceptic Sémka.* And have not the Germans such a law?

"*Teacher.* There are also laws with us about the gentry, the peasants, the merchants, the clergy (the word ' clergy ' perplexes them).

"*Sceptic Sémka.* And have not the Germans such a

"*Teacher.* In some countries there are such laws, and in others there are not. We have a Russian Czar, and in the German countries there is a German Czar.

"This answer satisfies all the people and even sceptical Sémka.

"Thinking it was now time to pass on to explain what is meant by the classes, the teacher asks them what classes of society they know. The pupils begin to enumerate them: the gentry, the peasants, the popes, the soldiers. 'Any more?' asks the teacher. 'The manorial servants, the burghers, the samovár-makers.' The teacher asks them to distinguish these classes.

"*Pupils.* The peasants plough, the manorial servants serve their masters, the merchants trade, the soldiers serve, the samovár-makers get the samovárs ready, the popes serve mass, the gentry do nothing. . . .

"Then in the same order and under similar difficulties there follows an explanation of the idea of 'Classes of Society,' 'frontiers,' and other terms applied to the State.

"The lesson lasts about two hours. The teacher is convinced that the pupils have retained a great deal of what has been said, and continues his subsequent lessons in the same strain, convincing himself only much later that his method was wrong, and that all that he has been doing has been the merest nonsense."

4. THE SECOND LESSON IN HISTORY.

"The holding this class has remained a memorable event in my life," says Tolstoy. "I shall never forget it. The children had long been promised that I should tell them history, going backward, while another teacher would begin from the beginning, so that we should finally meet. My evening scholars had left me, and I came to the class of Russian history. They were talking about Svyatosláv. They felt dull. On a tall bench sat in a row, as they always put themselves, three peasant girls, with their heads tied with kerchiefs. One was asleep. Mishka pushed me. 'Look there, our cuckoos are sitting there—one is asleep.' And they were like cuckoos!

"'You had better tell us from the end,' said some one, and all got up.

"I sat down and began to talk. As always, the hubbub, the groans, the tussling, lasted about two minutes. Some were crawling under the table, some on the table, some under the benches, and on their neighbors' shoulders and knees, till at last all was silent. I began with Alexander I, told them of the French Revolution, of Napoleon's successes, of his seizing the government, and of the war which ended in the peace of Tilsit. The moment we reached Russia there were heard sounds and words expressing lively interest on all sides.

"'Well, is he going to conquer us, too?'

"'Never mind, Alexander will give it to him!' said some one who knew about Alexander, but I had to disappoint them—the time had not yet come for that—and they felt uncomfortable when they heard that the Czar's sister was spoken of as a bride for Napoleon, and that Alexander spoke with him on the bridge, as if he was his equal.

"'Just wait!' exclaimed Pétka, with a threatening gesture.

"'Go on and tell us!'

"When Alexander declined to submit to him, that is, when Alexander declared war, all expressed their approbation. When Napoleon came against us at the head of twelve nations, and stirred up the Germans and Poland, their hearts sank from agitation.

"A German, a friend of mine, was standing in the room.

"'Ah, you were against us, too,' said Pétka (the best story-teller).

"'Keep quiet!' cried the others.

"The retreat of our army tortured my audience, and on all sides were asked questions why? and curses were heaped on Kutúzof and Barclay.

"'Your Kutúzof is no good!'

"'Just wait,' said another.

"'Well, did he surrender?' asked a third.

"When we reached the battle of Borodinó, and when in the end I was obliged to say that we did not gain a victory, I was sorry for them—it was evident that I gave them all a terrible blow.

"'Though our side did not win, theirs did not either!'

"When Napoleon came to Moscow and was waiting for the keys of the city and for submission, there was a burst of protest, as they had thought that they were unconquerable.

The conflagration of Moscow was, naturally, approved of by all. Then came the victory, Napoleon's retreat.

"'When he came out of Moscow, Kutúzov rushed after him and went to fight him,' I said.

"'He made him rear!' Fédka corrected me.

"Fédka, red in his face, was sitting opposite me, and was bending his thin, tawny fingers with excitement. That is his habit. The moment he said this, the whole room groaned with pride and delight. A little fellow in the back row was being badly squeezed, but nobody paid any attention.

"'That's better! There, take the keys now!' and so forth.

"Then I continued, describing our pursuit of the French. It pained the children to hear that some one was too late at Berézina, and that we let them pass; Pétka even groaned with pain.

"'I should have shot him dead for being late.'

"Here we even had some pity for the frozen Frenchmen. Then, when we crossed the border, and the Germans, who had been against us, joined us, some one remembered the German who was standing in the room.

"'How is that? At first you are against us, and when the power is losing, you are with us!' and suddenly all rose and shouted at the German, so that the noise could be heard in the street. When they quieted down I went on, telling them about our following up Napoleon as far as Paris, placing the real king on the throne, celebrating our victory, and feasting. But the recollection of the Crimean War spoiled the whole thing.

"'Just wait,' said Pétka, shaking his fist; 'let me grow up and I will show them!'

"If we had at that moment had a chance at the Shevardinó redoubt and Mount Malakhof, we should certainly have taken them back.

"It was late when I ended. As a rule the children are asleep at that time. No one was sleeping, and the eyes of the little cuckoos were burning. Just as I got up, Taráska crawled out from underneath my chair, to my great astonishment, and looked vivaciously, and, at the same time, seriously at me.

"'How did you get down there?'

"'He has been there all the time,' some one said.

"There was no need to ask him whether he had understood; you could see that by his face.

"'Well, are you going to tell about it?' I asked.

"'I?' He thought awhile. 'I will tell the whole thing.'

"'I will tell it at home.'

"'So will I.'

"'And I.'

"'Is that all?'

"'Yes.'

"All flew down under the staircase, some promising to give it to the Frenchmen, others scolding the German, and others repeating how Kutúzov had made him 'rear.'

"'*Sie haben ganz Russisch erzaehlt,*' the German who had been hooted said to me in the evening. 'You ought to hear how they tell the story in our country! You said nothing about the German struggle for freedom.'

"I fully agreed with him that my narrative was not history, but a fanciful tale to rouse the national sentiment.

"Consequently, as a study of history, this attempt was even less successful than the first."

To give a full picture of Tolstoy as a schoolmaster we must add his views on the teaching of music. He gives a concise summary of his conclusions in four short paragraphs.

"From the small experience which I have had in teaching music I have become convinced:

"(1) That the method which consists in writing the sounds down in figures is the most convenient.

"(2) That teaching time independently of sound is again the most convenient method.

"(3) That, in order that musical instruction should produce permanent effect and be cheerfully received, it is necessary from the very outset to teach the art and not the skill of singing and playing. Young ladies may be made to play Burgmüner's exercises, but the children of the people it is better not to teach at all than to teach mechanically.

"(4) That the aim of musical instruction must consist in giving the pupils that knowledge of the common laws of music which we possess, but by no means in transmitting that false taste which is developed in us."

Drawing occupied a conspicuous place in the school course, but Tolstoy did not teach it himself, as he did not think he was competent, and this task was undertaken by a fellow teacher.

In the spring of 1862 Tolstoy was very tired after his work as Peace Mediator and at the school, and, having some fear of consumption, he resolved to try the Koumiss treatment.

Accompanied by his man-servant Alexey and two schoolboys he went to the province of Samara in the middle of May.

He wrote from Moscow to his aunt Tatiana, informing her that he and his companions were all well, and giving her certain advice and messages in connection with the school.

They went by rail to Tver, and then on by a steamer which was to take them down the river Volga to Samara.

On the voyage Tolstoy probably was in that very happy mood which is so often enjoyed by all travellers upon the Volga. The great river in its spring overflow, the soft murmur of the steamer as it moved, the fascinating spring nights with their starlit skies, the mirror-like river, the lights of the shore and the vessel, the pilgrims, monks, Tartars, and other passengers, who, in spite of the great variety of types, conditions, nationalities, and religions, bear on them a distinctive Great Russian *cachet;* possibly thoughts of the great historic past of the river and its banks—all these make an incomparably gladdening and softening impression, and bring with them many thoughts and dreams.

Tolstoy probably had some similar sensations, for on May 20th he wrote in his diary:

"On board steamer. It seems as if I were again awakening to life and to the understanding of it. The thought as to the absurdity of progress pursues me. With the intelligent and the silly, with old men and with children, I keep discussing this one thing."

On his way Tolstoy stopped with his relation Vladimir Ivanovich Yushkof, in Kazan.

Then, from Samara itself, he wrote to his aunt:

"*May 27*, 1862.

"... I have had a splendid journey; I like the locality very much; my health is better, *i. e.*, I cough less. Alexey and the boys are alive and well, as you may tell their parents...."

He next wrote from the place where he was undergoing his treatment:

"*June 28*, 1862.

"... Alexey and myself have become stouter, especially Alexey, but we cough a little, and again especially Alexey. We are living in a Kibitka.[1] I found my friend Stolipin was an Ataman[2] at Uralsk, where I visited him. I brought from there a clerk, but I do not dictate or write much. Laziness quite overpowers one when taking koumiss. In a fortnight I intend returning home. I am troubled by want of news in these wilds, and also by the consciousness that I am dreadfully behindhand with the publication of the journal. I kiss your hands. Please write in detail about Seryozha, Masha, the students, whom I greet.

"Enclosed are letters from the boys to their teachers."

While he was spending a peaceful time in the Bashkir Steppes an unexpected event took place in the school at Yasnaya Polyana.

There can be no doubt that the powerful preaching of freedom of speech and action at the school could not but attract the attention of the authorities, and Yasnaya Polyana was denounced to those whom it concerned as a centre of criminal revolutionary propaganda. In the summer 1862 the police appeared in the school and made a perquisition.

A full description of this is to be found in the reminiscences of E. Markof in his article printed in *The European Messenger*.

"I cannot help mentioning a characteristic episode," says Markof, "known only to a very few persons, but which had been the cause of Tolstoy's giving up educational work. As a peace mediator of the first elected group, Tolstoy warmly sympathized with the liberation of the serfs, and naturally acted in a direction which provoked a large

[1] A Tartar tent.
[2] Cossack Commander.

majority of landowners against him. He has received a number of threatening letters; they threatened to knock him down or shoot him in a duel; and he has been denounced to the authorities. It so happened that just at the very time when the magazine *Yasnaya Polyana* was started by Tolstoy, proclamations of different revolutionary parties made their appearance in St. Petersburg, and the police were actively engaged searching for the hidden printing-press. Some one of Tolstoy's political enemies craftily insinuated that certain secret leaflets containing appeals for coöperation could be printed only in the printing-office of a magazine published—*horrible dictu!*—not in a town, as all respectable people would have it done, but in the country. In fabricating this, they only omitted to give a glance at the title-page, where it was stated in big type that the review was published in the most respectable printing-office of M. N. Katkof in Moscow. The denunciation, nevertheless, created a real storm.

"In the absence of Tolstoy, his house was being kept by his elderly aunt, and his sister, also married to a Tolstoy, was staying there with her children on a visit. Our common friend G. A. Auerbach and myself were spending the summer with our families at a distance of about five versts from Yasnaya Polyana, in a house let to us by a landowner in the same Raspberry Abattis where Yasnaya Polyana was. One early morning a messenger from Yasnaya Polyana arrived. We were requested to come as soon as possible on important business. Auerbach and I jumped into a wagonette and hurried on as hard as we could. On our entering the court-yard we were faced with a real invasion; there were post-chaises drawn by teams of three horses with their bells, conveyances of local inhabitants, the head of the police district, the commissary of rural police, local policemen, witnesses, and in addition to all this —gendarmes. The colonel of the gendarmes arrived with jingling and bustle at the head of this fearful expedition into Tolstoy's peaceful abode, to the great consternation of the village people. After some difficulty we succeeded in entering the house. The poor ladies were almost fainting. Everywhere there were watchmen, everything was opened, shifted about, and turned upside down—tables, drawers, wardrobes, chests of drawers, boxes, caskets, etc. Crowbars were used in the stables to lift the floors; the ponds in the park were searched by means of nets in order to catch the criminal printing-press, instead of which only innocent carp and crabs made their appearance.

"It need hardly be said that, in the first place, the unfortunate school had been turned upside down; but, finding nothing there, the searchers went in the same noisy, bustling procession, with sounding bells, to pay a visit apparently to all the seventeen schools of the peace districts, everywhere turning over tables and ransacking cupboards, carrying off exercise-books and school manuals, putting teachers under arrest, and creating the wildest conjectures in the heads of the peasants, who were generally unfavorable to schools."[1]

Prince D. D. Obolensky speaks of the same incident in his reminiscences, with the addition of some interesting details:

"The school of Yasnaya Polyana was getting on splendidly. But as most of the school-teachers were students, the authorities did not very much favor the institution, and suspected that there must be something politically unsound in Yasnaya Polyana. Even an officer of the gendarmes called, but of course could not find anything, for there was nothing to find. Only in one room in the house of Yasnaya Polyana, which was converted into a schoolroom, the attention of the officer was attracted by a photographic apparatus. In 1862 this was still a novelty, especially in the provinces and villages. 'What is that?' sternly inquired the officer. 'Whose photos are taken here?' The students, of course, did not like his visit, and one of them said for fun, 'Kergen's, from nature.' 'How Kergen?' inquired the officer. But the laughter explained to him that it was a joke, and he left the place biting his lips."[2]

Zakharyin Yakunin tells the following in his *Reminiscences of the Countess A. A. Tolstoy:*

"Relating to her this humiliating incident, Tolstoy added: 'I often say to myself, what a very lucky thing it is that I was not at home! If I had been, I should by this

---

[1] E. Markof "The Living Soul in School: Thoughts and Reminiscences of an Old Educationalist." *Messenger of Europe.* p. 584, February, 1900.
[2] "Sketches and Reminiscences by Prince D. D. Obolensky." The Russian Archive, Book X, 1894.

time have been tried for murder.' It is easy to explain these strong words used by Tolstoy forty-two years ago, if one remembers the great shock suffered by his dearest friends at the time—his aunt and his sister. It is enough to say that the Police Commissioner of Túla, Kobelyatsky, gave permission to Tolstoy's sister to leave the study for the drawing-room, and then to go to bed only after he had read before her, and in the presence of two gendarmes, all those intimate letters which we mentioned in their place, as well as Tolstoy's diary, and everything Tolstoy had written and kept hidden from all since the age of sixteen. . . .

"The owner of Yasnaya Polyana did not wish to leave such unnecessary harshness unpunished, so he cut short his medical treatment and went home. He wrote to Countess A. A. Tolstoy immediately upon receiving news of the police invasion, and asked her to communicate all the details of the affair to those in power who knew him well, and on whose protection he could rely, *i. e.*, to Count B. A. Perovsky, Countess H. D. Bludof, and others. What Tolstoy requested was, not the punishment of those who committed the outrage, but the restoration of his good name in the eyes of the peasants around him, and security against similar incidents in the future.

"'This affair I positively do not wish to and *cannot* leave alone,' he wrote; 'all the employment in which I had found happiness and peace is spoiled. Auntie is so ill from fright that she will probably not recover. The people look upon me no longer as an honest man—an opinion, on their part, which I have earned during many years—but as a criminal, an incendiary, or a coiner, who has escaped merely owing to his slyness. . . .

"'Ah, friend! you have been caught . . . you needn't talk to us any more about honesty and justice—you have almost been handcuffed yourself.'

"'As to the landowners, it goes without saying there is one outburst of delight. Please tell me at once, after consulting Perovsky or Alexey Tolstoy, or whom you like, how I am to write and to transmit my letter to the Emperor. I have no other choice than either to receive a satisfaction as public as the insult (it is too late for any redress), or else to expatriate myself, upon which I have firmly decided. To Herzen I will not go; Herzen has his own way, and

I have mine. Nor will I conceal matters, but will loudly proclaim that I am selling my estate in order to leave Russia, where it is impossible to know for one minute what you have to expect.'

"It is a long letter written on eight large pages. Informing her at the end that the colonel of gendarmes on leaving had threatened Yasnaya Polyana with a new search till he should find out 'what was hidden,' Tolstoy added:

"'Loaded pistols are in my room, and I am waiting to see how all this will end.'

"I remember Tolstoy telling me that he felt extremely hurt by this meddling of the police in his affairs, the more so as the visit and the search of the police were made during his absence. He made up his mind to complain of it to the Emperor Alexander II, and at the latter's visit to Moscow, when he met him in the Alexandrovsk Garden, he personally handed him a petition. The Emperor received his petition, and I believe sent one of his adjutants to apologize."

But the authorities were far from pacified, and a correspondence between the Ministers of the Interior and of Instruction ensued on the subject of the review *Yasnaya Polyana*. We quote extracts from this correspondence printed in the reminiscences of Oossof:

"The Minister of Interior informed the Minister of Instruction on October 3, 1862:

"The careful reading of the educational review *Yasnaya Polyana*, edited by Count Tolstoy, leads to the conclusion that this review, in preaching new methods of tuition and principles of popular schools, frequently spreads ideas which, besides being incorrect, are injurious in their teaching. Without entering into a full examination of the doctrines of the review, and without pointing out any particular articles or expressions—which, however, could be easily done—I consider it necessary to draw the attention of your Excellency to the general tendency and spirit of the review, which very often attacks the fundamental rules of religion and morality. The continuation of the review in the same spirit must, in my opinion, be considered the more dangerous as its editor is a man of remarkable and one may say even a fascinating talent, who cannot be suspected to be a criminal or an unprincipled man. The evil lies in the sophistry and eccentricity of his convictions, which, being expounded with extraordinary eloquence, may carry away inexperienced teachers in this direction, and thus give a wrong turn to popular education. I have the honor to inform you of this, hoping that you may consider it useful to draw the special attention of the censor to this publication."

Having received this report, the Minister of Instruction issued an order for the examination of all the printed books of the review *Yasnaya Polyana*, and, on October 24th of the same year, informed the Minister of the Interior that in accordance with the examination made by his subordinates, and the report presented to him, he saw nothing dangerous or contrary to religion in the review *Yasnaya Polyana*. One only came at times across extreme views upon the subject of education, which might very well be criticised in scientific educational reviews, but not forbidden by the censor.

"On the whole," continued the Minister of Public Instruction, "I must say that Count Tolstoy's work as an educationist deserves full respect, and the Minister of Public Instruction is bound to help him and give him encouragement, even though not sharing all his views, which, after maturer consideration, he will probably give up himself." [1]

The liberal Ministry of Public Instruction was mistaken. Tolstoy did not give up his ideas; but all those attacks had prevented the further development of his school work in Yasnaya Polyana.

---

[1] E. Solovyof, *Leo Tolstoy: His Life and Literary Activity*, p. 73. Published by Pavlenkof, St. Petersburg, 1897.

CHAPTER XVI

MARRIAGE—SHORT REVIEW OF TOLSTOY'S WORKS

Dissatisfaction of Tolstoy with his educational work—His account of it in *Confession*—The loss at play to Katkof—The selling of *The Cossacks*—Turgenef's letter—The narrative of the Countess S. A. Tolstoy—Fet's description of his visit to the family Bers—Account of Tolstoy's sister-in-law of his relations to her family—Account of same by the Countess S. A. Tolstoy—Declaration of love at card-table—The proposal—Reflection of these relations in his diary—Tolstoy's diary read by his *fiancée*—The wedding—Departure to Yasnaya Polyana—Letter to Fet—The new life—Review of the works *The Snowstorm, The Recollections of a Billiard-Marker, The Two Hussars, Family Happiness, Polikushka*—The attitude of the critics.

NOTWITHSTANDING the apparent success of his educational work, Tolstoy could not be entirely satisfied with it; however grand the building which he had so cleverly planned, he was not sure of the firmness of its foundation. For him this foundation was non-existent. His analytical brain prevented him from resting on unstable foundations, and a really firm one he had not found.

This dissatisfaction was expressed in his *Confession* in the following words in reference to that period:

"I believed that I had found a solution abroad, and, armed with that conviction, I returned to Russia the same year in which the peasants were freed from serfdom, and, accepting the office of a country magistrate or arbitrator. I began to teach the uneducated people in the schools, and the educated classes by means of the journals which I published. Things seemed to be going on well, but I felt that my mind was not in a normal state, and that a change was near. I might then, perhaps, have come to that state of absolute despair to which I was brought fifteen years later, if it had not been for a new experience in life which promised me safety—the home life of a family man. For a year I occupied myself with my duties as arbitrator, with the schools, and with my newspaper, and my work became so involved that I was harassed to death; my arbitration was one continual struggle; what to do in the schools became less and less clear, and my newspaper shuffling more and more repugnant to me. It was always the same thing, trying to teach without knowing how or what. So that I fell ill, more with mental than physical sickness, gave up everything, and started for the steppes to breathe a fresher air, to drink mare's milk, and live a mere animal life.

"Soon after my return I married."

The following incident in the life of Tolstoy took place about the same time:

Still a passionate gambler, he often fell a victim to his own excesses. Thus in the beginning of 1862 Tolstoy, in a game of billiards, lost 1,000 roubles to Katkof, the well-known publicist and editor of *Moscow News.*

He was unable to meet this debt, and, in lieu of payment, gave his unfinished novel, *The Cossacks,* to be printed in the magazine, the *Russian Messenger,* published by Katkof himself. It appeared in January, 1863, in its unfinished shape, and in consequence of disagreeable recollections connected with it, Tolstoy gave it up and never finished the story.

Being informed of this incident by Botkin, Turgenef wrote about it to Fet:

"Tolstoy has written to Botkin that he played against luck in Moscow, and got from Katkof 1,000 roubles as a deposit for his Caucasian novel. May God grant he returns to his true work, if even in this manner. His *Childhood* and *Youth* have appeared in an English translation, and it seems are popular. I asked a friend of mine to write an article on it in the *Revue des Deux Mondes.* One ought to have intercourse with the people, but to long for it like a woman who is *enceinte* is ridiculous."

At that time Tolstoy used very often to visit the house of Dr. Bers, with whom he was to be more closely connected by family ties.

"We were still little girls," said the Countess Tolstoy to the biographer Loewenfeld, " when Tolstoy first visited our house. He was then already a well-known writer, and lived in Moscow in a gay, noisy style. One day Tolstoy rushed into our room and joyfully informed us that he had just sold his *Cossacks* to Katkof for a thousand roubles. We thought the price very low. Then he explained that he had to do it; that he had lost that sum of money at a game of 'China billiards,' and that it was for him a matter of honor to settle the debt immediately. He intended to write the second part of *The Cossacks*, but he has never done it. His news so much upset us little girls that we cried, walking up and down the room."

About this time Tolstoy again became friendly with Fet, the estrangement from whom had been the result of the quarrel with Turgenef. Of this renewal of their friendly relations Fet speaks thus:

"If my memory—which keeps correctly not only events of importance in my life, but even the precise words used on any odd occasion—did not retain the circumstances of our reconciliation with Tolstoy after his ill-tempered postscript, it only proves that his anger against me was like a hailstorm in July, which was bound to melt by itself. Yet I suppose it did not occur without Borisof's help. However this may be, Tolstoy again appeared on our horizon, and with the enthusiasm peculiar to him began to speak of his friendship with the family of Dr. Bers.

Having accepted the offer of the Count to introduce me to the Bers family, I met the doctor, a polite and well-mannered old man, and a beautiful, distinguished looking brunette, his wife, who was evidently the ruler of the household. I refrain from describing the three young ladies, the youngest of whom possessed a beautiful contralto voice. Notwithstanding the careful supervision of their mother and their perfect modesty, they all possessed the charm which the French call *du chien*. The dinner table and the dinner of the domineering hostess were irreproachable.[1]

Of the attitude of Tolstoy to the Bers family and his gradual preparation for the marriage we learn from a private letter of Tolstoy's sister-in-law:

"His relations with our house are of long standing: our grandfather Islenef and Tolstoy's father were neighboring landowners as well as friends. Their families had been in constant communication, and it is through this that my mother and Tolstoy were like sister and brother in their childhood. He used to call on us when he was an officer. My mother was then already married and on very friendly

[1] A. Fet, *My Reminiscences*, vol. i.

The Countess S. A. Tolstoy in 1860, before her marriage.

terms with Tolstoy's sister, and at her house as a child I often met Tolstoy. He used to get up all sorts of games with his nieces and myself. I was about ten at that time, and have but little recollection of him. When he returned from abroad in the year of his marriage, he had not seen us for several years, and, coming to Pokrovskoye (near Moscow), he found my two elder sisters already grown up. He brought with him a teacher, Keller, from abroad, and engaged a few more teachers in Moscow for his school, which occupied his attention very much.

"He almost always came on foot to Pokrovskoye (12 versts). We went out with him for long walks. He took great interest in our life, and became very intimate with us. Once we—my mother and we three sisters—went for a fortnight to grandfather's country place in the province of Tula, of course driving, and he joined our company. On the way we called at Yasnaya Polyana. He lived with his aunt Tatiana Alexandrovna Yergolsky and his sister Marie, who were the ladies that my mother stopped with. The next day a picnic was arranged at Yasnaya Polyana, in the coppice, with the families of Auerbach and Markof. Haymaking was going on in the abattis, and we all climbed up a haystack. After this Tolstoy followed us to 'Tvitzi,' my grandfather's property, and there, at the card-table, occurred the declaration in 'primary letters,' as described in *Anna Karenina*. In September we moved to Moscow, where he too followed, and on the 17th of the month the intended wedding was made known in Moscow. During the whole of his stay in Moscow he was everywhere and always lively, gay, and witty—he was like a volcano throwing out sacred sparks and fire. I remember him often at the piano; he would bring music, rehearsed the cherubic song of Bortniansky with us, and many other songs. He accompanied me every day and called me Mme. Viardot, urging me to be always singing."

This is how Countess Tolstoy herself tells about her wedding, in a conversation with Loewenfeld. We amplify and correct the narrative which we heard from the Countess:

"The Count visited our house constantly at that time. We thought he was courting our elder sister, and my father was perfectly sure of it down to the last minute, when Tolstoy asked him for my hand. This was in 1862. We went with our mother in August to visit our grandfather *via* Yasnaya Polyana. My mother wanted to call on Tolstoy's sister, and we, the three sisters and our younger brother, therefore remained for a few days there. Nobody was astonished at the Count's attention to us, our acquaintance being, as I have told you, of long standing, and the Count had always been very kind to us. 'Tvitzi,' our grandfather's property, or rather that of his wife, *née* Islenef—for his own land he lost by card-playing—was fifty versts from Yasnaya Polyana. A few days later Tolstoy arrived and, in a word, here took place a scene similar to that described in *Anna Karenina,* when Levin made his love declaration in 'primary letters,' and Kitty guessed it at once. Up to the present, said the Countess with a smile, proving that the mere recollection of it caused her pleasure, I cannot understand how I made out the meaning of the letters then. It must be true, that souls attuned to one another give out the same sound even as do equally tuned chords."

The sentences exchanged by Tolstoy and the lady who became his wife, which had been written only in primary letters, were the following:

"I. y. f. e. a. f. i. a. t. m. a. y. s. L. Y. a. T. m. d. i." This meant: "In your family exists a false idea as to me and your sister Liza. You and Tanichka must destroy it."

The Countess guessed the sentence and nodded affirmatively.

Then he wrote thus:

"Y. y. a. d. f. h. r. m. t. v. o. m. a. a. t. i. o. h.," which meant: "Your youth and desire for happiness remind me too vividly of my advanced age and the impossibility of happiness."

Nothing more was said between them, but they understood and were sure of one another.

They went to Moscow, whither Tolstoy followed them. He lived in town, and the family of Bers were generally in Pokrovskoye-Glebovo, twelve versts from Moscow, where they had lived every summer for twenty years. Tolstoy was their daily visitor. All in the house were perfectly sure that he was going to propose to the elder daughter. But on September 17th, the Saint's Day of Sofya Andreyevna, Tolstoy handed her a letter in which he made her a proposal of marriage. Of course, this was joyfully accepted by her;

but her father was displeased; he did not like to give the younger daughter in marriage before the elder one, as it was against old customs, and he at first refused his consent. But the persistence of Tolstoy and the firmness of Sofya Andreyevna induced him to yield.

In Tolstoy's diary we find the following vivid reflections of these events.

After one of the visits to the family Bers, he wrote down on August 23d:

"I am afraid of myself. What if it is only the *desire* to love, but not love? I try to look only at her weak side, and yet I love."

At the same time he felt the loneliness of his public life.

"I got up in good health, with an especially clear head; my writing came easily, but the subject matter is poor. Then I felt so sad as I have not for long. I have no friends, none. I am alone. There were friends when I served Mammon, and there are none when I serve the truth."

At last on August 26th he wrote:

"I went to the Bers's at Pokrovskoye on foot. I felt at peace, comfortable. Sonia gave me a story to read. What energy of truth and simplicity! She is troubled with its indefiniteness. I read it all without agitation, without any symptoms of jealousy or envy, but the words 'of excessively unattractive appearance and inconstancy of views' hit me splendidly. I consoled myself by the thought that it was not about me."

Unfortunately this story was never given to the world; it was destroyed by the author.

On August 28th, his birthday, when he was thirty-four years old, we once more see in his diary marks of hesitation, self-accusation, and a struggle. He wrote:

"I got up in the usual sadness. I have planned a society for apprentices. A sweet, quieting night. You ugly face, don't think of marriage; your calling is of another kind, and much has been given for it."

But want of family happiness got the upper hand, and the *desire* of love turned at last into real passionate love, which knew no bars whatever. And yet notwithstanding the power of this passion, Tolstoy here too displayed his honesty and love of truth. After having already made his proposal and been accepted, he handed to his betrothed all the diaries of his bachelor days, with all his expressions of self-reproach and his perfectly sincere description of his youthful escapades, and the excesses and moral conflicts which he had gone through.

The reading of the diary was a blow which caused deep suffering to the young girl, who had seen in her hero the ideal of all virtues. The suffering was so great and the struggle she went through so hard that at times she hesitated, and wondered whether she should not sever the link. But love swept away all hesitation, and after nights of weeping she returned him his diary with a look in which he read forgiveness, and a stronger and still more courageous love than before.

The wedding was fixed for a very early date, the end of the week following the formal proposal—September 23d.

The marriage took place at the Kremlin in the Court church, and immediately after it the newly married couple drove away in a dormeuse to Yasnaya Polyana, where they were met by Tolstoy's brother and his aunt Tatiana Alexandrovna.

The brother of Countess Tolstoy, S. A. Bers, in his reminiscences thus describes his sister:

"My late father did not approve of schools for girls, so that Tolstoy's wife was brought up at home, but she went through an examination and received the diploma of a teacher. While a girl she kept her diary, tried to write stories, and showed some talent for painting."[1]

Soon after his marriage Tolstoy wrote to Fet:

"FETOUSHKA, DEAR OLD FELLOW—I have been married for two weeks and am happy, and a new, quite a new man. I wished to come to see you, but cannot manage it. When shall I see you? Having come to myself I value you very much indeed, and there is between us too much in common and unforgetable—Nicolenka and much besides. Come to make my acquaintance. I kiss Marya Petrovna's hands. Good-by, dear friend. I embrace you with all my heart."[2]

With his marriage Tolstoy entered upon a new phase of life, the family phase, " yet unknown to him, but promis-

---

[1] S. A. Bers, *Reminiscences of Count L. N. Tolstoy*, p. 13.
[2] A. Fet, *My Reminiscences*.

ing salvation," as he says in his *Confession.* We shall see in our further narrative how far these expectations of Tolstoy were justified. The spirit of analysis did not spare even this harbor of salvation, and destroyed this allusion also. But all-powerful reason lifted him a step higher. In the next volume we hope to peep into this mysterious process so far as is possible.

During this period Tolstoy wrote, besides those already mentioned, the following books: *The Snowstorm, The Recollections of a Billiard-Marker, The Two Hussars, Family Happiness,* and *Polikushka,* and he also began a new story entitled, *The Cloth-Measurer.*

The Snowstorm presents a winter landscape. While reading it you not only see before you the storm, the snow-bound road, and the wandering drivers with their vehicles, but you hear all the sounds of the storm, and feel in the elements a kind of soft, evanescent life.

In the *Recollections of a Billiard-Marker* is presented a pure, sweet, human soul gradually lost in the midst of town debauchery.

In *The Two Hussars* are pictured two generations: the old, which indulged in all kinds of excesses, but which at the same time was unsophisticated and sincere, and therefore lived in harmony with nature; and beside it the young generation—viciously cautious, calculating, and hypocritical. The harmony of nature is broken, and the harmony of consciousness not yet found, and the soul, depraved by vice, sounds with horrible discord.

Family Happiness is a quiet, touching story of family affection and the author's experience.

Polikushka—a tragedy of serfdom, the trifling of the sentimental gentry with the peasant's soul, which possesses, hidden under its coarse appearance, the finest moral traits, that break at the mere touch of the perverted and decadent nobility.

The critics of the sixties paid very little attention to these remarkable works.

They looked for a certain public standard, and had not enough sensibility to perceive the higher moral beauty with which these works were imbued.

This silence of the critics induced one of them to write an article entitled " The Phenomena of Contemporary Literature passed over by our Critics. Count Tolstoy and his Works."

We consider it out of place to enter into detailed criticism of these works, and we mention them only as facts, proving the unceasing inner creative work of Tolstoy.

CHAPTER XVII

CONCLUSION

Attitude to reality—Traits of Tolstoy's character resulting in his further development—Passionate nature—Truthfulness—Love of good—Dissatisfaction, absence of foundation—Search for it—Development.

IN this cursory review almost half of Leo Tolstoy's life lies before us.

Fearing to distort his original thoughts and the facts of his life by unskilled handling, I have tried wherever possible to let Tolstoy himself, or those nearest to him, his relatives and friends, his acquaintances and comrades, expound those thoughts and facts, reducing my part of the work to the presentation of a series of interesting pictures.

Notwithstanding the rawness of material, I believe that the nature of Tolstoy's personality during this half of his life must stand out clearly before the reader. To this end certain striking traits may be pointed out which impress one, and which appear as leading on to his further development.

One of these is his extraordinary capacity for being passionately carried away by anything brought within his sphere. Whether that happened to be hunting or card-playing, music or reading, school-teaching or farming, he exhausted to the very utmost each set of new impressions, transformed it in his artistic laboratory, and presented it to the world in lovely shapes, penetrated with high moral and philosophic meaning.

The same passionate ardor he carried into his search for truth, for the meaning of human life, and with the same power of genius he transformed and gave to the world the results of his work.

The other striking trait of his character is its truthfulness; a sincerity which feared nothing, which often caused disagreeable encounters, but more often, and finally, brought him to the God of Truth, whom he always served, however unconsciously overshadowed by varying temporary attractions.

The third and final trait of his character is the love of goodness; the enjoyment of it, and the incessant labor upon himself in view of widening the domain of goodness, the winning others over to the path of goodness, the striving to show to others all its beauty.

It is evident that these three traits, combined with his natural gifts, were sufficient to win for him the world-wide influence he now possesses.

But glancing at the first half of his life we notice yet one more remarkable trait—his constant dissatisfaction with himself, with his social activity, with his literary work. This dissatisfaction has been maintained in him by constant self-analysis, which never allowed him to find rest in any of the beautiful illusions floating before him.

This dissatisfaction was not a sickly, causeless complaining. Deep and real causes lay at the bottom of it. With all the great resources of his spiritual development, he was devoid of a substantial foundation—of the synthesis of all the ideas in which he was interested. He often approached the solution of the great problem, but could not get hold of it, passed on, and again suffered intensely and deeply.

These waverings round the one, the only possible, necessary, and satisfactory solution, explain all his apparent contradictions, his reasonings and self-accusations.

In the next volume we hope to narrate that current of events in Tolstoy's life which brought him to the moment when the thirst for truth, and the suffering occasioned by not finding it, culminated, and eventually led him to the only solution, the only foundation of life, and the only guide in his further exertions—*to religion.*

THE INTERNATIONAL EDITION OF
❧ ❧ THE WORKS OF LYOF N. TOLSTOY

TRANSLATED FROM THE MOSCOW EDITION

In 22 octavo volumes. Sold only by subscription
Special circular on request

CHARLES SCRIBNER'S SONS, PUBLISHERS

Mr. Nathan Haskell Dole, whose special study of Tolstoy has given him unusual qualifications for the work, supervised the preparation of this edition and himself made most of the translations. The following extract from a letter to him from Tolstoy's daughter sets the stamp of the author's personal approval upon his work:

"My father has read your translations, and approves of them very much—they are very faithfully and carefully made, to his mind.

"Yours truly,

"[Signed] TATIANA TOLSTOY."

A FEW SELECTED ENDORSEMENTS

"As you read on you say, not, 'This is like life,' but, 'This is life.' It is not only the complexion, the very hue of life, but its movement, its advances, its strange pauses, its seeming reversions to former conditions, and its perpetual change, its apparent isolations, its essential solidarity. It is a world, and you live in it while you read and long afterward; but at no step have you been betrayed, not because your guide has warned you or exhorted you, but because he has been true, and has shown you all things as they are."—W. D. HOWELLS, *in Harper's Monthly.*

THE INTERNATIONAL EDITION OF THE WORKS OF LYOF N. TOLSTOY

"I should agree with Mr. Howells in placing Tolstoy, with all his faults, at the head of living novelists."
—Thomas Wentworth Higginson.

"If Count Tolstoy's books have appeared in edition after edition and translation after translation, the reason is because the world learns from him to see life as it is."—Dean Farrar.

"His life, in its simplicity and its consecration to unselfish ends, is quite on a level with his art, and, in my judgment, he is one of the greatest artists of the century."
—Hamilton W. Mabie.

"Here is one of the great masters before whom ordinary merit must be dumb, whom to criticize is in vain, to admire alone is permitted."—*The Westminster Review*, London.

"No living author surpasses him, and only one or two approach him, in the power of picturing not merely places, but persons, with minute and fairly startling fidelity."
—*The Congregationalist*, Boston.

"It would be very fortunate if the complete works of Count Tolstoy were made accessible in an English form, above reproach as to their external parts, and deserving of full confidence as to their translation."—*The Dial*.

"The editorial work of Mr. Nathan Haskell Dole is satisfactory, and furnishes interesting introduction to those books that need it. The illustrations, too, are good, the novels being adequately and artistically pictured, while the essays and philosophical writings are presented with many portraits and views illustrative of the great man's life at different periods. The letter-press is excellent. . . . If one could possess only the works of one writer, Tolstoy, because he has touched human experience at so many different chords and from so many points of view, should be that one."
—New York *Times*.

THE INTERNATIONAL EDITION
OF THE
NOVELS AND STORIES
OF
IVÁN TURGÉNIEFF

Translated from the Russian

By ISABEL F. HAPGOOD

In 16 octavo volumes. Illustrated by S. IVANOWSKI, FRANK
VINCENT DUMOND, EDWIN POTTHAST and
MRS. M. WILSON-WATKINS

Sold only by subscription. Special circular on request

CHARLES SCRIBNER'S SONS, PUBLISHERS

THE "ENCYCLOPÆDIA BRITANNICA" SAYS

"Unquestionably Turgénieff may be considered one of the greatest novelists of our own or any other times, and worthy to be ranked with Thackeray, Dickens and George Eliot. His studies of human nature are profound, and he has the wide sympathies which are essential to genius of the highest order."

A FEW SELECTED ENDORSEMENTS

"Miss Hapgood has had much experience in translating from the Russian; she has entered into the spirit of Turgénieff, and the putting of his works into English has been for her, we imagine, a labor of love. Certainly she gives us prose

THE INTERNATIONAL EDITION OF THE NOVELS AND STORIES OF IVÁN TURGENIEFF

"that is as fluent as it is sound, prose with an atmosphere, prose that is delightful to read. Her prefaces are brief, intelligent, and in good taste. . . . The publishers have given the edition charming form. The typography is handsome and clear, the paper is light in weight and pleasant to the eye and to the touch."—New York *Tribune*.

"If it be asked: Who is Turgénieff? we may answer: One of the greatest novelists that the world has ever read. A novelist whose force and finish are now winning for him in English-speaking countries the popular appreciation that he has for many years enjoyed in Russia and in France."
—Baltimore *Sun*.

"It is probable that the passing years will add still greater fame to Iván Turgénieff, and that his work as a novelist will rank among the greatest intellectual achievements bequeathed to history by the nineteenth century. He is even now one of the few men of the Slavonic race whose reputation is worldwide, and as great among other people as among his own."—Boston *Transcript*.

"As satisfactory a presentation of the Russian novelist's work as exists in English. . . . A worthy edition of a great writer."—New York *Sun*.

"They are novels of power, containing profound studies of human nature and exhibiting genius of the highest order which has exercised an estimable influence on European prose."—Philadelphia *Press*.

"Here at last we have the entire work in fiction of perhaps the greatest of all novelists presented in admirable English and in beautiful mechanical form."—*The Dial*.

CHARLES SCRIBNER'S SONS
153-157 FIFTH AVENUE, NEW YORK

[A facsimile of a letter written by Tolstoy in 1860.]

BOOK JUNGLE

Bringing Classics to Life

www.bookjungle.com email: sales@bookjungle.com fax: 630-214-0564 mail: Book Jungle PO Box 2226 Champaign, IL 61825

The Two Babylons
Alexander Hislop
You may be surprised to learn that many traditions of Roman Catholicism in fact don't come from Christ's teachings but from an ancient Babylonian "Mystery" religion that was centered on Nimrod, his wife Semiramis, and a child Tammuz. This book shows how this ancient religion transformed itself as it incorporated Christ into its teachings....

Religion/History   Pages: 358
ISBN: *1-59462-010-5*   MSRP *$22.95*   QTY

The Go-Getter
Kyne B. Peter
The Go Getter is the story of William Peck. He was a war veteran and amputee who will not be refused what he wants. Peck not only fights to find employment but continually proves himself more than competent at the many difficult test that are throw his way in the course of his early days with the Ricks Lumber Company...

Business/Self Help/Inspirational   Pages: 68
ISBN: *1-59462-186-1*   MSRP *$8.95*   QTY

The Power Of Concentration
Theron Q. Dumont
It is of the utmost value to learn how to concentrate. To make the greatest success of anything you must be able to concentrate your entire thought upon the idea you are working on. The person that is able to concentrate utilizes all constructive thoughts and shuts out all destructive ones...

Self Help/Inspirational   Pages: 196
ISBN: *1-59462-141-1*   MSRP *$14.95*

Self Mastery
Emile Coue
Emile Coue came up with novel way to improve the lives of people. He was a pharmacist by trade and often saw ailing people. This lead him to develop autosuggestion, a form of self-hypnosis. At the time his theories weren't popular but over the years evidence is mounting that he was indeed right all along...

New Age/Self Help   Pages: 98
ISBN: *1-59462-189-6*   MSRP *$7.95*

Rightly Dividing The Word
Clarence Larkin
The "Fundamental Doctrines" of the Christian Faith are clearly outlined in numerous books on Theology, but they are not available to the average reader and were mainly written for students. The Author has made it the work of his ministry to preach the "Fundamental Doctrines." To this end he has aimed to express them in the simplest and clearest manner...

Religion   Pages: 352
ISBN: *1-59462-334-1*   MSRP *$23.45*

The Awful Disclosures Of Maria Monk
"I cannot banish the scenes and characters of this book from my memory. To me it can never appear like an amusing fable, or lose its interest and importance. The story is one which is continually before me, and must return fresh to my mind with painful emotions as long as I live..."

Religion   Pages: 232
ISBN: *1-59462-160-8*   MSRP *$17.95*

The Law of Psychic Phenomena
Thomson Jay Hudson
"I do not expect this book to stand upon its literary merits; for if it is unsound in principle, felicity of diction cannot save it, and if sound, homeliness of expression cannot destroy it. My primary object in offering it to the public is to assist in bringing Psychology within the domain of the exact sciences. That this has never been accomplished..."

New Age   Pages: 420
ISBN: *1-59462-124-1*   MSRP *$29.95*

As a Man Thinketh
James Allen
"This little volume (the result of meditation and experience) is not intended as an exhaustive treatise on the much-written-upon subject of the power of thought. It is suggestive rather than explanatory, its object being to stimulate men and women to the discovery and perception of the truth that by virtue of the thoughts which they choose and encourage..."

Inspirational/Self Help   Pages: 80
ISBN: *1-59462-231-0*   MSRP *$9.45*

Beautiful Joe
Marshall Saunders
When Marshall visited the Moore family in 1892, she discovered Joe, a dog they had nursed back to health from his previous abusive home to live a happy life. So moved was she, that she wrote this classic masterpiece which won accolades and was recognized as a heartwarming symbol for humane animal treatment...

Fiction   Pages: 256
ISBN: *1-59462-261-2*   MSRP *$18.45*

The Enchanted April
Elizabeth Von Arnim
It began in a woman's club in London on a February afternoon, an uncomfortable club, and a miserable afternoon when Mrs. Wilkins, who had come down from Hampstead to shop and had lunched at her club, took up The Times from the table in the smoking-room...

Fiction   Pages: 368
ISBN: *1-59462-150-0*   MSRP *$23.45*

The Codes Of Hammurabi And Moses - W. W. Davies
The discovery of the Hammurabi Code is one of the greatest achievements of archaeology, and is of paramount interest, not only to the student of the Bible, but also to all those interested in ancient history...

Religion   Pages: 132
ISBN: *1-59462-338-4*   MSRP *$12.95*

Holland - The History Of Netherlands
Thomas Colley Grattan
Thomas Grattan was a prestigious writer from Dublin who served as British Consul to the US. Among his works is an authoritative look at the history of Holland. A colorful and interesting look at history....

History/Politics   Pages: 408
ISBN: *1-59462-137-3*   MSRP *$26.95*

The Thirty-Six Dramatic Situations
Georges Polti
An incredibly useful guide for aspiring authors and playwrights. This volume categorizes every dramatic situation which could occur in a story and describes them in a list of 36 situations. A great aid to help inspire or formalize the creative writing process...

Self Help/Reference   Pages: 204
ISBN: *1-59462-134-9*   MSRP *$15.95*

A Concise Dictionary of Middle English
A. L. Mayhew
Walter W. Skeat
The present work is intended to meet, in some measure, the requirements of those who wish to make some study of Middle-English, and who find a difficulty in obtaining such assistance as will enable them to find out the meanings and etymologies of the words most essential to their purpose...

Reference/History   Pages: 332
ISBN: *1-59462-119-5*   MSRP *$29.95*

BOOK JUNGLE

Bringing Classics to Life

www.bookjungle.com email: sales@bookjungle.com fax: 630-214-0564 mail: Book Jungle PO Box 2226 Champaign, IL 61825

The Witch-Cult in Western Europe
Margaret Murray

The mass of existing material on this subject is so great that I have not attempted to make a survey of the whole of European "Witchcraft" but have confined myself to an intensive study of the cult in Great Britain. In order, however, to obtain a clearer understanding of the ritual and beliefs I have had recourse to French and Flemish sources...

Occult   Pages:308
ISBN: *1-59462-126-8*   MSRP *$22.45*

QTY

Philosophy Of Natural Therapeutics
Henry Lindlahr

We invite the earnest cooperation in this great work of all those who have awakened to the necessity for more rational living and for radical reform in healing methods...

Health/Philosophy/Self Help   Pages:552
ISBN: *1-59462-132-2*   MSRP *$34.95*

QTY

The Science Of Psychic Healing
Yogi Ramacharaka

This book is not a book of theories it deals with facts. Its author regards the best of theories as but working hypotheses to be used only until better ones present themselves. The "fact" is the principal thing the essential thing to uncover which the tool, theory, is used...

New Age/Health   Pages:180
ISBN: *1-59462-140-3*   MSRP *$13.95*

A Message to Garcia
Elbert Hubbard

This literary trifle, A Message to Garcia, was written one evening after supper, in a single hour. It was on the Twenty-second of February, Eighteen Hundred Ninety-nine, Washington's Birthday, and we were just going to press with the March Philistine...

New Age/Fiction   Pages:92
ISBN: *1-59462-144-6*   MSRP *$9.95*

Bible Myths
Thomas Doane

In pursuing the study of the Bible Myths, facts pertaining thereto, in a condensed form, seemed to be greatly needed, and nowhere to be found. Widely scattered through hundreds of ancient and modern volumes, most of the contents of this book may indeed be found; but any previous attempt to trace exclusively the myths and legends...

Religion/History   Pages:644
ISBN: *1-59462-163-2*   MSRP *$38.95*

The Book of Jasher
Alcuinus Flaccus Albinus

The Book of Jasher is an historical religious volume that many consider as a missing holy book from the Old Testament. Particularly studied by the Church of Later Day Saints and historians, it covers the history of the world from creation until the period of Judges in Israel. It's authenticity is bolstered due to a reference to the Book of Jasher in the Bible in Joshua 10:13

Religion/History   Pages:276
ISBN: *1-59462-197-7*   MSRP *$18.95*

Tertium Organum
P. D. Ouspensky

A truly mind expanding writing that combines science with mysticism with unprecedented elegance. He presents the world we live in as a multi dimensional world and time as a motion through this world. But this isn't a cold and purely analytical explanation but a masterful presentation filled with similes and analogies...

New Age   Pages:356
ISBN: *1-59462-205-1*   MSRP *$23.95*

The Titan
Theodore Dreiser

"When Frank Algernon Cowperwood emerged from the Eastern District Penitentiary, in Philadelphia he realized that the old life he had lived in that city since boyhood was ended. His youth was gone, and with it had been lost the great business prospects of his earlier manhood. He must begin again..."

Fiction   Pages:564
ISBN: *1-59462-220-5*   MSRP *$33.95*

Advance Course in Yogi Philosophy
Yogi Ramacharaka

"The twelve lessons forming this volume were originally issued in the shape of monthly lessons, known as "The Advanced Course in Yogi Philosophy and Oriental Occultism" during a period of twelve months beginning with October, 1904, and ending September, 1905."

Philosophy/Inspirational/Self Help   Pages:340
ISBN: *1-59462-229-9*   MSRP *$22.95*

Biblical Essays
J. B. Lightfoot

About one-third of the present volume has already seen the light. The opening essay "On the Internal Evidence for the Authenticity and Genuineness of St John's Gospel" was published in the "Expositor" in the early months of 1890, and has been reprinted since...

Religion/History   Pages:480
ISBN: *1-59462-238-8*   MSRP *$30.95*

Ambassador Morgenthau's Story
Henry Morgenthau

"By this time the American people have probably become convinced that the Germans deliberately planned the conquest of the world. Yet they hesitate to convict on circumstantial evidence and for this reason all eye witnesses to this, the greatest crime in modern history, should volunteer their testimony..."

History   Pages:472
ISBN: *1-59462-244-2*   MSRP *$29.95*

The Settlement Cook Book
Simon Kander

A legacy from the civil war, this book is a classic "American charity cookbook," which was used for fundraisers starting in Milwaukee. While it has transformed over the years, this printing provides great recipes from American history. Over two million copies have been sold. This volume contains a rich collection of recipes from noted chefs and hostesses of the turn of the century...

How-to   Pages:472
ISBN: *1-59462-256-6*   MSRP *$29.95*

The Aquarian Gospel of Jesus the Christ
Levi Dowling

A retelling of Jesus' story which tells us what happened during the twenty year gap left by the Bible's New Testament. It tells of his travels to the far-east where he studied with the masters and fought against the rigid caste system. This book has enjoyed a resurgence in modern America and provides spiritual insight with charm. Its influences can be seen throughout the Age of Aquarius.

Religion   Pages:264
ISBN: *1-59462-321-X*   MSRP *$18.95*

My Life and Work
Henry Ford

Henry Ford revolutionized the world with his implementation of mass production for the Model T automobile. Gain valuable business insight into his life and work with his own auto-biography... "We have only started on our development of our country we have not as yet, with all our talk of wonderful progress, done more than scratch the surface. The progress has been wonderful enough but..."

Biographies/History/Business   Pages:300
ISBN: *1-59462-198-5*   MSRP *$21.95*

BOOK JUNGLE

Bringing Classics to Life

www.bookjungle.com *email:* sales@bookjungle.com *fax:* 630-214-0564 *mail:* Book Jungle PO Box 2226 Champaign, IL 61825

QTY

☐	**The Rosicrucian Cosmo-Conception Mystic Christianity** *by Max Heindel*	ISBN: *1-59462-188-8* **$38.95**

The Rosicrucian Cosmo-conception is not dogmatic, neither does it appeal to any other authority than the reason of the student. It is: not controversial, but is: sent forth in the, hope that it may help to clear...
New Age/Religion Pages 646

Abandonment To Divine Providence *by Jean-Pierre de Caussade* ISBN: *1-59462-228-0* **$25.95**
"The Rev. Jean Pierre de Caussade was one of the most remarkable spiritual writers of the Society of Jesus in France in the 18th Century. His death took place at Toulouse in 1751. His works have gone through many editions and have been republished..."
Inspirational/Religion Pages 400

Mental Chemistry *by Charles Haanel* ISBN: *1-59462-192-6* **$23.95**
Mental Chemistry allows the change of material conditions by combining and appropriately utilizing the power of the mind. Much like applied chemistry creates something new and unique out of careful combinations of chemicals the mastery of mental chemistry...
New Age Pages 354

The Letters of Robert Browning and Elizabeth Barret Barrett 1845-1846 vol II ISBN: *1-59462-193-4* **$35.95**
by Robert Browning and Elizabeth Barrett
Biographies Pages 596

Gleanings In Genesis (volume I) *by Arthur W. Pink* ISBN: *1-59462-130-6* **$27.45**
Appropriately has Genesis been termed "the seed plot of the Bible" for in it we have, in germ form, almost all of the great doctrines which are afterwards fully developed in the books of Scripture which follow...
Religion/Inspirational Pages 420

The Master Key *by L. W. de Laurence* ISBN: *1-59462-001-6* **$30.95**
In no branch of human knowledge has there been a more lively increase of the spirit of research during the past few years than in the study of Psychology, Concentration and Mental Discipline. The requests for authentic lessons in Thought Control, Mental Discipline and...
New Age/Business Pages 422

The Lesser Key Of Solomon Goetia *by L. W. de Laurence* ISBN: *1-59462-092-X* **$9.95**
This translation of the first book of the "Lemegton" which is now for the first time made accessible to students of Talismanic Magic was done, after careful collation and edition, from numerous Ancient Manuscripts in Hebrew, Latin, and French...
New Age/Occult Pages 92

Rubaiyat Of Omar Khayyam *by Edward Fitzgerald* ISBN: *1-59462-332-5* **$13.95**
Edward Fitzgerald, whom the world has already learned, in spite of his own efforts to remain within the shadow of anonymity, to look upon as one of the rarest poets of the century, was born at Bredfield, in Suffolk, on the 31st of March, 1809. He was the third son of John Purcell...
Music Pages 172

Ancient Law *by Henry Maine* ISBN: *1-59462-128-4* **$29.95**
The chief object of the following pages is to indicate some of the earliest ideas of mankind, as they are reflected in Ancient Law, and to point out the relation of those ideas to modern thought.
Religion/History Pages 452

Far-Away Stories *by William J. Locke* ISBN: *1-59462-129-2* **$19.45**
"Good wine needs no bush, but a collection of mixed vintages does. And this book is just such a collection. Some of the stories I do not want to remain buried for ever in the museum files of dead magazine-numbers an author's not unpardonable vanity..."
Fiction Pages 272

Life of David Crockett *by David Crockett* ISBN: *1-59462-250-7* **$27.45**
"Colonel David Crockett was one of the most remarkable men of the times in which he lived. Born in humble life, but gifted with a strong will, an indomitable courage, and unremitting perseverance...
Biographies/New Age Pages 424

Lip-Reading *by Edward Nitchie* ISBN: *1-59462-206-X* **$25.95**
Edward B. Nitchie, founder of the New York School for the Hard of Hearing, now the Nitchie School of Lip-Reading, Inc, wrote "LIP-READING Principles and Practice". The development and perfecting of this meritorious work on lip-reading was an undertaking...
How-to Pages 400

A Handbook of Suggestive Therapeutics, Applied Hypnotism, Psychic Science ISBN: *1-59462-214-0* **$24.95**
by Henry Munro
Health/New Age Health Self-help Pages 376

A Doll's House: and Two Other Plays *by Henrik Ibsen* ISBN: *1-59462-112-8* **$19.95**
Henrik Ibsen created this classic when in revolutionary 1848 Rome. Introducing some striking concepts in playwriting for the realist genre, this play has been studied the world over.
Fiction/Classics/Plays 308

The Light of Asia *by sir Edwin Arnold* ISBN: *1-59462-204-3* **$13.95**
In this poetic masterpiece, Edwin Arnold describes the life and teachings of Buddha. The man who was to become known as Buddha to the world was born as Prince Gautama of India but he rejected the worldly riches and abandoned the reigns of power when...
Religion/History/Biographies Pages 170

The Complete Works of Guy de Maupassant *by Guy de Maupassant* ISBN: *1-59462-157-8* **$16.95**
"For days and days, nights and nights, I had dreamed of that first kiss which was to consecrate our engagement, and I knew not on what spot I should put my lips..."
Fiction/Classics Pages 240

The Art of Cross-Examination *by Francis L. Wellman* ISBN: *1-59462-309-0* **$26.95**
Written by a renowned trial lawyer, Wellman imparts his experience and uses case studies to explain how to use psychology to extract desired information through questioning.
How-to/Science/Reference Pages 408

Answered or Unanswered? *by Louisa Vaughan* ISBN: *1-59462-248-5* **$10.95**
Miracles of Faith in China
Religion Pages 112

The Edinburgh Lectures on Mental Science (1909) *by Thomas* ISBN: *1-59462-008-3* **$11.95**
This book contains the substance of a course of lectures recently given by the writer in the Queen Street Hall, Edinburgh. Its purpose is to indicate the Natural Principles governing the relation between Mental Action and Material Conditions...
New Age/Psychology Pages 148

Ayesha *by H. Rider Haggard* ISBN: *1-59462-301-5* **$24.95**
Verily and indeed it is the unexpected that happens! Probably if there was one person upon the earth from whom the Editor of this, and of a certain previous history, did not expect to hear again...
Classics Pages 380

Ayala's Angel *by Anthony Trollope* ISBN: *1-59462-352-X* **$29.95**
The two girls were both pretty; but Lucy who was twenty-one who supposed to be simple and comparatively unattractive, whereas Ayala was credited, as her Bombwhat romantic name might show, with poetic charm and a taste for romance. Ayala when her father died was nineteen...
Fiction Pages 484

The American Commonwealth *by James Bryce* ISBN: *1-59462-286-8* **$34.45**
An interpretation of American democratic political theory. It examines political mechanics and society from the perspective of Scotsman James Bryce
Politics Pages 572

Stories of the Pilgrims *by Margaret P. Pumphrey* ISBN: *1-59462-116-0* **$17.95**
This book explores pilgrims religious oppression in England as well as their escape to Holland and eventual crossing to America on the Mayflower, and their early days in New England...
History Pages 268

www.bookjungle.com *email:* sales@bookjungle.com *fax:* 630-214-0564 *mail:* Book Jungle PO Box 2226 Champaign, IL 61825

Bringing Classics to Life

BOOK JUNGLE

www.bookjungle.com email: sales@bookjungle.com fax: 630-214-0564 mail: Book Jungle PO Box 2226 Champaign, IL 61825

QTY

The Fasting Cure *by Sinclair Upton* ISBN: *1-59462-222-1* **$13.95**
In the Cosmopolitan Magazine for May, 1910, and in the Contemporary Review (London) for April, 1910, I published an article dealing with my experiences in fasting. I have written a great many magazine articles, but never one which attracted so much attention... New Age/Self Help Health Pages 164

Hebrew Astrology *by Sepharial* ISBN: *1-59462-308-2* **$13.45**
In these days of advanced thinking it is a matter of common observation that we have left many of the old landmarks behind and that we are now pressing forward to greater heights and to a wider horizon than that which represented the mind-content of our progenitors... Astrology Pages 144

Thought Vibration or The Law of Attraction in the Thought World ISBN: *1-59462-127-6* **$12.95**
by William Walker Atkinson Psychology/Religion Pages 144

Optimism *by Helen Keller* ISBN: *1-59462-108-X* **$15.95**
Helen Keller was blind, deaf, and mute since 19 months old, yet famously learned how to overcome these handicaps, communicate with the world, and spread her lectures promoting optimism. An inspiring read for everyone... Biographies/Inspirational Pages 84

Sara Crewe *by Frances Burnett* ISBN: *1-59462-360-0* **$9.45**
In the first place, Miss Minchin lived in London. Her home was a large, dull, tall one, in a large, dull square, where all the houses were alike, and all the sparrows were alike, and where all the door-knockers made the same heavy sound... Childrens/Classic Pages 88

The Autobiography of Benjamin Franklin *by Benjamin Franklin* ISBN: *1-59462-135-7* **$24.95**
The Autobiography of Benjamin Franklin has probably been more extensively read than any other American historical work, and no other book of its kind has had such ups and downs of fortune. Franklin lived for many years in England, where he was agent... Biographies/History Pages 332

Name	
Email	
Telephone	
Address	
City, State ZIP	

☐ Credit Card   ☐ Check / Money Order

Credit Card Number	
Expiration Date	
Signature	

Please Mail to: Book Jungle
                  PO Box 2226
                  Champaign, IL 61825
or Fax to: 630-214-0564

ORDERING INFORMATION

web: *www.bookjungle.com*
email: *sales@bookjungle.com*
fax: *630-214-0564*
mail: *Book Jungle PO Box 2226 Champaign, IL 61825*
or PayPal *to sales@bookjungle.com*

Please contact us for bulk discounts

DIRECT-ORDER TERMS

20% Discount if You Order Two or More Books
Free Domestic Shipping!
Accepted: Master Card, Visa, Discover, American Express

www.ingramcontent.com/pod-product-compliance
Lightning Source LLC
Chambersburg PA
CBHW080722230426

43665CB00020B/2582